The River Has Never Divided Us

Number   JACK AND DORIS SMOTHERS SERIES
Thirteen   IN TEXAS HISTORY, LIFE, AND CULTURE

Jefferson Morgenthaler

THE RIVER
HAS NEVER
DIVIDED US

A Border History of La Junta de los Rios

University of Texas Press, Austin

Requests for permission to reproduce material from this work
should be sent to Permissions, University of Texas Press, P.O.
Box 7819, Austin, TX 78713-7819.

∞ The paper used in this book meets the minimum
requirements of ANSI/NISO Z39.48-1992 (R1997)
(Permanence of Paper).

LIBRARY OF CONGRESS CATALOGING-IN-PUBLICATION DATA
Morgenthaler, George J.
    The river has never divided us : a border history of La Junta
de Los Rios / by Jefferson Morgenthaler.
       p.   cm. — (Jack and Doris Smothers series in Texas
history, life, and culture ; no. 13)
Includes bibliographical references and index.
ISBN 0-292-70166-7 (cl. : alk. paper) — ISBN 0-292-70283-3
(pbk. : alk. paper)
    1. La Junta de los Ríos (Tex.)—History.   2. La Junta de los
Ríos (Tex.)—Social conditions.   3. La Junta de los Ríos
(Tex.)—Biography.   4. Mexican-American Border Region—
History.   5. United States—Relations—Mexico.   6. Mexico
—Relations—United States.   I. Title.   II. Series.
F392.L33M67   2004
972'.16—dc22

                                                        2003026428

To my daughter Jean,
who waded the Big River
and brought back an idea

Contents

ix Acknowledgments

1 Forgotten

3 Junie

11 The Land

14 La Junta

21 Before 1830

25 The Promised Land

33 Anglos Arrive

39 In Doniphan's Wake

49 Jack Hays Gets Lost

56 Whiting Draws the Line

63 Forty-Niners

70 Scalp Hunting Redux

76 A Sudden Death

83 The End of Isolation

93 Railroads and Ranches

99 The Armies

108 Skillman's Raiders

115 The Rise and Fall of John Burgess

121 The End of the Mescaleros

131 Victor Ochoa

138 Toribio Ortega's Rebellion

158 Orozco and Huerta

168 Pancho Villa

185 Punitive Expeditions

201 The Spencers

207 Pablo Acosta

225 Rick Thompson

229 River and Border

234 Gilbert Spencer

239 An Afternoon with Enrique

247 Notes

289 Bibliography

299 Index

There is little point in attempting to recognize all the people who helped bring this book to be. Many had no idea at the time who they were helping or why, several never met me face-to-face and too many have slipped from my memory. It would be unfair to select a favored handful (such as Robert Mallouf, Glenn Willeford, Troy Solis, Claudia Rivers, Enrique Madrid and Gilbert Spencer) and thank them without mentioning all the others.

It is more important that thanks go to those who almost always go unmentioned: the anonymous founders, funders and hard-working staff of the institutions that we rely on for research material. In my case, the list of institutions includes the University of Texas (including the Center for American History, the Benson Latin American Collection, the Harry Ransom Center and the Perry-Castañeda Library), the University of Texas at El Paso (including the Library and its Special Collections Section), Sul Ross State University (including the Archives of the Big Bend and the Center for Big Bend Studies), the National Archives (including the depositories in Washington, D.C., and Fort Worth), the county clerks of Presidio, El Paso, Bexar and Menard Counties, the Marfa Public Library, the Houston Public Library (including its Texas Room and Archives and its Clayton Library Center for Genealogical Research), the El Paso Public Library (including its Southwest Collection), the Texas State Library and Archives and the Texas General Land Office. There are people at all these places whom I never saw but whose work was essential to my being able to do mine.

Most of all, thanks to Junie Hernandez, Ben Leaton, Toribio Ortega, Leonard Matlack, Pablo Acosta, Lucía Madrid, Jack Hays, Pancho Villa, Henry Skillman, María Gómez Gutiérrez, Victor Ochoa, José de la Cruz Sánchez, John Burgess, John Spencer and all the other historic characters who made this book such a pleasure to research and write.

Acknowledgments

The River Has Never Divided Us

Enrique Rede Madrid took them to the spot where his friend had bled to death. Prickly pears and ocotillos jutted from the loose, dry soil. Every footstep raised a puff of red dust. Standing exposed on the arid promontory, the reporters squinted across the river below, across the green fields on its flanks. They wondered whether people really lived in the weary adobe houses. They eyed the old border post, surrounded by splintered chairs, sun-baked bottles and scattered detritus of long neglect. They asked their questions, they learned what they wanted to know, then they climbed into their rental cars and left, sorting out details in their heads as they drove the long desert highways.

For five centuries there have been many reasons to come here, but few reasons to linger. Explorers, invaders, exploiters and enforcers have faded into history; ancient rhythms of life have endured. Rattlesnakes, javelinas and lynx still forage in the mezquital. Spindly ramadas lean into the midday sun, casting patches of shade across dusty plazas. People tend corn, squash and beans that struggle up from parched earth. Green swaths of alfalfa and cotton flourish where the river's waters have been trained to meander through the

Forgotten

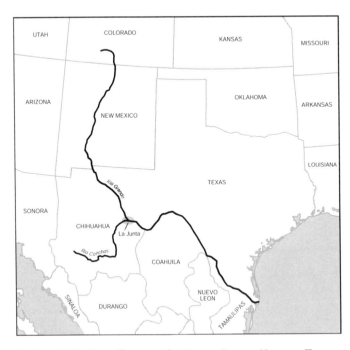

La Junta de los Rios. Illustration by Herring Design, Houston, Tex.

land. People work the fields, they pray and—gods permitting—they harvest.

The reporters came because this is where Clemente Bañuelos killed Junie Hernandez. You have already forgotten what they wrote about Junie's death—if you ever knew—even though it happened just a few years ago. That's understandable. Junie was nobody, and he lived in the middle of nowhere.

He lived in La Junta de los Rios.

President George Herbert Walker Bush looked over the crowd assembled in the White House East Room. His Ivy League–inflected Texas twang carried through the room as he related a story about Vincent Van Gogh volunteering to help victims of a mining disaster in a small Belgian town. He paused briefly, presidentially, then introduced a St. Louis teenager who fought to protect his neighborhood against crime and drugs, and a couple from Washington, D.C., who established an academy to tutor disadvantaged kids. These were some of President Bush's Thousand Points of Light, and he had invited nineteen of them to the White House on that April day in 1990.[1]

The Thousand Points of Light were a characteristic Bush mix of patrician altruism and corny populism. It was a way to reach out to the commoner, to connect with the electorate. Volunteerism is people helping people, not government helping people—a theme that foreshadowed the compassionate conservatism of the second Bush White House.

One of the nineteen points of light honored that day was Lucía Rede Madrid, a frail white-haired woman in a wheelchair. President Bush gave Mrs. Madrid two medals. The first was the President's Volunteer Action Award, designating her as one of the Thousand Points of Light. The other was the Ronald Reagan Award for Volunteer Excellence, a special recognition of the individual whose contribution is greatest among the Volunteer Action Award winners. The brightest point of light.[2]

Mrs. Madrid's grandparents were among the five founding families of an unattractive village called Redford, Texas. Their eleventh child, María Antonia Luján, was born in 1878. She became a schoolteacher but gave up the occupation when she married handsome Eusebio Rede. Eusebio took up farming in Redford and María Antonia became the local postmistress. Lucía Rede was their daughter. After graduating from college in Alpine, Texas, Lucía married Enrique Madrid, who worked as a diesel mechanic at a nearby silver mine. A few years later Enrique put down his wrench in favor of running the Madrid family's grocery store in Redford.[3]

Located near the Rio Grande, about a half-mile above the El Polvo river crossing, Redford is named for the red rocks

Junie

in the hills on either side of the valley. *Polvo* is the Spanish word for dust.

The oldest structures in the vicinity are down in El Polvo, on a mesilla above the river. The ruins of an adobe cavalry fort slowly dissolve in the infrequent rains. A stone watering trough crumbles next to the abandoned shell of a bandido-era border post. A dirt road leads down to a few houses at the crossing. Some yards boast colorful flowers; others harbor disabled automobiles.[4]

Redford is up the hill, by the farm-to-market road. Redford is barely a village. It has a small church and an elementary school. The front yard of the schoolhouse is paved, and there are basketball hoops at either end. A flagpole is planted at center court. An ancient flat-tired road grader rusts from yellow to brown along the side of the road.

Redford claims one hundred inhabitants. Maybe that's true. Maybe on a winter day when the crops don't need tending and a battered school bus has collected children into the cement-block school. Maybe then, maybe if you counted the people who live in El Polvo, too. Most days, though, you would be hard-pressed to spot a half-dozen people among the scattered mobile homes and adobe houses.

Lucía Rede Madrid was a schoolteacher like her mother. She spent decades working with kids from El Polvo, Redford and the surrounding ranches and farms, and she witnessed her students' disadvantages. Many local families were too poor to afford schoolbooks. County funds were so scarce that the elementary school couldn't maintain a proper library.

In 1979 Mrs. Madrid began collecting a few books for her students. She kept them in her home, where kids could come by to read, study and learn. Over the years her fledgling library grew. Mrs. Madrid knew how to gather donations and how to harness the charity of others. The books crowded her home, then overflowed into her husband's store. By the mid-1980s she had collected over 20,000 volumes.[5]

There is a picture of Mrs. Madrid in her library at about the time that she received presidential recognition. She is sitting at a rectangular wooden table next to a boy of about ten and a girl of perhaps twelve. Mrs. Madrid is showing a book to the young boy while the girl reads. There are books on shelves, books on tables, books stacked on the floor. The boy sitting with Mrs. Madrid is Esequiel Hernandez Jr. His family called him Junie; he would be killed by Clemente Bañuelos in a few years. The young girl is his sister, who would grieve.

Enrique Rede Madrid, the man who showed reporters where Junie died, is the son of Enrique Madrid and Lucía Rede Madrid. He is an anthropologist and a steward of the Texas Historical Commission. College students come to tiny, desolate Redford just to meet Enrique. They come from expensive private liberal arts schools. They sit with him and learn about desert prehistory and traditional native foodways. He shows them how to harvest and eat sotol, lechuguilla and other desert plants, and he teaches them the fine points of slaughtering and butchering goats. *Cabrito*—young goat—grilled over a wood fire is a West Texas delicacy. Goat's milk is nutritious and can be used to make traditional Mexican white cheeses such as *queso fresco* and *queso asadero.*[6]

People have lived down the road at El Polvo for hundreds, perhaps thousands, of years. Before it was El Polvo it was called Tapacolmes, and before that it was home to families that survived using the skills that Enrique Madrid now teaches. People lived in the place then for the same reasons that they do now—there are some lands along the river that are moist enough to be farmed, and there are shallows in the river where people can cross to the other side.

People like the Madrids, Valenzuelas, Hernandezes, Acevedos, Cataños and Evaros have lived here for generations, doing the best they can with the meager opportunities afforded them. They grow corn and cantaloupe and onions in their fields, and they raise goats that graze in the scrub. People come from the other side of the river to buy a half-gallon of milk or to mail a letter.

By twenty-first-century standards, this isn't enough of a community to support life. If it weren't for the family of families that stretches up and down both sides of the river, El Polvo and Redford would have been abandoned long ago. When children reach high school age, they take the bus to Presidio High School, sixteen miles up the road. For a night out at a restaurant or a cantina, families go into Ojinaga, across the river from Presidio.

La Junta de los Rios embraces an extended network of friends, family, partners and acquaintances on both sides of the Rio Grande. They are here because of the river, and they do not make distinctions among themselves on the basis of upstream or down, left bank or right. It is all La Junta. According to Lucía Madrid, "Anglos have tried to divide it, for a different country, but no, . . . the Rio Grande has never, never divided the people."[7]

The river binds La Junta. Denise Chávez, one of Lucía Madrid's daughters, says, "The river is a unifier to me in my heart and in my spirit because it is the primal source of life. It gives hope, nurture and sustenance, and so to me, La Junta de los Rios, when you talk about it, it seems to be a specific thing, but really it is a universal pipeline, the artery of life."[8]

Denise's brother, the remarkable Enrique Madrid, is somewhat less poetic: "The river is a minor inconvenience, something that will get your feet wet when you're doing your daily business."[9]

Unofficial border crossings like the one at El Polvo are a normal and accepted part of life in La Junta. People load their pickups with furniture, lumber, goats or beer and drive across the shallows. Families graze livestock on one side and raise vegetables on the other. The porosity of the border and the similarities of life on both sides make it difficult to maintain a mental distinction between the United States and Mexico. Denise Chávez recognizes the abstraction: "There's Mexico on one side, there's the United States on the other, and sometimes you're a citizen of both and yet by being both you're neither — you're something else."[10]

People in more populated places have a hard time understanding how things work along this stretch of the Rio Grande. They expect a border, and they don't expect unsupervised crossings. They believe that the United States should seal its perimeter. Politicians visualize a firm, bright barrier along the Rio Grande and consider it a place where some of the problems of Detroit and St. Louis can be nipped in the bud. "The border program is an absolute joke," said one Ohio congressman. "Our border is wide open. There's heroin and cocaine on every street corner, and it's easier to get than aspirin."[11]

Heroin and cocaine are not evident on every street corner in Redford. There are no street corners in El Polvo. Statistically, more than 85 percent of all illegal drugs enter the United States not through neglected low-water fords but through official ports of entry such as El Paso and San Diego. That is because the high volume of traffic at official checkpoints permits searches of only a small percentage of vehicles and because the trucking industry opposes delays from stricter enforcement. The best place for big-league smuggling is an international bridge swarming with customs agents.[12]

Admittedly, though, marijuana does come across the border at El Polvo, just as it does all along the West Texas border. And there are doubtless some marijuana traffickers in El Polvo or Redford, just as there are in every border town. Marijuana smuggling can be more profitable than herding goats, but it doesn't seem to be attracting a crowd to Redford. An article in the *Denver Post* called Redford a drug capital. When Enrique Madrid saw that, he laughed, saying, "We're a little town of one hundred people. We're not the capital of *anything*."[13]

Caught in a magnanimous mood, the chief United States Border Patrol agent once called the people of Redford "salt of the earth, hard-working people with good values," noting that "they have been there for generations." The task of the Border Patrol is to distinguish the troublesome few from the respectable many, and the local populace is generally content to leave that challenge to the government. In the opinion of Redford storekeeper Rosendo Evaro, "Drug smugglers never caused any trouble. They go on with their business and we go on with ours." Life is difficult enough in La Junta without looking for problems.[14]

One February day in 1997 Junie Hernandez herded forty goats through the brushy arroyos between El Polvo and the river. He was eighteen, the sixth of eight children, a high school sophomore given to wearing Western shirts and a white cowboy hat. Junie was a skinny teenager with a trace of a moustache who didn't smoke, drink or do drugs. He wasn't college material; he kept a United States Marines recruiting poster on his bedroom wall.

Like most people who grew up around El Polvo, Junie was comfortable on a horse and comfortable with a varmint gun. When he took the goats out of their pen to graze, he usually toted an ancient .22-caliber rifle that had belonged to his grandfather. A .22 is a plinker that uses little rim-fired shells less than a quarter-inch in diameter. Good for shooting squirrels, but there aren't many squirrels in El Polvo. There are rattlesnakes and compact peccaries called javelinas—a .22 is enough to deal with those, and it's enough to scare off a coyote. Mostly, though, a .22 is good for killing time while your goats forage, good for popping a few tin cans or for trying to snip a twig off a tree.

Without meaning to offend urban sensibilities, it should be noted that a varmint rifle is also an accepted distant early warning device in West Texas. People who go onto land that isn't theirs do so at the risk of hearing a couple of small-caliber rounds zing by them. It is a good idea to respect private property along the border. Of late, this traditional means of instilling territorial discipline has fallen into disfavor—not because of any risk to the targets, but because certain classes of trespassers (particularly those who smuggle people and controlled substances) have taken to arming themselves heavily. A friendly reminder from a rancher's .22 bolt-action carbine might be met with a rejoinder from a distinctly more urban 9 mm Glock semiautomatic pistol.

Junie was a young member of the old school, and when he heard noises in the brush on that February evening he figured it was someone or something that didn't belong there. He popped off two or three rounds from his old rifle—just enough to keep folks honest. A few minutes later Junie saw a Border Patrol vehicle drive slowly up the dirt road from the crossing, and he knew that he had committed an error in judgment.

The Border Patrol agents were almost to Redford when a beat-up pickup truck pulled up behind them and flashed its headlights in the descending darkness. They stopped. Junie hopped out of the old rig and ran up to their vehicle. "I'm sorry that I was shooting," he said. "I thought someone was doing something to my goats. I didn't know that you were back there."[15]

Agents Johnny Urias and James DeMatteo had heard the gunshots, but hadn't felt any physical risk. They figured no harm, no foul. Agent Urias remembers telling Junie, "Use more discretion when shooting your weapon, especially at night."[16]

Not "Assume the position," or "Holy Mother, you coulda killed me," or even "Don't be firing a rifle around here." Just "Use more discretion with your weapon, son." That's how it is in La Junta.

Three months later Junie stepped down from the school bus around four in the afternoon and walked down the dirt road to his family's homestead. He spent some time studying for his driving test and helped his father unload hay for the livestock. Then, as he did most evenings, Junie herded the goats out into the scrub to graze. He took his grand-dad's old .22 and headed along the dirt road toward the dilapidated shack where the army watched for bandidos during the Mexican Revolutions. The goats wandered through the sparse vegetation, bleating intermittently as they tugged at the dry browse.

A covey of Gambel's quail scurried across the dirt track, their silly topknots bouncing, their frantic twig-legs moving too fast to see. The afternoon sun warmed the windy day.

Raising his rifle, Junie plinked at something in the brush over toward the river, then resumed ambling behind the goats. Junie didn't know it, but he had repeated the mistake that he had made with the Border Patrolmen. There were people in that direction. Like the Border Patrolmen, they said nothing.

Junie circled behind the old border post and approached the square stone trough. He looked across the road and uphill, to his left. Was that something rustling around in the mesquite? Junie raised his rifle, but he never got a chance to fire.

From the other direction, 130 yards to Junie's right, Corporal Clemente Manuel Bañuelos, United States Marines, fired a single high-velocity 5.56 mm round from his M-16. Like the three other marines who had been invisibly trailing Junie—including Lance Corporal James M. Blood, who was in the general direction of Junie's aim—Bañuelos was wearing full guille-suit camouflage, and he was an expert marksman. The bullet entered under Junie's right arm, lifted him off his feet and blew him backward into the stone trough. Blood poured from Junie's wound.[17]

There are reasons and explanations, far too many of both. The shooting was investigated four times and it was reviewed by three grand juries. It came down to this. A decent young man was tending his sheep and doing what people do every day in La Junta. Four camouflaged, heavily armed, misinformed United States Marines were in a place where they shouldn't have been, badly executing a secret and ill-advised mission. They were supposed to be watching for drug smugglers, not goatherds. They were not supposed to arrest anyone or even reveal their presence, much less shoot citizens, but they were authorized by their rules of engagement to defend themselves, which is what Corporal Bañuelos said his squad was doing when they stalked, flanked and killed Junie.

Diana Valenzuela, wife of goat cheese promoter Jesus Valenzuela, asked the most poignant question: "What are these 'rules of engagement'? We had no idea we were being engaged in the first place."[18]

Enrique Madrid, the anthropologist and cultural resource of Redford, said, "I'm telling you, the only way they could have botched this up more was if they shot Mother Teresa. If there was one truly innocent man on the border, it was this young man." Later, holding his mother's two presidential medals in his hands, Enrique reminisced about how she had taught Junie in school, and remarked on the irony of what the federal government had brought her: "two presidential medals and an M-16 bullet in a kid's chest."[19]

Enrique Madrid and his wife, Ruby, along with the Reverend Mel La Follette, Jesus and Diana Valenzuela and Junie's sister Belen Hernandez, went to Washington, D.C., to visit with lawmakers. They asked for an end to armed military patrols on the border. They asked that the task force that killed Junie—called JTF6—be disbanded. After meeting with the citizens' committee, one solon said, "Of course I grieve with the family, but you know what they want in Redford? They don't even want the Border Patrol there—I don't agree with that."[20]

Junie's death spurred debates about militarization of the border and the use of federal troops on United States soil. It spawned arguments over drug policy and immigration and criminal responsibility. It prompted a withdrawal of armed soldiers from border duty. On the first anniversary of Junie's death Amnesty International issued a report accusing the United States Border Patrol of brutality.[21]

The Marine Corps never admitted any wrongdoing in the shooting, but it did pay almost $2 million to Junie's parents. Esequiel Hernandez Sr. used some of the money to buy a plot of land across the river for his goats. He still lives in El Polvo, but can't countenance grazing the flock where his son died.[22]

After Junie's funeral a crude wooden cross marked his grave. His name was misspelled. Some of the money from the United States

Marines went to buy a handsome new granite headstone for Junie. Behind it stands a modest white cross adorned with yellow plastic flowers. Junie's bandana is neatly folded at the base of the granite marker. His bolo tie hangs over the arms of the cross.

The reporters are gone. Dust devils swirl outside the Hernandez home. Burros find shade under acacia trees and stand motionless in the desert heat. No one watches Junie's father drive his pickup across the river to his goat pen.

The Chihuahuan Desert is high. Its low points are about one thousand feet above sea level, and extensive portions of its flatlands are above four thousand feet. Within its boundaries, craggy peaks rise several thousand feet higher—as high as ten thousand feet in its southern extremes.[1]

Winters in this desert are cool, and December brings snow and frequent freezes to its northern reaches. Summer is entirely different: temperatures can exceed 120° Fahrenheit.

The lowest portions of the Chihuahuan Desert are vegetated with desert scrub—creosote bush, cactus, yucca, agave, ocotillo, mesquite and acacia. Though sparse, this hardscrabble wasteland possesses a stark beauty, and a favorable spring can produce a show of blossoms that rivals a mountain meadow. The lowlands succor a remarkably diverse animal community—including over four hundred species of birds—but the terrain is hostile to people and can support only small populations.

The Land

The Chihuahuan Desert. Illustration by Herring Design, Houston, Tex.

As the desert rises, it progresses through grasslands where the soils are deep enough, then passes into woodlands of scrub oak, juniper, piñons and pines. At the highest elevations, coniferous forests harbor ponderosa pine and Douglas fir.

The most significant watershed in the Chihuahuan Desert is the valley of the Rio Grande. The river begins in the mountains of southern Colorado and flows south through New Mexico before it turns southeast at El Paso on its journey to the Gulf of Mexico. From El Paso to the Gulf, the Rio Grande marks what is today the border between Mexico and Texas.[2]

The other important waterway in the Chihuahuan Desert is the Rio Conchos, which gathers in the mountains along the west coast of Mexico, flows east through the foothills and the central plateau, then turns north and northeast. After coursing northerly for about two hundred air miles — many times that in riverbank miles — it meets the Rio Grande. The Spanish gave the river junction the most obvious name: La Junta de los Rios.

La Junta is surrounded by mountains. To the north are the Chinati Mountains — a jumble of igneous intrusions, uplifted lava flows, resistant sedimentary rock and metamorphic conglomerates. Further northwest stand the volcanic fault blocks of the Sierra Vieja, and to the southeast are the tilted lava peaks of the Bofecillos Mountains.[3]

On the west of La Junta, standing back from the Rio Grande, is a string of massive, structurally complex ridges that extends from northwest to southeast. The knife-edged Sierra Grande is the most imposing. To its north, on the other side of the Rio Conchos, the Sierra de la Parra segues into the Sierra Pinosa and the Sierra de Ventana. An igneous monolith called the Sierra de la Santa Cruz juts out of the land almost due south of the river junction, so alone and so large that it plays tricks on the eyes, moving first near the Rio Grande, then nearer the Conchos, when in fact it is more than two miles from either.[4]

Over time, soft rock and sedimentary overburden have washed out of the mountains into valleys. Millions of years of movement and erosion have created an undulating series of alluvial basins and craggy mountain ranges. In the southwestern United States and northern Mexico, basins and ranges often form *bolsons*. Similar to long depressions called grabens, bolsons are shallow valleys rimmed by mountains. Typically there is no natural water outlet in a bolson; if inflows and precipitation are adequate, a lake will form, flood the bolson and eventually overflow. Bolsons collect sediment from the surrounding heights. Lava flows and volcanic debris can contribute to bolson diminishment. Some bolsons have filled so completely that they have buried the sur-

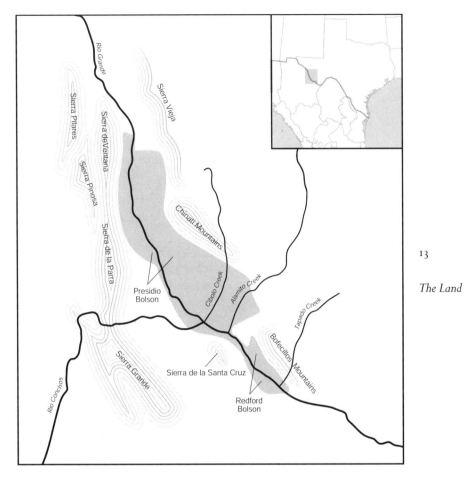

La Junta Mountains and Bolsons. Illustration by Herring Design, Houston, Tex.

rounding mountain ranges and form a continuous floor into adjacent basins. A beneficial aspect of bolsons is that their sedimentary floors can capture and hold groundwater.[5]

La Junta lies within bolsons, not canyons or plains. When the desert's infrequent but intense rainstorms strike the mountains around La Junta, they wash soil and soft rock into the valleys below. Massive alluvial fans flow out of the mountains, carrying sediment toward the rivers. The rivers rearrange the sediment into terraces and banks. In good years there is enough rain for agriculture; the bolsons' alluvial fill helps store precious moisture.

Of all the spots for scores of miles, the broad, level terraces and promontory mesillas of La Junta are the best place for people to build houses, grow crops and raise families. La Junta is an oasis.

La Junta de los Rios means "river junction." The junction is easy to reach if you have a key to the gate. The gate is at the west end of the Presidio-Ojinaga international bridge, just before the Mexican border control station. Open the gate, drive onto the gravel road that parallels the river and proceed a mile or so upstream to La Junta.

But you don't have a key to the gate. So you pass through the Mexican control point, drive straight up the hill into Ojinaga, turn right on Calle Trasviña y Retis, drive past the church and through scruffy cement-block neighborhoods to the edge of the mesilla, wander around on a few dirt streets until you descend to the level of the valley, then guess which ruts wind up at the river.

La Junta

When you reach the confluence, you realize that you have wasted your time. The Rio Grande that enters the junction is a stream, not a river. The Rio Conchos is a straight, disciplined irrigation ditch. The combined river is maybe three Buicks wide. There's a United States Border Patrol road on the other bank, and some plowed fields. Where you stand, on the Mexican side, is a patch of dirt littered with broken bottles. Twenty-foot dikes confine the rivers when they swell with rain and runoff, but the sky is clear today and the rivers are pitiful vestiges of themselves.

Both rivers have been tamed—no, they have been emasculated—by upstream water storage and diversion. The benefits of that development are evident on the Mexican flank of La Junta, and in the lush farmlands on the other side of the Sierra Grande. They are also evident far upstream on the Rio Grande, in the fields and orchards of New Mexico and Colorado. The cost of upstream irrigation is evinced by the modest, docile flow of the Conchos at the river junction. It is even more evident in the mudflats and dry gulches above La Junta where the Rio Grande used to be.

For centuries, the most common name for the Rio Grande in this region was the Rio del Norte. The added waters of the Rio Conchos so changed the Rio del Norte that people called the downstream stretch the Rio Bravo. Inevitably, the names sometimes mingled into El Rio Bravo del Norte. Today, locals just say El Rio, or maybe they use the derogatory *Rio Guapo*—dirty river. The Conchos is the clean river, *Rio Limpio,* or it is just El Conchos.

From the river junction, La Junta de los Rios extends

twenty-five miles or more along each waterway. The boundaries are easily visible. A green swath sprouts in the midst of the Chihuahuan Desert. The width of the green zone is anywhere from a few hundred yards to a few miles. The narrow segments are where mesillas confine the valley, or where people dry-farm, using the moisture that wicks up from the soil. Broad fields flourish where farmers are able to irrigate.

La Junta extends another couple of miles outside of the green swath. There have always been desert-dwelling community members who choose not to farm, and who rely on those who do. At one time the people who lived on the periphery were hunters and gatherers, and trade media included pottery, points and hides. Today the peripheral members are ranchers, laborers and people who hoard their privacy. The trade media are U.S. dollars, Mexican pesos and a few other things. There never has been a large population beyond the green zone, because life is difficult and unpleasant out there.

La Junta's upstream terminus along the Rio Conchos has not changed in a thousand years. Mexico's sheer, jagged Sierra Grande parallels the Rio Grande at a distance of about twenty-five miles. A few miles in front of the Sierra Grande is an abrupt mounded ridge, perhaps five hundred feet high, that sits astride the Rio Conchos. The river cuts a narrow canyon through the ridge. La Junta ends at the mouth of the canyon. Between the canyon and the Sierra Grande is rocky, brushy, uncultivated land.

La Junta's downstream limits along the Rio Grande are equally distinct. Tapado Creek enters the Rio Grande drainage about twenty-five miles below the river junction. Just downstream of that point, the land flanking the river rises. Jagged rocks crowd the riverbank. Eerie erosion-carved sandstone hoodoos loom over Colorado canyon, the river's outlet from the Redford Bolson. Here the green fields of La Junta come to an end and the rugged landscape of the Big Bend begins.

Going back upstream along the Rio Grande past the Conchos, the land gradually changes. About forty-five miles above the junction, on the Chihuahua side of the river, an angled gap opens between the Sierra de Ventana and the Sierra de Pilares. About halfway there, when the gap first becomes visible in the distance, the land takes on a different look and feel. Handsome farms give way to threadbare ranchitos. The broad river valley fills with dense mezquital taller than a man. The open terraces of La Junta dwindle away. Before the nineteenth century, La Junta ended here, in the vicinity of a native pueblo that the Spaniards called San Bernardino; archaeologists associate it with a site that today is endearingly known as Chihuahua E7–2. Beyond San Bernardino, the thick mezquital made farming difficult, but from the early nineteenth century onward, enterprising agrarians pushed La Junta another thirty miles up the river, above where the village of Candelaria is today.[1]

Presidio, Texas, feels like the closest town to the river junction. Ojinaga, Chihuahua, is actually closer, but it is perched on a mesa, and the vertical separation creates an illusion of distance. Presidio is an undernourished dirt-road town that claims five thousand citizens but appears to hold maybe half that many. It sits about a mile back from the Rio Grande. Not unlike several other settlements in the region, Presidio's preeminent characteristic is dust. Most homeowners do not bother trying to grow a lawn, perhaps because the grass would only disappear under a thick layer of wind-blown alluvium. Topsoil is highly mobile within the Presidio Bolson.

Presidio is proud to be in the U.S.A., but it prefers to speak Spanish. You can miss the best pie in town if you do not know that pecans are *nueces*. If you ask what kind of food a restaurant serves, the answer is likely to be "both kinds."

Like every small town, Presidio tries to attract tourists. Sadly for the local economy, there are no longer many reasons to visit Presidio. A few Big Bend travelers come through on their way back home; Chihuahuans driving to San Antonio or Dallas transit regularly. It's just enough to keep two weary motels in business.

The biggest employers in Presidio are the city, the school district and the Border Patrol. The town is too small for a Wal-Mart. A third of the Herrera family's supermarket is devoted to jeans, boots and work shirts. The grocery aisles are stacked with fifty-pound buckets of lard, twenty-pound sacks of pinto beans and twenty-pound bags of *masa harina* — corn flour.

The things that can be cooked with lard, pinto beans and masa harina will make you fat unless you work as hard as people do in Presidio. Perhaps because of the magnificence of their carbohydrate-laced, fat-soaked diets, La Juntans are a quietly friendly lot. When you pass an oncoming car on the highway, a two-finger howdy is appropriate. If you encounter an occasional standoffish sort, it is probably because your jangling urban ways grated upon the gentle and reserved local manners. Easy does it.

Ojinaga, in the Mexican state of Chihuahua, is the only settlement of any size within La Junta. Built atop a mesa in the southwest corner of the junction, about a mile back from the rivers, over the years it has spilled down to the Rio Grande. Ojinaga is connected to Presidio by an international bridge of proportions that dwarf the spindly river below.

The bridge is a quiet point of entry; it is unusual for more than a dozen vehicles to be backed up on either end.

There is a railroad bridge between the towns, too, but the railroad has fallen into disuse. An immense, dark, steel grate stands at the center of the span, blocking the tracks. It is possible to summon up all sorts of symbolism from this image, but at first look the overwhelming impression is of stupidity.

Ojinaga is a working town, not a tourist trap. It has some warehouses, some light manufacturing, some commerce, some banking, a fair amount of agricultural trade and a strong drug-smuggling subculture.

Most people who live in Presidio could just as well live in Ojinaga, and vice versa. Many of them divide their time and their families between the two. People who sleep on one side of the river may work, play and title their cars on the other.

In the manner of a traditional Mexican town, the highest point in Ojinaga is occupied by a pink adobe church that opens onto a plaza where people gather for fiestas. Festive banners ring the square, and a life-size bronze Benito Juárez gestures to his people. Brightly colored shops clutter the narrow streets adjoining the plaza. Peddlers set up stands, selling cold drinks, magazines and sweets.

Ojinaga's style may be uncomfortable for some citizens of the United States — it lacks convenience stores and Snickers bars, for example — but there is not a lot of qualitative difference between Ojinaga and Presidio. With 30,000 citizens, Ojinaga is basically eight or ten Presidios jammed together. Which is to say that it is not an attractive city.

In addition to Presidio and Ojinaga, there are several La Junta villages scattered along the rivers. On the Texas side, El Polvo and Redford are the only ones downstream of the river junction. Upstream, Ruidosa and Candelaria are part of the post-nineteenth-century La Junta that pushed beyond San Bernardino.

Ruidosa is a wide spot in the road thirty-eight miles above the river junction. A settler named William Russell built an irrigated farm there in 1872 and grew wheat. The Apaches killed four people on his farm and wounded three others. Cotton farming flourished around the beginning of the twentieth century. Then the water available for irrigation dwindled and Ruidosa did the same. Today there's a store, a tavern, a couple of houses and an abandoned adobe church.

Candelaria is another twelve miles up the Rio Grande. A plant called candelilla grows in the Chihuahuan Desert. People pull it up by its roots, boil it, add some sulfuric acid, boil it some more, and produce

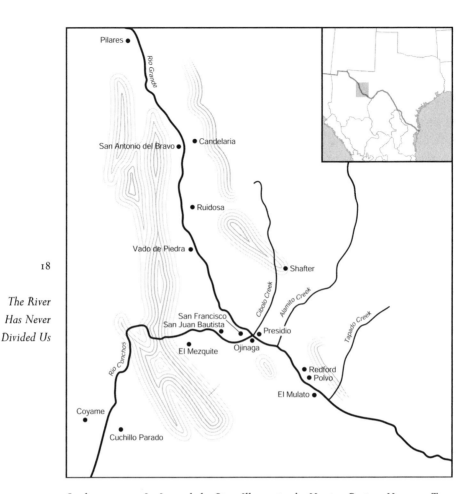

Settlements near La Junta de los Rios. Illustration by Herring Design, Houston, Tex.

a high-quality wax, second only to carnauba. A lot of candelilla was pulled up and processed locally. Some say that's how the town got its name, but Candelaria is a traditional woman's name, and it's easy to suppose that someone's wife or daughter was the inspiration. If Candelaria ever had glory days, they came to an end when its United States Army border post closed in 1919. Today it's a tiny farming pueblo centered around a one-room church.[2]

The pavement ends at Candelaria, and for the next ten dozen miles along the river there are no towns, no civilization. A road atlas shows nothing at all along that stretch — just blank paper with a dotted line where the Mountain and Central Time Zones meet.

On the other side of the Rio Grande, upstream and downstream from the river junction, Mexican farm pueblos scatter across the land: El Mezquite, San Juan, Valverde, San Antonio del Bravo, San Francisco,

La Esmeralda, Vado de Piedra, El Tecolote and El Mulato, to name a few. Some of these pueblos—certainly El Mezquite, San Francisco and San Juan—date back five hundred years, and possibly another five hundred or five thousand before that. Most are at a distance from paved roads and most consist of a church, a two-room elementary school and a smattering of adobe or cement-block houses. Sometimes there is a concrete plaza or a corral. These are subsistence agricultural villages. Because of the high cost of acquiring, fueling and maintaining farm equipment, much of the field labor is done by hand.

The few towns of La Junta comprise an isolated realm. Only a handful of other communities lie within a hundred miles of its borders. Those outside settlements are easily distinguished from La Junta not only because they fall outside the geographic limits that we have set, but also because they fail to meet some definitive standards: La Junta is a riverine agricultural community centered around the junction of the Rio Grande and the Rio Conchos; it has a rich heritage of nominally peaceful, largely sedentary, native settlements dating back more than a thousand years; it has a complex history of Spanish exploration and occupation; when Anglo pioneers first reached the community, they assimilated into the mestizo population. Places that violate one or more of those conditions fall outside La Junta.

A quick survey of the compass reveals a paucity of towns that could even be tested against those standards. To the west of La Junta is nothing. Desert. Rocks. Rattlesnakes. A few cattle. Yucca, sotol and ocotillo.

To the south and southwest, the Sierra Grande cuts off the world. On the other side of the divide are the village of Coyame, the little farming town of Cuchillo Parado and a dusty settlement at Julimes. Taken together, these pueblos have less than two thousand people.

To the east—the southeast along the river, really, and separated by thirty miles of rough country—is the old trading post at Lajitas (now a small, unfortunate resort). A flat slab of rock underlies the river there, making a good crossing. A dozen miles past Lajitas, Terlingua squats in ugly cuts slashed into rippling hills. The dilapidated former mercury-mining town exists today primarily to service an annual chili festival. The festival is held there because Terlingua is the most godforsaken place in the United States.

All of the sparse grazing land for seventy miles to the north and northeast of La Junta is within Presidio County, Texas. There are exactly two towns within Presidio County that are not in La Junta. Shafter, twenty-five miles from the river junction, is an old silver-mining ghost town. Ten, maybe twenty, people still linger there. Forty-five miles farther north is the iron-spike railroad town of Marfa, which is smaller than Presidio. The tall grasses inside the fence of the abandoned army base there make you wonder what the county might look like if livestock hadn't chewed it to a nub.

Presidio County, Texas, contains 7,300 people and 3,856 square miles. That's just under two people per square mile. The ratio in Montana is six people per square mile. In North Dakota, it's nine. Presidio County is larger than Delaware (population 783,600) and Rhode Island (population 1,048,319). If you took all the people in Presidio County to New York City and put them in Yellow Cabs, two in the back seat of each taxi, there would be more than eight thousand empty cabs left over.

Esequiel "Junie" Hernandez Jr. was an ordinary young man with an uncertain future.

Friends and family of Esequiel Hernandez Jr. erected a modest monument at the stone watering trough where he was shot. Photograph by author.

Wading across the Polvo crossing is easy when the Rio Grande is low. The Mexican rancheros on the far side are purchasing gasoline from a private party in El Polvo, who carries the fuel across the river in plastic jugs. Photograph by author.

Lucía Rede Madrid taught children for decades in the Redford Elementary School. Her daughter-in-law, Ruby Madrid, later assumed her duties. Photograph by author.

The Rio Grande brings life to La Junta. The ocotillo in the foreground is on a mesilla — an extension of a gravelly terrace. The irrigated fields in the right background are on a lower sedimentary terrace just above the riverbank. This spot is below Redford, approaching the southern limits of La Junta. Photograph by author.

North of the river junction the knife edge of the Sierra Grande segues into a series of more jumbled mountain ranges. The Rio Grande flows through the valley between the gravel terraces in the foreground and the ridges that rise in front of the mountains. Even a burro has a hard time finding browse in this ocotillo-strewn landscape. Photograph by author.

The railroad bridge across the Rio Grande between Presidio and Ojinaga is blocked by steel gates on the United States side. People sometimes come here to swim in the summer because the water is deep and cool under the bridge. Photograph by author.

Ruidosa boasts a bar, a small store and a crumbling adobe church. The church is not especially old, dating to the early twentieth century. Photograph by author.

Adobes bake in the heat at the ancient village of San Juan Bautista. The odd configuration of the building in the foreground suggests that it might once have been a church with a bell tower, but if that were the case there should have been a doorway beneath the spires. Photograph by author.

Two rurales pose outside a typical desert jacal. The walls and roof are of ocotillo stalks and sotol candles. An interior framework made of cottonwood timber supports the structure. Some jacals were coated with mud or adobe. Courtesy of Archives of the Big Bend, Bryan Wildenthal Memorial Library, Sul Ross State University, Alpine, Tex. Photograph by Glenn Burgess.

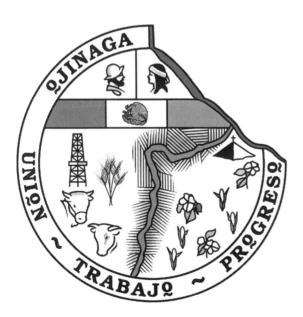

The seal of the Municipio of Ojinaga (similar to a county) shows the Rio Conchos and Rio Grande, the Sierra de la Santa Cruz, cultivated fields along the river, cattle, a native, a conquistador and other symbols of La Junta's past. Most revealing is the shape of the seal. Its upper right sector — the part of La Junta within Texas — is missing, as if it had been torn away.

La Junta is one of the oldest continuously occupied settlements in the Chihuahuan Desert, ranking in age and dignity with the Anasazi pueblos of New Mexico. The native people who inhabited La Junta were a complex and varied lot.[1]

Several tribes of sedentary or semisedentary agricultural people lived more or less permanently in La Junta. They built sturdy, square, flat-roofed houses of poles plastered with mud. They fell into two principal divisions: Abriaches and Otomoacos. The subclans that appeared most often in the historical record were the Julimes, Cabris, Mezquites, Púliques, Tapacolmes and Tecolotes.

Semisedentary hunters visited and sometimes settled in La Junta seasonally or more permanently. They fall into three principal groups: the Jumanos, the Cibolos and the people of the Cielo Complex. Within a given group, some members might remain seminomadic while others might become permanent La Junta residents. Most transient La Juntans lived in temporary huts, wickiups or tepees.

Groups of nomadic or seminomadic hunters and gatherers visited—or raided—La Junta but did not willingly settle there. They include Conchos, Chisos, Apaches and Comanches. Nomads lived in wickiups or tepees, or found shelter under ledges or in caves.

The Spanish had their own ways of classifying native people. Using the Spanish labels would provide a certain feel of authenticity, but wouldn't fit La Junta particularly well. Early Spaniards called La Juntans *Patarabueyes* (Pah-tahr-ah-boo-AY-yays), slang for "ox-kicker," but that broad label applied to all categories of La Juntans and was used far beyond La Junta's borders. Colonial Spaniards called desert nomads *Chichimecas,* but La Juntans weren't nomads, and the term was used less often as the Spanish explored northward and gained a more sophisticated understanding of native inhabitants.

Álvar Núñez Cabeza de Vaca was the first European to visit La Junta. In 1534, after an unimaginable seven-year journey that began on the Gulf Coast of Florida, he found himself in a La Junta village, accompanied by his last three surviving companions. They were completely lost in a land never before explored by Europeans.[2]

During his amazing journey Cabeza de Vaca had been a prisoner, a trader, a slave, a traveler, a shaman and a crafts-

Before 1830

man. He had relied on the generosity of natives for his survival and had accumulated a sizable entourage, for his new native friends were most curious about his destiny. He followed established trails and relied on natives for guidance, but never knew where he had been or where he was going.

The escorts that brought him to La Junta were hunter-gatherers — probably not Apaches, because no archaeological evidence exists to indicate their presence in La Junta that early. Jumanos are likely candidates. The Spanish parted ways with the nomads at La Junta and cast their lot with the La Juntans. This was the Spaniards' first encounter with sedentary agricultural natives; they had spent the last seven years among nomadic hunter-gatherers. To Spanish eyes, the natives along the Rio Grande "had the best physiques of any we saw. They were the liveliest and most skillful, and the ones who understood and answered our questions best." They grew beans and squash, but dry weather had forced them to trade for corn. They lived in square, flat-roofed habitations — simplified versions of adobe pueblos that Cabeza de Vaca called "the first houses that really looked like houses." [3]

Cabeza de Vaca and his companions were the first Europeans to venture into the interior of what is now the United States west of the Mississippi River. Spurred by Cabeza de Vaca's exploits, Friar Marcos de Niza scouted a path from Mexico City into New Mexico for Francisco Vasquez de Coronado, who soon followed on an expensive and ill-fated 1540 expedition. Coronado penetrated deep into the Great Plains without achieving his goal — conquest of the Seven Cities of Cibola and the Grand Kingdom of Quivira.

For forty long years after Coronado's debacle the Spanish largely ignored the northern deserts — the *Tierra Despoblada,* or uninhabited land — while they concentrated on other matters. Then, in 1581, a Spanish expedition into the unknown departed the northern mining town of Santa Bárbara. Led by Franciscan friar Agustín Rodríguez under the protection of Captain Francisco "Chamuscado" Sánchez, the Spaniards traipsed down the Rio Conchos and through La Junta before proceeding to New Mexico in search of silver and souls.

Rodríguez and Chamuscado never made it back to Santa Bárbara, the former having been murdered by natives and the latter dying of disease on the return trip. Two friars had insisted on remaining in New Mexico after Chamuscado's departure. Because they were obviously in peril (a peril that culminated quickly in their deaths), a quasi-rescue mission to New Mexico was mounted by Antonio de Espejo, who also took a route that passed through La Junta.

There are clear indications that soldiers, adventurers and slavers reached La Junta before either the Rodríguez-Chamuscado expedition or the Espejo mission, but unlike those unofficial visits the two sanctioned *entradas* provide written records of early native communities in La Junta.

Together with Cabeza de Vaca, the two expeditions add up to a remarkable fact: of the first five European forays into the western United States, three proceeded by way of La Junta. La Junta received this surprising distinction because of its defining characteristic: it lies at the junction of two rivers that could be followed from the farthest settled frontier of New Spain deep into the hostile desert.

As New Spain's frontier pushed north beyond the mining towns of what are now Durango and southern Chihuahua, the Spanish found it essential to establish a distant perimeter to protect their colonists from raiding Apaches, Comanches and other hostile peoples. Over many decades of Spanish indecision and gyration, La Junta emerged as a critical point of frontier defense. Captain Manuel Muñoz established the Presidio Nuestra Señora de Bethlem y Santiago de Amarillas there in 1760, but within a few years it had been abandoned under pressure from indigenous warriors. Though called a presidio, that first military establishment in La Junta was little more than a militarized village. Its 1773 replacement, the Presidio de los Ríos del Norte y Conchos, at least possessed basic adobe-walled defenses, though it was a crude structure at best. The Presidio del Norte, as it came to be known, grew and endured well into the nineteenth century; in effect, it remains today in the guise of a Mexican Army garrison in Ojinaga, and a few walls of the old presidio still stand adjacent to Ojinaga's square.

Though there had long been an ongoing effort by Franciscans to save La Juntan souls — six simple missions once dotted the valley — the arrival of a permanent Spanish military presence effectively doomed the existing native communities. A multitude of conflicts, pressures and practices — including Anglo settlement to the northeast that drove Comanches up against Apaches and pushed Apaches into and beyond La Junta — displaced traditional La Juntans from the valley, destroyed tribal relationships and engendered new hostilities. By 1787 Captains Domingo Díaz and Juan Bautista Elguezábal were embarked upon the first of three attempts to resettle La Junta with "pacified" Apaches.

Over time, La Junta and the Presidio del Norte became part of a fortified line of defense along the Rio Grande that flourished in the late 1700s and early 1800s. Its importance as a way station between Ciudad

Chihuahua and New Mexico, however, had disappeared years before, when the Spanish learned to cut directly through the desert from Ciudad Chihuahua to El Paso. That diagonal roadway became a vital *Camino Real* that bypassed La Junta. The Presidio del Norte was an isolated defensive point.

During the fifteen years between the independence of Mexico in 1821 and the independence of Texas in 1836, La Junta was an undisputed part of the Mexican state of Chihuahua. For another dozen years until the Treaty of Guadalupe Hidalgo, sovereignty over La Junta north of the Rio Grande was in dispute, but the valley's governance and loyalties were entirely Chihuahuan.[1]

Although Chihuahua — or at least its southern tier — was not exempt from the ongoing political machinations of Mexico City, and although the state busied itself with ejecting foreign capitalists while lamenting that its economy was in ruins, its greatest problem was exactly what it had always been: hostile nomads. Sensing Mexican weakness, Apaches and Comanches raided mercilessly, penetrating far into areas of the state that had once considered themselves free of predators.

As had been the case since the seventeenth century, Chihuahua needed strong frontier defenses and strong military leadership in the field. These familiar needs were intensified by rumblings from the Anglo colonies in Texas and the ill-concealed territorial greed of the United States. Establishment of a secure perimeter was imperative. Chihuahua had long realized that neither it nor the nation could defend a border beyond the Rio Grande; although Chihuahua extended much farther north before 1848, its only practical option was to draw the line at the river.

Relying on authority created under the Mexican colonization law of 1824 (the law that gave rise to the Texas colonies), Chihuahua promulgated its own colonization law in 1825, declaring the lands along the Rio Grande to be open to settlement. The terms were generous: colonists were required only to present a plan for settlement and establishment of industries, arts and machinery; if the government approved their plans, the land was free. Chihuahua's leaders wanted a breed of bold, hardy settlers to populate their frontier, and they meant to draw them there with free land.[2]

Free land proved to be an inadequate incentive; few if any colonies took root. In 1830 Mexico authorized the use of land for frontier fortifications and arsenals, and appropriated funds for construction of forts and transportation of colonists to the frontier. Money was also set aside to maintain the colonists for their first year, purchase agri-

The

Promised

Land

cultural tools and reward farmers who distinguished themselves. Duties on imported cotton were allocated to a special fund "to maintain the integrity of Mexican territory [and] to form a reserve fund against the event of Spanish invasion." Finally—and essentially—the decree provided that prisoners sentenced to hard labor in a garrison could instead be diverted to frontier military colonies, where they would work off their sentence. If, after completing their sentence, prisoners wished to remain as colonists, then they would be given land, tools and a year's support. Mexico had sweetened the pot for colonists and had offered the mixed pleasures of frontier life to a class of people who could not refuse.[3]

The exact date that a fortified military (prison) colony was established at *Vado de Piedra* (Rock Ford—a ford with a solid rock bottom, not a rocky bottom) is lost in the fog of history, but it is more than likely that its construction and operation were directed by the Presidio del Norte's Captain José Ignacio Ronquillo, a remarkable soldier who spent most of his career defending frontier presidios. As second lieutenant of a highly mobile "flying squadron" of cavalry, his first assignments were at the presidio in Janos and then the Presidio de San Francisco de Conchos. As he rose in the ranks, the government entrusted him with the sensitive task of reconciling presidial officers who had been loyal to the ousted Emperor Iturbide. After the flying squadrons were disbanded in 1826, he became the commander of the Presidio del Norte in 1829.[4]

Vado de Piedra was a pueblo at a river crossing about thirty miles upstream of Presidio del Norte, below and across (on the Mexican side) from Ruidosa. The Rio Grande forms a big, sweeping bend there, called *Ancón Grande* (Big Bend, but in the argot of La Junta *ancón* also refers to a swath of riverine subirrigated land on which crops can be grown). Vado de Piedra is in the stretch of country once occupied by people known as Tecolotes, near where Cabeza de Vaca stumbled into a village that the Spanish called San Bernardino. There's still a little Mexican pueblo near the ford.[5]

The fort at Vado de Piedra was rectangular and built of adobe. It had parapets at each end of a long wall with a crenellated top. As many as three hundred colonists (mostly convicts) and overseers were stationed there; they cultivated corn, melons and other crops in nearby fields. Only one of a line of military prison colonies strung along the border, it was complemented by similar installations upstream at Pilares, Guadalupe, San Ignacio and San Elizario and downstream at San Carlos and San Vicente. There are even reports that there was a prison colony at the Presidio del Norte; though this was not the presidio's origins, it is entirely possible that prisoners were added to its retinue at times.[6]

Captain Ronquillo was fortunate not to accompany the forced occupants of Vado de Piedra on their hunting trip to San Esteban, a spot considerably north of the river and just south of where Marfa is today. Buffalo were rare in the region, but the convicts came across a small herd, surrounded it quietly, then drove the bison into a trap where riflemen could slaughter the beasts. It was a bountiful kill, and the men were so preoccupied with skinning and butchering the game that a band of Comanches had no trouble executing their own stealthy surround and ambush, wiping out the hunting party. Some people called the convict colonists "condemned regiments," and that dramatic name combined with the Comanche ambush gave rise to inevitable folklore about the dead men returning each year to the site of their fatal hunt.[7]

Ronquillo was more than just another commander of the Presidio del Norte. Unlike Captains Muñoz, Díaz or Elguezábal who preceded him, Ronquillo fell in love with La Junta and made it his home. When he arrived in 1829, he brought along his wife, Rafaela, and his three girls — María de los Angeles, Paz and Josepha. His longtime mistress, Antonia Oros, and their three-year-old daughter, Trinidad, were already living in the village at Presidio del Norte. This may have come as a surprise to Rafaela.[8]

Like many military officers, Captain Ronquillo longed to retire to a big ranch. He wasted no time establishing a small spread that he called Tapacolmes (across the river and up a creek from the ancient native pueblo of Tapacolmes) and another called Álamo Chapo (twenty-five miles upstream on the Rio Conchos, near the Sierra Grande). But Ronquillo had something bigger in mind. The captain knew that he had performed valuable services for Chihuahua, and he intended to become even more valuable to the state during the remainder of his career. Sometime, somewhere in the future, he would secure a land grant worthy of his accomplishments — a grant more magnificent than his little farms at Tapacolmes and Álamo Chapo. It would be a grant far larger than the eleven square leagues permitted under the colonization laws. It would be a generous act of largesse bestowed by a grateful governor upon a loyal servant.[9]

It wasn't long after assuming the command of Presidio del Norte that Ronquillo decided that La Junta was where his land grant should be. But the time wasn't right for approaching the governor; Ronquillo needed to accumulate a few more career credits. In the meantime, he wanted to somehow stake out his claim, preempting any potential competitors until a formal grant could be obtained. This was neither unheard of nor inappropriate on the frontier, where the supply of land seemed inexhaustible and the demand was low. Many colonists marked their claims, built their houses and began growing crops in the expectation that the necessary paperwork would eventually work its way through Ciudad Chihuahua. Ronquillo's plan differed only in its grandeur.

The captain became good friends with the alcalde of Presidio del Norte, Cesario Herrera. Because the presidio and the community around it were under military command, Herrera technically reported to Ronquillo. More importantly, Herrera demonstrated an inclination to cater to the captain's wishes and had a reputation for being able to stretch his authority a bit when appropriately compensated. Herrera could provide the air of legitimacy required to set aside Ronquillo's lands.[10]

And so Ronquillo, Herrera and a few witnesses set forth on horseback, a wagon trailing behind, to establish the boundaries of Ronquillo's promised land. The first corner was at the junction of Cibolo Creek and the Rio Grande, about where the town of Presidio is today. From there, they rode thirty miles up the Rio Grande to the Ancón Grande, near the prison colony at Vado de Piedra. That was the second corner of Ronquillo's ranch. Then the crew took a seventy-mile overland jaunt north to a spring in a cottonwood grove called Los Álamos de San Juan, where the United States Army would establish Fort Davis twenty-five years later. That was the northernmost corner. Turning southeast, Ronquillo's party rode forty-three miles to the Sierrita del Álamo, another cottonwood grove and spring that later became known as simply "Cottonwood Spring" or "Ojo de Álamo." From there, the boundary extended fifty-three miles straight back to the confluence of Cibolo Creek and the Rio Grande.[11]

It was an enormous tract of land. Ronquillo and Herrera calculated it as 15 leagues square, or 225 square leagues, or 1,557 square miles. In fact, when it was accurately surveyed it turned out to be a rhombus of larger scale: 2,345.5 square miles, or 1,501,120 acres—almost half the size of Connecticut.[12]

Cesario Herrera lacked the power to bestow the grant upon his friend, but he did what he could to formalize Captain Ronquillo's claim. Every Sunday morning, after church services were over, the citizens of Presidio del Norte would gather in the plaza to hear the local officials announce new decisions and acts. One Sunday in 1829, Cesario Herrera proclaimed that the enormous tract of land had been set aside for Captain Ronquillo. Thereafter, people accepted that the lands were reserved, even though not yet formally conveyed. Ronquillo had his ranch.[13]

Captain Ronquillo moved his legitimate family into a stone house that he built on his new grant. The house and the huts of a few peons were about three miles northeast of the Rio Grande in a place that he called Cibolo, after the creek that ran nearby. But the ranch house wasn't safe when the captain was away pursuing Apaches across the landscape; during those times, his family would move back to the presidio. The arrangement wasn't practical, and soon the stone ranch house stood abandoned.[14]

Given that the protection of the presidio didn't extend even as far as Ronquillo's Cibolo house just three miles northeast, it is no surprise that the people who were trying to farm *ancónes* two or three miles downstream along the Rio Grande felt equally exposed. Because there were several families in that area (a mile or two below where Presidio is today), the army built a small outpost there—just a couple of fortified houses and an adobe-walled corral. It came to be known as the *fortín* (little fort). Locals dubbed the modest compound the Fortín de San José. Sometimes Ronquillo would leave the presidio and live in the fortín for a few days with his soldiers, perhaps because it put him closer to his farm at Tapacolmes, or maybe because it was near the southern edge of his enormous land claim.[15]

The fortín is one sign of the difficult life of La Juntans in 1830; they found themselves directly engaged in battles with Apaches in their midst. Reacting to events in La Junta, the Congress of Chihuahua, with the governor's blessing, passed a resolution "with the just purpose of alleviating in part the constant fatigue that frontier inhabitants experience due to the frequent aggression of the barbarous nations that surround them." Citing the praise given the citizens of Presidio del Norte in communications from the commandant general, the Congress declared that as soon as the state of the treasury would permit, they should be remunerated for their contributions in the military actions against the Apaches. Specifically, any horses lost by La Juntans in the struggles were to be replaced at state expense and any wounded civilians were to be treated without charge at the military hospital in Ciudad Chihuahua. Those that could not be transported to Chihuahua were to get the best available local care at the state's expense. The sons of the settlers in La Junta were to be given preference in allocation of state government jobs. Finally the Congress, ever short of funds, called on the state's hacendados and rancheros to contribute horses to the troops that garrisoned the border.[16]

For Rafaela Ronquillo, life at Presidio del Norte may have been better than out at Cibolo, but the hostile environment of La Junta was still a difficult place for a woman trying to raise three girls while her husband traipsed across the countryside and camped out with the guys at the fortín. Rafaela grew tired of life in La Junta. Perhaps she grew tired of José Ignacio Ronquillo. It is almost certain that in the tiny, gossipy community of the Presidio del Norte she grew tired of Antonia Oros. Rafaela took María, Paz and Josepha to Aldama, near Ciudad Chihuahua, and never returned.[17]

Captain Ronquillo stayed at La Junta even after his wife left him. He became a fixture of the community. His friends and supporters called him *Capitan* Ronquillo as a sign of warm respect even after he gained a promotion to lieutenant colonel. In 1832 Colonel José Joaquín Calvo, the new commander general and inspector of Chihuahua and Nuevo Mexico, gave Ronquillo command of all frontier troops engaged in fighting Apaches and Comanches. This required Ronquillo to operate out of the Nuevo Mexico town of Santa Rita. A later promotion to assistant inspector of Chihuahua and Nuevo Mexico, followed by a stint as military commander of El Paso, extended Ronquillo's absences from La Junta.[18]

When Apaches weren't raiding near the Presidio del Norte, Comanches were. In October 1831 two soldiers—Quiterio Rivera and Eugenio Heredia—were killed in a gunfight with more than one hundred Comanches who attacked a horse herd at the Vado de Piedra fort. Captain Ronquillo took soldiers, citizen auxiliaries and a group of pacified Apache guides in pursuit of the raiders. Exasperated, Commander General Calvo declared war against the Comanches and called on all of the citizens of Chihuahua to support the valiant efforts of the frontier citizens. Within a few months, Chihuahua also declared war on Apaches who had broken their peace treaties and called for collection of all peaceful Apaches near several key presidios, of which the Presidio del Norte was one. The situation was so dire that the government found it necessary to prohibit citizens from leaving their homes without firearms approved by the military.[19]

Calvo and Ronquillo were fighting a losing battle. Eight hundred Apaches swept into Chihuahua during 1835 and operated with relative impunity. In February of that year Lieutenant Colonel Ronquillo led a campaign against Apaches in the vicinity of Ojo Caliente, about halfway between the Presidio del Norte and El Paso. He died in combat on February 19, and his body was carried back to La Junta, where his onetime dreams of a ranching empire were now lost. His wrongful love, Antonia Oros, was there as soldiers buried their *Capitán* inside the presidio's church. His estranged wife Rafaela did not attend.[20]

Apache incursions during 1835 were relentless. In June, General Calvo—who had now become governor as well—gathered an army and marched to Presidio del Norte, where he prepared to attack Mescaleros north of the river, only to be called back again by President

Santa Anna, who was more concerned with the threat of French and Spanish invasions than with murderous Apaches.[21]

Because of the presence of the presidio and the military prison colony, no Apache raiding pathways led directly through La Junta, but the Chinati Mountains, the Sierra Vieja and the Bofecillos Mountains all harbored Mescalero Apache rancherías (temporary villages). Just upstream, at El Morrión Pass (beyond Candelaria, roughly west of Valentine, Texas), was a major thoroughfare for Mescaleros. Downstream, Apaches poured out of the Chisos Mountains, the Sierra del Carmen and their other Big Bend hideouts, drawn by opportunities to the south. As Comanches pushed into Apache territory, the region from La Junta to the Big Bend became a transition zone that saw both Apache and Comanche traffic. An important avenue for Comanche raids into Mexico crossed the Rio Grande near Lajitas, about forty miles below La Junta. Once across the river, the Comanches headed for the Rio Conchos and followed it into the rich interior of Chihuahua. Another Comanche pathway forded the Rio Grande farther down, at the apex of the Big Bend, then penetrated a hostile desert known as the Bolson de Mapimí and emerged in Chihuahua, Durango and Coahuila. It is roughly correct to say that Apaches dominated to the west of La Junta, Comanches prevailed to the east of the Big Bend and the two nations overlapped in the region between.[22]

It is no longer stylish to think of Native Americans as bent on harming peaceful settlers, but the facts regarding Apaches and Comanches in Chihuahua during the nineteenth century are difficult to avoid. They were raiders and predators. This accurate statement is not meant to obscure the perfectly good reasons for their aggressive tendencies, nor is it meant to suggest that the Mexicans were not equally guilty of intraspecies atrocities. We must, however, accept that in this particular place and time there was an established migratory pattern by which nomads would leave their summer hunting grounds to the north of the Rio Grande (where nonnatives were entirely absent), pass through lightly settled Mexican outposts on and below the river and penetrate more southern agricultural domains in search of food, livestock, captives and plunder.

September was the month when the raids would begin, and it became known as the month of the Mexico Moon. The weather cooled, the trails were dry and forage was still abundant. The nomads' pattern of autumnal migration was so predictable that settlers along the Rio Grande and to the south would post sentinels on hills, watching for telltale dust plumes. The watchers would light signal fires to alert their villages and sentinels farther south. Frightened rancheros would prepare their fortifications and weapons. Soon terrible pilgrims would appear on the trails that flanked La Junta. Thefts and murders and abductions would begin.[23]

The social dynamic between nomads and Mexicans was interesting and unfortunate. As was usually the case when nomads cast their eyes on sedentary societies, Apaches and Comanches saw the blend of Mesoamerican, Chichimeca, La Juntan, Spaniard and African that had become Mexicans of the north as a weak, inferior race, the legitimate prey of brave warriors. Mexico's nomads commonly captured Mexican women and children, treating them as lowly creatures, keeping and trading them as slaves and concubines. These were barbarous times.[24]

La Junta avoided the worst of the consequences not only because it was militarized, but also because it was an impoverished outpost on Mexico's Rio Grande perimeter. It was an easily avoided obstruction on a scattered frontier, quickly bypassed by nomads bent on penetrating to the wealth of the interior. There were no rich haciendas in La Junta—they lay beyond. Still, La Juntans had little to be thankful for; the predators' proximity was acute, the possibility of becoming a target of opportunity was apparent and the risk of venturing beyond the presidio's walls was high. Too poor and too miserable even to merit a major Apache raid, La Junta was doomed to stay in exactly that condition unless the threat of attack could be removed.

In time, the Mexicans became the predators, the raiders, the ones looking for trouble. At a complete loss to control nomadic raids, they turned to the most despicable possible solution: scalp hunting.

In 1837 Chihuahua began offering one hundred silver pesos—equal in value to one hundred silver dollars—for the scalp of a male over the age of fourteen who belonged to the Apache, Comanche, Kiowa or Navajo tribes. The scalps of women of those tribes brought fifty pesos. A child's scalp was worth twenty-five pesos. As an added incentive, scalp hunters were entitled to keep any livestock and plunder that they took from their victims.[1]

Chihuahua's treasury was stretched thin, so merchants and hacendados formed "war societies" that collected funds to pay for scalps. Governor Calvo entered into contracts with people like James Kirker to assemble miniarmies that would pursue Apaches full time. Kirker, who came to be known in Chihuahua as Santiago—sainted by his murderous trade—fell into and out of favor with the government over decades of scalp hunting, changing sides as circumstances required. At one amazing point Kirker became the leader of an Apache band in western Chihuahua, but when he heard that the governor had put a bounty of nine thousand pesos on his head, Kirker negotiated a deal under which he switched loyalties, raided his own Apache village and collected 168 scalps.[2]

Mexico's resort to scalp hunting represented a complete failure to manage conflict with the northern nomads. Burdened with an impoverished government, an ineffective army and an insufficiently armed citizenry, Mexico chose to unleash demons upon its foes. There is an unsettling Thomas Easterly daguerreotype of a gaunt Kirker in ill-fitting formal dress. His disturbed, wild-eyed look is eerily reminiscent of John Steuart Curry's mural of abolitionist John Brown holding a Bible in one outstretched hand and a rifle in the other, his tangled hair and long beard blowing in the firestorm of the Civil War. Kirker was haunted by wraiths we cannot imagine.[3]

Though contracts with scalp hunters were signed at the Presidio del Norte, and although scalp hunters did sometimes collect their coup in the region, most scalp hunting was done to the south (among more civilized and populous

Anglos

Arrive

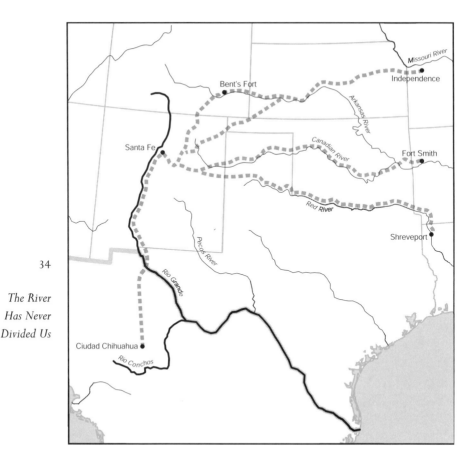

*Santa Fe Trail and Camino Real to Ciudad Chihuahua. Illustration by Herring
Design, Houston, Tex.*

settlements) and to the west (along the trail from Ciudad Chihuahua to
Santa Fe). There was no shortage of Apaches in the mountains north and
east of La Junta, but the mountains were a place where scalp hunters
found it more difficult to execute ambushes and more likely to have
one executed upon them.[4]

The scalp hunt was one of two activities that brought Anglos from
Santa Fe to Ciudad Chihuahua, the gateway to Presidio del Norte.
Trading was the second Anglo-attracting activity. By the mid-1830's
the Santa Fe Trail connected the fledgling United States with Mexican Santa Fe. Santa Fe was not especially important as a destination
in itself, for it was a modest frontier town, albeit with a thriving local
marketplace. Arguably the greater significance of Santa Fe was that it
was an established port of entry into Mexico, at the northern terminus of the venerable Camino Real that connected the most lucrative
frontier mining centers with Mexico City. About half of the freight

reaching Santa Fe from the United States continued south through El Paso to Ciudad Chihuahua, and some continued farther south into the Mexican interior.

As wagons came and went between Santa Fe and Ciudad Chihuahua, some Anglo merchants began to linger, setting up trading operations in Mexico. Gradually, Ciudad Chihuahua added more Anglos to its mix, and those Anglos began to learn about their surroundings.[5]

One successful merchant in Chihuahua was Dr. Henry C. Connelly. Born in Kentucky, he received a medical degree from Transylvania University in Lexington. Soon he moved his practice to Liberty, Missouri. Liberty is in western Missouri, just north of the Missouri River — meaning just north of Independence, where wagon trains gathered for the journey to Santa Fe. Soon young Doctor Connelly was in Santa Fe and then Chihuahua, where he changed professions and became a prominent and successful merchant and freighter.[6]

We find Connelly in 1839, before Texas statehood, before he moved back to Santa Fe, before Chihuahua jailed him as a spy, before Abraham Lincoln appointed him governor of the Territory of New Mexico, before he died of an accidental overdose of opium taken to ease the pain of his many illnesses. The Henry Connelly we find is young, entrepreneurial and adventurous.[7]

Connelly shrewdly analyzed Chihuahua's situation and his own. 1839 was a time when Chihuahua would reward creativity in bringing goods to market and in finding purchasers for the state's silver bullion. It was a time when a man who could cut his expedition's costs — perhaps by shaving a few hundred miles off his journey — could make a killing.

Connelly began making plans for a wagon train that would follow the Rio Conchos to Presidio del Norte and from there across Texas toward the Mississippi. It was an ambitious plan; his wagons would be the first to take that route. Because his caravan would begin at Ciudad Chihuahua, its cargo pattern would be the opposite of most: Connelly would carry silver bullion north and return with manufactured goods. He attracted two other merchants to his scheme, and together they decided that they would need only seven sturdy wagons on the outbound leg. The cargo — almost MEX$300,000 worth of silver — was compact, but demanded reliable transport: the merchants planned for fifty private guards, fifty Mexican soldiers and seven hundred mules.[8]

Enlisting Mexican soldiers into Connelly's entourage would require the cooperation of the government, but that cooperation was a sine qua non for other reasons, anyway. First, no freight entered or left Chihuahua or Mexico legally without official sanction. Second, because Connelly planned to exit Chihuahua's zone of control at Presidio del

Norte — rather than at the approved Mexican port of entry at Santa Fe — special permission would be required. And third, Connelly's trading expedition could not profit without an *arreglo*.[9]

An arreglo is a secret arrangement with the authorities who collect customs duties. Arreglos were common with local customs agents at Mexican ports of entry. Incompetence and corruption were rampant; even leaving those factors aside, the difficulty of enforcing Mexico's complicated and ever-changing tax laws drove officials to more expedient measures. Connelly's arreglo was unusual in that it was reached with the central authorities of Chihuahua, rather than with minor customs officials at a port of entry. It was said that Connelly made his arrangement with Governor Irigoyen de la O himself. Perhaps the governor felt it appropriate to lower the customs duties in advance because of the inordinate risk that Connelly was taking to open a new trade route for Chihuahua. Or perhaps the governor had some bills to pay.[10]

Whatever the official motivations, differences in how the United States treated shipments over land versus those by sea made Connelly's arreglo an essential element of his plan. At the time, U.S. laws provided for a debenture, or refund, of duties paid to import goods that were later transshipped to another country. This permitted ports in the United States to competitively receive, warehouse and reship cargo bound for foreign shores. Without the refund, ships with goods for Mexico and beyond would avoid American ports. Unfortunately for Connelly, the debenture laws would not apply to shipments over land until the passage of the Drawback Act in 1845. Connelly's wagons were already an expensive way to move freight; the tariff disadvantage made things even more difficult, so he negotiated Mexican tariff relief in advance with the governor of Chihuahua, offsetting the tax advantages of seaborne freight.[11]

Once the arreglo was cemented, Connelly's train left Chihuahua on April 3, 1839, traveled down the Rio Conchos to the Presidio del Norte and crossed the Rio Grande without incident, though the arrival and departure of such a large, heavily guarded caravan in La Junta — and the first appearance of Anglos in the valley — must have caused quite a stir. One local recorded it in his journal, granting an on-the-spot promotion to either Connelly or the leader of his military escort: "The 20th of [April] the General started his journey to the United States of America having with him one hundred men as guards."[12]

Connelly's crew had a remarkably easy time crossing the South Plains, but they did become lost at one point in Oklahoma and required the assistance of some Delaware Indians to set them back on course. They reached Fort Towson, near the Red River in far south-

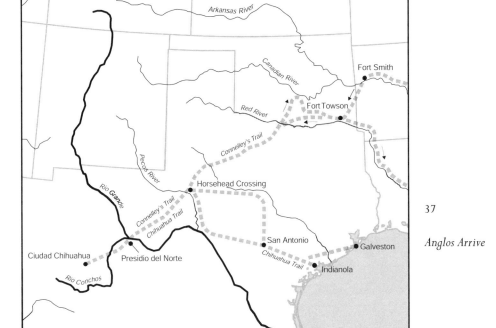

Connelly's Trail and the Chihuahua Trail. Illustration by Herring Design, Houston, Tex.

east Oklahoma, three months after departing Presidio del Norte. There they negotiated their entry into the United States. From Fort Towson they took a steamboat to Shreveport, thence to the Mississippi River and its rich opportunities for trade.[13]

Winter came upon Connelly sooner than he wished, and he was obliged to lay over until spring arrived. Departing Fort Towson again in April 1840, his wagons lost a great deal of time hacking and slogging their way through the Cross Timbers, a dense forested strip that bisects the plains of North Texas. It was August 27 when Connelly's wagon train returned to the Presidio del Norte. Surprises were in store for all.[14]

The La Juntans must have been startled by the transformation in Connelly's entourage. Outbound, it consisted of seven wagons of bullion and one hundred men. Coming back into La Junta along Alamito Creek, it had swelled to sixty or eighty wagons of cargo and more than two hundred people. Among the party was a company of American equestrian entertainers, complete with tents and circus paraphernalia.[15]

The surprise for Connelly and his fellow merchants was that in their absence civil governor Irigoyen de la O had died of a fever. His replacement was Chihuahua's commander general Francisco García Conde, who cared not the slightest about Irigoyen's arreglo. The commander general and governor, perhaps caught off guard when a wagon train appeared at his most remote presidio, insisted that full duty be paid.[16]

The Mexican national *derecho de internación* was a traditional form of duty, based on the value of goods and levied according to a schedule of tariffs. It was a steep imposition; cotton textiles might suffer a 15 percent levy, for example. In addition, there was the *derecho de consumo,* a state excise tax that varied from 3 percent to 20 percent over the years. And on top of that, the post-Irigoyen government surely wanted to inquire into whether Connelly's party had properly paid the *derecho de extracción de oro y plata* on the silver bullion that had left Chihuahua the year before. That tax would amount to 3.5 percent of the bullion's value.[17]

The complexity of the various customs levies invited simplification by negotiation. Even government officials were frustrated at the hassle involved. In fact, while Connelly was addressing his problem in Presidio del Norte, Governor Armijo of New Mexico had extralegally declared a flat rate of five hundred pesos per wagon in Santa Fe. But the simplicity of a flat rate was not available to Connelly. He faced a hard-nosed military administration, and he was at a distinct negotiating disadvantage, having no real option to take his goods elsewhere.

And so the wagons, the mules, the people, the circus tents and the trade goods languished at Presidio del Norte while Connelly negotiated. It took forty-five days. We can imagine bored entertainers performing stunts on horseback for gaggles of campesinos, imagine them putting on shows at the presidio in an effort to generate some goodwill with the customs officials. We can imagine them wondering how they had gotten stuck in such a desolate place.

The outcome was not what La Junta needed. When Connelly finally reached Chihuahua, all the profit had been sucked out of his excursion. Three months to Fort Towson was bad enough, but a nine-month layover on the Mississippi, followed by five months' travel on the return — and another six weeks in customs impoundment — was prohibitive. No one who heard Connelly's tales felt the urge to follow in his wagon tracks.

The Mexican-American War further stirred Anglo aware-ness of Chihuahua. The outcome of the war—creation of an international border through the center of La Junta—brought the first Anglo settlers to the valley.[1]

The genesis of these events was in Washington, D.C., and Austin, Texas, but for La Junta the critical location was Santa Fe. By the time that President Polk declared war on Mexico in May 1846, spring caravans to Chihuahua were al-ready being assembled in Independence, Missouri. Substan-tial sums had been invested in wagons, teams and goods; it was too late to abort the trip. Determined wagonmasters led their trains west into enemy terrain, figuring that a solu-tion would present itself sooner or later.[2]

President Polk decided to protect the valuable cara-vans, and integrated that goal into his plan of attack upon Mexico. He sent Colonel Stephen W. Kearney from Fort Leavenworth to take Santa Fe. Along the Santa Fe Trail, wagon trains were detained at military posts and were re-quired to fall in behind Kearney's Army of the West. One of those wagon trains was led by Edward Glasgow. His part-ner Henry Connelly—the man who brought the circus to La Junta—was coming from Chihuahua to meet him in Santa Fe.[3]

Kearney took Santa Fe in August without firing a shot, in significant part because of the efforts of Henry Connelly and fellow trader James Magoffin in mediating with Gov-ernor Armijo of New Mexico. In September Kearney left Santa Fe for a campaign in California. As he departed, he gave the traders in Santa Fe permission to go forward to Chihuahua at their own risk. Henry Connelly was one of those who decided to test the waters. The waters were hot: when he reached El Paso he was jailed and taken to Ciudad Chihuahua.[4]

Kearney had left Colonel Alexander Doniphan and his troop of Missouri volunteers in Santa Fe. Doniphan pre-vented the remaining traders from leaving New Mexico until Christmas Eve, when he began a march on Mexico, traders in tow. By the time he reached El Paso, Doniphan had 315 merchant wagons following his soldiers.[5]

There is no question but that trade and tariffs were on the list of grievances that the United States held against Mexico. Still, Doniphan's expedition is a most peculiar piece of mili-

In

Doniphan's

Wake

tary history. He was pursuing the military goal of securing New Mexico and Chihuahua, but there was an unusual transparency about the mission's concomitant commercial motives. Doniphan would have objected, but it is not entirely unfair to say that his task was to spearhead an attack of calico merchants.

On the first day of March 1847 Doniphan occupied Ciudad Chihuahua unopposed, Governor Trías having fled to Parral. Doniphan sent Henry Connelly, now free from the Mexican jail, to offer peace terms to the governor. Doniphan, wishing to be relieved of the need to guard the traders, wanted to negotiate a treaty under which the merchants could pay Chihuahuan duties and remain in Ciudad Chihuahua unmolested, setting up shop and engaging in their usual business. Trías was not amenable to the idea, however, and no agreement resulted.[6]

On March 20 Doniphan reported to his superiors that his volunteers were restless to join the American forces farther east in Mexico, but "we cannot leave this point safely for some days—the American merchants here oppose it violently, and have several hundred thousand dollars at stake. . . . I am anxious and willing to protect the merchants as far as practicable; but I protest against remaining here as a mere wagon-guard, to garrison a city with troops wholly unfitted for it, and who will be soon wholly ruined by improper indulgences."[7]

Doniphan's wish was granted. He received orders to march east to Saltillo. When he left Ciudad Chihuahua on April 28, most of the American merchants went with him, unwilling to risk the wrath of Governor Trías. In that group were five people who would soon inhabit a new La Junta settlement: John D. Burgess, John W. Spencer, Benjamin Leaton, Juana Pedraza and Edward Hall. Together, these future founders of what would become Presidio, Texas, followed Doniphan to Saltillo, Cerro Gordo and Monterrey.[8]

Henry Connelly was among a group of experienced Chihuahuan traders who elected to stay behind. Doniphan gave Connelly a letter for Governor Trías, advising the governor that if he would protect the American merchants, then Doniphan would see to it that Ciudad Chihuahua was not reoccupied. After negotiations between Trías and the merchants over the payment of Mexican tariffs, an agreement was concluded and Connelly's group remained in Ciudad Chihuahua.[9]

When hostilities ended in 1848, Burgess, Spencer, Leaton, Pedraza and Hall backtracked to Chihuahua and then traveled together to La Junta. Burgess, Spencer and Leaton were merchants and freighters. Pedraza was Leaton's lover; they had lived together for the last ten years in Ciudad Chihuahua. Spencer was an established merchant in

Chihuahua and had known Leaton and Pedraza for a decade. Hall was a teamster who worked for Leaton.[10]

We can only speculate about why the group decided to try their luck in La Junta. The rationale likely turned on four issues: the Presidio del Norte created a small umbrella of safety in the midst of the frontier; there were lands in La Junta that could be farmed; there was a road to La Junta that at least once had been used to access United States markets beyond; and there would soon be an international border through the center of the valley.

This was a powerful combination. The potential to grab a big parcel of land—by hook or by crook—was obvious. Impending Texas statehood to the Rio Grande made it likely that a road would be established from Presidio del Norte to San Antonio, which would turn La Junta into a port of entry for both nations—the kind of place where a trader could become wealthy.

The border created another benefit. A border permits clever people to play those on one side against those on the other. It becomes possible to conduct a business here that is prohibited over there, or to consort with people here who would be jailed over there.

David Torrey is a good example of a person who understood the profit potential in borders. Born in Connecticut in 1815, he came to Texas at age twenty-four and joined his brother John in operating a string of frontier trading posts.

There were two views of what it meant to operate a Texas trading post in the 1840's. To Texians (prestatehood Texans), traders were an important part of Sam Houston's policy of peace, friendship and commerce with Texas natives. Trading posts were places where indigenous people and immigrants could gather to barter, talk and commune. But Mexicans saw Texas trading posts differently. To understand their viewpoint, one need only answer this question: What were the Apaches and Comanches trading? They were nomads. They didn't grow crops, didn't breed cattle, didn't weave blankets and didn't work silver. What they did was hunt and gather, which—when talking about livestock, slaves and valuables—means that they were thieves. To the Mexican government, Texas trading posts were outlets where Apaches and Comanches could fence plunder taken at the expense of Mexican lives.[11]

One can be a fence anywhere, but a border maximizes the efficiency of such a business. In many cases, such as that of Texas and Mexico, a trader on one side of the border can deal with impunity in goods stolen on the other side. To gain maximum efficiency, it is a good idea to be close to the border. Admittedly, places like Bent's Fort in Colorado did well at some distance from Mexico, and the original Torrey trading post on the Brazos River (near present-day Waco) prospered, but in 1849 the Torreys sold their existing posts and headed for El Paso, which had suddenly become a border town.[12]

When they arrived, John set up shop, but David went looking for a place of his own. He did some trading with natives west of El Paso, then decided to travel down the Rio Grande. He came upon La Junta after Burgess, Spencer and the others arrived. Torrey recognized that La Junta offered everything he needed to ply his trade. He began operating near where Presidio is today, safely across the Rio Grande from the Mexican authorities. His customers were the Mescalero Apaches who prowled Chihuahuan settlements and then fled north with their booty. Torrey was only too glad to take cattle and horses in exchange for guns, ammunition, knives, cloth and food.[13]

Then David Torrey made a mistake. He began crossing the Rio Grande to trade with Mescaleros on the Mexican side of the river. There was an obvious risk that the Mexican government would disapprove of his activity, but that was not what brought disaster. In December 1849 Torrey was deep in Chihuahua on an extended trade mission among a band of eight hundred Mescaleros. He concluded his business satisfactorily and headed back toward La Junta. Shortly after he left the Apache camp, a group of Mescalero raiders arrived from Durango, where they had received a severe trouncing from Mexicans and Americans defending the settlements. In the mood for revenge, the raiders followed Torrey's trail north and caught up with him on Christmas day. Only one member of Torrey's party survived to tell the tale.[14]

Ben Leaton reached La Junta before David Torrey. He looked about for a suitable place to set up a trading post. Being among the first Anglos on the scene, he picked what turned out to be an ideal site: the old fortín downriver from the Presidio del Norte, where Captain Ronquillo used to camp with his troops. There were good farming lands there—after all, the fortín was originally built to protect farmers—and the site was close enough to the presidio's protection, yet far enough from its watchful gaze. Most importantly, it was almost a mile inside the new border of the United States of America.

There was just one problem. La Juntans were already farming the land around the fortín, as they had done for generations. These people may have been traditional La Juntans or offshoots of the Apaches who attempted reservation life in La Junta, or they may have staked out claims under Mexico's colonization laws. Whatever their origins, their plots had never been formally surveyed, and an official survey was a prerequisite to a Mexican land grant, so none of the tenants had paperwork for their lands. But there they were. These Mexican citizens and their formerly Mexican lands were now within the United States. What rights did they have?

If there were any rights, they would have been stated in the Treaty of Guadalupe Hidalgo, a most revealing document that ended the Mexican-American War. It declared peace (Article 1), appointed a commission to sort out the details (Article 2), and then got down to business, terminating the blockade of Mexican ports and settling how import/export duties and customhouses would be allocated (Article 3). The commercial question of duties—an essential element of governmental cash flow—came ahead of the military matter of termination of the American occupation of Mexico (Article 4) and the essential jurisdictional establishment of a new boundary line (Article 5).[15]

Either the Mexican-American War was about taking land and making money, or the treaty entirely failed to address the war's causes. Article 12 obliged the United States to pay $15 million for the land it was acquiring. Articles 13–15 concerned claims of citizens against one government or the other. Article 18 declared that supplies for United States troops still in Mexico would be duty-free. The next article dealt with merchandise of American traders taken into Mexico during the occupation. When Article 22 addressed what might happen if war broke out again ("which is not to be expected, and which God forbid!"), its first paragraph concerned how American merchants in Mexico would be treated. The second governed treatment of prisoners of war.[16]

The commercial underpinnings of the war and the treaty were further revealed in President Polk's 1847 State of the Union address, in which he complained angrily that the Mexican government was demanding to be paid import duties on the goods sold by United States merchants in occupied Mexico. In Polk's view, any United States goods brought to Mexico during the occupation should be duty-free. Whether he was being reasonable or not, raising the subject of import duties in the State of the Union address demonstrates the prominence of commercial issues in the shattered relations between the United States and Mexico.[17]

There were other important rights for the treaty to settle. What about Mexican citizens living on land that had suddenly become part of the United States? Articles 8 and 9 gave them the option of becoming citizens of the United States or remaining Mexicans. And what about their land? Article 8 said that Mexican citizens could keep their property and that their rights would be respected, but the language was remarkably brief and general for such an important topic. What about all the pending Mexican land grants? What about people who were prevented from meeting the terms of their grants by the outbreak of war? What about frontier colonists like those at the fortín — good-faith squatters, probably lured to the frontier by governmental promises of land, waiting for surveys and paperwork? Those topics were addressed by Article 10, which afforded broad protection to Mexican citizens. There was just one problem: the United States Senate rejected Article 10. The final treaty contained no specific provisions regarding Mexican land grants.

This was troubling. It amounted to an astounding gap in the treaty, but the Senate's view was that granting specific dignity to Mexican land grants would only encourage fraudulent claims. Besides, all the public domain in Texas belonged to Texas, not the United States, so it was a matter for state law to address. Land claims could be settled in court, or maybe by special commissions, but the Senate wasn't inclined to make any promises in advance.

The government of the new state of Texas took the position that the laws of Mexico relating to the colonization of lands in the former Mexican state of Coahuila y Texas remained in force, but La Junta (and much of the rest of the new state of Texas) had been within Chihuahua, not Coahuila y Texas, and the status of prestatehood grants in those regions was entirely unclear.[18]

As pressure for a more specific answer mounted, the treaty commissioners met in Querétaro, Mexico, and executed a secret protocol, stating that by rejecting Article 10 the United States did not intend to annul any Mexican land grants. Word of the secret protocol leaked and its provisions became controversial, so one of the U.S. commissioners met with the Mexican foreign minister to clarify what the protocol meant. They agreed that the protocol was not part of the treaty, the protocol did not change the treaty and the protocol correctly interpreted the treaty. When the United States Department of State reviewed the clarification, it immediately objected to the language about correct interpretation. That remains the official and not terribly helpful position of the State Department to this day.[19]

The confusion was great enough that in 1848 — about the time Ben Leaton came to La Junta — Texas governor Peter Bell called for an investigation of claims to lands that were within the state of Texas but outside the former Mexican state of Coahuila y Texas. Two years later, the legislature created a Texas board of commissioners charged with resolving disputes in those areas. When the law was enacted, La Junta had become part of Presidio County, which had been created only thirty-six days earlier and which was low on the list of land-claim resolution priorities.[20]

Ben Leaton would have boiled down all the international diplomacy and statehouse gyrations to this one point: in 1848 nobody knew what land rights were possessed by the Mexican citizens farming near the fortín. The land was up for grabs.

But how to grab it? Leaton could conceivably run off the Mexicans at the point of a gun, but then his rights would be no better than those of the first person to come along with a bigger gun.

Leaton needed some sort of legal right to the land. One option was to buy up Republic of Texas land scrip—coupons that entitled the bearer to claim land, usually in increments of 160, 320 or 640 acres. The Republic of Texas, and later the State of Texas, issued scrip for between fifty cents and two dollars per acre. Once issued, the freely transferable scrip represented the unconditional right to claim the stated amount of unappropriated public domain, sort of like a gift certificate for land. Scrip was often available at a deep discount to the price stated on its face, in part because there was a lot of high-quality counterfeit land scrip in circulation. But land had to be surveyed before it could be claimed with scrip, and La Junta was a long way from the nearest surveyor or state land office. Moreover, the existence of counterfeit scrip made purchasing it a risky business. In 1848 the use of scrip in La Junta was more theoretical than practical.[21]

It might seem that Leaton should have homesteaded the land he desired, but La Junta was unsurveyed and far beyond the regions where homesteading was active. Most Texas homestead laws, known as headright laws, benefited only those who had arrived before 1842. The only significant exception, the Preemption Act of 1845, limited preemption homesteads to 320 acres—much less land than Leaton had in mind.[22]

In the end, Leaton chose a course of action that might seem odd, but it was the only practical choice immediately available to him. That it was completely illegal and unethical is another matter. Leaton went to Esmerijildo Baiza, who was then the alcalde of Presidio del Norte, and asked him to forge up a Mexican land grant. Leaton was the living embodiment of the Senate's reasons for rejecting Article 10.

The idea was that the alcalde could backdate a grant to someone who was long dead, and then forge a transfer of the land to Leaton. Baiza agreed that the plan might be a good one, but he pointed out that he had not been alcalde during the necessary prior years; besides, he was feeling a bit squeamish. He suggested that Cesario Herrera—the flexible soul who had been alcalde back when Captain Ronquillo was in command—might be able to help.[23]

And so Ben Leaton went in search of Cesario Herrera. Leaton must have known that a Mexican land grant was dubious title, but he also must have figured that a Texas court would favor his dubious title over that of some dispossessed Mexican peons. The important thing was to get possession of the land and create appropriate documents of at least modest credibility; the details could be sorted out later.

Leaton had no trouble finding Herrera, for the former alcalde was now working as secretary to Alcalde Baiza. Herrera went back to Baiza and asked him to help with the fraudulent title, but Baiza refused, leaving Herrera to conjure up some papers for the man he knew as Don Benito Leaton.[24]

Leaton wanted a plot of land five miles long and over a mile wide — more land than the Mexican laws would have given to one person. Undaunted, Herrera applied his customary creativity and ingenuity. He forged a grant from Lucas Aguilar, the *juez de paz* (justice of the peace), to Januario Galindo dated in 1832 and another from Juez de Paz Eugenio Baesa to Tomas Garcia dated two years later. Then he forged transfers from Garcia to Galindo dated in 1846 and from Galindo to Leaton dated in 1849. Herrera executed an affidavit stating that the transfer to Leaton was made in his presence (instead of having a grantor execute and file a deed, the Spanish land system required the grantor to appear before an official and declare the transfer, which was then noted in the official records), and he made sure that each grant recited that a survey had been done first.[25]

Then Herrera forged an 1832 grant from Juez de Paz Aguilar to Crisanto Acousta, and an 1848 transfer from Acousta to Leaton. The transfer to Leaton was stated to have been made in front of Herrera. Next came an 1831 grant from Juez de Paz Baesa to Juan Bustillos and an 1832 grant — this one transferring the land where the fortín was located — from Juez de Paz Aguilar to Bustillos. As one might expect, Bustillos then supposedly transferred both tracts to Leaton in 1848, witnessed by Cesario Herrera. With that, Leaton's title to the lands around the fortín was fraudulently complete.[26]

Perhaps Leaton was sitting around with Cesario Herrera, enjoying a sip of whiskey and laughing about what they had done, when he first heard Herrera's story of the legendary Ronquillo land grant. Such a pity that the captain had died before he could receive his reward. It wasn't long before Leaton's ambitions extended far beyond the fortín. He had already bought so many forgeries from Herrera that he had needed a loan of $500 from John Spencer, but he just couldn't let this grand opportunity — backed by a poignant and credible story — slip through his grasp.[27]

And so Leaton had Herrera forge an 1832 grant under Herrera's own signature to "*el Teniente Coronel de ejercito, Don José Ignacio Ronquillo*" conveying the enormous ranch that Ronquillo had coveted. The grant bore the forged signatures of the people who surveyed the land for Ronquillo, though later no one would be so bold as to say that they were qualified surveyors. Then Herrera forged an 1832 transfer from Ronquillo to Hipolito Acosta, Ronquillo's loyal employee, and an 1833 transfer from Acosta to Juana Pedraza, Leaton's close personal friend.

Backdating the transfer to when Ronquillo was at the Presidio del Norte meant that Herrera could claim to have made the grant himself. A juez de paz might grant a small temporal to a common man, but it would take the act of the alcalde himself to attempt a Ronquillo-sized grant, and even then it would take additional formalities, as we will see. Making Pedraza the transferee was an elegant touch, for it distanced Leaton and his fortín grants from the Ronquillo grant. It was plausible that Pedraza might have done business with Acosta in 1833, before Leaton ever set foot in Mexico. Pushing the transfer to Pedraza that far back neatly made Pedraza and Herrera the only living witnesses to the events that did not occur.

Herrera included some customary conditions in the grant to make it appear authentic under the colonization laws: Ronquillo was obligated to live on the ranch for four years, construct improvements and man it with enough people to defend the area from attack by nomads. Since Ronquillo's military duties had forced him to leave La Junta before he could comply with the conditions (this being why Ronquillo supposedly sold his ranch to Acosta, his faithful majordomo), Herrera inked a waiver of the conditions, certifying that the captain had fully qualified for his grant.[28]

It was a glorious moment, but there was still work to be done. Leaton had to remove the pesky Mexicans from his farm. It didn't take long; he got Herrera's help in running them off, claiming authority under the forged grants. Their success in doing so might seem somewhat odd, since Herrera had no authority on the Texas side of the river and had very little on the Mexican side, but perhaps Ben Leaton contributed some firearms to the discussion.[29]

Unexpectedly, the Mexican farmers resisted Leaton's grab. In November 1849 six of them wrote the governor of Chihuahua saying that "Mr. Leaton presented himself . . . showing he had no rights in those lands that would incommode any neighbor, but a few days later he made an alliance with the alcalde who governed in this community, and both dispossessed us from the said property, the said judge showing to the said Leaton that we have not had title papers, that he could easily dispossess us of our lands." The Mexicans begged their governor for some kind of relief "in order that we may possess our lands, this being the only jewel which is all that is left us for our subsistence." [30]

The governor would provide little help. His reply nine days later said that if the farmers could prove legal title to the property, then Article 10 of the Treaty of Guadalupe Hidalgo would protect them. Otherwise, they were without rights. The governor was mistaken about Article 10, which had been rejected by the U.S. Senate, but it mattered not; the farmers had no legal title to uphold their claims, and the governor's jurisdiction did not extend beyond the river. And so Leaton prevailed.

The farmers never received their land back, and they were never compensated for its loss, but they did get a form of satisfaction. A message soon reached the presidio from the governor. Cesario Herrera was shackled and taken back to Ciudad Chihuahua for trial on charges of creating fraudulent land titles. [31]

Leaton, a United States citizen living on the Texas side of the river, was beyond the governor's jurisdiction; that circumstance elegantly demonstrates the dark beauty of a border. As a practical matter, there was no law of Texas or the United States in La Junta. There wasn't even a road into the United States from there. Leaton (and Burgess and Spencer and Hall and Pedraza) were exempt from the laws of Mexico and beyond the reach of the laws of Texas and the United States—a most interesting circumstance.

The situation was still precarious in the new borderlands. Chihuahua's combination governor and commander general Francisco García Conde—the man who had repudiated Connelly's arreglo—had yet again made peace with the Mescaleros living near La Junta, but the treaties had fallen apart in the spring of 1846. Even before the formal agreements failed, Conde recommended that Mexico's minister of war reinvigorate the less-than-successful practices of the 1830's, building a string of Roman-style military colonies along the Rio Grande to block Apache and Comanche raids, backed by a second line of military colonies hemming in the Bolson de Mapimí. Appropriate legislation passed in 1846, but the United States invasion pushed the plan aside.[1]

Citizens of Presidio del Norte asked Chihuahua for additional military protection in 1847 and again in 1851, and it wasn't because they feared occupation by the United States Army. Mexico had siphoned off soldiers from frontier posts to battle Americans in the interior; the Apaches and Comanches recognized the opportunity and made the most of it.[2]

After the Treaty of Guadalupe Hidalgo was inked in 1848, Mexico enacted another law for the establishment of military colonies along the border, including a colony at Presidio del Norte. That project, born of concerns about American expansionism as well as nomadic raids, didn't get under way until 1849 and was never completed. Since there was already a military garrison and a pueblo at Presidio del Norte, we cannot ascribe any great importance to its being declared a military colony, though generous provisions for land grants and supplies might have attracted new colonists. The law provided that each military colony should have a walled fortress measuring one thousand feet square to enclose the populace, but no such structure was built in La Junta. The garrison at Presidio del Norte was to be manned by seven officers, seven sergeants, twelve corporals, thirty-three infantrymen, ninety-four cavalry, one drummer and one bugler—a welcome restoration of the troops drawn away from the presidio during the war.[3]

In 1851, the Mexican minister of (foreign) relations urged intensified colonization of all the frontier states. Then veteran soldier and diplomat Juan Almonte published a proposal for colonization of the northern frontier by Euro-

Jack Hays

Gets Lost

pean immigrants from Germany, France, Belgium, Italy and wherever else hardy, industrious souls could be found. Under existing conditions, he warned, the frontier colonists were regularly "murdered, their houses are sacked and their fields burned by the various tribes of barbarians that ceaselessly invade their lands," and—alluding to the limited progress made under the law of 1848—he lamented that when it came to forging frontier settlements, Mexican citizens' "dispositions, habits and customs do not qualify them for this labor." Almonte felt that European immigrants could be induced to "found towns in the deserts which, until now, have served only as cover for wild beasts, assassins, and thieves." But no action was taken on his recommendations, other than the maintenance of existing garrisons.[4]

The first Anglos to arrive in La Junta faced a situation as dangerous as the valley had ever experienced. Nonetheless, Leaton, Spencer, Burgess and Hall all settled into trading, freighting, farming and ranching across the river from the military colony at Presidio del Norte.

Spencer was the most successful farmer, and over time his descendants became the most enduring merchants: Spencer's Department Store still sells boots in Presidio, which is situated near the old Spencer farm. As time went by, Spencer's property holdings expanded upriver and Indio—today an abandoned pueblo about halfway to Ruidosa—became his farm headquarters. Spencer tried horse ranching for a while, but thefts by Apaches made the business unprofitable. Raising cattle proved less prone to loss; beef was not part of the traditional native diet, and Apaches knew that lumbering cattle on the hoof could never keep pace with a raiding party. Reliable markets were provided by the presidio across the river, followed by the 1854 arrival of Fort Davis seventy miles north.[5]

Hall was the smallest player, always on the fringes, still in the employ of Leaton. Burgess seems to have stayed with the freighting trade in the early years. Juana Pedraza . . . well, we will see about her.[6]

Leaton was the earliest and most flamboyant trader. He had no sooner run the existing settlers off his land than he began expanding upon the old fortín, constructing what would come to be known as Fort Leaton. Built of adobe bricks that measured eighteen inches long (the thickness of the walls), twelve inches wide and five inches thick, it was an enclosed compound with stables, corrals, courtyards, work areas, living quarters and a trading post. Leaton's fort had forty rooms, corner parapets and immense exterior doors to permit horses and wagons to enter the courtyard.[7]

When they arrived in 1848, Ben Leaton and Juana Pedraza had three children: Joe (or José), Bill and Elizabeth (or Isabella, but known as La

Chata, meaning "pug-nosed" or "cutie"). La Chata was nine and the boys were a few years older. Their parents had been living together in Ciudad Chihuahua and elsewhere in Mexico.[8]

Life on the frontier remained harsh for many years, and the Leaton boys had a knack for getting into trouble. After he became an adult, Bill was killed by Ojinaga's chief of police during a gun battle. Francisca Ureta Leaton heard that her husband Joe died in prison in San Antonio, though she wasn't sure. Other people said Joe died somewhere in the California goldfields. La Chata was still alive and living in Ciudad Chihuahua in the 1880's.[9]

Leaton and Pedraza feathered their nest quickly. By 1851 they had two African slaves named Jacob (worth $500) and Peggy (worth $400), eleven mules, two horses, three hundred goats, ten oxen, twenty head of cattle and a handsome collection of wagons, firearms and implements.[10]

One must wonder exactly who Leaton planned to trade with at La Junta. An obvious answer is Apaches, for Leaton could sit safely on the United States side of the river and trade for booty taken in Mexico. But were hostile nomads really his targeted customers, or was he banking on the emergence of a wagon road to San Antonio?

It wasn't long before an itinerant trade of sorts emerged. The first group of travelers pulled into Leaton's compound on an October Sunday in 1848. The fort was still under construction, but it was a welcome sight to the battered expedition led by retired Texas Ranger and United States Army colonel John Coffee Hays. There were seventy men in his group, and they did not look good. Leaton provided food and supplies and helped them set up camp near an old adobe house about a mile away.[11]

Half the men had signed up with Hays in San Antonio, committing to an official expedition to forge a road to Chihuahua via El Paso. The other half were under the command of Texas Ranger captain Samuel Highsmith, who had been ordered to provide a military escort for Hays's group. Opening a road from San Antonio to Chihuahua had long been an active topic of discussion in Texas. As early as 1835, Stephen F. Austin had promoted "opening a road from Texas to the Paso del norte [El Paso], or in a direct line (or as nearly as the country will admit) to Chihuahua." Following the conclusion of the Mexican-American War and at the urging of the leading citizens of San Antonio, Hays had gone to Washington, D.C., to get federal support for the project.[12]

Hays set forth from San Antonio in late August 1848, relying on a guide named Lorenzo who claimed to know the way to El Paso. Lorenzo's expertise was based on his having been a prisoner of the

Comanches for fifteen years, but he turned out to be incompetent, leading the expedition into the rugged Big Bend region, where he finally confessed that he lacked any idea of where he was going. Hays and Highsmith ended up asking Mescaleros how to get to the Rio Grande; the Mescaleros pointed the wanderlings to the Comanche raiding trail. The San Antonians found the river near the apex of the Big Bend.[13]

By then, Hays's men were running out of food. They resorted to eating mustang meat, panther, bear grass, prickly pear tunas, the occasional polecat and four of their pack mules. When water was scarce, they chewed strips of boot leather to keep their mouths moist. A member of their party, a Doctor Wahm, entirely lost his wits — probably from starvation — and fled into the hills. One of the men in Hays's party made a laconic entry in his journal: "Dr. Wahm rode off in a fury last night. Suppose he is lost. Send back, for lame and crazy." A search party went looking for the doctor and found him, but he escaped again in the deep ravines of the Big Bend.[14]

The Texans crossed the Rio Grande on the Comanche trail and continued southwest, then — realizing that the trail was taking them away from the river — turned back northwest and followed a creek to the military colony at San Carlos, about forty miles below La Junta. They had been foraging off the land for twelve days and were grateful for the basic provisions available there — dried beef, cornmeal and milk. After a day's rest, Hays's crew followed the Rio Grande upstream to the Presidio del Norte, where they checked in with the commander and explained that they would not have crossed into Mexico but for their extreme hunger (not to mention their extreme disorientation). The explorers then crossed back into the United States and made their way to Leaton's fort.[15]

Colonel Jack Hays is a minor Texas legend, known for his leadership of Texas Rangers, his bravery in the Mexican-American War and his establishment of a trail to California. Fawning books have been printed about the man. Those books treat his journey to La Junta with some delicacy, for the fact is that he was totally lost. Hays never found a road to El Paso or Chihuahua. What he found was a terrible route to La Junta. He was fortunate that the Mexican military at San Carlos and Presidio del Norte decided that it wasn't worth the trouble to incarcerate his scraggly band of invaders.[16]

The arrival of Hays's expedition was treated with La Junta's version of pomp and circumstance. Hays had someone sew up an American flag, and he presented it to Leaton. After appropriate speeches, Leaton fired off a small cannon that he kept at the fortín and a party ensued.[17]

Hays's expedition rested at Fort Leaton. During the interlude their quartermaster, a man named Ralston, stocked up on food, powder, horseshoe nails and other provisions. He may have found some supplies in the village around the presidio, where almost two thousand people lived. At one point a priest from Ciudad Chihuahua, perhaps already in Presidio del Norte on ecclesiastical business, came to meet the new arrivals. He presented Hays with a mule and mentioned that the people in Chihuahua would welcome a new trade route through Presidio del Norte.[18]

The San Antonio party was a remarkable group. One member, Major Jack Caperton, had long served under Colonel Hays and would later follow him to California, where they both became prominent figures in Oakland and Woodside. George T. Howard was a noted soldier, businessman and public servant. As a member of an ill-fated Texian expedition to Santa Fe, he had once been obliged to escape from Mexican jail. Samuel Maverick, who had been a delegate to the Texas independence convention, had been thrown into a Mexican prison following a famous conflict with Mexican general Woll. He went on to become a cattle baron. "Maverick" cattle are named after one of his straying herds; television and movie characters Brett and Bart Maverick are his namesakes. Michael Chevallié had been a Texas Ranger under Hays and was known as a rough-and-tumble frontier sort. There is a tale about an Englishman complaining to an American general that Chevallié had beaten him; the general is said to have offered little comfort, warning the Brit to "keep a sharp look out or he will beat you again."[19]

The distinguished credentials and hardy frontier character of Hays's retinue helps explain why Ben Leaton made what would otherwise be an inexplicable decision. He asked Hays and James T. Peacock, a prominent San Antonio attorney in the expedition, to shepherd young Joe Leaton back to San Antonio for schooling.[20]

All signs are that Ben Leaton and James Peacock formed a lasting friendship during Peacock's brief visit to La Junta with Colonel Hays. They became partners in a San Antonio livestock operation, keeping forty Spanish mares, six hundred Mexican sheep and one hundred head of cattle at Peacock's ranch. At Leaton's death, Peacock became the executor of his estate.[21]

Though Leaton had his flaws and detractors, more than one traveler reported him to be a generous and caring host. After enjoying hospitality and commerce with Leaton for ten days, the Hays expedition headed back to San Antonio. Fortunately, they received some local guidance about the best direction to take; they proceeded up the gentle Cibolo Creek valley to the north.

The trip back to San Antonio was easier in the sense that they took a much improved route, but it was late October by the time they departed, and winter was coming. Though it had taken them sixty days to reach La Junta, they packed only thirty days' food for the return, which would end up requiring six weeks to complete. The party split up and the group of six that included Hays, Peacock and Caperton took an unproved direction against the advice of their guides. They ran out of food, suffered from the weather, endured native thefts of their horses and had been given up for dead by the time they straggled into San Antonio. With them was young Joe Leaton, who had been through much more than his father or he had ever expected.[22]

Because federal dollars had paid for Captain Highsmith's Texas Ranger escort, Hays was obligated to render reports to the United States secretary of war and to the army's commanding officer in Texas, Lieutenant Colonel Peter Bell, who would be elected the governor of Texas in the following year. In reporting to Bell, who had once served under his command, Hays admitted that he had not covered the entire route to El Paso (and discreetly made no mention whatsoever of his original goal, Chihuahua), but reported that he had discovered a route to the Presidio del Norte. From there, Hays said, the road up the Rio Grande to El Paso was easy going.

In his separate report to the secretary of war, Hays said he had mounted "an expedition to explore a route practicable for wagons to Presidio del Norte, and Paso del Norte, which I had the honor to conduct. We . . . succeeded in discovering a way perfectly practicable for wagons at all seasons of the year." Again avoiding the topic of Chihuahua, Hays conceded that "We did not examine the whole distance to the Paso del Norte, but having learned from information on which we fully rely, that there will be no difficulty whatever in going from one town to the other." He embellished beyond his knowledge: "Fifteen miles above the Presidio del Norte, on the Rio Grande, there is large timber in abundance, and the distance to Paso del Norte is generally level."[23]

Captain Highsmith also rendered a report to Colonel Bell. He was both optimistic and prone to overstatement, saying "it is my opinion that a first-rate road can be established on or very near the same route which we traversed on our return from Paso del Norte," despite the fact that he had never gotten within two hundred miles of El Paso. Perhaps it was a mere misstatement, or a Freudian slip. Perhaps he meant to refer to his return from Presidio del Norte, not Paso del Norte, for his report makes it clear that the group never ventured farther than Fort Leaton.[24]

The Hays-Highsmith viewpoint was that getting to La Junta was the hard part; from there it was all downhill to El Paso and Ciudad Chihuahua. True, it was possible to reach El Paso that way—Franciscan Friar Lopez had walked the reverse route barefoot in 1683, followed by Spaniard Captain Mendoza on horseback, and others would take that path later—but there was no wagon road along the river in 1848 and there is none today. The route that Hays promoted is a perfectly awful way to reach either El Paso or Ciudad Chihuahua from San Antonio.

Hays did opine that an alternate route could strike directly across the country to El Paso, bypassing Presidio del Norte and the Rio Grande. He figured that this route would shave hundreds of miles off the trip, and he was right (this more direct route later became a major thoroughfare from San Antonio to El Paso and beyond), but it must be observed that the good colonel had never in his life set foot on that path, nor had anyone else except members of the Jumano and Apache tribes.[25]

Ironically, Hays had bumbled into something worthy without realizing it. San Antonio needed (and would in a few years have) *two separate* routes—one to Ciudad Chihuahua and another to El Paso. Hays had accidentally discovered the former—an important result—but adhered to a false claim that he had found the latter. He was crippled by a connect-the-dots view of known waypoints.

Was Hays's misunderstanding of the transportation realities a significant failing? Put it this way: If he was trying to reach Ciudad Chihuahua, why didn't it occur to him to ask either Ben Leaton or the visiting priest how they had gotten to La Junta from there?

Several notables arrived in La Junta during 1849. The first was Lieutenant William Henry Chase Whiting, a twenty-four-year-old honors graduate of Georgetown College and valedictorian of his West Point class. Whiting's superior, Major General William J. Worth, ordered him to lead an expedition from San Antonio to Presidio del Norte. From there, Whiting was to proceed up the Rio Grande to El Paso and then back to San Antonio.[1]

Major General Worth was executing an order from the secretary of war calling for a reconnaissance of the left bank of the Rio Grande in search of a practicable military road from San Antonio to Santa Fe. Worth knew that roads existed from El Paso to Santa Fe and Ciudad Chihuahua, so he ordered Whiting to do what Hays had not: open the missing link from San Antonio to El Paso.[2]

Whiting

Draws

the Line

Worth's view of how the reconnaissance should proceed was colored by Jack Hays's report, which claimed that a river route from La Junta to El Paso was workable. Worth believed that the route through La Junta would attract settlers to a region where military posts would be necessary, and he recognized that settlements would lend critical support to his forts. So Worth commanded Whiting to proceed through La Junta — not as a gateway to Chihuahua, but as a waypoint to El Paso. On his return trip, Whiting was to explore the more direct route to the north postulated by Hays.[3]

Whiting left San Antonio in early February with nine men. Nine days later he was in Fredericksburg, where he employed Richard A. Howard, who had been on Hays's trip to Presidio del Norte. Howard acted as a guide, directing Whiting's group across the plains and down Cibolo Creek, the route that Hays had taken on his return trip. Four more men joined the entourage, making a total of fifteen.[4]

Whiting is the first diarist to refer to a settlement at La Junta as "Presidio." That may simply be shorthand for the Presidio del Norte, but Whiting makes remarks about a village near Fort Leaton, on the Texas side of the river, that suggest that today's town of Presidio was already taking on an identity of its own.

We will let Whiting tell his own story, for he tells it well, but let us first set the stage. It is late March 1849. Whiting's small party has survived a harrowing encounter with Mescalero chief Gomez, eluding his hostile surveillance only by sneaking out of their campsite in the dark of night. The expedition's daily food rations are down to coffee and a spoonful of pinole. They come across a prairie dog town along Cibolo Creek and make a breakfast of the varmints. Then they get lucky and kill a panther; the tough but substantial meal—Whiting called it "decidedly not good"—boosts their spirits. That afternoon they kill a small deer and another prairie dog, "very poor, but better than we had had for some time. We demolished it that night." The next morning they come across Hays's trail and begin following it to Presidio. They try to make it to Fort Leaton, traveling into the night, but lose the trail in the darkness. Here we join Whiting's narrative:[5]

Saturday, March 24. At daylight when we awoke we saw we were within two miles of Leaton's place. The little white church of the [Presidio del] Norte beyond had a very pretty effect below the dark mountains, with the morning sun shining lightly upon its walls. We soon came in view of the Rio Grande with its green valley and cottonwood groves. It was delightful to our jaded spirits to catch glimpses of the adobe houses. At seven we reached Fort Leaton, where we received a warm welcome and great hospitality. Leaton has performed severe labor and gone to much expense in his location. His fort is a collection of adobes, or earth-built houses, with a lookout and a wall which encloses also his corral. The rooms are surmounted by a crenelated parapet wall, and the place would make a strong defense against Indians. . . . [Our] party made their appearance about ten this morning. Leaton immediately allowed them to camp in his yard, had wood brought and a meal cooked for the rough and hungry travelers, and after an enormous dinner the remainder of the day was appropriated to rest.

Sunday, March 25. This morning I had the necessary subsistence for our next march put in a state of forwardness. All that can be procured—and that at high prices—is dried beef, pinole and cornmeal. Pinole is parched corn ground and sweetened, a very pleasant and nutritive article of food. But both it and the meal here have to be ground by hand and the beef must be dried. Three or four days will perforce be consumed. Everything brings enormous prices in this vicinity. Mr. Leaton has to supply himself entirely from Chihuahua. The neighboring village is a poor, stricken town, and the journey into Chihuahua is one of no common peril. We will require many new animals, nearly all ours being either sore backed or tender footed and unfit to proceed farther. Leaton is very active and enterprising in his assistance. His endeavors with small resources to promote our success lay me under many obligations.

Smith, Howard, Leaton and Delacy went over with me today to the Norte. It is a collection of one-story adobe buildings, situated on one of the gravel tables at the junction of the Conchos with the Rio Grande. It has a barren and desolate aspect. *The soil in the vicinity is sandy and sterile. Indeed, for farming purposes, Leaton has the only soil about, and his tract is confined. Gazed at with wondering eyes by the population as the strangers who had passed through the Apache country, we walked through the streets, and on coming to the Presidio, or Fortaleza, del Norte, we called on the commandant, Don Guillermo Ortiz. This fortress is a rude adobe structure, oblong in shape, without flanking defenses, containing the church and the barracks, and capable of accommodating five or six hundred men. Some miserable, ragged creatures, apparently half starved and called "soldiers," were standing about the gateway. A scarecrow was walking past with a bankrupt escopette [a broken carbine]. We were ushered into the commandant's room. A few chairs and a pine table were its furniture. He soon made his appearance, a short, slightly built man, dark mustache, and gentlemanly address. We were presented in form by Mr. Leaton afterwards to the alcalde and other officials of the place. The usual compliments passed, and whiskey and Pass brandy from Leaton's were handed round, and then a Mexican dinner brought in, in the usual style, one dish at a time—stewed chicken flavored hotly with chile colorado; tortillas; a roasted turkey exceedingly well cooked; and finally frijoles and coffee. We ate to repletion, as might have been expected of men with our late experiences. Adjourning, we visited Don José Rodríguez, recommended by Leaton as the only honest man in the place.*

The town of the Norte is said to contain from twelve to fourteen hundred souls but, like all Mexican towns on the frontier, is a miserable, Indian-blighted place. . . . Only an eyewitness can form an idea of the complete stagnation in every branch of industry produced by these terrible Indian depredations. The town of Norte, once a more flourishing place and occupying an important military position, now indeed enjoys in some sort immunity, but it is for the reason that its inhabitants have been stripped of their all, and, in the way of plunder, present no attraction for the Apache robbers.

Fort Leaton will become an important site to the United States in view of the treaty stipulation and the Indian aggressions. It will make a convenient post, or depot, and refuge for the roving camps of dragoons which must be placed upon the great warpaths. Presidio is at the western part of that large bend of the Rio Grande where most of these passes into Mexico exist. It is in convenient striking distance also of the upper passes of the Apache. With a proper and efficient system of mounted troops, heavy blows will at one day or other be struck upon the Comanche from this point. It will also become the customhouse for the Chihuahua trade, destined to pass, henceforth, if I mistake not, not by Santa Fe, but from New Orleans and the southern states. It appears to me one of the most important places on the Rio Grande.[6]

We can see why Whiting graduated at the top of his West Point class. Looking at a miserable adobe village, he saw customhouses and wagon trains carrying goods from the Gulf Coast to Ciudad Chihuahua. He had broken the pattern of looking to Santa Fe and El Paso for access to Mexican markets. He was exactly right about La Junta's future.

After a rest of only a few days, Whiting left La Junta, following the Rio Grande to El Paso. Wanting to travel light, and fearful of attacks from Gomez and his men, Whiting shed all unnecessary equipment and papers, leaving them in the custody of Leaton, who also agreed to care for some of Whiting's exhausted mules and horses. John Spencer, who had come to La Junta with Leaton and was developing a string of farms along the river, joined Whiting's party. Whiting's travelogue remains entrancing:

The Sierra Grande, as I believe the Mexicans called the mountain which for some twenty miles above the Norte lies parallel to the river, is very singular in appearance. A high, unbroken, narrow ridge from one end to the other, seems to form its summit. The side towards the river is very steep and is intersected at short intervals by huge furrows which extend from the summit to the base, terminating generally in ravines which course toward the water; and looks as if, when elevated, the mountain had been combed down by the teeth of some gigantic harrow. . . .

By twelve we reached a valley opposite the casa vieja or old fortaleza, which stands deserted, crowning the bluff on the opposite shore. Built for defense against the Indians, it is, in its crumbling desolation, a mournful monument of Mexican weakness. Two towers at either extremity of the site constitute its lookouts and flanking defenses. These are connected by a long curtain which on top shows the remains of a crenelated parapet wall. Here the Rio Grande runs for some distance over a rocky bottom, forming a very good crossing, Vado de Piedra, or rock ford. This point is about thirty-five miles above Leaton's.[7]

Whiting continued up the river beyond the now-abandoned military colony at Vado de Piedra, and noted that the fortified colonies at Pilares, Guadalupe and San Ignacio were just as empty. Unlike Hays, he succeeded in his mission of reaching El Paso. Departing for San Antonio, he took the route postulated by Hays, proceeding southeast along the Rio Grande for about one hundred miles, then crossing the countryside roughly due east to the Pecos River. Between the Pecos and San Antonio one either proceeded south then east (the route that Whiting took on his way back to San Antonio), or east then south (the reverse of the route that Whiting took on his outbound leg).[8]

While the main body of his command proceeded along the direct route from El Paso to San Antonio, Whiting dispatched Lieutenant Henry Skillman back to Presidio to retrieve the gear that had been left at Fort Leaton. Skillman had already gained a reputation for bravery during the capture of El Paso in the Mexican-American War, but his trip back to Presidio through Mescalero territory with only a three-man escort was extraordinary. Gomez might be lying in wait.[9]

Ben Leaton turned out to be the savior of Lieutenant Skillman and his three men. According to Whiting, Skillman "met with Gomez, but . . . that wily chief, finding that we had escaped him and reached El Paso, had in the mean time moved nearer to Presidio, and, fearing lest we might come back with a stronger party, had made a treaty with Mr. Leaton, and permitted Skillman to pass unmolested through his whole tribe."[10]

When Whiting returned to San Antonio and rendered his official report, he declared that he had met his orders to "ascertain if there be a practicable and convenient route for military and commercial purposes between El Paso and the Gulf of Mexico, passing by or near San Antonio or Austin, in Texas." In fact, he had discovered two. His outbound path to the Pecos would become the "lower" military road that departed San Antonio and skirted the lower Rio Grande, passing through Fort Inge, Fort Clark and Camp Hudson before turning north and terminating at Fort Lancaster, where it met the "upper" military road (his return route) that ultimately connected San Antonio, Fort McKavett, Fort Stockton, Fort Davis, Fort Hancock, Fort Quitman and Fort Bliss (El Paso).[11]

They were both good routes, but Whiting saw the upper road as the better. For travelers to El Paso, either road made a lot more sense than going through La Junta. But remember that Major General Worth had wanted Whiting to dip south to Presidio because a road along that stretch of the Rio Grande would attract settlers, which would help defend the frontier and supply the army. Whiting's report confirmed that "the importance of a river road between [Presidio and El Paso] had been strongly urged by General Worth," and—even though the subject of his report was the more direct military road to El Paso—he made his own pitch for a route through La Junta: "The difficulties in the way of communication by the Rio Grande bank between Presidio and El Paso are not sufficient to do away with its importance to the public interest. Bound to afford protection to our own settlements which in course of time [will] advance into this region, and by the stipulations of solemn treaty to restrain and punish Indian depredations upon Mexico, I regard the construction of a military road upon the river here as absolutely necessary to this end. Independent of the fact that communication between posts is itself one great and most efficient barrier to savage incursions, early secured, it induces settlements, which, in

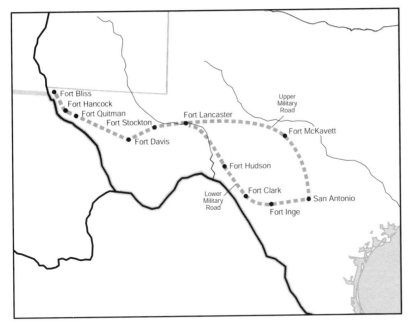

The Military Roads. Illustration by Herring Design, Houston, Tex.

time, peopled by our hardy pioneers, become the best defence of a frontier."[12]

Whiting was advocating two roads and two defensive lines, but he must have known that economics and logistics made that unlikely. The United States was not in a position to build one string of forts across the Texas plains and a second along the Rio Grande.

Only one line would be drawn, and that line would not pass through La Junta. Why would the direct road to El Paso get the nod? Not because travelers preferred to reach Ciudad Chihuahua through El Paso — that matter was ultimately settled in favor of La Junta. And not because there was a road from El Paso to Santa Fe — most travelers accessed Santa Fe along the trails that traversed the Great Plains. El Paso bested Presidio because it was 1849 and El Paso was on the way to the goldfields and dreams of California. The route west from El Paso through the gentle Mesilla Valley was so important that in 1853 the United States coerced Mexico into a border adjustment known as the Gadsden Purchase, allowing travelers to transit from El Paso to California without entering Mexico.

Nonetheless, Whiting's road through Presidio would emerge in time. It would not be the military road, which would remain far north, but a commercial road — just as predicted by Whiting — from ports on the Texas Gulf Coast, inland to San Antonio, onward to an international port of entry at Presidio and Ojinaga, and from there to Ciudad Chihuahua. It would be known as the Chihuahua Trail. For a brief time it would be a major thoroughfare, then it would lapse into obscurity.

Before moving our story in the direction of the Chihuahua Trail, we should linger for a moment to appreciate the impact of Whiting's reconnaissance of a military road along the east–west route to the north of La Junta. Think of the Big Bend—the most expansive definition of the Big Bend, that giant desert tenderloin that descends below West Texas—with a military road drawn across its northern edge. Thirty years later the Southern Pacific Railroad would draw another east-west line, a few dozen miles farther south. Towns would spring up along the military road and along the railroad. Stores, ranches, mills and churches would gather close to the nurture and safety of the transportation corridors. In the harsh realm of the Trans-Pecos, that line would be the perimeter of civilization, the furthest extent of effective transportation, the de facto border of the United States. Everything below would be trimmed away as excess, waste, tierra despoblada. Whiting was an advocate of La Junta's importance and an advocate of a river road, but he was arguing against geography, logistical realities, the Chihuahuan Desert and the irresistible lure of California gold. The longitudinal military road—and then the railroad, and finally the interstate highway—sliced La Junta off of the United States of America.

Lieutenant Whiting came to La Junta during the spring of 1849. That year also brought a much less welcome visitor: cholera. Caused by an organism named *Vibrio cholerae*, cholera is spread by eating food or drinking water that has been contaminated by the feces or vomit of an infected person. It is an astoundingly deadly disease; a healthy adult can die from loss of fluid and salts within a few hours after the onset of profuse diarrhea and vomiting. Only the rapid killer fevers — yellow fever, dengue fever — can match its swift lethality.[1]

Medical science in the early nineteenth century had no idea what caused cholera. The most popular theory was that bad air — known as miasma and thought to be found in wet, low-lying places — brought on the disease. The critical linkage between cholera and drinking water was not understood until 1854.[2]

Cholera first appeared in Texas in 1833, but the epidemic of 1849 was by far the most severe. Infections began along the Gulf Coast and moved inland. Five hundred San Antonians died of the disease in the first five months of that year. Cholera's spread was swift and extensive, broadcast by increasing migration across the continent. Ciudad Chihuahua was battered by the disease in the same year as Galveston and San Antonio.[3]

In La Junta, cholera struck in the fall of 1849. Here are the October entries from the diary of Francisco Colomo, a simple soldier in the tiny community of Presidio del Norte.

The year of 1849 was the year of the Cholera. The day of October 1849 Rafael Salas died in Coyame. Prudencio Valenzuela died. Francisca Baeza the wife of Nabor Sanchez died. A daughter of Pedro Sotelo died. The 8th of the said month the soldier of Coyame died, Salgado. Tomasas the son of Marcos Sanchez died. In the said day, month and year Lino Baeza married. Pifanio Salgado and La Chona of the Americans died. The 11th Tomas Chavarria died. Jose Maria the twins died. The son of Jose Deanda died. Gordono Carrasco died. A son of Antonio Madrid. A son of Naisisia. The son of Jesus Jimez died. The 11th of October 1849 Rosa the wife of Eugenio Baeza died. The 13th of the same Juan Villanueva and a son of the deceased Gordono Carrasco died. The Grand-daughter of Quintela died. The rich soldier from Coyame died. Joaquin Hernandez died. The 13th Guadalupe Salgado died. El Señor Antonio La Alallo. The

13th of October Gregorio Olivas died. And the widow of Amancio died. In the said day and month Señora Rosa la Dias died. The 15th Santiago Valenzuela died. The 16th Abaristo died. The said day and month Nestora the mother of Villas died. The 16th the wife of Lujan died. Jose Talomontes died. The 19th the son of Eugenio Baeza and the brother of Encaranacio Franco died. The 19th of October Matias Olguin died. The 30th of the said the mother of Jesus Anaya died.[4]

Texas in the mid-nineteenth century was a hotbed of disease. Cholera, yellow fever, smallpox, dengue fever, measles, influenza, diphtheria and whooping cough took their toll. In small Texas towns the faded dates on modest tombstones still tell the story; the infants succumbed first, followed by their brothers and sisters and finally their parents — all within a matter of months. In 1831 a smallpox epidemic claimed the lives of forty-four La Juntans; smallpox struck again in 1857. More than twenty died of an unknown disease during March and April 1845; another unknown plague took more than forty lives in the early months of 1854. In August and September 1847, measles swept through La Junta, taking a dozen lives. In the spring and summer of 1848, thirty-three people — mostly children — died during a fever epidemic.[5]

During that same spring, just before his trip to La Junta, Samuel Maverick was away from his San Antonio home, surveying a new homestead on Las Moras Creek, when his daughter Agatha became ill. Maverick's wife Mary wrote an account of her life on the Texas frontier, and it reflects the ignorance, confusion, frustration and heartbreak that followed in the wake of frontier epidemics:

Sunday, April 30th, my dear little Agatha took fever. Lizzie and I with the girls and Betsy with the baby were out walking and we were near the Mill Bridge when she first complained. . . . At this time Agatha was a large and very beautiful child of seven years. She was the idol of her father, and in return for his devoted affection for her, she idolized him. The sentiment of love between Mr. Maverick and the sweet child was something extraordinary, something beautiful and touching to behold.

When I got home, I bathed her in tepid water and cared tenderly for her, but on the following day she grew much worse, and I called in the services of Dr. Cupples. He gave her an emetic and then powders and enemas, but nothing seemed to reduce the fever or overcome the stupor. Day by day, Dr. Cupples encouraged me to hope, but I lost my appetite and passed many sleepless nights, for a terrible fear took possession of me. My fears whispered in my heart, "Agatha is dying," and I lost hope.

The poor child, with crimson cheek and shining eyes, sometimes raved wildly — once she screamed out in agonizing manner: "Oh, Sam," she thought she saw Indians about to kill Sam. When she took her medicine (the first in her life), she would say: "Mamma, will you tell papa I was good and took my medicine?" . . . On May 8th, the poor child breathed her last. Even now, in 1880, after thirty-two years, I cannot dwell on that terrible bereavement. The child was the perfection of sweetness and beauty and possessed such a glad and joyous disposition that her very presence was a flood of sunshine.[6]

Friday, May 26th, Mr. Maverick returned. Eleven miles west of town, he met an acquaintance who told him of Agatha's death! He went to the grave and threw himself down upon it, and remained there until it was dark. No one but God could tell the depth of his anguish. He was crushed and broken when he came home. . . . In his deep anguish he said: "Cursed land, cursed money, I would give all, all, only to see her once more."[7]

Four days after Agatha Maverick died, her sister Augusta came down with the same fever, but another doctor was somehow able to nurse her to recovery. Physicians were woefully underequipped to deal with the fevers that swept Texas, and they shared their patients' complete ignorance of the diseases' causes. Mrs. Maverick continues:

We now learned from the servants that our nurse Lavinia and Mrs. Bradley's nurse had taken Agatha and Augusta and Mrs. Bradley's girls Pauline and Ada, on April 25th, out walking and had allowed them to eat as many green mustang grapes as they would. I have always attributed Agatha's death and Augusta's deadly sickness to the grapes. Pauline and Ada had similar attacks about the same time but not as severe as Augusta's. . . .

In August [1848] Colonel Hays was ordered to open a shorter and better trading route through the wilds to Chihuahua, Mexico. Colonel Hays asked me to persuade Mr. Maverick to go with the expedition. I answered: "Oh, no, he is not well enough for such a hard trip." Then Hays replied, "Don't you see Mr. Maverick is dying by inches? Every one remarks how gray he has grown, how bent and feeble he looks, and this will be the very thing for him—he always thrives on hardships, and his mind must be distracted now from his grief."

I recognized the truth and force of this reasoning and that Hays loved him dearly and I set to work to persuade him to go. My husband was quite reasonable, and quickly saw that the trip had become a necessity for him. . . .

On Sunday, August 27th, Mr. Maverick left with Colonel Hays, fifty men and fifteen Delaware Indian guides, to run out the new route to Chihuahua.[8]

And so Samuel Maverick—deeply bereaved over the loss of his daughter—became among the first visitors to Fort Leaton. Sadly, his life in San Antonio has another tragic link to our story. In 1849, the year when cholera struck La Junta, Augusta Maverick—the child who had survived fever the year before—succumbed to the disease. She was dead in less than a day.[9]

How did cholera reach the isolated community of La Junta? It could have come with Hays's expedition, or Whiting's. It could have traveled with wagons from Chihuahua, or have been brought by one of the visitors from San Antonio that were beginning to trickle through in the wake of Hays and Whiting.

It wasn't just pathfinding expeditions and the Chihuahua trade that were drawing attention—and cholera—to border crossings. Forty-niners took all sorts of odd paths to their destiny. George Evans kissed his wife goodbye and left Defiance, Ohio, on February 20, 1849, bound for California. His party of fifteen adventurers traveled down the Ohio and Mississippi Rivers by steamboat to New Orleans, which was in the grip of cholera. They sailed for Galveston, then Port Lavaca; two people died of cholera en route. From Port Lavaca, they took the trail inland to Victoria and San Antonio.[10]

When Evans reached San Antonio, Lieutenant Whiting's expedition was still in Presidio del Norte. That is worth noting, because it means that Evans found himself in a place from which no one had yet discovered a direct route to El Paso, much less California. Note that we say that no one had discovered a "direct" route, for there was a route of sorts—but not one that would make any sense when looking at an accurate map. The recognized path to California from San Antonio—a path that a surprising number of people took—proceeded south to the Rio Grande at Eagle Pass, then followed a Mexican-American War trail to Saltillo, in Coahuila. From there it circled westward below the Bolson de Mapimí and turned toward Ciudad Chihuahua. From that point, the forty-niners took the Camino Real to El Paso, turned west through the Mesilla Valley to California and followed the coast north to gold country. It was a long, long journey.[11]

Evans decided to forge a new shortcut. In Eagle Pass he hired a guide to take his group due west, into the harsh Bolson de Mapimí. They reached the pueblo of Santa Rosa, an old Spanish border outpost. From there, they headed toward the fortified colony at San Carlos. The words "headed toward" are not meant to suggest any conscious decision. In his diary, Evans wrote, "We have very unexpectedly got within ten miles of this town without the knowledge of the fact."[12]

San Carlos was where the wandering Colonel Hays had found only basic provisions several weeks earlier, and the food situation seems to have been about the same: "With the exception of [green] wheat and a very few beans just ripening, there is nothing to supply our wants, and eighty-four men must live five days longer without bread. . . . I strolled from hut to hut and made a personal inspection of the state of provisions, which, I have already told, were found extremely low, and with one or two exceptions the citizens occupied the same level." After resting for a day, they set forth on a road southwest to Ciudad Chihuahua.[13]

On their second day out of San Carlos, Evans's group met a local denizen who informed them that they were on the way to Presidio del Norte, not Ciudad Chihuahua. Frustrated, they backtracked ten miles and started over on a new road. Their guides—who appear to have outlived their usefulness—returned to Santa Rosa, but Evans was confident that his party was on the right path. Two days later, despite their best efforts, they found themselves on the outskirts of Presidio del Norte, off course again. Evans, the accidental tourist, gives us a good picture of life in La Junta's largest pueblo:[14]

Presidio del Norte is considerable of a mud-built town; the only respectable build-ing in town is the Catholic Church. This is a large mud building, of mud brick, neatly whitewashed. The town is laid out with some little regularity on a hill, at the bottom of which flows the Rio Conchas, a stream of fine water and con-siderable size. On this river's bottoms are small gardens, closely cultivated by the Mexicans. . . . With the exception of the small fields on the Conchas, the whole country is a pebble bed, with nothing in the world growing upon it but small chaparral. This town numbers about 2,500 inhabitants, the most of whom are almost naked and of a copper color; and in each house may be seen a revolting image, representing the crucifixion of our Savior, which is worshiped instead of God. Mary, the mother of Christ, also occupies a conspicuous place at the family altar, and a rude picture of St. Wan [Juan], or St. John, and the other apostles fills up the background. On our arrival, we were escorted to the customhouse, where our packs underwent [scrutiny], and when night came on, a guard of sol-diers was placed around our camp to prevent smuggling. Preparations were made, and our boys enjoyed themselves at a Mexican fandango, or Spanish dance, where rude things were indulged in, although the fandango was held at the residence of the city alcalde, or mayor.[15]

Evans mentioned Ben Leaton and misspelled his name: "There is on the American side of this river a fort owned and established by a Mr. Seaton for trading purposes. The amount of business done at that fort is said to be very great, and he pays his clerks from forty to sixty dollars per month, and controls almost the entire Indian trade." He also mentioned David Torrey, "who is engaged in trade through this country, and is making vast profits on his merchandise." As we already know, Torrey would be murdered by Mescaleros before the year's end.

Evans noted the presence of Mescaleros in Presidio del Norte, saying that they were looking to buy liquor. It was Evans's opinion that the Apaches and Comanches had the upper hand in frontier relations; if the Mexicans did not concede any of their demands, the nomads could easily wreak murderous havoc.[16]

Evans seems to have made the rounds of La Junta, for he also encountered Ed Hall, the drover who had arrived with Leaton, Burgess and Spencer. Evans's relation of his business with Hall is distasteful in some respects, but reflects the realities of life in Presidio del Norte:

I went into Presidio today, and while there was much assisted by a young American by the name of Hall. This gentleman has spent some time in trade in this country and is master of the Spanish language and ever ready to interpret for those who do not understand this tongue, and is very obliging and affable in his manners. The alcalde was seeking to make me pay the sum of dos pesos (or US$2.00) for countersigning my passport, when Mr. Hall told him that he had no right under the sun to do it; and by this interference my US$2.00 were saved and Mexican rascality exposed to the scorn of strangers. Conscience has nothing to do in a Mexican's estimate of the value of his property or his services, and when an attempt is made by any of these harpies to extort money for real or imaginary services, the only thing necessary to be done is to take a firm stand at your own price and give them that or nothing. I have said that with few exceptions the Mexicans met with on this route are of the lower order, of Negro and Indian origins, and if they seek to do you a kindness, you may rest assured that there is a motive and that your confidence will be misplaced if you place any in their acts.[17]

George Evans was not the sort of person who would be comfortable in La Junta. As soon as his unintended visit was complete, he gathered up his entourage and headed for Ciudad Chihuahua.

The spring and summer of 1849 were a traffic jam by Presidio del Norte standards. After Hays, Whiting and Evans came a group that included a Texan by the name of Robert Hunter, a farmer from Fayette County, Texas, east-northeast of San Antonio. When he decided to seek his fortune in the goldfields, he knew there was a cholera epidemic raging in San Antonio, so he bypassed the city. Forty-niners usually traveled in groups for safety; by the time Hunter's company entered the frontier it consisted of ninety men and twenty-one wagons. Hunter had gathered intelligence from Hays's reports and chose to follow the route to Presidio del Norte that Hays had taken on his return journey. Hays, who we know was prone to exaggerate a bit, had extolled the virtues of the path, saying that there was plenty of grass and water for livestock and men. It did not turn out that way. By the time Hunter reached the presidio, he declared, "We have traveled two hundred and forty miles without seeing any timber and at two different times we drove two days and nights without water over mountains and ravines on the route that Jack Hays said he found water so plenty, and if he had been in sight he would not have lived one minute. Our mules suffered immensely, but the men done very well as we had gourds and kegs." [18]

Hunter's group left its wagons at Presidio del Norte and switched to pack mules. The wagons were dilapidated from their long journey, and the mules were better suited to what lay ahead. The deciding factor, though, may have been that each Mexican state charged duty of three dollars per wagon, so there was considerable savings to be had by leaving them behind.

Hunter was a pretty tough specimen. In a letter to his wife, he spent only a few words reporting that "we have seen a great many Comanches, Apaches, etc. but they generally left us in a hurry. We also had a fight with some Kioways on the Concho [of Texas] and killed several of them. They had stolen some horses from us but we got three for one in the winding up." He was also not terribly demanding about cuisine: "We get plenty of milch, wheat bread or flour and green snap beans from the Mexicans, so you may know that we are doing verry well in the eating way." Hunter mentioned something else that might explain his sparse literary style: "My hands are so full of prickley pears that it is with great difficulty that I can scratch a few lines for you." [19]

Like Evans, Hunter proceeded to Ciudad Chihuahua along the Rio Conchos, then followed the Camino Real to El Paso and from there traveled to California. It seems an impossibly indirect way to reach the goldfields of northern California, but in 1849 there were few alternatives for someone commencing the western part of their journey in Texas. [20]

The groups that included Whiting, Evans and Hunter are the only people known to have passed through La Junta in 1849, but there must have been others who left no diary or report to evidence their passage. Evans said that Ben Leaton was already doing substantial business at his fortín. While it is clear that a significant amount of that business was with Apaches, it is more than possible that we are aware of only a small portion of the Anglo merchants, freighters and forty-niners who came to Leaton's trading post in 1849. Over a period of just a year or so a trickle of commerce had begun, and it would soon turn into a torrent.

Among the many notable events of 1849 was a resurgence in Apache and Comanche raids. Chihuahua's legislature, overriding a veto by Governor Angel Trías, enacted legislation known as the "Fifth Law," which resurrected the scalp hunt, paying MEX$250 for a live captive warrior, MEX$200 for scalps of men over the age of fourteen and MEX$150 for all other scalps (thus eliminating any incentive to preserve the lives of women or children). Trías opposed the scalp hunt on constitutional and moral grounds, preferring a carrot-and-stick approach; he formed a pacification committee charged with enticing Apaches to cease hostilities, and he encouraged efforts to maintain the peace among Apaches who had accepted reservation life, but he also took the field personally as commander general of a military campaign against hostile Apaches and Comanches.[1]

The Chihuahuan legislature was encouraged to renew the scalp hunt by the lobbying efforts of former Texas Rangers who saw an opportunity to handle some frontier dirty work and profit handsomely at the same time. Among these proponents of a scalp harvest were ex-Rangers Michael Chevallié and John Glanton. Chevallié was the fist-fighting frontiersman who had come to La Junta with Hays. Glanton served under Hays and Chevallié in the Rangers, and gained an unsavory reputation. He was rumored to have once been banished from Texas by Sam Houston.[2]

There is evidence that newly arrived La Juntans John Spencer and Ben Leaton were themselves former scalp hunters. Spencer is said to have been with the notorious James Kirker when he turned traitor upon his own Apache village; Leaton supposedly was among a group that massacred a band of Mimbreño Apaches by using gifts to lure them before a concealed cannon. There are no credible indications that they participated in the 1849 hunt, however. In fact, all signs are that the La Juntans managed to strike an independent peace with the Apaches and viewed the scalp hunt as a threat to local equilibrium.[3]

Glanton, Chevallié and their ilk sometimes found it convenient to collect scalps that were outside the scope of those targeted by the Chihuahuan legislature. There were persistent rumors that they scalped peaceful natives and exploited the similarity between Apache scalps and those of Mexican campesinos. From the point of view of Leaton and others at

La Junta, however, the biggest problem with Glanton and Chevallié was that they would not stay on the Mexican side of the Rio Grande.[4]

A letter written by Brevet Major E. B. Babbitt from his San Antonio post in October 1849 describes the problem:

A party of Americans has engaged in the service of the State of Chihuahua to kill and destroy Indians, for whose scalps they are to receive from US$50 to US$500 according to the official importance of the victims; these men have recently crossed into our Territory near the Presidio del Norte and killed and scalped a number of peaceable and friendly Indians; which has so exasperated the Indians along the whole frontier, that the life of every white man who may fall into their power must pay the cost — Nothing short of a very general hostility on the part of the Indians against the whites is anticipated as the result of the shameful conduct of those degraded mercenaries who bear the name of Americans.[5]

The army may have longed to punish the scalp hunters for their incursions, but they received contrary signals from Washington, D.C., as evidenced by an August 1849 letter from the adjutant general of the United States Army to Major General George Brooke, the army's commander in San Antonio. In response to an inquiry from Brooke, the adjutant general remonstrated that "you do not, as Military Commander, possess the authority to restrain the conduct of evil-disposed white persons, whether acting individually, or in bands. . . . It may be presumed that the Executive of Texas under the laws of the State, will regulate and control the intercourse of her citizens and traders with the Indians, and restrain any improper conduct on the part of the whites toward them." Brooke was reminded that he was "to employ the troops to protect the peace of the frontier by repelling the incursion of Indians; and this is the leading purpose of the military force under your command on the frontier of Texas."[6]

Leaton became an opponent of the scalp hunters, despite his background. In November 1849 he traveled to the site of the future Fort Bliss, opposite the Mexican town of El Paso, to meet with Brevet Major Jefferson Van Horne, commander of the army post there. Leaton advised the major that he had spent the last year or two getting Apaches to settle peaceably in La Junta, hoping that a United States Indian Agent would be sent to formalize a peace treaty with them. He let the major know that it was only through his good offices that eight hundred assembled Apaches had permitted Captain Skillman's squad to reach Presidio unmolested. Immediately thereafter, Glanton's band of scalp hunters had crossed the Rio Grande and attacked the Mescaleros. Glanton had some trouble disengaging from his foes and took shelter at Fort Leaton, leading the Apaches to conclude that Leaton had become their enemy. According to Leaton, all the settlers in La Junta had fled to the safety of the Presidio del Norte except for his family and employees, who remained safe inside Fort Leaton. At some peril, Leaton traveled to El Paso to report the incident and to urge the army to establish a post in La Junta.[7]

Van Horne agreed with Leaton in one regard: he recommended an army post in La Junta, advising his superiors in San Antonio that "it is highly probable that the Presidio del Norte will be an important point on the great route of trade from San Antonio, Lavaca, Corpus Christi, &c, to Chihuahua, Durango, &c, which is an additional reason why troops should be stationed there."[8]

Unfortunately for Ben Leaton, Van Horne hadn't even finished his letter to San Antonio when another missive arrived—this one from Colonel Emilio Langberg, Mexico's inspector of military colonies, based in El Paso. Enclosed in Langberg's letter was another from Governor Trías of Chihuahua. Langberg complained about "a person, residing opposite the Presidio del Norte, calling himself Ben Leaton, and the place of his residence, Fort Leaton. Among the complaints . . . is the trade, which he continually carries on with the Apache and Comanche Indians. I need hardly state the fact to you, that these Indians are continually engaged in murdering, robbing and plundering the citizens of this country; it is not therefore, not only probable, but positive proof is in the hands of the Commandant General, that a great portion of the illicit traffic consists in the selling and purchasing of the very goods and property of the citizens of this country and of which they have been robbed by the Indians. But the evil consists not only in this: In return for the plunder which this person takes from the Indians, he furnishes them with arms, powder, lead, and other articles of ammunition."[9]

The enclosed letter from Governor Trías pulled no punches: "The American, Leaton, who resides on the opposite bank of the Rio Grande, near Presidio del Norte, has, for some time past been committing a thousand abuses, and of so hurtful a nature, that he keeps an open treaty with the Apache Indians, in opposition to what he has been expressly advised not to do. He has been repeatedly charged with this depraved conduct, but it has been impossible to put a stop to it in a satisfactory manner, as he does as he pleases, without respecting either the authorities of that Presidio, or the laws of the country."[10]

One reason for Governor Trías's anger was that Chihuahua's congress had anticipated exactly this kind of problem and had beseeched the national authorities to address it adequately in the treaty with the

United States. Any treaty would be unacceptable, Chihuahua advised Mexico City, "if it does not establish a sufficient mechanism so that neither the government of the United States, nor the citizens of that nation, can buy the property that savages have stolen in Mexican territory, nor provide them with any instruments of war, nor push them onto our territory by buying them land or by other means, nor directly or indirectly facilitate their incursions."[11]

Were the Mexicans' charges just? Major Van Horne thought so. He reported up his chain of command that "there is no doubt but that Leaton deals extensively in buying mules and horses, stolen by the Indians from the Mexicans, and in trading them off. The Torreys, and others, carry on the same traffic, and the Indians are extensively supplied by traders to Santa Fe, San Miguel, &c, with arms and ammunition in exchange for animals &c. Many of those traders rove about among the Indians, and live with them." (The clock was still ticking for David Torrey: six more weeks until his murder while trading among the Mescaleros.)[12]

The controversy over scalp hunters in La Junta made its way to the highest echelons in Washington. In November Secretary of War George Crawford wrote Secretary of State John Clayton urging that the scalp hunters' incursions into Texas be stopped. Clayton in turn alerted the United States ambassador to Mexico to the situation. Secretary of War Crawford put the problem this way: the scalp hunters in Texas would inflame the Apaches and Comanches, who would take out their frustrations first on Americans and later upon Chihuahua, which would complain that the United States had not observed its treaty obligation to stem cross-border incursions.[13]

Crawford's remarks made it clear that he understood that the root problem was the inherent counterproductivity of scalp hunting, not where the hunt was held. He doubtless referred the problem to the secretary of state because—as the commander in San Antonio had been reminded—the army lacked any authority to stop scalp hunting. Crawford and Clayton were both unaware of the complaints against Leaton, thus it would not have occurred to them that pushing the scalp hunters back into Mexico would benefit border traders, which would further inflame relations with Chihuahua.[14]

For all his perspicacity, Lieutenant Whiting had overlooked something when he observed that La Junta "enjoys in some sort immunity, but it is for the reason that its inhabitants have been stripped of their all, and, in the way of plunder, present no attraction for the Apache robbers." La Junta was exempt from Apache attacks because Ben Leaton, David Torrey and the other border traders formed a symbiotic relationship with the Mescaleros. Without the traders, the Mescaleros could not convert the property that they seized in Mexico into food, weapons, ammunition, blankets, whiskey and other goods. The Texas side of La Junta and the mountains that ringed it were the Apaches' sanctuary. Even though the commandant of the Presidio del Norte was among those who executed scalp-hunting contracts under Chihuahua's Fifth Law, the Apaches could safely fence their loot just a few miles away on the Texas side of the river.[15]

So, given that the commander of the Presidio del Norte could not cross the river without causing an international incident, and given that his presidio was in the business of exterminating Apaches, we are left to wonder who came up with the idea for Glanton's and Chevallié's men to cross the river and rout the Mescaleros. Was it really an act of overzealousness by the Americans, or was it a clever move by the Mexicans, who figured out that the lack of civil law on the Texas side of La Junta, combined with the absence of military authority to restrain the conduct of American citizens, effectively granted American-citizen scalp hunters (but only American-citizen scalp hunters) immunity to work both sides of the river? In all likelihood, the work of Glanton and Chevallié in La Junta was Mexico's answer to Leaton and Torrey.

The duplicity of Leaton's business helps us understand why Leaton —the Apaches' valued trading partner—was obliged to build a sturdy fort. When things went sour, as they did when Glanton and Chevallié crossed the river, Ben Leaton was the one man who could not expect sanctuary at the Presidio del Norte. When Leaton went to El Paso to complain to Major Van Horne about Glanton and Chevallié, everyone in La Junta was taking shelter at the presidio except Leaton's outcasts, who were hunkered down in his fortín.

Leaton was wise enough to extend generous hospitality to every Anglo who visited his home. They were good customers and they were beneficiaries of Leaton's ability to create a peaceful eye at the center of an Apache storm. Leaton's was a four-way game, and only the Mexicans were necessarily opposed.

The United States Army did nothing to curb Leaton's trading, for it was as powerless to restrain him as it was to punish Glanton and Chevallié. But the Mexicans continued to keep a close eye on his activities. In April 1850 a new captain arrived to take command of the Presidio del Norte. In May Inspector Colonel Langberg paid a personal visit to La Junta, touring the settlements on the Mexican side of the Rio Grande, not departing for Ciudad Chihuahua until early July.[16]

It had been less than two years since the Treaty of Guadalupe Hidalgo had been signed, but it had already brought a sea change to La Junta.

People on both sides of the border still mingled and married and traded and visited, and for most purposes the border still did not exist, yet there were new legalities and new distinctions. The social dynamic was no longer as simple as Spaniard versus native, or ranchero versus nomad. The new border had introduced subtleties and complexities. It had shifted allegiances, alliances and advantages.

We must briefly step back to 1846, when General Stephen Kearney occupied Santa Fe during the Mexican-American War. While he was there, he replaced the Mexican administration with a temporary civil government to oversee New Mexico. This ruffled some feathers in Texas, which claimed jurisdiction over all land to the Rio Grande, including much of New Mexico. As the territorial tug-of-war between free and slave states heated up in Washington, lawmakers became acutely interested in whether proslavery Texas would control New Mexico.

Texas staked out its claim in March 1848 when it created Santa Fe County. The Rio Grande delimited the county on the south and west and the Pecos River on the east and northeast. To the north, Santa Fe county extended into what is now Wyoming. Texas declared Santa Fe to be the county seat of Santa Fe County, Texas, and adopted joint resolutions letting the United States know that Texas meant business.[1]

In reaction, the citizens of Santa Fe asked the United States to include New Mexico within a new federal territory. Texas responded by dividing preposterously gigantic Santa Fe County into four less preposterously gigantic counties and sending out an expedition to organize them. The expedition, headed by Robert S. Neighbors and John "Rip" Ford, didn't so much organize the counties as it did discover another bad way to get from San Antonio to El Paso and (learning from experience) a good way to get from El Paso to San Antonio. The good route, which followed the Rio Grande downstream about eighty miles (to the vicinity of the future Fort Quitman) before turning east, became known as the Ford-Neighbors Trail.[2]

Presidio County was one of the three new counties carved out of Santa Fe County. Created on January 3, 1850, it began at the junction of the Pecos River with the Rio Grande, followed the Rio Grande upstream to the Ford-Neighbors Trail junction, then cut across country in a straight line northeast to intersect the Pecos River (near Roswell, New Mexico), then ran downstream on the Pecos to the Rio Grande—smaller than the original Santa Fe County, but still a huge expanse of land. There weren't any real towns in Presidio County, so the Texas legislature declared the county seat to be Fort Leaton.[3]

A Sudden

Death

Texas and the United States continued to wrangle over borders. Proposals before the United States Congress called for splitting Texas into two or three states, which didn't help matters any, but finally a compromise was reached that established Texas borders where they are today. Cash-strapped Texas decided to accept the Compromise of 1850 because it involved payment of $10 million to the state—most of which went to its creditors, who were lobbying hard in Washington for the financial settlement.[4]

In 1858 the legislature adjusted Presidio County's borders to make it smaller, moved the county seat to the town of Presidio del Norte (today's town of Presidio, not the actual Presidio del Norte) and called for election of county officials and opening of county offices. It looked good on paper, but the elections never happened and the offices never opened. In 1870, the legislature again adjusted the county boundaries and again called for the organization of the county, this time with Fort Stockton as a temporary county seat until the citizens of the county chose another. Again, no effective county government emerged. In May 1871 the legislature adjusted the boundaries again and ordered county organization again, but this time it specifically named three commissioners to carry out the task. Still no luck. In 1875 the legislature named five new county commissioners and directed them to organize the county. This time it finally worked, and Presidio County existed in fact as well as in law.[5]

The first functioning county seat (disregarding the fictional county seats at Fort Leaton, Presidio, and Fort Stockton) was Fort Davis. When the Southern Pacific Railroad came through in 1883 the county population balance changed; in 1885 the courthouse was moved twenty-five miles to the new railroad town of Marfa. The citizens of Fort Davis were none too happy about the move and raised allegations of vote fraud. The acrimony was intense, and the upshot of the internal strife was that Presidio County was divided into five counties in 1885. Fort Davis became the county seat of newly formed Jeff Davis County, and Marfa retained dominion over a shrunken Presidio County.[6]

For La Junta, the practical effect of these gyrations was that the Texas side lacked even a pretense of local government—it had no sheriff, no judge, no jail, no county commissioners—until 1875, and by that time the preponderance of the county's population and commerce had shifted from La Junta to Fort Davis (where the military road crossed), leaving La Junta an orphan community eighty long horseback miles from the county seat. When the railroad came through and Marfa became the county seat, little changed, at least in terms of government, which stayed far north of the border. La Junta remained a land apart.

Now we must again step back a few years. The temporal locus of our story remains 1850, when Benjamin Leaton was given the honor of having his fortín declared the nonexistent county seat of barely existent Presidio County. Once the trail to San Antonio was open, Leaton began hauling freight to and from the Gulf Coast via San Antonio. We find him in San Antonio and Indianola (a Gulf port) during those years. This is probably when he struck up his business partnership with attorney James Peacock in San Antonio, and we know that Peacock began working on perfecting Leaton's title to the fortín and surrounding lands. We cannot tell whether Peacock knew that Leaton's underlying grants were fraudulent.[7]

Leaton doubtless already understood the advantages that derived from recording his bogus paperwork in the county courthouse. Since the days of the Republic of Texas the rule had been that even a questionable deed (color of title) properly recorded in the county courthouse could ripen into legal ownership after five years' unchallenged possession. Only there wasn't a Presidio County courthouse yet. At first, filings were made in San Antonio (Bexar County). After El Paso County was formed and organized, filings were made in the El Paso Courthouse until Presidio County was organized. Leaton began working his filings in 1849, when Bexar County was the appropriate place to file, and San Antonio lawyer James Peacock was the perfect person to assist.[8]

When Peacock looked over Leaton's papers, one significant obstacle emerged: There was no point in taking the papers to the courthouse unless the county clerk would accept them for recording, and not just anything could be recorded. For a deed to pass muster, the validity of the grantor's signature had to be proven. That required a personal acknowledgment by the grantor before a county clerk or a notary public. If a personal acknowledgement was impractical (as in the case of Leaton's dead grantors), then a subscribing witness to the document was required to testify to proper execution and delivery. Since there were a lot of old grants and deeds floating around Texas, the law went even further to accommodate potential deaths: if the subscribing witnesses were dead, or their place of residence unknown, or if they lived out of the state, then two or more "disinterested witnesses" could execute a verification that they recognized the signatures of the grantor and at least one of the subscribing witnesses.[9]

Leaton and his helpful friend Cesario Herrera had carefully picked the signatories and witnesses to their forged deeds so that there would be no one living to dispute Leaton's claim. Now Leaton needed two people to verify that the forged signatures were valid. Herrera might have been a good choice—assuming that the county clerk hadn't heard of his land-fraud trial in Chihuahua—but he had died in the year of the cholera. Leaton needed to find two credible souls who could verify that the signatures on his deeds were genuine, which of course they weren't.[10]

In 1849 Leaton was in San Antonio on business. He had Peacock draw up a will for him and persuaded Cesario Ureta, former secretary to Cesario Herrera, to go with him to the Clerk of the Bexar County Court to verify several of the (forged) signatures on the land grants. There are signs that the Leaton and Ureta families were close: Ureta's daughter later married Joe Leaton. Ureta signed affidavits verifying the signatures of more than a half-dozen people, all of whom—as luck would have it—were either dead or out of the state.[11]

Leaton needed a second verification, but the project languished, as is understandable given the difficulties of travel then. In the summer of 1851 Leaton was back in San Antonio. With him was Ed Hall, the teamster who had long worked for Leaton. Two interesting things happened on this trip: Ed Hall provided the verifications lacking on the forged Spanish land grants and Ben Leaton died. We do not know the order in which those things occurred, because we do not know the date of Leaton's decease; death certificates were not required in 1851, and the original petition in Leaton's probate is missing. It is not unreasonable to assume that Leaton's unexpected death (likely from a fever or cholera, possibly caught in Indianola) caused a flurry of activity to clean up his affairs.

Attorney Peacock addressed two problems in getting Leaton's estate tidied up. The first was the need to complete the land grants. Peacock had learned a thing or two since Cesario Ureta provided his verifications; Hall's was on its face of a higher quality. Texas law was evolving toward saying that it was not enough that a county clerk accepted a deed for recording; it was also necessary that it be clear on the face of the instrument that it was entitled to be recorded—which, in the case of Leaton's forged grants, meant that two signature verifications were required and the verifications had to recite facts that demonstrated their reliability. To put a finer point on it, Ed Hall's verification needed to state exactly how Hall had come to be familiar with the signatures in question.[12]

And so Ed Hall summoned the creativity that was the hallmark of Leaton's land grants. His signature verifications recited that he had been employed by the Mexican government as an interpreter and customhouse officer, and that he had done business with the signatories. His claim to have been a customs officer was a blatant fabrication.

His claim to have interpreted is plausible, but his having been employed by Mexico as an interpreter is doubtful. And it is most unlikely that any of the dead-or-vanished 1832 signatories had done business with Ed Hall since his arrival in La Junta in 1848.[13]

Hall added his fraudulent verifications of the fraudulent signatures on the fraudulent deeds on July 10, and the Bexar County Clerk recorded them on July 11. Leaton's will was filed for probate on August 15. In the interim, Peacock had probably been mulling over his second problem: Leaton and Pedraza were not married. There were people who thought, or assumed, that they were married, but those who knew them best said otherwise. The most revealing document on this point is Leaton's will. A will is the one place where it is essential to be clear about relationships, because those relationships are material in determining who gets what. Leaton identified his children by name and specifically stated that they were his and Pedraza's offspring. But he identified their mother as simply "Juana Pedraza," without mentioning any marital relation. He left all his property to "Juana Pedraza and our three children." And he provided for "the support of the said Juana Pedraza and for the proper maintenance and education of the children." Coldest of all is this: "I appoint the said James Peacock also the Guardian of the said children, enjoining upon their mother to permit him to direct and control in regard to their education."[14]

Peacock was looking at a will that left Leaton's property to his lover and their three illegitimate children. If Leaton had any other living relatives—and there are mentions of brothers in at least two contexts—his legitimate family might try to strip the estate. And so Peacock performed an immaculate postmortem marriage, bestowing the title of "widow" upon Juana Pedraza, who now began calling herself Juana Pedraza y Leaton.[15]

The estate was burdened with debt, and Ben Leaton's death had left a complete management vacuum at the trading post, which quickly ceased business. Peacock looked after getting the Leaton conveyances recorded in San Antonio and El Paso and took care of the expenses of the departed's final illness, but the probate consisted mostly of liquidation. Juana Pedraza, ensconced in a rented house, evidenced little interest in returning to Presidio.

The probate dragged on, and there may have been a falling out between Peacock and Pedraza. By June 1852 Peacock resigned as executor of the estate. Hall may have fomented the apparent unrest: when Juana Pedraza replaced Peacock, qualifying as executrix on September 4, she signed her name Juana Pedraza Hall. The paperwork trailed the declaration: five weeks later Pedraza and Hall received a marriage license in

Bexar County. By April of the next year, Pedraza and Hall were claiming to be the joint administrators of Leaton's estate, though there is no evidence of Hall's appointment.[16]

Regardless of the estate's debts, under Texas law the "widow" Pedraza was entitled to retain the fortín and a surrounding two hundred acres as her homestead, exempt from the claim of creditors. Pedraza kept that land while selling off other parcels. Then in the spring of 1853 Pedraza decided to sell off all of her homestead except the fort itself and five acres surrounding it. The purchaser was Joseph H. Devine, who paid US$1,600.[17]

Less than five years after Ben Leaton cut a swath through the valley, his fortín stood empty. Juana Pedraza, now married to Leaton's former teamster Ed Hall, was unwilling to venture back into the difficulty and danger of La Junta, but she held on to the fort, hoping that she—or Hall, or one of the Leaton children—might one day reopen a trading post there.

James Kirker, notorious scalp hunter, was a man possessed by demons. Thomas Easterly daguerreotype, courtesy of the Missouri Historical Society.

Ben Leaton expanded Ronquillo's old fortín below Presidio, creating a fortified home for his family. Apache raids were a constant peril; venturing beyond sight of the fortín was risky. Photograph by author.

In 1926 modest efforts to preserve crumbling Fort Leaton were under way; another attempt was made in the 1930's. Today it is a state historical park. W. D. Smithers Collection, Harry Ransom Humanities Research Center, the University of Texas at Austin.

When the Rio Grande was high at the Presidio-Ojinaga crossing, wagons and automobiles would use a ferry to cross the border. People often made the trip in rowboats; that practice continues at inconspicuous crossings. W. D. Smithers Collection, Harry Ransom Humanities Research Center, the University of Texas at Austin.

This *ancón grande* above Candelaria is similar to ones found elsewhere in La Junta. In the spring, the entire ancón floods. As spring gives way to summer, it holds enough moisture along the riverbank to grow crops. The river gradually dries, but water continues to migrate beneath the surface, leaving mudflats and small pools. Photograph by author.

Maurice von Hippel was a small cog within a dysfunctional international machination. In early 1852, sitting in his dusty El Paso office, the lowly draftsman looked with disgust at the maps produced by incompetent appointees of United States Boundary Commissioner John Bartlett. Depictions of the topography along the Rio Grande were deficient or entirely absent. There were no bearings to the tops of prominent mountains, no description of their forms, heights or characteristics. Roads were seldom described. Irrigation ditches were uniformly and improbably shown as connecting to the river at right angles. The maps were useless.[1]

Hippel knew that there had been problems with the survey from the outset. The politicians and lawyers that drew up the Treaty of Guadalupe Hidalgo had described a border west of the Rio Grande that followed perfectly straight lines across the curving surface and rugged features of the earth. They had adopted a map published in New York with boundaries that varied markedly from reality on the ground. They had called for the border on the Rio Grande to run "up the middle of that river, following the deepest channel, where it has more than one," leaving surveyors wondering whether to chart the middle of the deepest branch (its median) or the deepest line through the deepest branch (its thalweg).[2]

Commissioner Bartlett and his Mexican counterpart, Pedro García Conde, had reached a compromise on the location of the border west of the Rio Grande, and in theory their decision was final under the treaty, but the issue had quickly become politicized and influential people in Washington were clamoring for a renegotiation. In sum, the border was uncertain, the surveys establishing its compromise location were flawed and a movement was afoot to reject the compromise. And now, in response to Hippel's complaints about the river surveys, Hippel—a draftsman, not a surveyor—had been ordered to go into the field and survey the topography of the Rio Grande himself.[3]

Dutifully setting forth into the desert, Hippel began surveying at the point where the cross-country boundary first intersected the Rio Grande—the "initial point" that (according to the García-Bartlett compromise) was about eight miles upstream of El Paso. Hippel worked his way downstream to El Paso, where he learned that Major William H. Emory—a skilled engineer and surveyor—had arrived to

The End of

Isolation

replace both the chief astronomer and the official surveyor, men who had proved quarrelsome and overly political. Emory would later be credited with salvaging a project that threatened to become a political and managerial fiasco. After meeting with Hippel, Emory instructed the draftsman-turned-surveyor to move forward aggressively on the Rio Grande survey with the goal of reaching the Presidio del Norte as soon as possible. Emory wanted to let the controversial boundary to the west simmer while he advanced the project downriver.[4]

After dispatching Hippel toward La Junta, Emory sat down with his Mexican counterpart, José Salazar Ylarregui, surveyor for the Mexican Border Commission. Salazar had his hands full. Underfunded and understaffed, his burdens had been compounded by the recent death of Commissioner García. The Mexican government had named Salazar as interim commissioner, adding more responsibilities to his portfolio.[5]

The original concept of the two boundary commissions had been for them to work side by side, reaching concurrent agreement on the border's location, but inadequate resources and funds on the Mexican side, matched by incompetence and bickering on the United States side, had reduced the two organizations to working sporadically and separately. When Emory and Salazar met in El Paso during the spring of 1852 they agreed to accept the work done by Hippel from the town of Frontera (north of El Paso, near the initial point) to the place eighty miles downstream where the military road to San Antonio left the river. After reviewing pending projects, they made plans to meet again in Presidio del Norte during August "for the purpose of signing and marking a red line shewing the Boundary on all the maps of surveys now unfinished from the Initial point to that Presidio."[6]

Hippel reached Presidio del Norte by the middle of May. His duties were confined to a topographical survey—establishing contours, monuments, lines and distances—and did not include determining latitudes and longitudes along his route. The latter task—astronomical work—was undertaken by Emory personally. Accompanied by an assistant, Emory followed in Hippel's path and reached La Junta in early July. Salazar, who had gone to Ciudad Chihuahua for supplies, had not yet arrived in the valley.[7]

Emory's survey report contains his first impressions of La Junta:

We arrived in front of the Presidio del Norte July 8, 1852, and found watermelons ripe and the corn in tassel. The town, isolated and very remote from any other settlement, had been suffering from famine. The Indians had run off most of the cattle, and the drought for the three preceding years had caused a failure in the corn.

The Presidio is a miserably built mud town, situated upon a gravelly hill, overlooking the junction of the Conchos and the Rio Bravo — the latter called here the Rio Puerco, no doubt from the contrast of its muddy waters with those of the Conchos, which, except during freshets, is limpid. The town, which contains about eight hundred souls, is one of the oldest Spanish settlements in northern Mexico; but from the barrenness of the soil, an attempt is making to settle a military colony forty miles higher up the Rio Bravo [at Vado de Piedra], where the land is supposed to be better adapted to agriculture.

The church is within the walls of the Presidio, or fort, and contains one or two paintings of a better class than are usually found disfiguring the walls of frontier churches. In almost every house is found, in addition to the cross, a figure of our Saviour, which is sometimes so very grotesque that piety itself cannot divest it of its ridiculous appearance.[8]

Emory spent some time in La Junta, waiting for Salazar, working on survey details and investigating his surroundings. He visited the fort at Vado de Piedra that Whiting had characterized as miserable and abandoned three years earlier. Emory found it to be a military colony with a population of three hundred persons. According to Emory, the citizens of Vado de Piedra tended large cultivated fields watered by *acequias* (irrigation ditches), yielding abundant crops of wheat and corn. The contrast between the two men's descriptions can be explained: when Whiting passed through, the fort was in disrepair; if any settlement remained, its military character had greatly diminished. One purpose of the 1850 visit to La Junta by Colonel Emilio Langberg, inspector of military colonies, was almost certainly to reinvigorate (or reestablish) the colony at Vado de Piedra. Emory was viewing the result.

Reinvigorated or not, Vado de Piedra was in harm's way; during Emory's stay in La Junta, Apaches attacked there, killing two men, wounding four residents and grabbing as much loot as they could carry. Only a week earlier Apaches had killed two other people in the valley.[9]

We cannot be certain, but the Apache attacks suggest that the deaths of Ben Leaton and David Torrey had altered the equilibrium in La Junta. Reading Emory's account, the role of outlaw haven seems to have shifted to another pueblo: "The relations between the Indians of this region and several of the Mexican towns, particularly San Carlos, a small town twenty miles below, are peculiar, and well worth the attention of both the United States and Mexican governments. The Apaches are usually at war with the people of both countries, but have friendly leagues with certain towns, where they trade and receive supplies of arms, ammunition, &c, for stolen mules. This is undoubtedly the case with the people of San Carlos, who also have amicable relations with the Comanches, who make San Carlos a depot of arms in their annual excursions into Mexico."[10]

Mexican representative Salazar soon arrived in Presidio del Norte. Despite the plans to agree on the border from El Paso to the Presidio, Emory's maps were not yet ready and Salazar's team had not even begun work on that stretch of river. They were only able to sign off on a map from the initial point established by the García-Bartlett compromise to the town of Frontera, a short distance downstream. Because of the storm brewing in Washington, D.C., Emory carefully avoided certifying the initial point as correct under the treaty; he only certified that it was the point agreed to under the García-Bartlett compromise.[11]

The inability of Emory and Salazar to accomplish their goals in Presidio del Norte led to a sensible change in their operating protocol: from that point on, no maps were to be considered finished in the field. The two commissions would do their work, compare and check each others' surveys and later — in a proper facility — prepare final maps for confirmation.[12]

Over the coming months La Junta would receive several more visits from survey teams. In the autumn of 1852, two U.S. surveyors attempted to map the rugged canyons below Presidio del Norte, but they got only as far as San Vicente before their boats were destroyed and their supplies ran short. Salazar returned in early 1853 on a trip to establish points of longitude along the Rio Grande. He was proceeding alone and without government funding, and experienced a number of problems. His trip concluded when he was robbed in the vicinity of Presidio del Norte, necessitating a return to El Paso. In 1855 a Mexican team attempted to survey from Presidio del Norte to Laredo, but their supplies ran out by the time they reached San Carlos. The difficulty of following the river downstream from La Junta was a lesson that had to be repeatedly learned.[13]

From La Juntans' perspective, Emory's greatest contribution was the effort he undertook on this and subsequent trips to improve the trail along Alamito Creek. "This road," said Emory, "was opened for the double purpose of communicating with my [survey] parties on the lower Rio Grande, and of shortening the distance from San Antonio to Chihuahua. The route followed by the merchant trains is by the way of El Paso, a distance greater by 300 miles. It is possible a shorter route may be found, but our explorations led us to believe this was the shortest one where a permanent supply of water could be obtained."[14]

The entirely unheralded 1850 trip of Ben Leaton from Presidio to Indianola by way of San Antonio — evidenced only by the debts he owed James Peacock when he died — may have been the first commercial trip from La Junta to San Antonio and thence to the coast (remember that Connelly did not pass through San Antonio and that he proceeded to the Mississippi River, not the Gulf). It is impossible to tell whether that trip included a leg to Chihuahua, but Leaton had a history of traveling that route, and Whiting noted that Leaton customarily obtained his supplies from that city.

Some say that in the fall of 1849 Francis Xavier Aubrey, a Santa Fe trader known for his high-speed dashes across country, took an eighteen-wagon caravan from San Antonio through La Junta to Chihuahua, then took the Camino Real to El Paso and the military road back to San Antonio. Unfortunately, there is no proof of his going through Presidio del Norte, and his route must be deduced from the eight weeks that it took him to travel from San Antonio to El Paso—slim evidence at best.[15]

We must accept that many historic data points have been lost. Not all freighters and traders kept diaries; most were of the type noted by forty-niner George Evans after he left La Junta: "We met ten American wagons, drawn by ten splendid mules each, and loaded with corn and whiskey for Presidio del Norte, intended by the traders to hit the California emigration. These men are making a speculation upon their wares and merchandise, and should there be as many emigrants on the Sante Fee route as have already gone through here, they are in the way of realizing a splendid fortune." It was undocumented traffic of that sort that quickly turned the route through La Junta into the Chihuahua Trail and made Presidio del Norte a significant port of entry between the United States and Mexico. As we will see, wagon traffic diminished during the Civil War and was dealt a heavy blow by the completion of the Southern Pacific Railroad, but between 1851 and 1883 wagon trains were a constant presence. The road forged by Connelly and Emory along Alamito Creek saw heavy traffic, and the two towns called Presidio (Presidio, Texas, and Presidio del Norte, Chihuahua) flourished in a modest, unattractive way.[16]

In 1853 a German traveler named Julius Fröbel decided to join a wagon train from Ciudad Chihuahua that was taking a load of silver pesos to San Antonio by way of La Junta. Fröbel was a leisurely professional tourist of the scientific sort who spent seven years inspecting North America, and he traveled in style. His description of the landscape near Julimes turned unexpectedly culinary: "The Rio Conchos, near which Julimas is located, is a clear stream in which soft-shelled turtles are found. One measuring 1 ½ foot in diameter was caught by one of our servants. It happened that a French gentleman living in this part of Mexico, the Marquis de V——, was then in our camp, and he offered to make us some turtle soup of superior quality. We possessed the ingredients he required, namely, Bordeaux, Madeira, vinegar, and spices, and, as the Marquis was a skilled gastronome, we had a dish literally fit for a king and which was not the less enjoyed from being eaten out of tin plates, and lying on the ground."[17]

We might not expect a man of such refined tastes to appreciate the rough and dubious pleasures of La Junta, thus his take on the valley is not entirely surprising: "I never, either then or subsequently, saw an inhabited region which so strongly retained the character of a savage wilderness. The Rio Conchos unites its clear waters here with the muddy stream of the Rio Grande. The junction of these rivers is surrounded by rocks and remnants of the alluvial masses. . . . Afar, the eye rests on nothing but gloomy mountains of the most irregular and varied forms, while near, a high, thick, thorny chaparral obstructs the road and the view, as if guarding a paradise."[18]

Fröbel's view of La Junta's citizenry was hardly more sympathetic: "The people here are savages, and their habits as rude as the nature around them. The Norteños—as the inhabitants of the Presidio del Norte are called in Mexico—are the allies, spies, powder purveyors, the receivers and buyers of stolen goods, of the Texan Comanches. Necessity may have driven them to this, for, isolated and exposed as they are, they could scarcely otherwise have held their ground between the Comanches and Apaches." This remark, taken with Emory's comments about San Carlos, suggests two changes since Ben Leaton's departure—the local peace was now with the Comanches, not the Apaches (who favored San Carlos), and the Presidio del Norte was an active participant in the Comanche peace. This raises an interesting question: Was Chihuahua's complaint about Leaton that he traded with hostile, thieving nomads, or that he did so with the *wrong* hostile, thieving nomads?[19]

The empty wagons in Fröbel's caravan were driven across the Rio Grande, but the loaded ones were taken on a ferry—a sign that commerce through Presidio del Norte was increasing. The group camped near Fort Leaton, and Fröbel was regaled with stories of the deceased trader. One tale had an enemy of Leaton's named "the Doctor" trying to kill Leaton from ambush, but the Doctor's rifle misfired. Leaton supposedly drew his pistol, captured his would-be killer and took him to the fortín, where he tied the Doctor to a post and made a mockery of him. After a few days of indignities, Leaton set the man free. Fröbel claimed to have met the Doctor, whom he found dislikable. The principal problem with this tale is that Leaton—like anyone else in La Junta at the time—would not have tied up the Doctor and tormented him. He would have shot the varmint dead and taken his horse.[20]

Stories of raiding Apaches and ambushing doctors left Fröbel and his compadres jittery. "During the night we had several alarms in our camp. First, one of the watch fired — more in joke I think than in earnest — upon a human figure which immediately took to flight, and was followed by several others who appeared to rise out of the ground; some other shots were fired; but they proved to be some common Mexican women, who had visited our drivers during the night. A few hours later there was another shot again upon a human figure, but this time a more dangerous one. A regular chase ensued, and wherever a shadow was seen among the bushes it was fired at. I can only hope that no harmless passer-by was injured." [21]

Fröbel survived the dangers of sleeping in La Junta, and his remarks upon departing demonstrated that knowledge of the various routes to Chihuahua was spreading through the frontier: "The road we took from hence is known as Connelly's Trail, after a Dr. Connelly, who a few years since made the first carriage track through the wilderness. This road, at the watering-place Agua Delgada [Fort Stockton], joins the more frequented one which connects El Paso with San Antonio in Texas." [22]

A freighter named August Santleben made at least four trips through Presidio del Norte beginning in 1869. On his first trip out of San Antonio he took the lower road through Fort Clark to Fort Lancaster — which was abandoned at the time — then proceeded west on the upper road to Fort Stockton. Nine miles west of Fort Stockton, exactly where U.S. Highway 67 intersects Interstate Highway 10 today, his train turned south for Presidio del Norte. [23]

Santleben made his way along Alamito Creek. When he reached Presidio del Norte, he estimated the distance that he had traveled from the military road turnoff as two hundred entirely uninhabited miles. In fact, it was probably closer to 150 miles, but it surely must have felt like more. He found that "the road is tolerably good excepting the last forty miles, which is hilly, and the sand is heavy, but its principal recommendation is an abundance of grass that affords good pasturage." [24]

Santleben took the two towns of La Junta in stride, making none of the derogatory remarks that other early travelers offered. He noted that both nations had established customhouses, and commented on the large volume of goods passing through. "The river at that point is always fordable," he observed, "except when the water is high, and then the passage is made on ferry-boats." [25]

"After submitting an inventory of my freight for inspection to the United States officials, who approved it," Santleben continued, "I crossed at the ford into Mexico, and my train was placed under guard until the inspectors verified my manifest and the duties on the bonded goods were paid. I received courteous treatment from the officials of both governments and was not unnecessarily delayed."[26]

Santleben, like many freighters to Chihuahua, was carrying bonded goods, meaning that his cargo had come ashore without paying import duty. The importer and freighter were required to post substantial bonds with the United States government to guarantee that the merchandise would be promptly exported—in this case, at Presidio del Norte—instead of being sold or consumed within the United States. Santleben picked up the goods from a firm of commission merchants in Indianola and hauled them on contract into Mexico.[27]

When Santleben reached Ciudad Chihuahua, he off-loaded his cargo, then took his wagons to the mining town of Parral, where he filled some of his wagons with bars of silver and others with crude copper ore. He hauled the metals to Chihuahua, where the silver's owner had contracted for it to be coined into Mexican pesos at a licensed private mint. Santleben waited ten days while the silver was minted into coins, then headed back for Presidio del Norte with 180,000 Mexican silver pesos and a few tons of copper ore, which he delivered to waiting customers in Texas. Just as Connelly and Fröbel had hauled silver coins before him, Santleben was part of an interchange that had not changed since the days of the conquistadores: Mexico was importing manufactured goods and exporting silver.[28]

Santleben was party to another coinage-hauling episode that did not turn out as well. On his third trip through Presidio del Norte, he attempted to execute an arbitrage. In Mexico, five-centavo and ten-centavo pieces had been made of copper, and were considered a poor person's coin. The government, for reasons that made perfect sense in the nineteenth century, attempted to eradicate copper coinage and required the licensed private mints to stamp 10 percent of their silver output in five-and ten-centavo denominations. Citizens resisted the change; merchants found that they were receiving the new coins but could not push them back to their customers. The result was an accumulation of unwanted small-denomination silver coins.

Meanwhile, in San Antonio, a shortage of small change existed, whether copper or silver. Merchants there were willing to pay a 10 percent premium for five- and ten-cent pieces and—because coins then held their worth in metal—were perfectly willing to accept silver. If an entrepreneur could purchase silver small change in Mexico at a slight discount and sell it in San Antonio at a 10 percent premium, there was money to be made. The only problem was that the Mexican government charged a 10 percent export duty on coins. Combined with the cost of transportation, the duty wiped out the potential profit. "Therefore," said Santleben, "certain persons [including Santleben himself, as it turned out] determined to avoid the imposition by smuggling this money across the Rio Grande."[29]

There is no doubt that Mr. Santleben was a creative entrepreneur. He once hauled a complete brewery, along with yeast and hops, into Mexico in partnership with a man who set about making the best beer ever brewed in Chihuahua — "best" in the sense that it was the first beer brewed there. Beer in corked bottles, six dollars for a dozen quarts. The business went well until his partner absconded with the profits. And as if carting an entire brewery across eight hundred miles of Apache-infested wilderness wasn't imaginative enough, Santleben later lost money on a scheme to haul a giant meteorite from Mexico to Texas and ship it to Philadelphia for exhibition at the World's Fair.[30]

The coin-smuggling venture was a simpler plan. Santleben hid MEX\$1,100 in small change in a sack of beans and loaded it on his wagons in Chihuahua. When he reached the pueblo of La Mula, almost to La Junta, his wagon train was inspected without incident, but the town alcalde appeared just as the wagons were about to roll and demanded a second inspection. Someone had ratted on Santleben; the alcalde pointed directly to the silver-bearing sack of beans and the trouble began.

A messenger hurried to Presidio del Norte and returned with a squad of customhouse guards. The squad's commander put Santleben under arrest and escorted the wagons to the presidio. Invoking a defense that remains popular to this day, Santleben claimed to know nothing of the smuggled coins. A number of the men in his wagon train testified to his innocence, and he was acquitted — "honorably acquitted," in his words.

The tension was not entirely relieved, however. Regardless of Santleben's personal innocence of smuggling, Mexican law required that the entire train and its cargo be confiscated. In addition to the beans, nickels and dimes in his custody, Santleben was carrying a legitimate cargo of 180,000 Mexican silver pesos and he was responsible to its owners for safe delivery. A little bit of influence was applied, the MEX\$1,100 in small change was left in the custody of the customs officials, the full 10 percent duty was paid on the legitimate pesos, a few more coins changed hands and Santleben's cargo was released. The relieved freighter reported that "the government officials were liberal in their exactions, and courteous treatment was shown me, especially by Henrico Peña, who was in charge of the custom-house, from whom I received an unusually lenient inspection when passing through his department."[31]

One might think that Santleben's next hurdle would be United States customs, perhaps interested in taking a close look at his troubled cargo. As it turned out, the inspection in Presidio, Texas, was uneventful. That night James Clark, who was in charge of the United States custom-house, appeared at Santleben's camp. In his company were his wife, two young ladies and six men on horseback. They had come to party. Fortunately, Santleben's company included one Professor Manuel Manso and his orchestra troop from Chihuahua. Santleben danced until dawn.[32]

During the years when traffic flourished along the Chihuahua Trail, the most notable changes in La Junta occurred
within the Anglo-initiated community that would become
Presidio. In the late 1850's—some say around 1856, others
say around 1859—Edward Hall and Juana Pedraza returned
to Fort Leaton and resumed operation of the trading post.
Their decision to return might have been motivated by the
founding of Fort Davis in 1854, for though it was eighty
miles north, the post heralded a regional security presence.
The more important event in terms of La Junta's safety,
though, was a formal peace treaty reached in June 1856 by
Mexican colonel José Quintanilla with the Apaches. Signed
in Presidio del Norte by Mescalero leaders Cisneros, Espejo,
Metal, El Gordo, Marcos and El Chino, the treaty resulted
in an exchange of captives and a return of livestock and
plunder that the Apaches had stolen.[1]

Hall and Pedraza's willingness to return to La Junta coincided with a greater general awareness of the potential
for settlement west of the Pecos River. In the last half of the
nineteenth century Anglos became conscious that desirable
West Texas land was both available and finite. The state of
Texas was doing all within its power to accelerate the pace
of occupation. More citizens and more towns meant more
revenue and more safety.

The Texas legislature, like the rest of the nation, saw railroads as the universal catalyst of dominion and wealth. The
United States had been granting land to help finance the
construction of roads and canals since 1808, and made its
first railroad right-of-way grant in 1832. Although the semi-
nal Pacific Railroad Act would not be adopted until 1862,
Congress began granting 100–foot railroad rights of way in
1835 and authorized railroad companies to construct their
improvements using earth, stone and timber from public
lands. When Stephen A. Douglas sponsored an 1850 measure to grant railroads free land in addition to rights of way,
a new era of railroad finance began. By the end of 1853, almost 2,700 miles of railroad construction had been planned
and over 8 million acres of public land had been granted to
finance the projects.[2]

Texas was entirely outside this process because it had retained title to all of its lands upon admission to the Union.
There was no federal public land in Texas, which meant that

Railroads

and Ranches

railroads would bypass Texas unless the state promulgated its own railroad land-grant laws. Texas began making piece-by-piece railroad land grants in 1852, when it chartered nine railroad companies (each by a separate act) and granted each company eight sections of land for every mile of completed railroad. Eight sections per mile proved an inadequate financial incentive, however, and no construction resulted.[3]

The rationale for these "give-aways" of public land was not unsound. The fact that eight sections per mile of road was not enough to result in construction testified to the economic challenge faced by railroad companies. If the state of Texas wanted railroads, and if it wanted them before population growth made construction economically attractive, then the state was going to have to provide a strong incentive. The cost to Texas might be negligible: railroad land grants were typically in a checkerboard pattern; the coming of a railroad would increase the value of the squares retained by the state, potentially offsetting the cost of the land grant.

In 1854 Texas adopted its first general railroad land grant law—a law that applied to any qualified railroad company, as opposed to specific laws for specific companies. A railroad company that constructed at least twenty-five miles of road could receive sixteen sections of land for each mile of road constructed. A section of land is 640 acres—one square mile—thus, each linear mile of iron tracks would be subsidized by a grant of 10,240 acres of land.[4]

Though the Texas land-grant system was rational as designed, it became excessive and corrupt in application. Between 1853 and 1858 Texas chartered thirty-eight railroad companies and qualified them for grants of more than 77 million acres upon construction of a projected 7,500–plus miles of railroad. By 1882 Texas had issued certificates that could permit location of railroad land claims upon 8 million more acres than the state owned. Not all of these acres were granted, because not all of the projected lines were constructed. In fact, in 1858 fewer than one hundred miles of railroad were in operation in Texas. But the effect of the railroad land rush was this: millions of acres of land were surveyed, often at great distances from any projected railroad lines; a checkerboard of land within the surveys was preempted by the railroads, preventing entry by any other claimant unless the railroad lost its rights; the surveys were often hastily done and there was no coordination between competing railroad surveys, resulting in gaps, overlaps and errors in land boundaries; and settlers became aware that the days of unlimited free public domain were coming to a close.[5]

Railroad land surveyors began appearing in La Junta long before any rails drew within three hundred miles of the valley. The surveyors were advance men for land speculation, laying down surveys that gave them claims to the best lands and water sources, so it is not unreasonable to conclude that part of the motivation for Ed Hall and Juana Pedraza's return to La Junta may have been the need to keep a watchful eye on their own land claims. After all, they had sold the acreage around the fortín, but they still had a paper claim to the huge Ronquillo grant. We know that they hadn't abandoned that dream, because when Milton Faver wanted to establish a ranch on 640 acres north of La Junta in 1858, he ended up having to buy the land twice: once from Archibald Hyde, who had filed a survey and location on the land (but had not yet received a patent) and again for two thousand dollars from Hall and Pedraza to clear their claim under the Ronquillo grant.[6]

Faver was one of the first La Juntans to venture outside the relative safety of the valley into the unprotected grazing lands beyond. He had come to Presidio from Meoque, Chihuahua, where he had worked for a flour miller. While there, he fell in love with Francisca Ramirez and won her hand. Faver was ambitious, and he left his job at the flour mill to try freighting on the Chihuahua Trail. He enjoyed early success and moved his family and his center of operations to Presidio del Norte, where he opened a general store in the early 1850's. After Fort Davis was constructed in 1854, Faver participated in the surge in freighting.[7]

The historical consensus is that Faver moved into cattle ranching in 1857, a year before he flanged up the paperwork with Hyde, Hall and Pedraza. The land coveted by Faver was centered upon a well-known spring investigated by Spanish Captain Joseph de Ydoiaga in a 1747 tour of La Junta. Ydoiaga's account of his travels suggests that Faver's ranchstead, which Faver called *El Ojo Grande del Cibolo* (the Big Spring of the Cibolo), included the site of an early native village where a Franciscan had once made a futile attempt to found a mission.[8]

Like the railroads, Archibald Hyde and Milton Faver were following an established strategy in West Texas land rights: get control of the water. The surrounding dry grazing land was worthless without water and could be used by the water owner without competition. Hyde snagged first rights to the spring, so Faver had to clear him out of the way. Hall and Pedraza had color of title to everything between Presidio and Fort Davis, so they had to be dealt with too. But once Faver controlled the 640 acres around the spring, he had unfettered use of tens of thousands of acres of surrounding dry ranchland.

Faver used this strategy not once, but three times. In addition to gaining control of Ojo Grande del Cibolo, he laid claim to 640 acres around a spring called *La Ciénega* (the marsh) and bought another 320-acre watered spread that he named *La Morita* (the little mulberry). Soon he had stocked his ranches with rough, wild Mexican longhorn cattle that thrived in the harsh Chihuahuan Desert.[9]

Being more than twenty-five miles north of the green zone, Ojo Grande del Cibolo, La Ciénega and La Morita are not part of La Junta. We follow Faver north because movement into grazing territory by La Juntans is part of the valley's evolution. Even if that were not the case, we might stretch our story to include Milton Faver, because he was a most remarkable person. His decision to found three ranches in 1857 was distinctly risky. Apache and Comanche raids were a weighty menace even with the presence of Fort Davis. Faver's ranches were along Cibolo Creek, not Alamito Creek, thus they were away from the somewhat safer main trunk of the Chihuahua Trail. His only chance of survival was to follow the lead of the late Ben Leaton and that is what he did, building a private fortín on each of his three ranches.[10]

First to be built was the fortín at Ojo Grande del Cibolo—the Fortín del Cibolo. Adjacent to a 90-by-140-foot adobe corral, it was served by an acequia that ran from the spring to the fortín. The walls of the fort were twenty to thirty inches thick and fifteen feet high. Round towers twenty feet high rose above the northeast and southeast corners. The roof was of typical pueblo construction—sturdy cottonwood beams (*vigas*) at two-foot intervals, crossed by a layer of branches (*rajas*) and topped with a thick layer of compacted brush and adobe mud.[11]

There are grand legends about Milton Faver. As is the case with many frontier figures, the stories paint a man who was at times harsh and at other times gentle. Though short of stature, he was indubitably brave. The most often repeated stories, and thus the most likely, concern the peach orchard he planted and the peach brandy that he distilled.[12]

Over the years railroad surveys and other settlers' claims gradually encroached on Faver's open-range ranches. For some reason, he never extended his legal holdings beyond the three spring-fed tracts. He and his fellow open-range adherents did what they could to keep the old system in place, actively fostering the belief that land titles were so unreliable in Presidio County that only a fool would attempt to locate a land entry there, but it wasn't enough. Newcomers dug wells and fenced their land, and Faver's range was gradually constricted. In 1883, at age sixty-four, he sold his herd of seven thousand head of cattle for a paltry US$18,000 and transferred La Morita to his wife's cousin, Juliana Ramirez de Dawson.[13]

At his death in 1889, Faver left the Cibolo and Ciénega ranches to his widow Francisca and son Juan. Francisca died soon, leaving both ranches to Juan. The estate left by his father was sufficient to support an affluent lifestyle even after Juan Faver suffered a stroke and was no longer able to actively manage the ranches. At his death, heirs and claimants squabbled and the ranches were sold.[14]

We have stated that during the florescence of the Chihuahua Trail the most notable changes in La Junta were within the Anglo-initiated community. The adjective "Anglo-initiated" acknowledges that people named Spencer, Burgess, Leaton, Russell and Landrum spurred the emergence of a second town across the river from Presidio del Norte, but purposely leaves room to recognize that the new subcommunity's Anglo founders assimilated into the larger Hispanic populace.

Admittedly, La Junta was never a mystical place where Virginia blue-bloods happily shed their cultural backgrounds and disappeared into a mellow mestizo melting pot. Early Anglo settlers assimilated to a great extent, later settlers to a lesser degree. Anglos who joined the mix maintained their contacts with Anglo communities to the north. The several stripes of La Junta Hispanics maintained their relationships with those of similar heritage. The divisions between Anglos and Hispanics were often apparent and sometimes painful.[15]

It is notable, however, that La Junta is among a select group of borderlands communities where a minority Anglo population easily accepted long-standing northern Mexican traditions of interethnic marriage. Anglos joined La Junta's blend without drastic disruption, just as Spaniards, Mesoamericans, Chichimeca, Africans, Patarabueyes, La Juntans and Apaches had already mixed on the Spanish and Mexican frontiers.

Ben Leaton's companion Juana Pedraza was from Ciudad Chihuahua. Joe (José) Leaton married Francisca Ureta, who did not speak English. John Burgess's wife was Tomasa Baeza. John Spencer married Tomasa's sister Jesusita and after her death remarried to Felicitas Molina. Milton Faver married Francísca Ramirez. Juan Faver attended school in Germany but returned to La Junta, where he married twice: first to Gavina Ramirez, then to Gumercinda Zubia.[16]

Juan Faver's two marriages demonstrate that the ease of relations between Anglos and Hispanics created its own set of problems. La Junta's first U.S. customs agent was Moses Kelly, who married a Mexican woman and fathered three children. Kelly took a liking to Juan Faver's first wife Gavina, and intimacy ensued. Juan did the natural thing; he waited stealthily outside his home in Ojinaga until Kelly dropped by for a liaison with Gavina, then he shot the rascal dead. Some say that Juan's father asked Juan why he hadn't shot Gavina too. Then Faver *padre* delivered Faver *hijo* to the police, but paternally purchased his freedom after a respectable period of time. Or so the story goes, but the story has a fatal flaw: at the time, Mexican and Texas law permitted a man to kill his wife's paramour without punishment. Juan Faver acted intelligently and legally in shooting Kelly and then divorcing—but not killing—Gavina. We learn from Juan's experience that Anglos and Hispanics melded well—perhaps too well—in La Junta, and that traditional Spanish notions of family values existed on both sides of the river.[17]

Hispanics labored, succeeded and failed shoulder-to-shoulder with the newly arrived Anglos. Milton Faver owed a good deal of his prosperity to the management skills of his brother-in-law Carmen Ramirez, whose hands-on abilities with cattle, sheep and vaqueros were indispensable. Ramirez lived in the fortín at La Morita with his wife and two sons. Around 1870, when his children were four and six, Apaches struck at La Morita, taking the entire family captive. Word of the attack reached Carmen's brother Pancho on the next day, and Pancho gathered four men to pursue the attackers. Two miles out of La Morita they found Carmen's body wedged into a rock ledge. Pancho continued on the raiders' trail. Soon he noticed bits of fabric in the dust—Carmen's wife was tearing pieces from her dress and dropping them to guide hoped-for rescuers. That afternoon, Pancho and his companions came to a creek where the Apaches had crossed. The rocks were still wet. There were fresh hoof prints in the mud. Many fresh hoof prints. The prints of a party much larger than Pancho's five-man posse. Pancho's men balked, unwilling to ride into such a dangerous confrontation. He was left with no choice; the five La Juntans turned back, never to see the family of Carmen Ramirez again.[18]

It took the United States Army a number of years to install its way stations on the military road from San Antonio to El Paso. The closest fort to San Antonio appeared in 1852 as Camp San Saba, twenty-two miles southwest of today's Menard, in Menard County. It was abandoned in 1859, then reoccupied in 1868 as Fort McKavett. Fort Lancaster, far to the west near the Pecos River (near today's Sheffield, in Pecos County), was erected in 1855. From there, the road was unprotected until it reached Fort Stockton, which was not built until 1859. At the far end of the road, there had been a military camp at El Paso since 1848. Those troops were moved forty miles north in 1851 to Fort Fillmore (in New Mexico), then four companies of infantry founded Fort Bliss at today's El Paso in 1854. Eighty miles back downstream to the southeast, where the military road left the river, was Fort Quitman, built in 1858.[1]

Other than Camp San Saba, the earliest military establishment on the road was almost midway between its endpoints. That was Fort Davis, eighty miles northeast of La Junta. Founded in 1854, it was later linked on the east to Fort Stockton by eighty miles of wagon road (a sixty-mile crow's flight) and to the west to Fort Quitman, 150 miles distant. Fort Davis and the military road influenced, but never threatened to redefine, La Junta. The dominant military presence in the valley remained Mexico's Presidio del Norte.

Not only was the nineteenth-century United States Army physically remote from La Junta, its tenure was insignificant in duration. The era of army posts on the military road was but a brief interlude tacked on to three hundred years of post-Columbian history that had already transpired at La Junta. The forts endured between twenty and forty years, interrupted by a five-year Civil War hiatus—similar to the incarnations of the prison colony at Vado de Piedra. In contrast, the Presidio del Norte was founded in 1773 and outlasted all of the forts along the military road except Fort Bliss.

Official government traffic on the military road did not wait for the appearance of the military. When Fort Davis was established in 1854, Henry Skillman—the Henry Skillman who had figured prominently in Doniphan's capture of El Paso and who had doubled back to Fort Leaton to retrieve

Whiting's gear—had already been operating a government mail route between San Antonio and El Paso for four years.[2]

Jefferson Davis, who was then United States Secretary of War, ordered the founding of Fort Davis, at the foot of the Davis Mountains in what would become Jeff Davis County. The Army selected the site for its "pure water and salubrious climate," and the fort initially hosted a garrison of six companies of the Eighth United States Infantry under Colonel Washington Seawell.[3]

Second Lieutenant Zenas Bliss, after whom Fort Bliss is *not* named (but who became a distinguished general and was awarded the Congressional Medal of Honor), arrived in Fort Davis in 1855. After a few months on station, he concluded that no one in their right mind would venture more than three or four miles from the post, and even within that distance an armed escort was advisable. Small parties were vulnerable to attack beyond a two-mile radius; in his estimation, something like half of the stages crossing the military road came under attack.[4]

Fort Davis was important to La Junta because anything that increased the safety of Trans-Pecos travel also increased the volume of traffic along the Chihuahua Trail. Though the fort's primary mission was to reduce attacks on the main military road, the soldiers could not do so without gaining better control of the territory between Fort Davis and Presidio del Norte. Of necessity, army patrols ventured up and down Alamito Creek; many times they would travel to Presidio, Texas, resupply and rest, then return to Fort Davis. There may have been an element of R&R involved; the modest pueblos in La Junta were the only civilization within two hundred miles.[5]

Fort Davis also mattered because it provided a market for La Junta's farmers and ranchers, giving them an incentive to expand their enterprises. The fort was surrounded by excellent grazing lands, and was next to prolific springs, but there were few local farmers and ranchers, so its fruits, grains and livestock had to be imported. La Junta readily supplied melons, squash and a limited amount of corn. More corn came from Mexico through La Junta. Cattle came from Chihuahua, but it wasn't long before La Juntans such as John Spencer and John Burgess were providing horses, mules and cattle to the fort. When the Mexican government placed an embargo on grain exports during an 1855 drought, the United States military encouraged La Juntans to grow wheat, which led to the construction of a flour mill in Presidio.[6]

A prominent theme in La Junta's history is the tendency of expeditions—sometimes quite unusual expeditions—to arrive, look around, and depart without a trace. Such was the case with the retinue of United States Army Lieutenant William H. Echols, who rode into the valley on July 19, 1860, with thirty-one infantrymen and a crew of herders and attendants. Echols had left Fort Davis five days earlier, trailing a day behind a detachment led by a Colonel Bomford from Fort Quitman. Both groups followed Alamito Creek to La Junta; Echols called the road "magnificent" and mentioned passing a load of watermelons on its way to Fort Davis. He reached the Rio Grande and turned upstream toward Fort Leaton, "an olde ranche established for a trading post, &c., on a grant from the Mexican government, made about twenty-five years ago; several fine ranches along the river before reaching the town owned by Americans; camped on the river bank in a coral, good camp."[7]

No doubt there was a crowd at the corral that evening, because Echols's entourage included twenty camels—bellowing, cud-chewing, malodorous camels. These were not the first camels to visit La Junta, but the last herd had been accompanied by giant ground sloths and woolly mammoths several thousand years earlier. The alcalde of Presidio del Norte came to Echols's camp and spent an hour marveling at the beasts. Echols in turn marveled at the Mexican women who carried seventy-pound *ollas* (jugs) of water on their heads.[8]

Echols was part of a United States Army experiment to determine the suitability of dromedaries for duty in the arid western United States. His judgment, and the judgment of most people connected with the project, was that they were far superior to mules and horses for many tasks. Future Confederate general Robert E. Lee, then a brevet colonel commanding the army's Department of Texas, commented on Echols's "train of camels, whose endurance, docility, and sagacity will not fail to attract the attention of the Secretary of War, and but for whose reliable services the reconnaissance would have failed." Despite the support of Lee and others, cultural prejudices and organizational inertia prevented the project from garnering the support necessary to survive. La Junta is only a footnote in the overall camel experiment, which involved travels from the Gulf Coast to California, but the appearance of dromedaries in Presidio del Norte must have been a most peculiar moment.[9]

Echols stayed only a day before leaving the valley. For a man who traveled in the company of camels, he was unduly disdainful of Presidio del Norte: "saw a good deal of the place, but found very little worth seeing. All the buildings are of adobe, and present much the appearance of a large mud dauber's nest. The population is 3,100, according to the alcalde; but about half, or less, are a den of thieves. The few Americans settled around the place seem to be gentlemen, and treated us with much cordiality."[10]

Lieutenant Echols reported that on his way out of town he "stopped to dine with Mr. Leaton, and had a magnificent dinner, and abundance of water melons; plenty of them and musk melons in the vicinity." Since Ben Leaton had been dead nine years at this point, the Leaton involved was probably Joe or Bill, living in the household headed by Ben Leaton's marital successor Ed Hall.[11]

Echols also found problems with the labor market in La Junta, which viewed him as an invading soldier from a foreign country: "We have been trying to employ a guide ever since our arrival at Presidio del Norte, and only succeeded in obtaining one to-day after we left camp. I hear they work for twenty-five cents a day with rations, and thirty-seven and a half without, but would not hire to us for two dollars a day and rations; most of them are afraid that we will hang them, so I learned, and were anxious to be paid in advance."[12]

Following his high-priced guide, Echols proceeded down the Rio Grande, looking for a spot near San Carlos to site a fort; the United States Army still had no desire to locate a post across the river from the Presidio del Norte, even though that must have been the most favorable position. As he exited La Junta into the Big Bend canyons, Echols learned what every traveler before him knew. He found the road to be "the roughest, most tortuous and cragged one I have ever seen. . . . I never conceived that there could be such a country. The guide says he could have brought us a little nearer route, but that it would have been rougher. I cannot conceive it possible. I cheerfully concur with all who regard this region as impassable." The trip was so rocky that it revealed the camels' one weakness: the pads of their feet were soft, suited to sand, and became sore walking over jagged terrain. Echols recommended rawhide camel shoes.[13]

Just eight months after Echols's visit, the Civil War came to West Texas, pushing La Junta backward twenty years in time. San Antonio was the center of gravity for the United States Army in Texas; Brevet Major General David Twiggs commanded the Department of Texas from that post. Twiggs was an advocate of states' rights, but recognized the importance of the oath he had taken to defend the Union. Knowing that Texas would almost certainly secede, and reluctant to engage in combat with the same citizens that he had been defending, he repeatedly asked for instructions on how to proceed in that event, but received little clear guidance.[14]

In February 1861 Texas adopted an ordinance of secession and formed a Committee of Public Safety to provide interim governance. Samuel Maverick, who had visited La Junta with Jack Hays, was one of three commissioners representing the committee. The commissioners, recognizing that the Union troops had long been friends of the community, also hoped to avoid violence, but were determined to sweep them from Texas soil.[15]

Texas secessionist volunteers soon took possession of the arsenal and storehouses at San Antonio. Twiggs, after a stormy conference with Maverick and the other two commissioners, agreed to move his Union troops to a camp outside San Antonio pending evacuation to the coast, allowing the Texans to take San Antonio without a shot being fired. Given his sympathies, Twiggs earnestly desired to avoid bloodshed, but his duties as an officer of the United States Army made him adamant on one point—his soldiers would not surrender or disarm. The commissioners agreed to this condition, resulting in the odd circumstance of an armed force making a peaceful exit from its territory under the courteous but watchful gaze of armed rebels. Twiggs's amenability was not favored in Washington; within a month he was dismissed from the Union army "for his treachery to the flag of his country." Among Texans, the idea of permitting the Union troops to retain their arms was not universally embraced; one Texas volunteer captain referred to the commissioners as "a set of jackasses" for making that decision.[16]

After some confusion about exactly how the evacuation should proceed, Union troops from the forts along the military road made their way east, congregating at Indianola. The army abandoned Fort Bliss on March 31 and Fort Davis on April 13. At Fort Davis, Union captain E. D. Blake peacefully turned over command to the infamously violent and mercurial Lieutenant Colonel John R. Baylor of the Second Texas Mounted Rifles, who was on his way west.[17]

Texas has always taken its own path; the course of the Civil War in Texas—particularly in West Texas—is no exception. Events from San Antonio westward are difficult to fit into the overall struggle over secession. The first concern in West Texas was not the threat of Union troops, but the threats of Mexicans, Apaches and Comanches in the *absence* of Union troops. Sam Houston and other influential Texans were prepared to revert to the status of an independent republic rather than join the Confederacy; in the public mind, the question of which way to go hinged in no small part upon whether the Confederacy could deliver men to replace the 2,800 Union soldiers that had protected Texas and Texans from predators.

Postsecession governor Edward Clark wrote Jefferson Davis, President of the Confederate States, to emphasize the importance of providing troops to protect Texas from Mexicans and nomads. He explained that rather than wait for Confederate soldiers to arrive, Texas had already formed its own military units because, "having 1,700 miles of frontier, with the ungoverned Mexicans on the west, who bear no love to us, and the Indians on the north and west, who are our perpetual foes, we were forced to take some steps for immediate protection." Clark warned that if the Confederacy did not promptly accept the Texas cavalry into their army and did not provide supplemental troops, then Sam Houston's advocates of an independent republic might prevail.[18]

In the minds of Texans, protection of the Rio Grande border was an essential element in defense of the state. Texas delegates to the Provisional Confederate Congress briefed the Confederate secretary of war on the importance of defending the Rio Grande "to preserve good order on the line and prevent lawless incursions across it," reminding him that "the upper settlements on this line are exposed to Indian depredations from the wild tribes of the plains and from Mexico." In response, the Confederate secretary of war reassured the Texas delegates that a regiment of troops would be sent to the Rio Grande and that his department would "exert all its energies and exhaust all the means at its command to secure the citizens of Texas against Indian and other depredations." The Confederacy, he pointed out, "has so far acted fully up to the measure of its ability, and as its capacity and resources are increased it will continue to augment and perfect the system of frontier defense." The secretary was making all the right noises, but one must wonder whether he shook his head in disbelief at the self-centered, provincial expectations of Texans who worried only about Mexicans, Apaches and Comanches when the true mutual enemy was the Yankees.[19]

The Confederacy established two lines of defense across the western frontiers of Texas. One was a jagged cordon from the Red River northwest of Fort Worth to San Angelo, west of San Antonio. The other followed the lower military road from Fort Inge (near Uvalde) to Fort Bliss. Colonel John "Rip" Ford (of the Ford-Neighbors Trail linking San Antonio and El Paso) was given command of the military road. Colonel Van Dorn, who commissioned Ford, made it plain that Fort Bliss was a critical point of defense in the west, though he suggested Fort Clark — far to the east — as a headquarters post.[20]

Colonel Ford assigned the reliably belligerent Lieutenant Colonel John Baylor to secure the former Union forts on the military road. It was in that capacity that Baylor accepted the surrender of Fort Davis in July 1861, turning it into a Confederate post. Baylor then began looking beyond the Texas borders. Immediately taking the fight into New Mexico, he captured Fort Fillmore, near Mesilla, where he redrew territorial boundaries to his liking, established the Confederate Territory of Arizona and proclaimed himself its military governor. The

Confederacy was fighting a war of secession; Baylor was fighting a war of aggression. For that he was promoted to full colonel.[21]

Disturbing news reached Baylor's ear in the fall of 1861—there were Union spies in Presidio del Norte, just across the river from the territory that he ruled. In particular, there was a fellow named Wulff that was of some concern. Baylor sat down at his desk in Doña Ana, Confederate Territory of Arizona, and penned a succinct order to Captain W. C. Adams, the commanding officer at Fort Davis: "Sir: I am informed that there is a man at Presidio del Norte by the name of Wulff who is a spy. I want him enticed over on this side of the river and taken prisoner and sent to these headquarters in irons."[22]

Captain Adams was absent when the order arrived. It was intercepted by Lieutenant Emory Gibbons, who was a fool. Handed the order from Baylor in the post office at Fort Davis, and rather than reading it himself (for perhaps he was an illiterate fool), he passed it to an acquaintance to read aloud. The man did as instructed, which meant that everyone in the post office knew that Wulff was in the Confederate crosshairs.[23]

Wulff was not a stranger in Fort Davis. He was a trader in Presidio del Norte and had a contract to provide a merchant named Murphy in Fort Davis with hay, wood and corn, which Murphy then sold to the Confederate garrison. As fate would have it, the acquaintance that Gibbons chose to read Baylor's order aloud was Murphy's clerk. By the time Gibbons and nine enlisted men saddled up, Wulff and everyone else in the two towns called Presidio were probably waiting for Confederates to arrive, though the confusion that ensued leaves some room for doubt on that score.[24]

When Gibbons reached the Rio Grande, he headed for Fort Leaton. There his men unsaddled and made their plans. He sent a detachment of four soldiers to reconnoiter and report back. The four advance men abandoned subtlety and went directly to Wulff's store in Presidio del Norte. Wulff recognized one of them as Tom Krain, who used to run a bar in San Antonio, and they struck up a conversation. Extemporizing, Krain said that he was looking for Lieutenant Gibbons and Murphy. He asked whether Wulff had any corn for the fort. Because his contract was with Murphy, not directly with the fort—and because he wasn't sure what Krain was getting at—Wulff said that he did not. The soldiers raised a few other peculiar questions—such as how a man could make a living in La Junta—that led Wulff to wonder whether they might be deserters.[25]

The four scouts returned to Fort Leaton and announced that they had found their man. The tricky part was going to be getting him to cross the river without raising his suspicions. Helpfully, Joe Leaton—by now twenty-four years old—announced that he had an idea about how to lure Wulff back to the Texas side.[26]

It was a lamebrained plan, predicated on Leaton bumping into Wulff at a dance. Joe Leaton figured he could convince Wulff to come to Fort Leaton to sign some papers regarding lands that Mexicans were supposedly trying to take away from the Leaton-Hall family (probably due to continuing problems with Ben Leaton's fraudulent land grants). Wulff did have some links to Leaton-Hall real estate matters—he witnessed a mortgage of the fortín to John Burgess—but the idea of him leaving a dance to handle business on the other side of the river was dubious. By three o'clock in the morning, Leaton and the four soldiers were danced out and Wulff was still safely at home.[27]

Disinclined to go to the trouble of coming up with a better plan, Krain and another man went directly to Wulff's house and banged on the door, claiming that they needed a place to sleep. Wulff, doing his part to contribute to a comedy of stupidity, opened his door to the men, who grabbed him by the hair and dragged him off. Wulff howled. The Confederates stuck their pistols in his chest. Wulff's wife cried out. His brother-in-law jumped over the back fence and went for help.[28]

Understandably, Wulff begged his captors to know what was going on. They told him that he was being taken back to Texas to sign some real estate papers for Joe Leaton and Ed Hall. Imagine Wulff trying to make sense of that.

But all did not turn out according to the Leaton-Krain plan. When Lieutenant Gibbons awoke the next morning at Fort Leaton, two of his men were missing and Wulff was nowhere to be found. The men who made it back said there had been some trouble. Gibbons sat down and penned a disingenuous note to the president of Presidio del Norte (an elected Mexican mayor, as opposed to an appointed Spanish colonial alcalde): "I gave my men permission to come on your side of the river to see the place, and one of your citizens invited them to come and pass the night, and as they were treated so well in the forepart of the day I gave them permission to come and spend the night and there are two of my men missing. You will please let me know what became of them. You will also please let me know about all the difficulty."[29]

Benigno Contreras, president of the pueblo of Presidio del Norte, replied in the most polite way: "Your favor was received and I am sorry to state that your two men are now killed and buried on this side of the river." Contreras spelled out the events of the prior evening, informing Lieutenant Gibbons that "I felt it my duty to order the citizens to go after Mr. Wulff; not with the intention to fight or kill anybody, but as [my] men caught up with them they asked for Mr. Wulff, and the first thing [the Confederates] did was to get out their pistols. They shot one of my citizens and came very near killing him. [Four of the men] showed fight. The other one ran through the bushes with J. Leaton and escaped; also the two that came behind escaped. If they had given up the man and had not shot first nothing would have happened. The balance of the particulars you will find out from the commanding officer at Fort Davis."[30]

The border was creating unexpected consequences. The Texas side of the river had become Confederate territory. Union supporters had fled to Presidio del Norte. Confederate soldiers were skulking into Mexico, looking for Union sympathizers who lived in safety there, and were finding themselves at odds with Mexican officials who didn't want troublemakers of any persuasion. The new border on the Rio Grande was not *creating* divisions among people, but it materially facilitated their enactment of those divisions. The red line drawn by surveyors Emory and Salazar through La Junta allowed people to physically divide themselves into opposing camps.

Confederate colonel Henry Sibley marched across Texas to Fort Bliss, where President Jefferson Davis directed him to occupy adjacent federal territories—an expansion of the push begun by Baylor. Sibley drew up an ambitious plan to capture New Mexico and the Colorado Territory, then march west through Salt Lake City and take Los Angeles and San Diego. Sibley, a noteworthy drunk, botched a few skirmishes, overextended his supply lines, got pounded at Glorieta Pass and was further battered on a retreat through Peralta. The campaign began in the fall of 1861 and dragged to a close in the spring of 1862, which Sibley's force spent recuperating at Fort Bliss. The whipping that his force had taken was so obvious that merchants near the fort refused to accept Confederate money. Needing supplies and horses for the trip back to San Antonio, the Confederates resorted to theft, which did nothing to endear them to the locals. The last of Sibley's forces withdrew from West Texas in July, leaving the field open for Union troops.[1]

Union brigadier general James Carleton led a column of California soldiers to Fort Bliss. He found twenty-six Confederate stragglers in the vicinity. Rather than take them prisoner, he sent them on their way to San Antonio with provisions and an escort. Hearing a rumor that the Confederates had left fifty or sixty wounded men behind at Fort Davis "guarded by a company of troops of Mexican lineage," he sent a detachment to investigate, but they found Fort Davis abandoned and in disarray. One dead Confederate soldier lay in the hospital with a gunshot wound in his head and an arrow in his body.[2]

When the Confederates evacuated Fort Bliss, they believed that Carleton was in hot pursuit and chose not to encumber themselves with heavy artillery pieces. To Carleton's subsequent distress, they sold their artillery to Confederate sympathizers on the Mexican side of the river. Carleton feared that the guns might later be used against him, and he wrote Luis Terrazas, governor of Chihuahua, protesting that the cannons had been permitted entry into a country that was supposed to be sympathetic to the Union cause.[3]

Soon matters got worse. Rumors began to spread that Baylor was organizing six thousand Texans to retake West

Texas and New Mexico. Union lieutenant colonel Edwin Rigg reported from Fort Bliss that "the party of secessionists in El Paso are in high glee, being much elated by the news; their party has increased to about eighty from different directions." Carleton began to prepare, reinforce and fret.[4]

Into this case of the jitters rode Henry Skillman: Texan, soldier, explorer and postman. After Sibley withdrew, Skillman, now a Confederate captain, gathered a dozen grizzled Texans to prowl West Texas and northern Mexico. One resident of El Paso put it this way: "Bad news; troublesome times again ahead. Skillman dropped from the clouds night before last, and his crowd were considerably excited all day yesterday. . . . The authorities made no effort, as I know of, to stop Skillman. He was met this morning tight as the devil . . . and of course sleeps to-night in Guadalupe." Concerned about the potential for violence, the correspondent worried, "I don't know what to do, whether to go to Chihuahua or get out by Tucson to California."[5]

Union intelligence was good; by the morning after Skillman's arrival in El Paso, Captain Edward Willis was passing word from Fort Bliss to the Union command in New Mexico:

Skillman is a noted desperado, and the man of all others that would be chosen as a spy. He knows every inch of this country well; he is also a fugitive from justice in Mexico for murder. Mr. Uranga sent last night to try to arrest him, but the birds had all flown. Dr. Samaniego tells me this morning that Skillman has a company of Texans at Presidio del Norte; that he has gone there to return with them in six days, when those across the river will join him to make a dash at this place.[6]

Skillman had already gotten a reputation as a guerrilla fighter. Captain Willis reported that "they do not expect to hold [Hart's Mill, today's downtown El Paso], but to plunder and retire immediately. It is in character with the man. He once with ten men held the plaza of El Paso for two hours." The Mexican citizens of El Paso had not forgotten the incident: "There is much excitement in El Paso with regard to these matters. The authorities are purchasing all the arms that they can. They are very much afraid of the Texans."[7]

In January 1863 Brigadier General J. R. West, the commander of the District of Arizona (which included Fort Bliss), followed up on General Carleton's letter to Governor Terrazas by sending Major David Fergusson to meet personally with the Chihuahuan leader. Fergusson was given explicit instructions to raise "the abuses against the Government of the United States which have been committed by certain rebels who have taken refuge in Mexican territory." The centerpiece of West's concerns was that

> one Skillman (with others in the military service of the so-called Confederate States to the number of fifteen persons I am informed) crossed from Texas into Mexico; that these men were as fully armed as when acting in the field against our troops, and that during their stay in Mexican territory they maintained a military organization; . . . that Skillman and his party then visited El Presidio del Norte, remained there several days, and made an effort to capture and convey into Texas certain American citizens temporarily sojourning in that town.[8]

From this we learn that there were still Union sympathizers in Presidio del Norte, and that Confederates, unbowed by the outcome of the Wulff incident, were still trying to kidnap and interrogate them. West's complaints received a sympathetic hearing from Governor Terrazas, who welcomed Fergusson with great hospitality. Terrazas reassured the Union officer that he had already heard of the problems in Presidio del Norte and had issued orders to prevent a recurrence. Then, according to Fergusson, "His Excellency expressed a hope that some measures might be adopted to rid the neighborhood of the Presidio del Norte of a gang of Mexican and American desperadoes who live at Leaton's Fort, on the Texas side of the Rio Grande." After briefing Fergusson on the attempted Wulff kidnapping sixteen months earlier, Terrazas reported that "Outrages of this nature are reported as frequent there by these villains, the chief of whom is one Edward Hall, living at Leaton's Fort." Fergusson informed General West that "Hall, the American desperado, recently robbed Fort Davis of much public property, I was informed, and sold it in Chihuahua. He claims to be an agent of the so-called Confederate States, and exhibited a paper signed by a notary public to the effect that he was legally empowered to dispose of property taken from Fort Davis. Justice has a strong claim on this bad rebel."[9]

Union commanders must have been confused. They had sent an emissary to complain about Skillman raiding into the United States from sanctuary in Mexico, and had in return received a complaint about Ed Hall and Joe Leaton raiding into Mexico from sanctuary in the United States. The problem was that the lessons being learned by the Union army in El Paso did not translate to La Junta. In El Paso, Union forces and sympathizers were gathered at Fort Bliss, on the Texas side of the Rio Grande, and Confederate sympathizers had fled to the town of El Paso on the Mexican side. Exactly the opposite obtained in La

Junta: the secessionists remained in Presidio, Texas, and the Union sympathizers were ensconced in Presidio del Norte, Mexico.

The Union commanders lacked another key piece of information: though Skillman and his men roamed from El Paso to San Antonio and sometimes dipped deep into Mexico, their base of operations was initially at Vado de Piedra, and later on Spencer's farm near Presidio. Skillman was using trails along both Alamito Creek and Cibolo Creek to maintain communications between Confederate forces in San Antonio and points of resistance in Presidio and El Paso. How was Skillman financing his operation? He had set up a border post in Presidio and was collecting duty on goods that came across the river from Chihuahua. Fort Leaton and the village at Presidio were Confederate havens.[10]

Cooperation between Governor Terrazas and the Union command blossomed. Terrazas seized the Confederate artillery pieces that General Carleton had worried about, and Carleton proposed a solution to Mexico's problems with Joe Leaton and Ed Hall (note that Wulff's travails seem to have worsened in the telling):[11]

I have understood that a band of outlaws and desperadoes reside at a place called Leaton's Fort, in the State of Texas, and that it is their habit to cross the Rio Grande near that point and commit outrages upon the citizens of Presidio del Norte, in the State of Chihuahua.

Should Your Excellency desire to send across the river and seize by force the ruffians alluded to this shall be your authority for so doing, and more particularly shall this be full authority for you to send across the Rio Grande and arrest for trial those who seized on the Chihuahua side a naturalized American citizen named Wolfe and bore him across to the Texas side, and there hung him until life was nearly extinct, simply because he was a Union man.[12]

Joe Leaton was now at the mercy of the commander of the Presidio del Norte. Sadly, he was not a significant enough historical figure for us to know exactly what ensued. We do know that at some point he went to San Antonio and never returned. His wife heard that he died in prison there. Carleton's letter may provide the reason why Joe Leaton decided to leave La Junta: a stroke of General Carleton's pen had made the border disappear.

That Skillman was not the only Confederate in La Junta was proven in April 1863, when local merchant John Burgess wrote Confederate general William Scurry in San Antonio:

I have understood privately from Captain Skillman that the presumption was that your command would move toward Arizona and New Mexico this spring.

Should such be the case, I am in such a position here that should you require
any army supplies, such as flour, corn, beans, soap, shoes, &c., I would be glad
to furnish the same, for which I am willing to take cotton at a fair price in ex-
change, as you are aware that it requires specie [bank notes] to purchase those
things in this country.[13]

Burgess and Skillman were right: the Confederacy *was* contemplat-
ing a campaign to the west. Burgess's letter addressed an important
issue with the Confederate army—where would they obtain supplies,
and how would they do so given the weak state of Confederate currency? Within a week of receiving the overture from Burgess, the
Confederate command at San Antonio received material reassurance.
Colonel Baird of that post reported that:

to-day thirty-odd wagons and carts owned by Messrs. Solis & Munis, of Santa
Cruz, near Chihuahua, loaded with flour, shoes, and blankets, discharged and
stored their freight at this place.
The above puts the question of supplies for Arizona and New Mexico at rest.
Messrs. Solis & Munis crossed the Del Norte at Presidio del Norte and came
by way of Fort Lancaster. I beg leave to suggest the importance of keeping this
route open.[14]

The Solis & Munis caravan was only the beginning of what became
a significant flow of cargo out of Mexico through La Junta to San
Antonio. Captain Henry Skillman was almost certainly the facilitator
of this backdoor trade route. The cartage moving up the Chihuahua
Trail did not escape the notice of Union commanders in El Paso and
New Mexico. During the spring of 1863 the two subjects most on their
minds were the risk of a Confederate invasion and the supply route
maintained by Skillman. Writing from Albuquerque to an informant
in Ciudad Chihuahua, General Carleton discounted the likelihood of a
full-scale invasion, but opined, "That Skillman may attempt a raid upon
El Paso and Franklin is possible, so I pray you will procure through
an eye-witness information as to Skillman's present whereabouts, his
exact strength, how his men are armed, how mounted, by what means
of transportation they have, and what quantity of provisions. . . . If
Skillman remains in Presidio, what appears to be his present business
and what is supposed to be his purpose?" Carleton then mentioned a
related concern: "I beg you will do me the favor to ask the Governor of
Chihuahua if he cannot prohibit the exportation of any more provisions
from his State to Texas or the Texans."[15]

At about the same time, the commanding officer at Fort Bliss was sending "a trusty Mexican to Presidio del Norte to ascertain what supplies are being taken from Chihuahua to Texas." His information that the Confederates were "placing considerable supplies upon the Fort Davis road" convinced him that a Confederate invasion was in the works.[16]

A year passed without a Confederate campaign coming to pass in West Texas. The bulk of the Confederate army was occupied to the east, but Skillman continued to be a Trans-Pecos thorn in the side of the Union troops. The idea of a spy and provocateur operating with impunity so close to Fort Bliss was unacceptable, as was the idea of his maintaining a supply route to rebel forces in San Antonio. The Union decided to put an end to Henry Skillman's days in La Junta.

At Fort Bliss Colonel G. W. Bowie dispatched Captain Albert H. French with twenty-five soldiers, a scout and two guides to intercept Skillman. Leaving the Union post at San Elizario, a few miles downriver from El Paso, Captain French took the military road until he intercepted the Alamito Creek section of the Chihuahua Trail. There he turned south and, finding fresh tracks of eighteen or twenty horses and mules, moved cautiously toward La Junta. On April 14, 1864, he reached Cottonwood Spring, where he found that Skillman had carved one of the giant cottonwoods with his name and a date only eleven days earlier. French sent the guides ahead to La Junta, advanced his troops another nine miles, dismounted and waited.[17]

In a few hours the guides returned; Skillman and nine other Confederate soldiers were camped on John Spencer's ranch, on the Texas side of the river crossing. French's men saddled up and rode forward quietly in darkness. At 12:30 A.M. they left their horses at a deserted ranch house a mile from Skillman's camp and crept toward their enemy. Skillman had unaccountably failed to post a watch, and the Union troops easily surrounded his camp.[18]

Out of the night, French shouted an order for the graycoats to surrender. A handful of the Confederates grabbed their pistols and carbines, but French was ready. Gunfire broke out. The rebels' horses stampeded. Men shouted and scrambled. Skillman and another Confederate were killed on the spot. Two others were mortally wounded. Four were taken prisoner and two escaped across the Rio Grande in the confusion.[19]

French was gratified to find a packet of mail and dispatches that Skillman was carrying from San Antonio back to El Paso. He gathered up what other spoils he could: five horses, four mules and an assortment of arms and provisions. According to Captain French, "The people here were delighted at seeing the Northern troops, expressed their satisfaction at the results, and escorted us several miles up the river." Whether the locals' celebrations were sincere or not, Skillman's Confederate customhouse was now officially closed.[20]

The Chihuahua Trail remained open during the Civil War, at least until Henry Skillman died. Overall, however, the effect of the war — more exactly, the effect of abandonment of the forts along the military road — was to return West Texas to the Apaches and Comanches. Only a few resilient merchants and ranchers had taken root around the forts; when the Union army departed, virtually all of those pioneers departed as well. La Junta remained habitable because of the protection afforded by the Presidio del Norte and the Mexican military colonies. Outside their limited sphere of influence, nomads could roam from San Antonio to El Paso almost entirely unchallenged.

With West Texas drained of settlers, the Apaches and Comanches intensified their raids upon the ranches and haciendas of Chihuahua. The few cattle that were not taken by force were withdrawn by their owners to safer enclaves further south. By the end of the Civil War, the expansive grazing lands of West Texas and northern Chihuahua were almost vacant. Returning from his meeting with Governor Terrazas, Major David Fergusson reported only four active ranches near Ciudad Chihuahua. Closer to El Paso he observed that "with the exception of a few head of stock owned at Carrizal and about two thousand head of cattle and sheep to the number of about 30,000, owned by Terrazas and Müller, there is not a hoof of stock in this great valley, where formerly they were innumerable."[1]

The notorious Ed Hall returned to La Junta shortly before the Civil War and remained through the conflict. The war did nothing to improve his character. Afterward, Joseph Magoffin, a pillar of the El Paso community who ran wagons to Presidio, said, "I know of his having run away from Fort Davis to El Paso, Texas, with the wagons and mules belonging to Don Francisco de Lao. Upon reaching El Paso he was captured, and the property was secured to the owner. He was regarded by the people as a bad character, and he was a sporting man and a horse racer."[2]

John Burgess remained in La Junta during the Civil War. In the summer after the Confederate army assumed command of Fort Davis, Burgess found himself on the receiving end of a promissory note from Ed Hall and Juana Pedraza Hall for $1,707.46. They secured the debt with a mortgage on all of the Leaton lands on the east side of the Rio

The Rise

and Fall of

John Burgess

Grande. (This is the mortgage that kidnap victim Wulff had witnessed.) The Halls agreed to repay the loan by December 30, 1862.[3]

It cannot come as a surprise that Hall did not pay the money as agreed. Foreclosure was a simple matter in those days—a mortgage was essentially a deed to the lender, and the borrower didn't get title to the land back unless he paid off the loan. That Hall never got a deed back tells us that he defaulted. We have even more vivid evidence of that, however: in the summer of 1862, five months before Hall's note came due, John Burgess purchased railroad land scrip, used the scrip to file land claims in Austin and obtained perfectly good Texas land patents to the same lands that Ed and Juana Hall had mortgaged to him— the lands that Ben Leaton had stolen from Mexican rancheros. Either Burgess was cementing his foreclosure or he was claim-jumping.[4]

Despite defaulting on their debt (or perhaps there was some dispute on that point) Ed and Juana Hall refused to vacate Fort Leaton. They had a fort and a cannon and they weren't going anywhere. This doubtless annoyed John Burgess. It is a testament to his patience, and perhaps to the relatively small amount of money at stake, that the situation was left to simmer unhappily for years.

After the Civil War, the ranches of West Texas and northern Chihuahua had to be restocked, but many cattlemen, freighters and traders hesitated to travel the Chihuahua Trail until the United States reoccupied Fort Davis in 1867. Not all merchants were so cautious—a man named George Crosson ran twenty wagons south through Presidio del Norte in 1865 and returned safely with a load of silver bullion—but most waited. As the region grew safer, cattle, goods and people surged forth to restore the ranches of the Chihuahuan Desert.[5]

In October 1868 San Antonian David Poor, who had gone to El Paso and back on Sibley's failed invasion of New Mexico, ran a herd of one thousand cattle to Presidio del Norte, arriving a month later. The venture was financed by Gustave Schleicher of San Antonio and was coordinated through John Burgess, who had already resumed trading at least as far as Fort Stockton. Poor's cattle drive was entirely speculative; he began looking for buyers after reaching Presidio del Norte. Leaving the cattle in La Junta, he traveled to Chihuahua, where he met with Governor Luis Terrazas. Over a bottle of wine, Terrazas agreed to buy part of Poor's herd. Surprisingly—especially given his access to the powerful governor—Poor had a difficult time selling his cattle and ended up spending Christmas in La Junta, or as he put it in a letter to his wife, "this miserable God forsaken country." By the time he finished up, Poor—a veteran of military expeditions in West Texas— was calling his drive to La Junta "the hardest trip I have ever made yet," even though he drove the cattle only as far as Presidio del Norte. Lucre had a way of overshadowing hardship, however (Poor hoped to make eight hundred dollars from his work), and soon vigorous freighters like August Santleben began trafficking on the Chihuahua Trail. La Junta was back in business.[6]

John Burgess resumed providing cattle and supplies to the army when Fort Davis reopened. Expanding businesses require capital. In 1868, he borrowed US$8,000 from the firm of Halff & Levy and another US$2,400 from Norton & Deutz. The two lenders required Burgess to mortgage the Leaton farm as security—the farm that Ed Hall and Juana Pedraza were still defiantly farming; it must have been a delicate topic. Then in 1869 Daniel Devine, successor to Joseph Devine, surfaced. Hall and Pedraza had purported to sell Fort Leaton and the farm to Joseph Devine back in 1853, while they were settling Ben Leaton's estate. Daniel Devine deeded the land to someone named Robert H. Nielson. So now Burgess had another fortín claimant to deal with— surely something that he wouldn't want his lenders to know.[7]

Then things started going sour for John Burgess. Business was bad. In addition to the money he owed on the US$3,200 mortgage, he was in debt to a man named Koenigham on two more notes of US$3,000 each and had mortgaged some upstream lands to William Russell to secure a debt of US$1,500. Burgess managed to pay off the Norton & Deutz note, but he defaulted on the notes to Koenigham, Russell and Halff & Levy. Koenigham filed suit in El Paso. Russell threatened foreclosure. In December 1873, Halff & Brother (successors to Halff & Levy) foreclosed on Fort Leaton. And still Ed Hall was defiantly ensconced in the fortín. Burgess watched, frustrated, as his business affairs crumbled and Ed Hall remained intransigent. It ruined Burgess's life; one observer said that "Burgess, from the loss of property, and trouble all around had become very reckless and rough."[8]

The image of Ed Hall getting away with this kind of behavior may defy logic. The idea that John Burgess and his lenders were powerless to eject Hall may seem improbable. But remember that it was 1875 before anyone made a successful effort to organize Presidio County. During the time that Burgess and Hall were struggling over Fort Leaton, the nearest law was in El Paso, two hundred miles distant. State patent certificates looked nice, and a recorded mortgage had an authoritative ring to it, but north of the Rio Grande La Junta was still operating on the principle of *pedis possessio*.[9]

Something snapped inside John Burgess. He knew that Ed Hall would never let him inside the walls of the fortín, so he sent his son Tomás with two other men, H. W. Tinkham and Santiago Baisa, to reason with the scoundrel. Reasoning was a volatile business in that time and place. The outcome was that Ed Hall died of gunshot wounds. Juana Pedraza gathered her small family and fled to Fort Davis, where—thanks to the notorious gambling habits of the deceased—they lived in poverty.[10]

In January 1874 the El Paso County Grand Jury indicted John Burgess, Tomás Burgess, H. W. Tinkham and Santiago Baisa for murder. The four men posted bonds and, in a clever move orchestrated by attorney J. J. Teel, applied for a change of venue to Menard County. Menard County had two advantages over El Paso. First, it was even farther from La Junta than El Paso, making it hard for witnesses to appear. Second, the circuit judge in Menard County was one Patrick Mies. Not only was Judge Mies the sort of man who would twice be indicted for neglect of official duties, but he owed $325 to none other than Halff & Brother, who knew that their troubled loan to John Burgess would never be paid if Burgess went to the penitentiary.[11]

In June Judge Mies scheduled murder trials for November and ordered five witnesses—Andrew Espinosa, Esculpio Gonzales, Feliciano Pais, Jesus Subia and Juan Gonzalez—to appear. Only two of the five witnesses did so in November, but that was not the court's biggest problem: all four of the accused failed to show up. The judge ordered bond forfeitures, but he did not order arrests of the defendants and permitted the bondsmen to appear at the next court term to show cause why the bond forfeiture should not be enforced. This is approximately the approach that a court might take today if a defendant failed to appear for trial on a jaywalking charge.[12]

In March 1875 the four defendants repented and appeared for trial. The court, being in a forgiving mood, nullified the bond forfeitures. John Burgess announced himself ready for trial, but the district attorney's witnesses were nowhere to be found. Burgess moved for dismissal, and the court set him free. In July the other three defendants executed exactly the same maneuver and they, too, went home free men. Other than having to make a couple of trips to Menardville, and other than the various routine and unconventional expenses that they might have incurred, John Burgess and his cohorts went unpunished for the death of Ed Hall.[13]

Or at least they went unpunished by the judicial system. In late 1876—local lore says Christmas day 1876, but historic dates in December have a way of migrating toward Christmas—Bill Leaton caught up with John Burgess. Bill was the son of Ben Leaton and Juana Pedraza and the stepson of Ed Hall. He and his mother had fled from Fort Leaton to Fort Davis after Ed Hall was murdered. Bill bore a grudge against John Burgess, and fate brought them together in Fort Davis.[14]

There is one oral history that says that Burgess was in Fort Davis because he had chased a black man there for suspected thievery. He found the accused in a barroom; it turned out to be a barroom in which Bill Leaton was having a drink. Leaton spotted Burgess, pulled a gun and shot him dead, which was not the outcome that Burgess had in mind when he came through the door.[15]

Another version goes this way: Burgess came to Fort Davis to do business. He left town to return to his ranch, and "after getting out on the road some miles he discovered that he had left a pistol at some place near the Post, and he told his driver he would go back after it. He rode back on horseback, and approaching a store kept by a man named Keezy, he was asked by Keezy what he was back for. He said, 'to kill the scoundrel who stole my pistol.' Bill Leaton was standing near and pretended to think Burgess meant him. He drew his pistol and shot Burgess three times in the head killing him instantly. In proof of Leaton's skill with a six-shooter it was said that any one of the shots would have killed Burgess, and he commenced to fall when hit by the first shot but Leaton put the other two shots in his head before he struck the ground."[16]

It looks like John Burgess wasn't the only person shot by Bill Leaton that day. In April 1877 Leaton was indicted for two counts of murder and a third count of assault to murder. After much pretrial maneuvering, one murder count was reduced to manslaughter. Leaton was convicted of assault to murder (two years in the penitentiary) and manslaughter (three years in the penitentiary). Trial on the remaining murder charge was repeatedly delayed, and we find no record of its resolution.[17]

Even though his prison term was short, Bill Leaton never had to serve it out. The governor pardoned him, although it wasn't a very pretty pardon. Leaton got to go home "because he has served part of his time and is afflicted with a loathsome and dangerous disease of permanent character." The report of the superintendent of the penitentiary was more specific: "Secondary and Tertiary Syphilis, in very bad form—cannot be cured—is of no service in the penitentiary." So Bill Leaton went back to La Junta (to chase down the three other men who went unpunished in Hall's death?), where he was promptly killed in a gun battle with the chief of police of Presidio del Norte.[18]

Thirty years after they first arrived in La Junta together, Ben Leaton, Ed Hall and John Burgess (and some of their offspring) had been laid to rest. Their role in founding Presidio, Texas, had sputtered to an unbecoming end. Looking back after more than a century, it seems like something out of a Louis L'Amour novel—bad guys, badder guys, feuds and gunfights—but even rough men like these left loved ones behind. There was one particularly poignant moment when finances finally compelled John Burgess's son and namesake to sell the family homestead. The legal description of the farm begins: "a certain tract of land known as the John D. Burgess Home-stead containing two hundred acres more or less and bounded as follows: Commencing at the grave of John D. Burgess, thence south 650 varas . . ." He had sold his father's grave.[19]

In addition to the war imposed upon it by the United States in 1846, Mexico fought a war over internal reform from 1858 to 1860. When that conflict ended, while the United States was grappling with its Civil War, Mexico suffered a French invasion that endured from 1861 to 1867.

The 1858–1860 War of the Reform pitted conservative, centralist, church-oriented interests against advocates of a liberal, federalist, secular government. The conservative movement was associated with General Felix Zuloaga; Benito Juárez led the liberal movement, but it was a fragmented alliance of divergent views.

In the 1861–1867 French Intervention, Mexicans who favored a Hapsburg monarchy led by imported Emperor Maximilian (obeisant to Napoleon III and backed by the French army) waged war against republicans committed to a more democratic model under the leadership of Juárez and the young Porfirio Díaz. This conflict distinctly echoed the conservative-liberal split of the earlier war.

In both nineteenth-century Mexican confrontations the liberal faction—a liberalism that cannot fairly be matched with current notions of liberalism in the United States—prevailed. The emergence of Mexican liberalism coincided with the rise of regional oligarchies—vortices of money and power that gave liberalism its national influence.

Regionalism was a subplot in these wars, and in virtually every other Mexican political engagement, because it appealed to the masses as much as to the dominant class. The sense of regional identity was as strong in Chihuahua as anywhere. The problems, solutions, policies and priorities of Mexico City were incongruent with those of the frontier. Just as the Apache problem in Texas was difficult for the Confederate command to grasp, so were Mescalero predations in Chihuahua far from the minds of lawmakers in the Valley of Mexico. West Texas and Chihuahua had a great deal in common, much more than they did with either Washington or Mexico City.

Another subplot, which endures today, was the matter of communal and traditional landholding. A lifestyle based on communal agricultural land was ingrained in Mesoamerican traditions. It was foreign to the Chichimeca but Mesoamericans and mestizos had brought it north, Franciscans nurtured it and it fitted comfortably with traditions that lin-

The End of the Mescaleros

gered in La Junta. In addition to sharing communal lands, many Mexicans farmed or ranched lands that their families had occupied for generations without formal legal title. In a typical case, the lands would have been occupied under one of the Mexican frontier colonization programs, but the formal paperwork would never have been delivered—usually because surveys had never been performed. Respect for ancestral landholdings was a paramount concern in rural areas. Local land ownership issues blended with other local concerns under the umbrella concept of local autonomy—the right of local communities to observe their local customs and apply their local sensibilities.

It is possible to look at Mexican politics as having three movements—national, regional and local—each competing with the other two movements and each movement harboring competing factions within itself. This is one source of Mexico's bewildering political complexity.

Regional and local movements were definitive determinants of allegiance on the northern frontier, but they did not define the two dominant national political factions. For someone living in Chihuahua, whether a hacendado, a ranchero or a campesino, regionalism and local autonomy complicated the choice between liberals and conservatives at the national level. Neither party promoted regionalism, though the federalist words of liberals could be construed that way. Neither advocated protecting communal and ancestral lands, though there might be a wisp of protection under conservative paternalism.

Out of this volatile concoction emerged Chihuahua's Governor Luis Terrazas, a complicated man. Terrazas—an oligarch first, a liberal second—understood the transcendent influence of money and power. Distributing those commodities wisely among several contentious liberal factions and the state's conservative opposition, and focusing his largesse on influential families rather than sprinkling it across society, he was able to dominate Chihuahua politically and economically for decades, eventually passing his mantle to son-in-law Enrique Creel.[1]

The foundation of the Terrazas empire was laid between 1860 and 1885 by manipulating political factions, military forces and state government to solidify economic and political power. Terrazas began with land and cattle, forming a partnership with Henry Müller, a German entrepreneur. It was Müller who owned the private mint where August Santleben converted a load of silver ore to pesos. Müller and Terrazas were the two hacendados that Major David Fergusson singled out as still having livestock amid the desolation of northern Chihuahua. As his wealth grew, Terrazas branched out into textile manufacturing, flour milling, banking, transportation, urban real estate and heavy industry. When his work was complete, Luis Terrazas could rightfully claim stature equal to that of Rockefeller, Carnegie, Gould and the other Robber Barons of the age. His was a fabulous wealth.[2]

The term "Robber Baron" fits Terrazas well, even though he did not do his robbing in coal, iron, oil or transcontinental railroads of the United States. Terrazas stole a great deal of land. He stole it through manipulation and abuse of systems meant to colonize *tierras baldíos* (vacant lands) and programs intended to reallocate church holdings. He stole it by relocating peons and appropriating their fields. His surveying companies, backed by his police, stole land from small rancheros, then his military forces protected Terrazas lands from Apaches while others suffered merciless attacks. When stealing land was impractical, the Terrazas banks were in a position to benefit by foreclosures. The Terrazas family ultimately controlled more than 10 million acres of Chihuahua—including Enrique Creel's Hacienda Los Angeles near San Carlos and his 1.2-million-acre Hacienda de Orientales near La Junta, which he acquired by foreclosing upon longtime political foe Celso González.[3]

It was not only land that Terrazas stole. During a time when the central government and the states were arguing about the allocation of customs duties (which were the primary source of government finances), Terrazas was appropriating a significant amount of the duties collected at El Paso and Presidio del Norte for his personal account.[4]

The Terrazas dynasty has its supporters, and that is not entirely without reason, for in the course of amassing a personal empire Terrazas revitalized a devastated regional economy, created tens of thousands of jobs, attracted millions of dollars of foreign investment and—not insignificantly—finally put an end to Apache predations. Terrazas lorded over an oligarchy that shepherded Chihuahua from the nineteenth century into the twentieth.

Benito Juárez held the presidency of Mexico when the French arrived in 1861. He called upon Governor Terrazas to provide two thousand men to help repel the French invasion. Terrazas decided that his state needed protection from Apaches more than it needed protection from Frenchmen, and he kept his troops at home. Juárez was enraged. Soon he had been run out of Mexico City by the French and was forced to set up a government in exile in Monterrey. From there, the livid Juárez removed Terrazas as governor and installed a replacement. Terrazas took refuge in El Paso.[5]

In July 1863 thirty-year-old José Manuel María Dionisio León Ojinaga y Castañeda took up arms against the French and became lieutenant colonel of Chihuahua's First Battalion. (It was not that Ojinaga's battalion was the first ever formed in Chihuahua, but the original First

Battalion of Chihuahua had already been taken prisoner by French Imperialists, so the name was available.) Ojinaga was a good soldier, a respected leader and a decent polemicist. He was ordered to retreat after a battle in 1865, but his battalion was short of horses. To provide an example to his men, he led them on foot across the desert, declining the privileges due his rank. When President Juárez—who had been driven out of Monterrey to Chihuahua and then to El Paso—learned of Ojinaga's leadership, he promoted him to brigadier and named him governor and military commander of Chihuahua.[6]

Things did not go well for Ojinaga, however. On his orders, Lieutenant Colonel Rafael Platón Sánchez left Ciudad Guerrero to capture the pueblo of Temósachic. A group of Imperialist sympathizers were waiting in ambush and took 140 men prisoner. A few days later, his troop strength reduced to seventy, Ojinaga fled Ciudad Guerrero before the advance of troops loyal to Emperor Maximilian. On the road to Arisiachi, while Ojinaga was breakfasting at a villager's house, a scout rushed in and told him that the French were only a half-hour away. The brigadier went to organize his troops, but was intercepted by four enemy soldiers. He shouted, "I do not surrender, traitors!" pulled his pistol, killed three and wounded the fourth.[7]

But no sooner had he dispatched the four than three more opponents appeared under the command of Lieutenant Carmen Mendoza, who shot Ojinaga in the abdomen. The brigadier, who had been governor less than a month, died two and a half hours later. His last words were "Everything has been lost. With my death the national cause is going to suffer enough."[8]

It was perhaps not the most selfless or lucid thought ever uttered, but Ojinaga had been under a lot of stress. Juárez, who was now in the process of reconciling with Terrazas in El Paso, honored his fallen brigadier by changing the name of the Pueblo of Presidio del Norte to the Villa of Ojinaga. The connection between the late Governor Ojinaga and Presidio del Norte is murky at best. From a distance, it appears that Benito Juárez picked a town that would not particularly mind having its name changed. Today there is a larger-than-life bronze statue in Ojinaga's plaza. It is Benito Juárez, not Manuel Ojinaga.

Luis Terrazas may have had his disagreements with Benito Juárez, but when the French backed them both into a corner at El Paso during 1865, Terrazas rallied to the liberal-nationalist cause and helped organize a new resistance, putting him back into Juárez's good graces. Juárez returned the governorship of Chihuahua to Terrazas in November of that year. When the French began to retreat and Juárez marched forth toward Mexico City, Terrazas personally escorted the President to Chihuahua's border.[9]

France pulled out of Mexico in 1867. The Emperor Maximilian decided to stay. Juárez captured and executed him in June of that year. Juárez endured as president and was elected to his fourth term in 1871. Onetime ally Porfirio Díaz ran against him and took defeat ungraciously, declaring a revolution under a set of principles called the *Plan de la Noria*. Because the Juárez reign had demonstrated the ability of an incumbent to perpetuate power, a central principle of the plan was a prohibition against reelection of national officeholders.

Díaz invaded Chihuahua and defeated Governor Terrazas's troops. Federales under Juárez scattered the rebels, but Juárez died suddenly of a heart attack, eliminating the impetus for rebellion. The chief justice of Mexico's Supreme Court, Sebastián Lerdo de Tejada, succeeded to the presidency. When Lerdo took power and the revolution fizzled, Governor Terrazas met with Díaz to negotiate the terms of an amnesty. Once agreement was reached, Terrazas personally escorted Díaz to Chihuahua's border. Unlike when Terrazas escorted the victorious Juárez to the border, his trip with the failed rebel was in the nature of a humiliation; Díaz never forgot the insult.[10]

President Lerdo scheduled elections for October 1872, ran against the rehabilitated Porfirio Díaz and won handily. When Lerdo announced his campaign for reelection four years later Porfirio Díaz again railed against reelection. In March 1876 he issued a new antireelectionist call to rebellion, the *Plan de Tuxtepec*. Like the first Díaz takeover attempt, the ensuing struggle was brief, but the outcome differed. President Lerdo fled to the United States, and Porfirio Díaz declared himself president. Given its antireelectionist roots, it came as a surprise that the *Plan de Tuxtepec* launched a thirty-four-year dictatorship known as the Porfiriato. It was less surprising that one of Díaz's first presidential acts was to take control of Chihuahua and oust Luis Terrazas, installing Angel Trías Jr. as governor.

Back in La Junta, the Texas community across the river from Ojinaga had grown to nearly one thousand citizens. Joseph Dianda and Clato Aradia told the census taker that they were miners. Edward Foster, Pedro Juárez, Ruperto Orneles, Juan Keller and Refugio Gonzales were laborers. Joe Leaton was nowhere to be found; his wife Francisca had moved back in with her parents, Cesario and Jesusa Ureta, bringing her four children Ohamita, Manuelita, Bino and Joseph. Samuel Terrell was a carpenter, Raphael Mendoza was a gardener, Margarita Rodriguez was a weaver, David Geddis was a miller and George Brooks was an engineer. Most people had been born somewhere else, usually Mexico. Only children claimed to have been born in Texas.[11]

Even though the Presidio del Norte was active and Fort Davis had been reopened for three years, life remained dangerous. William Russell, whose farm was upstream of Presidio near Ruidosa, reported in May 1874 that the "Indians made their appearance a few miles below this place yesterday, carrying off a woman and her two children, and also several head of horses, and about ten days since they made a raid about four miles above here, killing some cattle and driving off several head of horses, and for the last six months during every moon, they depredated upon the ranches above and below here, killing and driving off stock. There are some three hundred families settled in the valley of the Rio Grande, within a distance of forty miles above and the same distance below here, on the American side of the river, and if they had any protection against the incursions of depredating bands of Indians, the number of settlers would be doubled within a year."[12]

A few months later Richard Daly, another of the Presidio founders, relayed the following status report to a frontier newspaper:

It is not very long since that the Indians came down upon the people of this neighborhood and did great damage.

They took off two children with them and when the elder of the two was no longer able to travel as rapidly on foot as they on horseback, they killed him.

Soon after they came again and raided on the ranch of Mr. Smith, killing him and burning his house.

About the same time another party of Indians, or maybe the same party, went to Mr. Milton Faver's ranch and ran off twelve of his oxen and this too not more than an hour after they had been turned loose from the plow.

The same night they attempted to get the cows from the corral, but somehow failed. They succeeded in cutting the rawhide bindings, but did not get the pickets out.

A few days afterward the Indians tried to get the sheep from the herding grounds, but the herders saw them and prevented them.

A few days before this the Indians tried to steal my animals from me while I was in camp at night, but they did not succeed. Not their fault, however. Here we have plenty of "reds" but no troops.

Another item by the way. I had forgotten to say in the body of the letter that only four or five days ago the Indians came within a mile of the Custom House here and stole some twelve or fifteen animals and got away with them as easy as you please.[13]

Six months later the news was no better. Russell's ranch was hit again and his men pursued the marauders, only to be surrounded. They managed to escape and began a running campaign against the nomads.

In June 1878 United States Army Colonel Benjamin Grierson visited Presidio del Norte and met with his Mexican counterpart, General Ortiz, who was commanding a hundred cavalry troops at the presidio. Grierson was pleased to learn that the Mexican Army would "cheerfully co-operate with the United States troops to prevent further depredations along the Rio Bravo in that vicinity," but the rest of the news was mixed:[14]

Of late considerable suffering has prevailed throughout the state of Chihuahua on account of the great scarcity of bread stuffs and provisions.

An abundant supply of wheat and corn will be produced this year in the valleys of the Rio Concho[s] and Rio Bravo which will be given to the destitute inhabitants.

Indians from the vicinity of San Carlos have of late been crossing into Presidio del Norte, Mexico, to trade for wheat or to beg to obtain grain and provisions in any manner possible. Many of these Indians are poor in appearance, but are well armed and correspondingly insolent and surly.[15]

The Apaches were under pressure. Being at best subsistence farmers, their crops were the first to fail. As ranchers pushed west, land and buffalo vanished. Worst of all was the complete disconnection between the expectations of nomads and settlers. Apaches did not want to become sedentary; it was not their way.

As early as 1854, United States Special Indian Agent Robert S. Neighbors (who had pioneered the Ford-Neighbors Trail to El Paso) advised Governor Bell of Texas that the Mescaleros "will not willingly remove from their old planting grounds between the 'Presidio del Norte' and the 'Horsehead Crossing' of the Pecos where they have planted corn for several years, and we cannot resist the strength of our own convictions that the course which will secure the most speedy, peaceable and permanent settlement of these people is, that of giving them the lands which they have already cultivated and which from the best information we can obtain are at the present vacant." In response, the state of Texas allocated land for a West Texas reservation and called upon the United States to establish and manage the facility (as it had done in two other Texas locations), but the national government never acted. The U.S. Army began pushing Apaches onto reservations in New Mexico. The Mexican Army began pushing Apaches into the United States for collection. When Apaches did not respond appropriately, both armies waged wars of extermination.[16]

In Chihuahua, Joaquín Terrazas, cousin of Governor Luis Terrazas, led the battle. His focus was a large band of Mescaleros led by a man named Victorio. Victorio's followers had once settled on a designated reservation in New Mexico, but found the situation intolerable. In 1878 he took eighty Apaches into West Texas and northern Mexico; soon their number grew to three hundred. Governor Terrazas put a price of two thousand pesos on Victorio's head, in addition to the usual scalp bounties. On the United States side of the border, Victorio was pursued by Colonel Benjamin Grierson, who had earlier assessed the situation at Presidio del Norte.[17]

Grierson scuffled with Victorio in July and August, chasing Mescaleros along the border northwest of La Junta. Joaquín Terrazas, backed by five hundred armed men, pursued Victorio's band across Chihuahua, catching up with them at Tres Castillos, in the northwestern part of the state. Terrazas killed seventy-two Mescaleros on October 14 and 15, 1880, including the brave and terrible Victorio. Most of the remaining warriors were wounded or taken captive.[18]

In early 1881 Mexico sent a column of federal soldiers led by General Carlos Fuero to Chihuahua, where they operated under a new compact with the United States that allowed both nations to cross the border in hot pursuit of Apaches. The federales fought pitched battles with the nomads; in April 1882 twenty-two soldiers were killed in a fight with warriors led by a Mescalero named Ju, who lost seventy-eight men in that same skirmish.[19]

Soon the troops focused on Apaches that remained in the mountains around La Junta. The most infamous band—known as the Chisos Apaches—was led by a man named Arzate, said to be the son of a captured Mexican from the locally prominent Músquiz family. Arzate roamed the stretch of the Rio Grande that included La Junta, but obtained greater notoriety to the south, near San Carlos and Santa Rosa. His band was finally subdued by trickery. The Mexican government hosted a fiesta for them in San Carlos, promising them easy life on a new reservation. Early in the morning, after most of the Mescaleros had passed out from drinking, Fuero's soldiers (who had been operating out of Presidio del Norte) swooped into San Carlos and took the entire clan captive. The Apaches were marched back to Presidio del Norte and confined. Most of Arzate's followers were divided up into small groups and sent south to be resettled in pueblos far from their homelands. The leaders—Arzate, Colorado and Zorillo—were lined up, shot and then buried at Presidio del Norte.[20]

Steam engines dealt the final blow to the Apaches. As the railroads pushed into Texas from the east and west and the Mexican Central Railway pushed north toward El Paso, the ranching invasion flourished and armies of both nations gained increased mobility. Severe drought in 1885 and 1886 compelled nomads to surrender to reservation life. There were no significant clashes with Apaches after 1886.[21]

The railroad was the agent of many changes. In 1870 the Texas legislature gave the Galveston, Harrisburg and San Antonio Railway the right to build a line across the state. Seven years later the first train pulled into San Antonio. The arrival of the railroad increased traffic on the Chihuahua Trail, benefiting La Junta. In fact, the surge of traffic was great enough to justify opening a new, more direct wagon route between San Antonio and Fort Davis, known as the New Military Road. The old route had looped from waterhole to waterhole; the new road cut directly across the plains, but was unsuitable in hot, dry weather.[22]

At about the time that the GH&SA reached San Antonio, future railroad baron Colis Huntington began constructing his Southern Pacific Railroad across California, Arizona and New Mexico, heading eastward to El Paso. Huntington negotiated a deal with the GH&SA under which the two lines would meet somewhere between San Antonio and El Paso. Huntington's Southern Pacific cut eastward across Texas below the old military road, stimulating the construction of a whistle-stop at Marfa and another at what would become Alpine, then picked up the new military road and proceeded east to the Pecos River. About three miles beyond the Pecos, Huntington's road met the western extension of the GH&SA on January 12, 1883. The line and its feeders connected San Francisco with New Orleans.[23]

The Southern Pacific Railroad is one-half of the reason why the villages at El Paso (Juárez) and Franklin (El Paso) grew into a metropolis. The other half of the reason is the Mexican Central Railway Company. A group of Boston financiers funded the construction of the railway in a both-ends-to-the-middle effort to link Mexico City and El Paso. The line from El Paso to Ciudad Chihuahua was operating by the autumn of 1882; when the east-west Southern Pacific drove its silver spike a few months later, the glory days of the Chihuahua Trail ended. The route through La Junta was still shorter than going far west to El Paso, but the railroad was faster and cheaper.

The Southern Pacific, cutting across the top of the West Texas tenderloin, illustrates La Junta's isolation, but was not its cause. Had the Mexican Central Railway run through La Junta to Marfa instead of northwest to El Paso, Presidio and Ojinaga might today have populations in the millions. Why did the Mexican tracks go where they did? Because the Mexican Central was not stretching to El Paso or San Antonio any more than was the Southern Pacific. Both railroads were about opening up California. California was north and west of Ciudad Chihuahua, so the Mexican Central followed the northwest trace of the Camino Real, which had spawned freight-generating ranches and towns along its path. True, there was still a need for freight carriage between San Antonio and Ciudad Chihuahua, but that need was secondary and could be accomplished by going through El Paso. If the need grew, a second line could be built through Presidio-Ojinaga.

Victor Ochoa's reported birth year of 1850 is certainly wrong. Victor was the son of Isabella Leaton, known as La Chata. Isabella was the child of Ben Leaton and Juana Pedraza, and was born in 1839, before they came to La Junta. She was still single, childless and living with her parents in 1860. Taking those and other facts into account, a more likely birth date for Victor Ochoa is somewhere between 1860 and 1870.[1]

Born in Ojinaga, Victor was the offspring of thrice-married Isabella's first union. His father, Juan Ochoa, was a customs collector who later operated a sawmill in Fort Davis. The extended Ochoa family owned a ranch in Chihuahua during the tumultuous 1880s and 1890s.[2]

Luis Terrazas had snatched back the governorship of Chihuahua from Angel Trías Jr. in 1879. When the Mexican Central Railway opened in 1882, Porfirio Díaz's central government could exert more control over Chihuahua than before. Under pressure from Díaz, Luis Terrazas stepped down from the governorship. Anti-Terrazas Porfiristas governed an unruly Chihuahua for eight years. By 1892 Terrazas had pragmatically swung over to the Porfirista side, and Díaz installed a Chihuahuan government that was less hostile to the Terrazas clan. Luis Terrazas returned to the governorship in 1903.[3]

While the Terrazas family was out of power, oligarchic land seizures continued unabated against a background of Terrazas-fomented political unrest. The grievances that would launch the Mexican Revolution of 1910 were emerging. The Ochoa Ranch was one of the homesteads seized in an oligarchic power play, and it must not have been the only one appropriated in the vicinity, for Victor Ochoa soon assembled several hundred armed men to rebel against the Porfiristas. It was a naïve but frustrated effort; the rebels attacked the Mexican Army at the towns of Palomas and Ascensión, but the federales ultimately routed the angry rancheros. In one of the final battles, Ochoa put on the uniform of a dead federal soldier and fled for the border.[4]

Porfirio Díaz did not take Ochoa's rebellion lightly, placing a MEX$50,000 reward on the young man's head and protesting loudly to the United States government about his continuing freedom across the Rio Grande. Texas authorities captured Ochoa more than once, but he was a sympa-

Victor

Ochoa

thetic figure who somehow always managed to escape. The Pecos County sheriff once found himself on the wrong end of an arrest warrant for complicity in Ochoa's disappearance from the county jail.[5]

United States marshals finally caught up with Victor Ochoa in 1895 and charged him with violation of the Neutrality Act. He ended up in the Kings County Penitentiary in Brooklyn, New York, and was discharged in 1897. After his release, he remained in the northeast and became an inventor. Ochoa received U.S. patents for two adjustable wrenches, a vertical turbinelike windmill for generating electricity, an electric brake, a pocket clip for a fountain pen and a reversible electric motor. His most remarkable invention was something given the dubious name of the OchoaPlane—a collapsible glider built of canvas supported by steel springs and tubes. The contraption looked like two bicycles being attacked by a pterodactyl. The wings were supposed to flap. There is no clear evidence that the OchoaPlane ever took flight.[6]

Victor Ochoa lived quietly in Paterson, New Jersey, for a few years, manufacturing fountain pens and working on his inventions. It was hard to rid himself of his revolutionary past. The muckraking *Everybody's Magazine* (in which Upton Sinclair condemned the meatpacking industry) published an article describing him as a human Gatling gun and a bloodthirsty revolutionist. Paterson's local paper reassuringly reported that Ochoa was "anything but a bloodthirsty looking individual, and when he says that his acts were just the contrary from those described in the magazine, he is apparently telling the truth."[7]

One day Ochoa suddenly departed New Jersey, leaving a prototype of the OchoaPlane behind. He next surfaced in a gold-mining venture in the state of Sinaloa, where he was double-crossed by two partners who left him to die in the desert. He survived. The story goes that sometime around 1936 he was walking down the street in El Paso with the chief of police when he saw the two blackguards approaching. The villains pulled guns. Ochoa was unarmed, but he grabbed the chief's pistol and killed both of his opponents. Ochoa was taken to jail and tried, but the judge set him free with a recommendation that he get back to Mexico. Some part of the story is probably true. His grandson and namesake, who became the sheriff of Hudspeth County, Texas, thought that his grandfather died around 1945 in parts unknown.[8]

From this we can conclude that Victor Ochoa was smart, industrious, ambitious, aggressive and willing to bend the rules on occasion. That makes it easy to understand his thought processes after he learned that John Spencer, who had come to La Junta with Ochoa's grandfather Ben Leaton, had discovered a vein of silver twenty-five miles north of

Presidio, near Milton Faver's Cibolo Creek Ranch. This was in 1883, before Ochoa turned revolutionary. Spencer took some rock samples to Fort Davis for assay and the results were so promising that the fort's General Shafter joined Spencer and two others in forming the Presidio Mining Company. Soon a town of a few hundred miners, laborers, merchants, bartenders and whores sprung up around Spencer's mine, which would ultimately yield over US$20 million in silver.[9]

Somewhere, probably from his mother, Victor Ochoa had heard about his family's claim to Captain Ronquillo's land grant. The grant covered virtually the entire county, but most importantly it covered the lands from which the Presidio Mining Company was extracting silver ore. In 1885, just as the mine was gearing up, Ochoa consulted his friend John R. Randolph about whether to assert a claim to the mine. Randolph contacted prominent San Antonio attorney T. T. Teel—the same lawyer who had gotten John and Tomás Burgess off the hook for shooting Ochoa's notorious step-grandfather, Edward Hall.[10]

Teel found the Ronquillo land grant most interesting, and he set about putting together a syndicate to challenge the Presidio Mining Company. He collected all of the descendants of Ben Leaton and Juana Pedraza as clients under an arrangement in which Teel and Randolph each received one-eighth of the grant. Another quarter was distributed to J. S. Dougherty and W. O. Ellis, who would finance the litigation. The Leaton-Pedraza heirs kept half, but Victor Ochoa deeded another eighth to Randolph for his services, leaving the family with three-eighths. To round out the party, Randolph sold one of his eighths to H. R. Hilderband and Rosina Sealy for US$5,000.[11]

After looking over the paperwork, attorney Teel advised Victor Ochoa that there was a problem. The grant said that Cesario Herrera waived Captain Ronquillo's obligations to occupy and defend the grant for four years; Teel doubted that an alcalde had that kind of authority. In Teel's opinion, only Chihuahua's legislature could waive statutory conditions. This is the point at which Victor Ochoa's bloodlines became obvious. Taking a cue from Teel, Ochoa went to Juárez, where he immersed himself in a set of Chihuahuan archives. After a period spent studying the formalities of Mexican legislative procedure, Ochoa conjured up a forged legislative decree and slipped it into the records. His first invention, as it were. A few days later he returned to the archives and boldly asked the clerk for a certified copy of the phony decree.[12]

Teel took time to clean up the title, study the law and watch how business was progressing in the mining town that was now called Shafter. He probably also spent some time pestering John Spencer for a piece of the silver mine, but nothing came of that. In the summer of 1889 Teel filed suit against the Presidio Mining Company in federal court in El Paso.[13]

An attorney in Juárez noticed the filing. It caught his attention because his name was Estanislado N. Ronquillo and his grandfather was José Ignacio Ronquillo. Recognizing that the transfer from Captain Ronquillo to Hipolito Acosta (who then purportedly sold it to Juana Pedraza) was probably void (Mexican law prohibited transfers for four years after the grant), Estanislado Ronquillo set about gathering up deeds from all of his grandfather's descendants. Then, rather than invest time and money in protracted litigation, Ronquillo sold his family's interest to James J. Fitzgerrell of Las Vegas, New Mexico, for US$100,000. Fitzgerrell laid off two-thirds of his interest to a Chicago attorney named Seth Crews, who paid US$150,000. Then, bringing Crews' partner Ernest Dale Owen into the venture, they tapped a group of investors for US$4.5 million, formed the Chicago & Texas Land & Cattle Company, and sold the Ronquillo rights to Owen as trustee for the C&TL&CC. They moved quickly; it had been only fifty-five days since T. T. Teel had filed his suit in El Paso.[14]

Teel was predictably upset when he heard of Ronquillo's claims. He checked out Ronquillo's background, then, not one to pussyfoot around, had Ronquillo arrested and jailed in El Paso. Ronquillo applied for a writ of habeas corpus, which meant that he wanted out of jail. At the hearing on Ronquillo's application, Teel pointed out a problem with Ronquillo's claim: his grandfather, José Ignacio Ronquillo, had never been in the Mexican Army, had never lived at Presidio del Norte and had died in San Elizario twenty-five years after Captain Ronquillo's death at Ojo Caliente. Same name, different person. Owen, representing the C&TL&CC, had some serious explaining to do to his investors: he was betting on the wrong horse.[15]

On the other team, Victor Ochoa, who had hired Teel almost four years earlier, was getting angry over the complications that had arisen. Ochoa had his mother and the other Leaton heirs fire Teel as their attorney and revoke the powers of attorney that they had given him. Teel responded by dropping the lawsuits he had filed on their behalf. Owen, who was definitely not a quitter, filed seven new lawsuits. Five were against the mining company and some railroad companies that claimed lands within the Ronquillo grant. The sixth was against the heirs of Ben Leaton. The seventh was against the heirs of the real Captain José Ignacio Ronquillo. Owen claimed with a straight face that his citizen José Ronquillo, not the esteemed Captain José Ronquillo, was the grantee named in the land grant.[16]

The Presidio Mining Company's lawyers had been looking over the Chihuahua decree invented by Victor Ochoa, and they advised the court that it looked like a bad forgery. It wasn't long before everyone admitted that it was a fake, but the three usurper groups (Leaton heirs, Owen's Ronquillo heirs and Captain Ronquillo's heirs) took the position that there had once been a legitimate decree in the Juárez records but someone had pulled the original decree and replaced it with a forgery. T. T. Teel testified that he had gone to Juárez in 1887 and gotten a copy of the original decree, but the copy had somehow gotten lost. That, according to Teel, was why Victor Ochoa had later been sent to get a copy in Juárez, only to have a forgery foisted off on him.[17]

Owen—now relying on an admitted forgery—was in hot water again, and he had US$4.5 million worth of Chicago investors to explain things to. Fortunately Estanislado Ronquillo had an idea. He would go find the missing original decree. Taking an El Paso attorney with him, Ronquillo set off for the official state archives in Chihuahua, only to find that the necessary records from 1834 had somehow been lost or destroyed. A former manager of the state printing office suggested that copies of the decree might be found in the records of any of the various Chihuahua districts. Ronquillo went to El Valle, but it was in vain. He went to Parral, but found nothing. Then his luck changed at the old mining outpost of Santa Bárbara. At first the archives' custodian refused Ronquillo access to the records, but Ronquillo had a private conversation with the secretary of Santa Bárbara's ayuntamiento (city council), who agreed to conduct a personal search. A copy of the decree was miraculously found in the right bundle of documents in the right sequence. The copy lacked any signatures or seals, but that was in a way a good thing—Victor Ochoa's forgery had been given away by obviously falsified signatures and seals.[18]

Owen, cheered by Ronquillo's good fortune in Santa Bárbara but weary of litigation against an array of diverse interests, decided to simplify his life. He went to the Leaton heirs and the Captain Ronquillo heirs and bought them out. Now it was just Owen as trustee versus the Presidio Mining Company.[19]

Owen got pounded at trial. He had to admit that the first decree was a forgery. Then Spencer's mining company brought in a string of expert witnesses who persuaded the court that the Santa Bárbara decree was a forgery too. A key piece of evidence was that all Chihuahua state decrees were numbered; lawyers for the mining company produced the real decree with the appropriate number, bearing authentic signatures and seals. It had nothing to do with any land grant.[20]

Then the mining company produced a string of witnesses who said that Ronquillo never received his promised land grant, that the people named in the grant as surveyors were common soldiers, that Cesario Herrera was a scoundrel, that Ben Leaton was a scoundrel, that Ed Hall was a scoundrel, that Cesario Herrera had been taken to Chihuahua in shackles for forging land grants, that enormous land grants were illegal, that the conditions to the purported grant had never been met or waived and that the supposed land grant was at best a bad copy, not the original. The court concluded that the Ronquillo land grant had been a scam from start to finish. Owen appealed the decision in 1892, but was thoroughly rebuffed by the Fifth Circuit Court of Appeals.[21]

The Ochoa-Leaton-Ronquillo-Owen attempt to snag a piece of a silver mine thudded to its conclusion at about the same time that Victor Ochoa was taking up arms against the Porfiristas.

In the last years of the nineteenth century, ownership of land was an uncertain proposition on both sides of the Rio Grande. Victor Ochoa was the loser in two different land squabbles that illustrate key differences between the two sides of La Junta.

Peons had been, and were being, pushed off their land on both sides of the Rio Grande. The Chihuahuan oligarchy may have been distinctive, but there is little point in pretending that land-baron oligarchies were not emerging in Texas. The Anglo-versus-Hispanic theme on the Texas side was not materially different in effect from the criollo-versus-Indio distinction in Chihuahua. What was the difference that would push La Juntans on only one side of the Rio Grande into revolution?[22]

A facile answer is that the laws and government emerging in Texas were more balanced than those in Chihuahua. The system in Texas unfairly favored Anglos over Hispanics, but perhaps there was enough inconsistency to maintain a façade of fairness. For example, did the battle between Owen and the Presidio Mining Company represent a triumph of Anglo settlers' mining claims over Hispanic settlers' land grants, or did it signal that even poor Hispanics in Texas could access the Anglo system, gain representation by lawyers in Juárez, El Paso, San Antonio and Chicago, and vigorously prosecute a dubious claim? After all, the only people who made money from the bogus Ronquillo land grant were the Leaton and Ronquillo descendants who sold their claims to Anglo lawyers.

A related possibility is that the governmental machinery of Chihuahua was seen as an active agent of oppression on behalf of a ruling class, which it was. The police, the surveyors, the armies, the courts—all were involved in transferring land from the poor and weak to the rich and powerful. There was an identity between the representatives of powerful economics and those of powerful government. Of course, the same can be said of Texas or the United States in general, but there the linkage was less overt. Predictably, when U.S. police power did align openly with the ruling class, insurrection was often the result. Early union struggles are one example: the 1914 massacre at the Ludlow Mine, Washington's 1916 Everett Massacre and Chicago's 1937 Memorial Day Massacre, for instance. Early race-riot massacres are another: East St. Louis, Chicago and Tulsa from 1917 to 1921. But early class struggles in the United States were over labor and race, not land, and — because the emergence of those issues trailed land distribution — came later than the Mexican conflict. Was it the presence of a balanced land allocation and adjudication system in the United States that made the difference?

Our hypothesis, which we will limit to the confines of La Junta, is almost the opposite. Unlike the Villa of Ojinaga, the state of Chihuahua and the nation of Mexico, the Texas side of La Junta managed to work through its confrontational land issues without insurrection because of the absence of government. Millionaires from Chicago might battle in federal court over silver mines, but at the ground level there was only scant evidence of municipal, county or state infrastructure. The complex, bureaucratic and ultimately oppressive mechanisms of Spanish and Mexican rule had reached as far north as Ojinaga, and had stopped there. There had never been active government on the far side of the Rio Grande, and nothing had yet transpired to change that circumstance. Ojinaga — and the other towns of northern Chihuahua — were controlled by a spate of local and state officials beholden to the oligarchy and backed by police and the military. Presidio — and everyplace else in West Texas more than a few miles from the railroad — offered no government to resent, no police to resist, no army to battle, no officials to string up. The battle was *mano a mano*.

Revolution never arose in Presidio because its continuing isolation offered no fixed target to revolt against. Revolution came to Ojinaga because its isolation was being stripped away.

When Mexican dictator Porfirio Díaz came to national power in 1876, Luis Terrazas found himself facing a national regime opposed to regional independence. Díaz sidelined the Terrazas political machine during most of the 1880's and 1890's, but did not curb the family's accumulation of wealth. Terrazas retained the economic might to finance continuing opposition to the Díaz administration; the resulting struggle endured until a cautious Díaz-Terrazas reconciliation began in 1886. Once in the same camp with Díaz, Terrazas set about attracting substantial foreign investment (primarily from the United States and primarily for mineral exploitation) and solidifying control of the Chihuahuan economy, but he did not return to the governorship until 1903.[1]

Toribio Ortega's Rebellion

Investors from the United States poured millions of dollars into Chihuahua's mining industry during the Terrazas and Díaz years. Much of the investment was diverted to the benefit of the oligarchy through legitimate and illegitimate channels. In northern Chihuahua, where ranching and farming were the dominant industries, William Randolph Hearst and other foreign investors worked alongside the local land barons to assemble vast blocks of land.[2]

In the summer of 1900, during the process of reconciliation between the Terrazas clan and Porfirio Díaz, Enrique Creel (son-in-law of Luis Terrazas) met with Arthur Stilwell, a promoter from Kansas City. Stilwell had built the Kansas City Southern Railroad, which terminated at a new port on the Gulf Coast that he named in honor of himself: Port Arthur, Texas. He knew what every industrialist knew: it is exceedingly difficult to make money running a railroad, but it is astoundingly simple to become wealthy building one. The wealth-generation potential of a railroad lies in siphoning off investors' (and governments') funds through a myriad of companies engaged in surveying, engineering, construction, land development, tie production, timber provision, rail manufacturing and any of a hundred other services required to lay track across thousands of miles of prairie, valley and ravine. Once a railroad has been built — or even partly built — its promoter can leave it to rust along with the investors' dreams. Enrique Creel was within the circle of capitalists who understood this fundamental truth.[3]

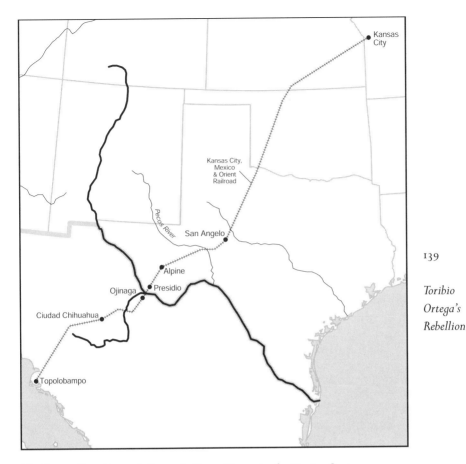

The Kansas City, Mexico & Orient Railway. Illustration by Herring Design, Houston, Tex.

A few months earlier Stilwell and his associates had invited 350 potential Kansas City investors to a dinner honoring none other than Stilwell himself. Taking the podium, the entrepreneur reminded his audience that he was the visionary who had opened a railway from Kansas City to the Gulf of Mexico. (He did not mention how he had been pushed out of the Kansas City Southern during a series of financial crises.) Now, he said, it was time to reveal his latest idea: a 1,600-mile rail link from Kansas City to the Pacific Ocean. Using a map and a piece of string, Stilwell demonstrated that the shortest route to the Pacific from the Midwest was not west to California but southwest, to an obscure Mexican port called Topolobampo. Stilwell's Kansas City, Mexico & Orient Railway to Topolobampo would cross the Rio Grande at Presidio-Ojinaga.[4]

When Stilwell met with Enrique Creel a few months later, he found a ready audience. Creel already owned a company known as the Ferro-caril Chihuahua al Pacifico that held the rights to build a line from Chihuahua to Topolobampo. The company benefited from some favorable government guarantees and subsidies and had laid 124 miles of rail, but it lacked the finances to take on the challenging inclines of the Sierra Madre Occidental. It was not the sort of project on which Creel wished to risk his own substantial fortune, and Stilwell understood Creel's thinking—better to build it with investor money.[5]

Creel provided an introduction so that Stilwell might meet with President Porfirio Díaz in Mexico City. There, with the dictator's blessing, Stilwell obtained a concession to build his railway from Ojinaga to Creel's Ciudad Chihuahua railhead. After a side trip to Topolobampo, where he visited with local landowner and promoter Albert Kimsey Owen—who had once tried to assemble something called the Texas, Topolobampo & Pacific Railway & Telegraph Company—Stilwell returned to Ciudad Chihuahua, where he resumed talks with Enrique Creel. The sizzle of Creel's influence and Stilwell's access to investors was manifest; in just days they inked an agreement to join their railroads.[6]

This was not the first time that promoters had talked of laying rails to Ojinaga: Mexico granted a concession from Ojinaga to Guaymas in 1853, another to Mazatlán in 1868, and a third to link to Piedras Negras, Topolobampo, Mazatlán and Alamos in 1881. Those tracks had never been built, but this was the twentieth century; railroads were reaching to every corner of the continent. Not only was the Kansas City, Mexico & Orient led by a proven railroad builder, it was in partnership with Enrique Creel and had been blessed by Porfirio Díaz. Something would happen this time.[7]

But ten years later there still were no railroad tracks in La Junta. Track had been laid from Ciudad Chihuahua to Falomir, about a third of the way to Ojinaga, and Stilwell had built and purchased somewhat more than four hundred miles of road from Wichita, Kansas, to San Angelo, Texas. A third disconnected piece had been built from Miñaca (ninety-five miles west of Ciudad Chihuahua) to the top of the Sierra Madre. The Mexican trackage added up to 237 miles, including the 124 miles that Creel had built before Stilwell arrived. Two-thirds of the railroad remained a dream. Stilwell had originally estimated the cost of the entire project to be US$8.5 million; he had issued US$25 million in stock, had incurred almost US$30 million in long-term debt, owed more than US$13 million to related companies and was out of money. The company was headed into a difficult receivership.[8]

Nonetheless, Presidio remained optimistic that the railroad would be built. Railroad fever also remained high in Marfa, which coveted the chance to become an iron crossroads. If anything, it was Marfa, not Presidio, that most anticipated a boom from the KCM&O, because the arrival of the Southern Pacific had already made Marfa the county's center of gravity.[9]

La Junta had never been entirely beyond Terrazas ambitions, but the promise of a railroad markedly increased its attractiveness. From a Terrazas viewpoint, it was logical and important—perhaps even inevitable—that the KCM&O cross the Rio Grande, but it was not essential. The project would profit the oligarchy even if it failed. And if the road reached Ojinaga but did not span the river, La Junta would still be drawn into the central Chihuahuan marketplace. Crops, cattle, timber, hardware, machinery, labor and money would flow between Ojinaga and Ciudad Chihuahua. The stretch of iron from Ciudad Chihuahua to Ojinaga—already one-third finished—would bring La Junta out of its isolation, into the Terrazas fold.

The expectation that Ojinaga would grow prompted the oligarchy to snatch lands in the town. The realization that cattle from the northern frontier would more easily move to market accelerated the pace at which land barons—*latifundistas*—acquired local ranches. Recognition that La Junta's fruits and vegetables could reach Chihuahua before spoiling prompted acquisition of farms and construction of irrigation projects to benefit them. The improved economics of transportation increased interest in La Junta's mineral potential. The Terrazas organization even began thinking about building a spa at the hot springs across from Candelaria, prompting local papers to conclude that La Junta would become "the greatest natural health resort the Old or New World has ever known." Though the resort was only a dream, the Terrazas name was magic: D. D. Kilpatrick, who farmed in Candelaria and ran a small general store there, began advertising "Groceries Sold to Hot Springs Visitors at Marfa Prices."[10]

Most expansions of the oligarchy's holdings were accomplished at the expense of unwilling victims. Mining claims were registered on communal Ojinaga lands. Water rights in the Rio Conchos were diverted from campesinos to more powerful interests. Pueblitos were burned to force villagers to abandon their ancestral farms, making them available to the oligarchs or their favored investors from the United States.[11]

There were two principal institutions of local oppression during the Díaz-Terrazas era: the *rurales* and the *jefes*. Rurales were a mounted national police force charged with enforcing the will of the oligarchy and suppressing dissent; they were distinct from the *federales,* who were the regular Mexican Army. *Jefes politicos* (district political chiefs) were appointed toadies of the Díaz and Terrazas apparatus. Their authority was reinforced by the 1904 replacement of elected municipal presidents with appointed *jefes municipales*. The jefes—political and municipal—were community outsiders that represented the Chihuahuan political machine, not local interests. Rurales and jefes exemplified the loss of precious local autonomy, treasured by communities all over Mexico—particularly those on the northern frontier, and particularly La Junta.[12]

Ojinaga was the largest town on the downstream Conchos. It was the headquarters for jefe municipal Ciro Amarillas and it hosted a garrison of federales—the same garrison that once occupied the now-defunct Presidio del Norte. To this was added a *comandancia de rurales*. Ojinaga became the center of authority and oppression for northeastern Chihuahua, much as Ciudad Juárez served the same role in the northwest.

The railroads, the expanding haciendas, the growing cattle herds, the increase in irrigated acreage—all of these reflected the economic boom that Chihuahua enjoyed from 1898 to 1908. It was a time when the wealth of the elite multiplied and a fledgling middle class began to emerge. Shopkeepers, craftsmen, small manufacturers and skilled workers fared better than before. Their ranks grew. Rancheros who managed to have their land purchased instead of stolen benefited from soaring real estate prices: agricultural land that was worth thirty cents per acre in 1879 could be sold for almost ten dollars per acre in 1908. But most rancheros never saw those prices; they saw rurales demanding to know by what right they occupied their family farm. Some Terrazas prosperity trickled down, but the trickle seldom reached peons. Agricultural wages stubbornly refused to budge from thirty-five centavos per day. Meanwhile, corn and chili doubled in price and the cost of beans rose sixfold.[13]

In 1908 the United States suffered a recession and its effects rippled into Mexico. Imports and exports slumped, railroad traffic fell and mineral prices plummeted. Expatriate Mexicans in the United States lost their jobs and returned home; competition for employment rose, pushing wages down. Capital from the United States dried up. Banks raised interest rates to as high as 24 percent. By 1909 Chihuahua was in a deep economic depression. Wealthy elites can survive depressions with only minor damage, but the depression of 1909 devastated the middle and lower classes. Salaries fell 60 percent. Between 1906 and 1909 the number of small industrial companies and artisan shops in Chihuahua dropped by 35 percent. Only one quarter of Chihuahuan businesses founded in 1907 and 1908 were still alive in 1910. Compounding the problem, drought swept Chihuahua in 1909, wiping out small farmers and ranchers and driving up prices of corn and beans another 70 percent.[14]

In this troubled time, rumblings began about the tenure of President-forever Porfirio Díaz, who had afforded the nation no alternative but to reelect him repeatedly since his ascension to power. Even loyal Porfiristas felt that it was time to think seriously about a successor to the eighty-year-old president. In 1908 Díaz gave an interview to journalist James Creelman and dropped a bombshell: "No matter what my friends and supporters say, I retire when my presidential term of office ends, and I shall not serve again. I shall be eighty years old then. I have waited patiently for the day when the people of the Mexican Republic should be prepared to choose and change their government at every election without danger of armed revolution and without injury to the national credit or interference with the national progress. I believe that day has come. I welcome an opposition party in the Mexican Republic."[15]

Francisco Madero believed Porfirio Díaz. Born into a family of wealthy Coahuilan hacendados, Madero studied in Paris and the United States and became something of a scholar in social, economic and political affairs. A little man with a squeaky voice, Madero was a democrat and he took the opportunity afforded by Díaz's pronouncement to write a treatise titled *The Presidential Succession in 1910* in which—while pronouncing himself loyal to Porfirio Díaz—he argued that the era of military dictatorships was over and that principles of effective democratic government, including the creation of an opposition party, should rule. In particular, and in response to the seemingly interminable reign of Díaz, Madero advocated strict one-term limits, as Díaz himself had done before settling into a lengthy dictatorship.

Madero's ideas caught on. He found himself the candidate of the new Anti-Reelectionist Party, and he took a liking to the idea of becoming president. Though the reforms he advocated were moderate and in line with Diaz's statements to Creelman—Madero was, after all, a hacendado—his campaign became a vehicle for the oppressed and dispossessed.

After making the mistake of believing Porfirio Díaz, who of course decided to run for reelection, Madero compounded his error by staying in the race and campaigning against the elderly dictator. When Madero's political rallies began to draw enough participants and enough fervor to make Díaz uncomfortable, Díaz took the logical step of putting Madero in prison, where he languished on election day in July. Madero was incarcerated at San Luis Potosí when Díaz announced his own reelection by a margin of 99 percent. Madero managed to get out of jail under a bond that required him to remain in San Luis Potosí. He was kept under close watch by Díaz agents, but when rumors surfaced that he was about to be rearrested and executed, he managed to slip his surveillance and cross into Texas at Laredo. From there he fled to San Antonio.[16]

Once safely in San Antonio, Madero met with his supporters and drew up his roadmap to revolution, the *Plan de San Luis Potosí,* in which he complained of the Díaz dictatorship, called for democracy, pronounced the recent election illegal and declared himself interim president until honest elections could be held. Finally, winding up for the most telegraphed punch in history, Madero called for all towns in Mexico to rise up in arms at precisely six o'clock P.M. on Sunday, November 20.[17]

Exiles and revolutionaries began massing on the Texas side of the border. There were rumors that groups of armed Mexicans were crossing the Rio Grande in La Junta and marching toward Marfa. The Mexican government complained to the United States that "bands of revolutionists are being recruited in various places along the frontier of Texas, the following points being mentioned as dangerous: Naso, El Paso, Presidio, Boquilla and Eagle Pass."[18]

Madero's call to arms was heard by Toribio Ortega. At age thirty-three, the tall, lean, dark and intense Ortega was already an influential citizen of Cuchillo Parado, a little town just across the Sierra Grande from La Junta. He led the local agricultural society — the voice of rancheros — which had been engaged in a futile attempt to prevent usurpation of lands by the criollo oligarchy. With the rising prominence of Madero, Ortega had founded a local Anti-Reelectionist chapter that coordinated its activities with Chihuahua's Anti-Reelection Party leader, Abraham González.[19]

After talking with his fellow rancheros, Ortega decided to organize the local populace for the big events of November 20. On the night of November 14 he gathered some loyal followers — nine members of the Navarrete family, eight from the Quiñónez clan, three Zubiates, seven named Juárez and thirty other community stalwarts — and set forth to change lives.[20]

The first item of business was running local Terrazas crony and jefe politico Esequiel Montes out of town. Then the band of rebels turned toward La Junta. Once across the Sierra Grande, their plan was to alert nascent insurrectos in Mezquite, San Juan and the other villages along the rivers, calling for a November 20 attack on Ojinaga. But as Ortega's men passed near Ojinaga they were discovered by federal troops; a skirmish ensued in which several federales were killed. The Mexican revolutions had begun.[21]

People like having data points. They like to know the date, time and place where things happened. There are textbooks that say that the Mexican Revolution of 1910 began on November 18 in Puebla, but we know that shots had already been fired in Ojinaga by then. Of those who accept Toribio Ortega's uprising on the fourteenth as the inception of the revolution, some peg the place as Cuchillo Parado and others focus on the confrontation with federal troops in Ojinaga. The more interesting question, though, is *which* revolution of 1910 was begun by Toribio Ortega.

Mexican history is messy. It is a river of rapids, eddies, subcurrents and undertow. Toribio Ortega may have been involved in the Anti-Reelectionista Party, but keep in mind that the Anti-Reelectionistas were by election day the only alternative to supporting the status quo. Unlike Francisco Madero, Toribio Ortega was not driven by a philosophical commitment to constitutional single-term representative democracy. He didn't disagree with Madero on the point, but a fervor for abstract political science was not why he gathered sixty men in the middle of the night and rode from village to village stirring up insurrection. Neither was Toribio Ortega consumed by the long-standing Mexican conservative-liberal split; at his level, the argument between nationalist centralism versus federalist regionalism boiled down to whether Cuchillo Parado should be oppressed by Mexico's Díaz oligarchy or by Chihuahua's Terrazas oligarchy.

The revolution begun by Toribio Ortega was rooted in his leadership of Cuchillo Parado's agricultural society. Ortega's followers wanted their land back. And because they knew well by whom the land had been taken, they wanted the jefes politicos and jefes municipales and all the other agents of the state and the nation removed. They wanted local autonomy. They wanted the outsiders to go away.

The revolution was not Toribio Ortega's any more than it was Francisco Madero's. It was the same insurrection raised by Victor Ochoa eighteen years earlier. It had belonged to Cholome general Francisco Arroyo, who tried to evict the Presidio del Norte from La Junta in 1759. It had been carried on the shoulders of a native general named Juan Antonio Príncipe, who warned Spanish captain Joseph de Ydoiaga to stay out of La Junta in 1747. It was prosecuted by the mystic native rebel Taagua, who sought to rain stones upon Spanish soldiers in 1684. Its brunt had been felt by friars Acevedo, Zavaleta, Colina, Hinojosa, Osorio, Lipián, Aparicio and all the other Franciscans repeatedly driven from the valley by natives who tired of efforts to change their ways.

La Juntans—and citizens of nearby towns on Mexico's northern frontier—wanted to be left alone, and that desire had become progressively more acute over the centuries.

To make matters worse, the Mexican government had spent seventy-five years neatly stacking social kindling along the border before applying an open flame. Northern Chihuahua was the land of government-sponsored military colonies. Rancheros in La Junta were descendants of tough, brave frontier pioneers who spent decades battling Apaches and Comanches at the behest of the nation. Mexicans on the northern frontier developed military savvy and a habit of going armed—the government even mandated that they arm themselves and taught them to fortify their communities. The last battles with the Apaches had been fought only thirty years earlier. Community elders remembered building fortíns in their fields for protection. They remembered loved ones who died defending their families and their lands. They remembered fighting alongside Joaquín Terrazas to rout Victorio and Arzate. To the military colonists who settled the murderous frontier, the government had promised lands. These were the lands that families were occupying at Vado de Piedra, El Mulato, Ojinaga and San Carlos. These were the lands farmed near Cuchillo Parado by families named Navarrete, Quiñónez, Zubiate, Juárez and Ortega. Now, because the Mexican government never honored its pledge to formally grant lands to the military colonists, the Terrazas oligarchy was declaring their hard-won farms to be *tierras baldíos*—lands where no one held legal title, lands that could be surveyed and usurped. It was the stuff of revolution.[22]

On November 20 Francisco Madero crossed the border into Piedras Negras (then ironically known as Ciudad Porfirio Díaz). To his embarrassment, and despite the premature commitment in La Junta, the remainder of his revolution failed to materialize. With obvious relief, the United States consul there reported that the "night passed without invasion from American side of border line owing to the vigilance of all federal officers, few of whom had any sleep." Gathering his wits and his supporters, Madero returned to San Antonio.[23]

Francisco Madero named Abraham González provisional governor of the state of Chihuahua and gave him the rank of colonel, in charge of the revolutionary army in Chihuahua and Durango. Consulting with revolutionary comrades Francisco "Pancho" Villa and Pascual Orozco, González decided to establish his headquarters somewhere on the international border so that he could import munitions and help finance the revolution with duties on imports and exports. Ciudad Juárez was his first choice—the railroad was an obvious asset—but the Juárez police

146

*The River
Has Never
Divided Us*

had swooped down upon the Anti-Reelectionista organization there and scattered it to the wind. Abraham González chose to site his provisional capital at Ojinaga.[24]

In early December González traveled to La Junta in the company of rebel Colonel José Perfecto Lomelín. The two men met with Toribio Ortega in his camp along the Rio Grande above Ojinaga. González gave Ortega the rank of colonel in the rebel army. Even Ortega recognized that he was as yet an unproven military leader, and the three men agreed that Perfecto should take command of the rebels in La Junta for the time being.[25]

Abraham González and his growing cadre of rebels established their headquarters—the first insurrecto capital of the state of Chihuahua—at El Mulato, across from El Polvo. El Mulato was far enough downstream from Ojinaga to be safe, and the crossing there permitted unofficial commerce across the river.[26]

Concern was mounting on the Texas side of the Rio Grande. The Marfa newspaper reported that on December 8 "U.S. Consul Luther T. Ellsworth [whose normal station was Ciudad Porfirio Díaz] and Immigration Agent Meng left in an auto for the river. Armed Insurrectos are reported all along the river front there. The Diaz people are flocking to the American side." Consul Ellsworth found only one hundred federales defending Ojinaga and concluded that the town would fall as soon as the rebels attacked. "Latest report says that all women and children in Ojinaga have been ordered to come to this side as a fight is hourly anticipated at Ojinaga."[27]

Some of the most reliable observers on the Texas side of the Rio Grande were customs officers—as a practical matter, the only daily law-enforcement presence in the area. They reported exceptionally heavy ammunition sales in local stores and noticed bands of armed men on both sides of the border. Concerned that a rebel attack on Ojinaga might be followed by raids into Texas, Consul Ellsworth ordered two of the customs agents to penetrate the border and scout out the situation. When the agents returned on December 10, they reported more than five hundred rebels poised to engage the federales. The next day Mexico reinforced the garrison at Ojinaga with 120 cavalrymen and ten artillerymen.[28]

A few days later Toribio Ortega led a squad of fifty men upstream to a ranch owned by the Vanagas family, near Vado de Piedra, where his rebels cut telegraph wires running to Ojinaga. Ortega figured that a detachment of federales would be sent out to make repairs, and he planned to wait in ambush. Federal colonel Alberto Dorantes set forth to investigate the situation with 175 soldiers plus a few dozen rurales and armed citizens. The size of the telegraph repair detail suggests that Dorantes had been warned of Ortega's planned ambush. Likewise, Ortega knew that Dorantes was approaching long before he appeared, giving the rebels time to auger into secure positions.[29]

Neither side incurred many casualties in the ensuing fight, but the rebels scored a moral victory. One witness who observed the clash from the Texas side of the river reported that "when the first shots were fired sixty Federals and Countrymen of the force in Ojinaga deserted and left their horses on the American side of the river, and also there ran away the mules of the Ametralladora [machine gunners], and they left cutlasses, blankets and hats on the horses." Frustrated at their loss, "the Federals ransacked and burned [the Vanagas ranch], killing all the pigs, goats and calfs, leaving it in a horrible state." The federales were later reported to "have been offering for sale on the streets of Ojinaga womens apparel taken from the family trunks."[30]

The rebels' success — if it can be called a success — was in no small part due to the poor quality of the soldiers that they faced. As had long been the case, frontier military garrisons included petty criminals who were given a choice of military service or jail. Because there were no more Apaches to pursue, border guards spent most of their time playing cards and drinking. Colonel Dorantes's troops were among the least trained and least qualified of all Mexican soldiers.

After the upstream clash with Dorantes's slovenly forces, the rebels skirted around Ojinaga, passed through San Juan on the Rio Conchos, then headed toward El Mulato. Partway there, near a village called Haciendita, the federales caught up. The rebels counterattacked and drove the federales into retreat. In the confusion of the fight, thirty more federal horses bolted and crossed the Rio Grande into the waiting lariats of the United States Customs Service. The rebels took almost one hundred federal troops prisoner; many of the captives promptly defected to the rebel cause.[31]

Francisco Madero went into hiding after the fiasco of November 20. Abandoning San Antonio, Madero took up temporary residence in New Orleans. Knowing that his revolution would sputter out unless he could reenter Mexico, Madero reviewed his options. Briefed by Abraham González on the rebel successes in La Junta, Madero declared that in Ojinaga "I have an open door." In preparation for his reentry he wrote his wife in San Antonio, telling her to "have my felt hat ironed, assemble my blanket and feather pillow, my cotton khaki clothing and my books, as well as a package with some oatmeal, cooking oil and all that which is most indispensable."[32]

Being in New Orleans, Madero would take a route through San

Antonio to Marfa on the Southern Pacific Railroad, then south by car, carriage or horseback to Presidio and Ojinaga. Though he had not seen his wife in weeks, he cautioned in a December 14 letter to her that he could not risk stepping off the train in San Antonio: "I will be very sad, but it is indispensable that I do not stop on my way to Ojinaga." Madero knew that Abraham González could not take Ojinaga without a fight, but he predicted that "before one month is over we will be masters of the city."

But González had his hands full in La Junta. Though his rebels had rebuffed two attacks, the Mexican Army was demonstrating a complete willingness to engage the insurrectos. It became obvious that the federales intended to take the fight to the rebels' home turf: El Mulato. González and Ortega ordered their men to construct defensive positions. The pueblo's civilian population fled across the river to El Polvo. On December 21 two hundred federales attacked the rebel base. A gaggle of Texas officials and citizens watched from the other side of the river; a stray bullet pierced a child's leg in El Polvo and several rounds fell among the observers. On the Mexican side, seven federales died and another dozen were wounded; one rebel lost his life and seven suffered wounds. The rebel lines held, and the Mexican Army was compelled to turn back to Ojinaga.[33]

It was a victory for the rebels, but a defensive victory that brought them no closer to control of Ojinaga. By the end of December Madero was beginning to wonder whether the town was an open door after all. He began talking about entering Mexico through Coahuila, while waiting to see whether González could turn up the heat in La Junta.[34]

In the first days of 1911, an FBI agent reported that Colonel Perfecto was in El Paso to buy armaments, and that "a band of Mexicans with ninety mules, loaded with arms and ammunition, left Marfa, Texas, to cross the border. . . . Numerous reports have come to Government officers here to the effect that arms and ammunition were being taken in various ways across the border for the use of the revolutionists." Consul Ellsworth picked up a rumor that two rail carloads of weapons and ammunition were on their way to Marfa, thence to El Mulato.[35]

In the first week of January 1911 Mexico reinforced the garrison at Ojinaga with two hundred men under the command of General Gonzalez Luque. His force set up camp in the town plaza, and another 150 men joined them during the next week. In total, there were now about six hundred federales in Ojinaga. General Luque soon reported to President Díaz that rebel Colonel José de la Cruz Sánchez had arrived in La Junta. Sánchez, a bearded and mature ranchero who was widely respected in the region, had assembled a rebel army of some six hundred men from the vicinity of San Carlos. According to Luque, Sánchez had recently been harassing Coyame and was directing the defense of the rebel outpost at Cuchillo Parado. Luque's prime complaint, though, was that Sánchez had been in Texas buying weapons and ammunition under the eyes of the American authorities — a violation, in Luque's opinion, of United States neutrality laws. President Díaz took the matter seriously enough to refer it to Foreign Secretary Enrique Creel, who forwarded it to Mexico's ambassador to the United States in Washington, D.C.[36]

U.S. laws did require neutrality in the conflict, but neutrality was a sensitive and complex topic, fostering ongoing debate about whether it required helping both sides, helping neither side or helping a favored side with a nod and a wink. The policy being applied in theory varied from reality, reality itself varied from place to place and from person to person and policies changed as the revolution evolved.

In Presidio, Consul Ellsworth detected strong support for the rebels, noting that La Juntans were "ardent sympathizers with law breakers generally, but particularly revolutionists and smugglers." Virtually all Hispanics in Presidio and other border towns supported the revolution, with the backing of most Anglos along the river. There were strong commercial motives for maintaining links with rebel forces: Kleinman's store in Presidio and Young Brothers Hardware Company in Shafter were among the merchants doing a booming business in munitions. People in the borderlands understood the insurrecto viewpoint and facilitated their uprising. Sentiments farther north and south differed.[37]

The state of Texas, swayed by influential pro-Díaz sentiments that existed even in Madero's chosen refuge at San Antonio, took a neutral stance that was calculated to disfavor the rebels. When Governor Colquitt issued a proclamation calling for neutrality, it emphasized prohibitions on shipping munitions to Mexico or enlisting supporters in Texas. One of the governor's staffers, accompanied by the Mexican consul to San Antonio, assured Luther Ellsworth that the proclamation would "have a dampening effect on the spirits of the Mexican exiles and Revolutionists now operating in Texas." Colquitt's proclamation did not, however, reflect any consensus of Texans, who, as one newspaper put it, "would do as we damned pleased about it anyway."[38]

United States Consul Luther Ellsworth's attitudes reflected those of the federal government generally. The United States found instability on its borders distasteful. Federal arrest warrants were issued for Francisco Madero and Abraham González. People on the Texas side of the Rio Grande who attempted to cross and join the rebellion were detained. The ability of the United States to enforce these policies was, however, limited—much too limited to control the long border through La Junta. While Consul Ellsworth and the Treasury Department were prohibiting sales of arms to either faction, and while customs agents in Presidio attempted to stem illegal exports, the only reason why Kleinman's store refused to sell ammunition to Ojinaga's jefe politico was that he couldn't pay cash.[39]

Francisco Madero remained in New Orleans, postponing his trip to Ojinaga until the situation settled. Provisional Governor Abraham González traveled to El Paso in early January 1911 to meet with other rebels and review the possibility of using Juárez—instead of Ojinaga—as an entry point for Madero. Concluding that a Madero entry at Juárez was impossible, González returned to La Junta and issued a letter staking out his principles: "free ballot and no reelection of the president and the governors. . . . We stand for fair taxation, diffusion of public instruction, a well paid small army made up of volunteers, instead of culprits and men impressed by force into service on account of their having incurred the displeasure of officers or men influential with the government officers; in short, we stand for a popular government, based on the law, instead of the caprice or will of a man or a gang of men, as has been the case in Mexico for over a third of a century."[40]

Skirmishes between rebels and federales continued in La Junta. In the most significant encounter, insurrectos led by José de la Cruz Sánchez lured two hundred of General Luque's troops into a deep canyon in the foothills of the Sierra Grande, sealed both ends of the defile and commenced an attack on the trapped soldiers. The rebels inflicted savage punishment that was stanched only by the arrival of federal reinforcements from Ojinaga. But despite gaining the advantage in this battle and others, the rebels could not dislodge the garrison at Ojinaga, and La Junta remained contested ground.[41]

Unable to establish enough control over a border point to ensure a safe reentry to Mexico, Francisco Madero returned to San Antonio from New Orleans then, concerned about spies, relocated to Dallas. On February 2 he finally made a move toward the border, but he did it incognito. Shaving his beard, he caught a train to El Paso, hid out there with a friend and summoned his rebel leaders.[42]

The United States harbored growing concerns about the potential for rebel success, fearing that a completed revolution would endanger American lives and businesses in Mexico. There were rumblings about intervention. In February, the United States Army began deploying along the border. A cavalry troop under the command of Captain Andrew Williams departed San Antonio's Fort Sam Houston to patrol up and down the Rio Grande near Presidio.[43]

Neither Governor González nor Colonel Sánchez were in their El Mulato rebel stronghold on February 7, because they were meeting with Francisco Madero in El Paso. General Luque must have known of their absence: his federales chose that day to attack. Toribio Ortega rallied two hundred rebels to oppose a force twice that size. Rumor had it that Ortega was being advised by an American (according to the Marfa newspaper) or Scottish (according to the El Paso newspaper) soldier of fortune named F. S. McCombs.[44]

The outnumbered rebels were determined. Luque could not penetrate their lines, even though reinforcements arrived from Ojinaga. The battle continued into a second day, at the end of which the federal attack collapsed and Luque's soldiers slunk back to their garrison. The insurrectos had successfully defended themselves, and the federal troops were reported to have suffered heavy losses, but the rebels' victory may have been Pyrrhic: the town of El Mulato was, according to one account, "battered to pieces" and Luque had vividly demonstrated that Ojinaga was not going to become the Maderista capital any time soon.[45]

Sánchez and González returned to El Mulato from El Paso. After reviewing the consequences of the fight that had transpired in their absence, they concluded that pitched battles with federales were the wrong strategy; the rebels would adopt a plan of roving guerrilla warfare. Planning to use the sympathetic village of Cuchillo Parado as a forward base, they targeted Coyame for their first attack. On February 14 General Luque (who always seemed to have excellent information about rebel movements) dispatched 250 federales from Ojinaga in pursuit. Leaving the safety of Ojinaga, the soldiers crossed the Sierra Grande and followed a canyon through foothills toward Cuchillo Parado. On the sixteenth about 175 insurrectos attacked as the federales emerged from the foothills. More familiar with the territory, the rebels gradually gained the upper hand, forcing the federales into positions on a small conical hill known as the Cuesta de Peguis. Insurrectos surrounded the hill and began picking off the Mexican soldiers. The battle continued for more than a day before a federal rear guard commanded by Colonel Dorantes arrived from Coyame, forcing the rebels to fight on two fronts simultaneously. Unable to control two fields of battle against superior forces, the insurrectos fell back across the Sierra Grande to their stronghold at El Mulato, suffering only a handful of casualties themselves but leaving more than one hundred dead federales in their wake.[46]

There were local political overtones to the attempt by Ortega and Sánchez to take Coyame. The town was known for holding loyalist sympathies in a region where loyalists were rare. An insurrecto from Cuchillo Parado put it this way: "While Cuchillo Parado distinguishes itself in having liberal ideas and a love of liberty, Coyame has always been a follower of tyrants, despotism and dictators." Sentiments of that type aside, attacking Coyame had the beneficial effect of drawing government troops out of Ojinaga and across the Sierra Grande, putting small federal detachments into vulnerable positions in open country. That was a matter of tactics—changing from conventional warfare to guerrilla operations—but the rebels' strategic goal remained control of Ojinaga, even though it was no longer Madero's open door to Mexico. Ojinaga held the only significant government presence for hundreds of miles, it had the only garrison of federales in northeastern Chihuahua, and its station on the Rio Grande meant that whoever possessed it had few worries about watching their back. The imposing Sierra Grande formed a magnificent defensive perimeter for those who knew its ways. La Junta had food, water, cattle and an international port of entry. It was a perfect enclave for Abraham González's rebel governorship.[47]

The Mexican government understood this—that is why they repeatedly reinforced the garrison at Ojinaga—but they faced a growing array of adversaries. Two hundred Coahuilan rebels settled into El Mulato; another two hundred arrived in San Carlos. An Associated Press correspondent reported in late January that "Outgeneraled and defeated, the forces of Mexican Federal General Luque are divided and cooped up. . . . Rebel General Jose de la Cruz Sanchos, says: 'We could take Ojinaga any time, but we have been able to use our Forces to a better advantage in the open and have no desire to tie them up in a permanent Garrison; however the time is near when we will take it.' "[48]

An unusual quiet descended over the valley. U.S. Cavalry Captain Williams was far upstream of El Mulato, riding along the border near Candelaria (territory that the local paper called "wild and wooly country, inhabited by many thieves, murderers and tough characters") when his men spotted twenty or thirty riders on the other side of the river. Customs officers in Williams's retinue identified the band as one led by Antonio Carrasco, a known horse thief and murderer. Border bandits were opportunists without entrenched political philosophies, but they sometimes joined the political fray. Because it was usually inconvenient for a bandido to pretend loyalty to the oligarchy, most of these misfits oscillated between banditry and rebellion. Such was the case with Carrasco, who had aligned himself with the insurrectos. On the day that Williams spotted him, however, Carrasco seemed more intent on robbing merchants Francisco Perez and Manuel Sánchez, who lived in the little Mexican settlement of San Antonio del Bravo. Carrasco may have been foraging for supplies for rebel troops; as Williams watched, he gathered up horses and cattle, posted a guard at a corn storehouse, then disappeared back downriver.[49]

With the cavalry patrolling the Rio Grande and confident insurrectos prowling the countryside, it wasn't long before the Mexican Army was in fact cooped up in Ojinaga. The confrontation had turned into a siege.[50]

No supplies could reach Ojinaga from Ciudad Chihuahua. General Luque found it difficult to develop a reliable source of provisions from Presidio. Like Kleinman, the other merchants were demanding cash; when Luque had cash, traversing even the short mile of open plain between the town and the river could be dangerous. Luque was not truly short of food, but fresh meat and produce were scarce, animal feed was dwindling and conservation of ammunition was mandatory. A growing bunker mentality led to conflicts between the civilian government and the military command. Ciro Amarillas was removed as jefe municipal and replaced with Viviano Jiménez. Tempers grew short.[51]

The siege of Ojinaga formally began on March 12, when six hundred rebels began peppering the town with long-range rifle fire. Shorter-range, more intense attacks ensued near the river crossing. There were reports that "from all directions [rebel] reinforcements are marching to Ojinaga. White-haired men with old smooth-bore guns they used in fighting Maximilian are marching in the ranks with their sons and grandsons." Forty Yaqui natives enlisted in the rebel cause, promising that one hundred more would join.[52]

Toribio Ortega's rebels assaulted federal forces at the riverside customhouse on March 15 and took control of the position. Rebels and government forces both built entrenched positions nearby, making it impossible for either side to use the ford except under a hail of gunfire. With the cooperation of U.S. customs agents, General Luque opened a second ford farther upstream, in the shadow of Ojinaga's protection and guarded by entrenched federal forces. The rebels, operating from the far side of the Rio Conchos, established flanking positions, then crossed the Conchos to put the new ford in a better field of fire, but still Luque used it to provision his garrison.[53]

Rebel General Sánchez ordered sometimes-bandido Antonio Carrasco to seize the new crossing. Over a period of days Carrasco dutifully reported to Sánchez that he was in control of the situation, but at heart Carrasco was a scoundrel, not a rebel, and he found it more profitable to double-cross Sánchez and warn Ojinaga's General Luque, giving him time to beef up his defenses at the new ford. The subterfuge could not hold up forever; in a few days Carrasco fled the rebel camp with a handful of followers, revealing his duplicity.[54]

Carrasco's treachery infuriated General Sánchez. He reported the incident to rebel President Madero, who issued a death warrant for Carrasco. A squad of Sánchez's men chased Carrasco down, brought him back to Sánchez's camp and placed him before a firing squad. Cigarette dangling from his lips, the defiant Carrasco told the firing squad to aim for his heart. His executioners had no objection to the suggestion.[55]

The insurrectos established a command post at the old pueblo of San Francisco, on the high mesa across the Rio Conchos from Ojinaga. Rebel forces began creeping closer to the town, but artillery barrages kept them at bay. A gap opened in rebel lines to the north. Seventy federales slipped across the Rio Grande, rode up the Texas side of the river, crossed back into Mexico and scouted the rear of the rebel deployment. It looked like a promising point of attack. The federales returned to Texas and rode downstream to the ford that they had used earlier, but they were met by Captain Williams, who cautioned them that no attacks would be launched using American soil.[56]

As rebels continued to move toward Ojinaga and federales continued to resist their approach, people in Presidio began standing on rooftops to watch the action across the river. An enterprising Presidian erected a grandstand and charged entrance fees to battle observers. Stray bullets would sometimes fall around town; after a while it began to look like the federales were taking deliberate aim at Presidians and U.S. soldiers. The danger of being wounded didn't quell the circus atmosphere that was taking over the town. Soon it was more than just atmosphere—a circus did in fact come to Presidio and put on a show. The federales took potshots at the tents from across the Rio Grande.[57]

The ranks of the insurrectos continued to grow. Armed women— soldaderas—fought alongside the men. Soldiers of fortune from the United States (including a man nicknamed "Dynamite Slim") aided the rebels. A machine gun brought with the mercenaries intensified the fire that could be brought to bear on Ojinaga. The hired guns also hauled in two artillery pieces. One of them, known as the "Blue Whistler," had been stolen from a display in front of the El Paso city hall. It only managed to whistle out two rounds before becoming unusable, perhaps because it had spent three weeks buried in an El Paso back yard between its theft and its return to service.[58]

Elsewhere, Madero's rebel army exerted pressure on Ciudad Chihuahua, then turned to attack Juárez. Maderista generals Pascual Orozco and Pancho Villa successfully challenged federal troops throughout the north. The rebellion spread to the states of Coahuila, Guerrero, Morelos, Puebla, Sinaloa, Sonora, Veracruz and Zacatecas.[59]

Ojinaga remained under siege. In April one thousand Mexican soldiers commanded by General Antonio Rábago boarded the Kansas City, Mexico & Orient in Ciudad Chihuahua and headed north. It was at about that time that Madero's forces turned toward Juárez, though, and the Díaz government redirected Rábago's troops to that battle. Ten days later a somewhat smaller column of infantry and cavalry reached Cuchillo Parado under the command of veteran Mexican general Manuel Gordillo y Escudero. Sixty rebels harassed the federales into immobility for a few hours, but withdrew. The next day Colonels Ortega and Sánchez attacked. After a few hours of fighting, Sánchez fell back toward Ojinaga with two hundred rebels, leaving Ortega to maintain pressure on the federal troops.[60]

General Gordillo's aim was to rout the rebel stronghold at El Mulato, then to turn north and relieve Ojinaga. To do so, he angled east from Cuchillo Parado to enter La Junta in its lower stretches. At the town of La Mula, still on the far side of the mountains from La Junta, Sánchez rejoined Ortega, and their combined forces struck again. The rebels held the high ground, but a squad of loyalist Zaque natives climbed the mountain behind the rebels and attacked from the rear. The battle lasted all day; the insurrectos were forced to fall back across the cordillera to El Mulato with Gordillo close behind. The rebels who were still positioned around Ojinaga abandoned their stations and fell back to El Mulato, preparing for Gordillo's strike.[61]

But Gordillo did not attack El Mulato. Instead, after crossing the Sierra Grande he turned upriver and marched unopposed into Ojinaga on the morning of May 2, 1911. The siege was broken. Relieved citizens cheered. General Luque's soldiers greeted their compatriots with warm embraces.[62]

On May 6 Gordillo returned his attention to El Mulato, overrunning rebel positions and scattering La Junta's insurrectos into the hills. Gordillo may have been gaining the upper hand, but the war was not going as well for Mexican forces elsewhere. Generals Pascual Orozco and Pancho Villa took Ciudad Juárez on May 10, allowing Madero to finally return to his homeland. Encouraged by the capture of Juárez, insurrectos across Mexico redoubled their attacks. Federales began deserting the Mexican Army.[63]

Isolated in Ojinaga, Generals Gordillo and Luque recognized the importance of the fall of Juárez. They were acutely aware that Madero's rebellion was sweeping Mexico; alone on the border, they could easily become stranded in a land entirely dominated by rebels. On May 19 — just more than two weeks after Gordillo arrived — the Ojinaga garrison packed up and fled to Ciudad Chihuahua. They had correctly anticipated events; under pressure from all sides, Porfirio Díaz accepted peace terms on May 22 and resigned three days later.[64]

Toribio Ortega and José Sánchez regrouped their battered armies and rode into Ojinaga. And then there was a quintessentially La Juntan event: hundreds of Porfirista loyalists in Ojinaga fled en masse to Presidio; as they straggled down the riverbank and across the Rio Grande, they were passed by flocks of Madero's supporters leaving Presidio to reclaim their homes and businesses in Ojinaga.[65]

Pascual Orozco was only twenty-nine when Porfirio Díaz resigned the presidency. From Guerrero in western Chihuahua, Orozco rose through Madero's antireelectionist movement to become one of the rebellion's most prominent and popular military leaders. More than six feet tall and weighing 180 pounds, he was an unusually intimidating physical presence. His horse skills and marksmanship made him the kind of man that Chihuahuans naturally followed.[1]

Differences arose between Madero and Orozco during the final stages of the 1910–1911 revolution because Madero failed to include the military in the post-Díaz redistribution of power. The failure was entirely intentional: Madero prophetically saw rebel military leaders as a threat to his own position.[2]

Orozco and

Huerta

Orozco had a loyal following of personal political supporters; with new presidential elections scheduled, he was favored by more than one faction as a candidate to oppose Madero. The campaign got rough. By early 1912, Pascual Orozco was the leader of a Chihuahuan counterrevolution that sought to overthrow the revolutionary Madero presidency. The mixed-bag Orozquista movement was backed by the Terrazas oligarchy, possessed strong anarchist overtones and opposed a concurrent Zapatista counterrevolution.[3]

Orozco's rebels took Juárez and a few small Chihuahuan towns. They trounced Pancho Villa's forces outside Ciudad Chihuahua. Orozco announced his intent to march on Mexico City. Ever protective of the status quo, even a recently established status quo, the United States imposed an arms embargo and closed the border at Juárez. Orozco occupied Parral. Then a column of federal troops arrived and pushed Orozco into the hills above Rellano. The Orozquistas pushed back (at one point using an unmanned locomotive loaded with dynamite) and defeated the federales. Feeling threatened, former-rebel-now-President Madero placed experienced general Victoriano Huerta in charge of the anti-Orozco campaign. On April 10 Huerta began a formidable effort with well-trained soldiers. He put Orozco on the run, defeating him at Conejos, Rellano and Ciudad Juárez. Like Madero's rebels had done a year before, Orozco began avoiding head-to-head clashes of massed soldiers, splitting his army into smaller units and making guerrilla strikes across northern Chihuahua.[4]

The new Madero government had not reinstalled a garrison of federales or rurales in Ojinaga, but venerable Colonel José de la Cruz
Sánchez commanded a few hundred volunteers there, as did Colonel
Toribio Ortega in Cuchillo Parado. (Like Sánchez and Ortega, the volunteers were former Maderista rebels, transformed into government
loyalists by the success of their revolution.) Understandably, Sánchez
and Ortega became jumpy when Pascual Orozco's insurrectos began
prowling in their vicinity.[5]

Five hundred Orozquistas assembled at Coyame, on the other side
of the Rio Conchos from Cuchillo Parado. Toribio Ortega was relieved
to discover that the rebels were afraid to ford the rushing river. Their
leader couldn't force them to cross, because they were notably undisciplined and insubordinate, but there was a risk that they would go back
upriver to Falomir, cross a bridge there and march down the right bank
to Cuchillo Parado and Ojinaga.[6]

Orozco's hot-blooded rebels fired into Cuchillo Parado from across
the river. This raised an alarm as far away as Ojinaga, but the opinion
of the Mexican consul in Marfa, Salvador Martinez del Toro, was that
the real risk was to small villages with no protection, not towns like
Cuchillo Parado and Ojinaga where local militias were on guard.[7]

If there was anything that gave Consul del Toro concern about the
safety of Ojinaga, it was the behavior of Colonel Sánchez, who seemed
to be engaged in unorthodox transactions with known gunrunner J. L.
Kleinman of Presidio. The rifles carried by Mexican soldiers and provided to volunteers were .30-40 caliber, and the American authorities
had approved exports of .30-40 ammunition to Ojinaga, but a boatload
of ammo taken across the river by Kleinman turned out to be Winchester .44-caliber cartridges. Customs officers confiscated the odd-
sized ammunition. Del Toro wondered whose guns the cartridges were
meant for; he made inquiries in El Paso and Mexico City about the
details of arms and munitions ordered by Sánchez. Checking with the
customs agents in Presidio, del Toro learned that Kleinman had applied
for permits to export eight hundred rifles and machine guns and a million cartridges for the account of the Mexican government, and that
those munitions were already stored in Kleinman's warehouse. Asking
around, del Toro found rumors in Presidio and Ojinaga that Kleinman
and Sánchez were up to something. There were stories of arms and
ammunition crossing the river at night. According to the grapevine,
if Orozco's rebels marched on Ojinaga there would be no resistance,
allowing them to capture all the armaments in the town. Who were
Sánchez and Kleinman arming?[8]

In August, after driving Orozco out of Ciudad Juárez, General Victoriano Huerta bragged about the immense strength of his military machine. According to Huerta, he held the power to dethrone Madero and put Orozco in his place, not that he would do such a thing. This was not the sort of idle chat that Madero wanted to hear; the president's wrath grew when Huerta was unable to account for a million pesos from the military budget. Madero removed General Huerta and disbanded his Division of the North. In its stead he created the Second Military Zone, run by old-line Díaz federal army officers—men who were not particularly loyal to Madero but who wanted to trounce someone (Orozco was as good a candidate as any) to make up for their defeat in the revolution of 1910. Huerta was offended by his removal. He began to scheme.[9]

As August turned to September, Orozco's rebels closed in on Ojinaga. Fifty La Juntans returned from Cuchillo Parado, where they had been helping Toribio Ortega fight the Orozquistas. They reported that Ortega had been wounded, and that the enemy had attacked in swarms. Colonel Sánchez sent out scouts; that night the men returned, having beaten a hasty retreat after a firefight with a rebel force that they generously estimated at four thousand men. Sánchez conferred with municipal officials, then announced that Ojinaga would be evacuated and that he would lead his men to confront the enemy. In a panic, the citizenry gathered their belongings and fled to Presidio. On Sánchez's orders, Ojinaga's twenty-three mounted policemen rode for safety to Ciudad Juárez; fifteen foot patrolmen threw their weapons into the Rio Grande and fled to Presidio.[10]

Informers brought word that Pascual Orozco was at the village of San Antonio del Bravo (across from Candelaria) with seven hundred men; his father, Pascual Orozco Sr., commanded six hundred at Cuesta del Gato, near Cuchillo Parado; other rebel leaders had assembled seven hundred more insurrectos on the outskirts of La Junta. Sánchez prudently did not take his few hundred irregulars to confront that many rebels. Instead, he retreated down the Rio Grande to familiar redoubts in the hills above El Mulato. On September 4 El Paso's morning newspaper reported Ojinaga's evacuation as a capture by Pascual Orozco, Sr., but in fact the town was empty, up for grabs.[11]

Preparations stirred on the Presidio side of the Rio Grande. Customs agents, United States marshals and Texas Rangers congregated. U.S. cavalry troops spread out along the border. Five hundred refugees came across the river to Presidio. Mexican consul del Toro arrived from Marfa, still concerned about Colonel Sánchez's loyalties. U.S. marshals investigating arms traffic intimated that Kleinman was aiding the rebels. A municipal official from Ojinaga admitted to del Toro that

Sánchez sometimes acted inexplicably, but the Mexican official felt that his actions were always in the best interests of the government.[12]

After rallying their spirits in the field for a few days, Sánchez and his men returned to the still unclaimed Ojinaga. On September 9 Orozco's rebels opened fire on the town. Sánchez excused himself from the scene, saying that he had to go to Presidio to pick up some equipment. Most of the other officials in Ojinaga followed suit, leaving the town's defense to about twenty-five armed irregulars, most of them young. The rebels attacked on the next day, but were repulsed. Fighting was intermittent on the eleventh, but when the rebels assaulted the town that night the defenders ran out of ammunition—the city's leaders had taken what they could to Presidio and had hidden the remainder.[13]

Consul del Toro found Colonel Sánchez and several other Ojinaga officials in Presidio. They seemed oddly relaxed. What, del Toro asked, was Sánchez doing on the Texas side of the river? Sánchez replied that because of the shortage of munitions in Ojinaga he had crossed the Rio Grande to resupply and would be returning to the front. Del Toro protested that a shipment of 25,000 cartridges had reached Presidio for export to Ojinaga only a month before—what happened to all that ammunition? Sánchez explained that the export paperwork was incomplete and thus the cartridges were still in Kleinman's warehouse. Sánchez appeared in no hurry to return to Mexico, though even Kleinman, surely a devotee of situational ethics, urged Sánchez to "return, Sir—you're covering yourself with shame."[14]

Three hundred rebels invaded Ojinaga. Once they secured the town, more rebels followed. In total, about seven hundred Orozquistas arrived, but many of them were wounded or unarmed. There were the usual executions of resisters and the usual murders of innocent old men. The rebels may have taken Ojinaga easily (thanks to the lack of resistance from Sánchez), but they were hardly a conquering army. They were on the run; government troops led by General Trucy Aubert and supplemented by Toribio Ortega's men were in hot pursuit. Weary rebels threw down their rifles and swam the Rio Grande. United States officials did their best to gather them up as they came ashore, deciding how to dispose of them on a case-by-case basis. Consul del Toro alerted the U.S. officers that the Orozcos *padre y hijo* were probably in Ojinaga and asked them to detain the rebel leaders if they attempted to cross into Texas.[15]

Watchfulness paid off. The United States Army captured nine men who crossed the Rio Grande in a boat and were attempting to hide. Among their number was Pascual Orozco Sr. A federal grand jury in El Paso had indicted the Orozcos for Neutrality Act violations in April;

the army passed the elder Orozco to a U.S. deputy marshal in Presidio, who arranged transportation to El Paso.[16]

The junior Orozco was more fortunate. Though reportedly wounded in the battle, he escaped across the river and made his way to St. Louis, then Los Angeles, leaving his followers to carry on a lingering guerrilla campaign without him.[17]

On September 15 federal colonel Manuel Landa, leading 350 of General Aubert's troops, attacked Ojinaga. The Orozquistas quickly collapsed and fled, permitting Aubert to peacefully occupy the town with one thousand cavalry the next day. The few remaining residents reported that the rebels had seized large quantities of arms and ammunition during their stay—the munitions bought, cached and left behind by Colonel Sánchez. Witnesses told of rebels abandoning their battered carbines and replacing them with new rifles from Sánchez's supplies; others said that the rebels had made off with more than fifteen thousand rounds of ammunition. Consul del Toro concluded that "it is perfectly certain that the defensive tools given to José de la Cruz Sánchez by the federal government were badly misused, this being the principal reason why the Orozquistas decided to attack Ojinaga."[18]

Between the battering that Ojinaga had taken in early 1911 and its bruising in 1912, the town was in desperate straits. Del Toro concluded that "all of Ojinaga is completely in ruins, and the pueblo needs a complete reconstruction." When a thunderstorm struck on the night after the rebels took Ojinaga, homeless families sought shelter under a few miserable trees. The suffering of the populace was considerable.[19]

Despite Pascual Orozco's exile, anti-Madero rebel bands continued their raids across northern Chihuahua through 1912 and into early 1913. Three hundred pro-Madero federal soldiers commanded by Colonel Landa remained in Ojinaga to protect the town, supplemented by volunteers under the durable (if not entirely reliable) Colonel Sánchez. The situation remained troubled. Government was in chaos. Municipal president Cipriano Márquez Aguirre took office through a rigged election and attempted to resume the old pattern of abusing the peasantry—imposing illegal taxes, restricting civil rights, executing suspected rebels and ignoring crimes. Only Colonel Landa's presence maintained a semblance of authority and responsibility in the town.[20]

Then, in early December, the government ordered Landa to close the Ojinaga garrison and report for duty elsewhere. In Marfa, Consul del Toro sounded the alarm: "The absence of a military commander in Ojinaga is dangerous. . . . After the upheavals that the frontier region, with Ojinaga at its center, suffered from the invasion of rebel forces, the confidence that was reborn there will disappear immediately when the population of Ojinaga realizes that the federal garrison is going to be closed." Del Toro predicted that the rebels who roamed the countryside would increase their incursions and that Sánchez's volunteers wouldn't be able to resist their attacks. Besides, the Sánchez volunteers were loyal to Sánchez, not the government, making it difficult to predict their reaction to a rebel attack — as del Toro had learned just three months earlier.[21]

Del Toro's concerns went unheeded. Perhaps that was because Orozco enjoyed military victories in early 1913, threatening Ciudad Juárez and Ciudad Chihuahua; the federal troops in Ojinaga may have been needed elsewhere. But there may have been something else afoot. Decommissioned but still influential, former general Victoriano Huerta was talking to the army and others about Madero's future. The secret military-based anti-Madero movement knew that any enemy of Madero's was a friend of theirs. Orozco's rebel army might prove useful; better to keep it around for a while.[22]

Madero attempted to negotiate a peace with Orozco, but failed. Orozco returned to the front in Chihuahua, and his counterrevolution flared larger across northern Mexico. Powerful business interests from the United States grew disillusioned with Madero; the conservative days of Díaz had served their interests better. United States Ambassador Henry Lane Wilson began pulling strings. A military coup was launched in Mexico City. Armies battled in the streets for ten days. Madero, unsure of who to trust, turned to his old friend Victoriano Huerta, restoring his rank and putting him in charge of the nation's defense. Facilitated by Ambassador Wilson, Huerta sat down with the reactionary army generals and cut a duplicitous deal. Madero was arrested by his own army. Huerta assumed the presidency on February 18, 1913, and had Madero executed three days later.[23]

Now everyone had to choose up sides again. Huerta and the reactionary (originally pro-Díaz) federal army were aligned. Most state governments attorned to the new power structure but not, of course, Chihuahua. Governor Abraham González, a staunch Maderista, refused to recognize the new federal government. Maderistas believed in democracy; in González's view, Huerta's coup was unconstitutional. Huerta had González arrested, murdered and replaced by a pro-Huerta military governor, General Salvador Mercado. In El Paso, Pancho Villa, who had been largely sidelined since a run-in with Huerta that resulted in Villa's brief imprisonment, took a vigorous Constitutionalist (anti-Huerta) stand, crossed the river to Juárez and rallied his troops. In Cuchillo Parado, the ever-loyal (or ever-anti-oligarch) Toribio Ortega joined the Constitutionalist movement. In Ojinaga, the ambiguous

Colonel José de la Cruz Sánchez was an unknown quantity: he commanded the remaining garrison of fifty men at Ojinaga, which was presumptively a federal, thus Huertista, presence, but his loyalties were local, not national. Somewhere in the deserts of northern Mexico, Pascual Orozco remained devoutly pro-Orozco, but he soon reconciled with Huerta, based on shared anti-Maderista, anti-Constitutionalist sentiments.[24]

Which of these factions controlled La Junta? The federal army, which had changed from pro-Díaz to uncomfortably pro-Madero to warily pro-Huerta, no longer manned its Ojinaga post. Sánchez's fifty volunteers were a visible paramilitary presence, but their loyalty was to their town and to Sánchez, uncomplicated by larger agendas. Toribio Ortega's Constitutionalist influence still extended over the Sierra Grande from Cuchillo Parado; his consistently local and regional viewpoints were not at odds with those of Sánchez's volunteers in Ojinaga. Coyame traditionally harbored centralist and oligarchic tendencies, but Orozco's rebels had left town. In effect, La Junta was unclaimed.

Constitutionalist rebel activity in central and northwest Chihuahua cut off Ojinaga from Ciudad Chihuahua; the only way for the government to attend to its interests there was to take the train through Ciudad Juárez and El Paso to Marfa and via roads from there to Presidio and Ojinaga. Huerta's government sent a Captain Ortiz to Presidio with orders to contact Sánchez and direct him to come to Ciudad Chihuahua (by train from Marfa) for meetings regarding reimbursement of expenses that he had incurred. It is not clear whether these were expenses that Sánchez had incurred working for the Madero government (as Madero's consul del Toro thought Sánchez should have been doing) or expenses incurred secretly working for Orozco's counterrevolution (as del Toro suspected Sánchez was doing). Sánchez was also supposed to talk to former comrade-in-arms Toribio Ortega and ask him to come to Ciudad Chihuahua for peace negotiations, giving the restive Ortega whatever guarantees he might require to ensure his safety.[25]

Consul del Toro had been ejected from his office in the Huertista takeover. When Captain Ortiz found things unexpectedly delicate in Ojinaga, he could only get in contact with Avilés Licéaga, the resident consulate manager in Marfa. Licéaga hurried to Presidio, where he found Ortiz, whom the United States Army would not permit to cross the river into Ojinaga lest it be construed as a violation of the Neutrality Act. As it turned out, it wasn't necessary to go to Ojinaga to meet with the appropriate municipal officials — because of a rumor that Toribio Ortega was going to take Ojinaga, all of the government representatives fled to Presidio, bringing along the town's funds and documents as well as its small arsenal. The U.S. authorities politely impounded the weapons, letting the Ojinagans know that they could have them back if and when they returned to Mexico. The municipal representatives that Ortiz and Licéaga talked to were willing to work for the Huerta government, but not until Ojinaga was secure.[26]

Also in Presidio was the good Colonel Sánchez, who was in a candid mood: he wasn't going to fight Ortega, he wasn't returning to Ojinaga, and he wasn't going to command troops. As he was getting up in years, he had decided to become a private citizen—and to hell with revolutions. Ortiz and Licéaga tried to talk Sánchez into making pretense of leading his volunteers to defend Ojinaga—just put on a show, even if you don't ever confront Ortega—but Sánchez would have none of it. He was finished. Licéaga, feeling a bit sarcastic, referred to Sánchez not as the Jefe de Militia or the Jefe de Voluntarios, but as the Jefe Accidental.[27]

Checking around, Licéaga learned that a teacher from Ojinaga named María Gómez Gutiérrez had been going around pueblos in La Junta stirring up support for Ortega's Constitutionalists. In the absence of a federal presence, the Constitutionalists were winning the propaganda war, and they were doing it with rebels in skirts.[28]

Ortiz and Licéaga found fifteen neutral men who weren't identified with either the Huertistas or the Constitutionalists, gave each of them a gun and sent them back to Ojinaga to maintain some semblance of order, protecting shopkeepers and citizens. After that there wasn't much to do except watch as Toribio Ortega and his men appeared on the evening of March 23, 1913, discharged their weapons a few times for effect and took over Ojinaga unopposed. Licéaga sent a telegram to his superiors at the Ministry of External Relations and to Chihuahua's military governor urging the government to send soldiers to retake Ojinaga.[29]

Ortega held Ojinaga for the only reason that anyone would hold what was surely by then a moonscape. He collected customs duties and smuggled arms into Mexico from the United States. His possession of Ojinaga went largely unchallenged; during the early months of 1913, Huerta's government controlled only a few towns in Chihuahua and lacked the strength to penetrate the rebel territory between Ciudad Chihuahua and Ojinaga.

Huerta's foes were not united; at first the Constitutionalist rebellion had many leaders. Not long after taking Ojinaga, Ortega—whose vision remained local and regional, not national—added his five hundred fighters to Pancho Villa's army, making it the strongest Constitutionalist force. Leaders of other disparate rebel bands gradually coalesced around Villa, thrusting the revolution into yet another phase.[30]

To get our bearings, let us briefly review Ojinaga's revolutionary history. In 1910 a newly militant Toribio Ortega skirmished with dictator Porfirio Díaz's federales near La Junta, but did not take the town. Because Francisco Madero wanted to reenter Mexico through Ojinaga, and because Abraham González wanted the town for his revolutionary capital, Ortega and Perfecto laid siege to the federal garrison there. The federales successfully broke the siege with the assistance of General Gordillo, only to desert Ojinaga, allowing Ortega and José de la Cruz Sánchez to occupy the town. Once Madero took power, Pascual Orozco and his ragtag 1912 counterrevolutionaries seized Ojinaga over the mild opposition of the ambiguous Sánchez. Toribio Ortega and federal colonel Manuel Landa almost immediately took Ojinaga back again for Madero. Landa remained in Ojinaga, heading the federal garrison there, but he was ultimately ordered to abandon the post, leaving it under the unreliable protection of Sánchez. When Orozco's counter-revolution lagged, then was eclipsed by Huerta's betrayal of Madero in 1913, local firebrand Ortega rose against the new Huerta central government, seizing La Junta for the post-Madero Constitutionalists. Sánchez sidelined himself in that change of possession.

It is difficult to slot José de la Cruz Sánchez. Taking everything into account, he appears to have been a local stalwart and a realist who assumed a small command out of a sense of obligation. He sought to protect the people of La Junta and didn't see any purpose in getting his band of La Juntans killed trying to protect themselves. When his volunteers were adequate to meet a challenge, they rode forth. When they were overmatched, they hid out. We lack the facts to make a fair judgment about his transactions with Kleinman. He may have been arming rebels — Orozquistas at that moment. Believing that requires believing that Sánchez was not a Madero loyalist but an apolitical local opportunist, which is possible. We prefer to conclude that he was spreading arms among the local rancheros and campesinos so that they could better resist the outside forces that were using La Junta as their battlefield. That seems more consistent with his local perspective and his distaste for unnecessary personal risk. Sánchez just doesn't come across as the gunrunner type.

Toribio Ortega is much easier to diagnose. At the risk of being overly dramatic about it, Toribio Ortega fought for the rights of the poor, disadvantaged and dispossessed — plain and simple. He fought for rancheros and campesinos against oligarchs, hacendados and dictators. He had no national agenda; he barely had a regional agenda. He was a Madderista because Madero stood for representative democracy and constitutional order, which in Ortega's eyes meant that Madero stood for a fair shake. He wanted his people's land returned. He wanted an end to government oppression. He wanted to be left alone. Toribio Ortega, as much as any figure of the time, exemplifies the root cause of the Mexican revolutions that began in 1910.

Despite the amount of time that Ortega spent fighting battles in La Junta, and despite the fact that he was a local-interests advocate first and foremost, it should not surprise us that Ortega was not, strictly speaking, a La Juntan. Nor should it surprise us that the same is true of José de la Cruz Sánchez, a man from San Carlos who spent almost a decade fighting over La Junta in a perfectly baffling way. For hundreds of years, native rebellions in La Junta had been catalyzed by people from the valley's penumbra, where, for some reason, flash points were lower. When someone told priests or soldiers to get out of the valley, the person doing the talking was usually a Chiso, Cholome or Apache, not an agricultural Tecolote, Mezquite or Tapacolme. Even La Junta's more peaceful leaders sometimes were not true La Juntans—a highly nomadic seventeenth-century Jumano named Juan Sabeata being the perfect example. Historically, the peaceful, agricultural La Juntans had to be stirred up by an outsider.

Pancho Villa led the military thrust of the Chihuahuan Constitutionalist revolution. Venustiano Carranza, former governor of Coahuila, exercised national political oversight of the struggle. Carranza favored Manuel Chao for the rebel governorship of Chihuahua. Chao had once competed with Villa for Chihuahuan military leadership. Villa disliked Chao, but tried to respect Carranza's opinions while asserting that it was the right of a state's liberators, not the national political movement, to appoint governors. This created friction between Carranza and Villa.

Pancho Villa

The problem was not a lust for political power on Villa's part. He was a peon and a rebel and was comfortable in his skin. "I am a fighter, not a statesman," Villa told a journalist. "I am not educated enough to be President. I only learned to read and write two years ago. How could I, who never went to school, hope to be able to talk with the foreign ambassadors and the cultivated gentlemen of the Congress? It would be bad for Mexico if an uneducated man were to be President. . . . There is only one order of my Jefe [Carranza] which I would refuse to obey—if he would command me to be a President or a Governor."[1]

Just as there was Carranza-Villa-Chao friction within the Constitutionalists, so was there a schism within the Huertistas. Pascual Orozco's rebels were noticeably more political, aggressive and unruly than the federales, and they generally enjoyed greater success on the battlefield. Over many months of difficult guerrilla warfare, the Orozquistas distilled themselves into a core faction of "Colorados," named for the red flags they carried and the red ribbons that they wore in their lapels or on their hats. Colorados traced themselves to the anarchist elements of the original Orozco coalition. The terms *Orozquista* and *Colorado* became interchangeable in northern Chihuahua, and the line between guerrilla warfare and banditry sometimes blurred. The scrappy Colorados felt that the federal troops led by General Salvador Mercado lacked a fighting spirit.

Pancho Villa defeated federal forces at Ciudad Juárez and Tierra Blanca. The federales fell back to Ciudad Chihuahua and were reinforced by Orozco's Colorados. The capital was under strain; though rebel attacks had not begun, communications and supply routes had been cut off and the city was becoming anxious. The army had not received its payroll in months, and the soldiers were restless. The relationship between the federales and the Colorados remained tenuous: Mercado, as commander of the federal Second Military Zone and military governor of Chihuahua, was Orozco's superior, which did not sit well with the self-centered and independent rebel. When Mercado openly considered abandoning the state capital to Villa's Constitutionalists in late November 1913, Orozco's blood boiled. Mercado and Orozco argued. Mercado—whom one observer described as "a fat, pathetic, worried, undecided little man"—held his ground. Or perhaps we should say that he refused to hold his ground, insisting on evacuating to Ojinaga.[2]

The military pretense for flight to Ojinaga was that Chihuahua's federal forces could mass there and wait for a Huertista push from the south, catching Villa's Constitutionalists in a pincer. On a grittier level, Mercado was reluctant to rely on the Orozquistas for loyal and obedient support in defense of the capital.[3]

Chihuahua's merchants and wealthy citizens begged the army to stay. Those with property that could never be moved out of the Constitutionalist rebels' reach even offered to fund their defense—but to no avail. A minimal garrison of two hundred men remained behind to maintain order, but fled after a few days. Local opinion held General Mercado to be a coward; citizens speculated about whether he managed to pocket the state's treasury on his way out of town.[4]

Pancho Villa's reputation pushed many civilians to abandon Ciudad Chihuahua. The capital was the bastion of the oligarchy, and Villa was unambiguous about his antipathy toward the ruling class and their supporters. His detractors painted him as a man prone to murder and pillage. Even his admirers admitted that he had a temper that sometimes exploded in violence. As he took possession of Ciudad Chihuahua, the *New York Times* described him this way: "Gen. Villa, who now assumes military command of all the North, . . . entered the revolution five months ago with only a borrowed revolver. He is a former bandit, and for twenty years under Díaz was sought as an outlaw." Bandit, outlaw or revolutionary, one thing is certain: when Villa's forces won a battle, they lined up all the Colorados and shot them, because they were peons and good peons did not fight against the cause of liberty. Then they lined up all the federal officers and shot them, because they were educated men and should have known better than to oppose freedom. Only the federal enlisted men, who were seen as ignorant conscripts fighting for their fatherland, were allowed to survive.[5]

It was not the military merits of Ojinaga that prompted Mercado and Orozco to move their armies there. They moved because Ojinaga was a better place—almost the last place—to escape Pancho Villa. Understanding that motivation, United States Army troops, customs agents and marshals patrolled the Rio Grande.[6]

From November 27 to 30, 1913, the Kansas City, Mexico & Orient Railroad carried hundreds of civilians and thousands of troops from Ciudad Chihuahua to Falomir, where they disembarked for the remainder of the trip to Ojinaga. Soldiers' families evacuated alongside them. Long lines of desperate people struggled along the Rio Conchos. Some were on foot; some rode horses or mules; a few had wagons or carriages. There were men, women, children, livestock and chickens. People carried their belongings on their backs, or in their hands. As cold weather, short rations and scarcity of water took their toll, the caravan slowed to a pace of ten to fifteen miles per day and stretched to dozens of miles in length.[7]

A garrison of five hundred Constitutionalist troops under the command of Colonel Emilio Chivara protected Ojinaga. Chivara and Villa both realized that Chivara's unit was far too small to confront the federal army headed his direction. Villa ordered Chivara to abandon Ojinaga at the first sign of the federal approach. Residents began packing their belongings yet again.[8]

Among the last citizens to evacuate Ojinaga was María Gómez Gutiérrez, whom we last saw stirring up support for Toribio Ortega when he occupied the town without resistance in the early months of the Constitutionalist movement. The *El Paso Morning Times* reported that "Gutiérrez . . . put on a khaki suit, three belts of cartridges, took a rifle and a six-shooter and joined her brother with the rebel troops, notwithstanding the fact that they expected to fight their way out."[9]

American officials in Presidio waited for Mexican travelers to arrive. Oddly, the first caravan to reach Ojinaga was from Parral, not Ciudad Chihuahua, and was not under federal control. Sixteen wagons, drawn by sixteen mules apiece, followed by a remuda of another two hundred mules, appeared with US$740,000 in silver bullion produced by two American-financed mines. When the silver left Parral, its guard of 150 men kept watch against bandits and roving Constitutionalists; halfway to Ojinaga they learned that the federal army was on the move and they realized that Mercado and Orozco were just as likely to confiscate their bullion as any rebel or bandido. They were relieved to reach the relative safety of the United States. The silver kept going to Marfa, where it was loaded on the Southern Pacific and sent to New York.[10]

The first wave of refugees from Ciudad Chihuahua brought Colorado general José Ines Salazar and his advance guard. Constitutionalist colonel Chivara was nowhere to be found. Neither were any of the citizens of Ojinaga, who had abandoned the city to the federales. One of

Salazar's first official acts was to establish a customhouse and collect duties on imports from Presidio.[11]

The next wave of evacuees were members of the ruling class—among them, families named Terrazas, Creel, Escobar, Cuilty and Falomir. Luis Terrazas traveled by automobile; though he left Ciudad Chihuahua a couple of days after the army, he arrived with its vanguard. His property was carried by a caravan of twenty prairie schooners. The cargo in the wagons included several million pesos in gold. Rumors of his treasure prompted stray bands of rebels and bandidos to harass the flanks and rear of the refugee procession, increasing the danger to innocents; as the refugee caravan crossed the Sierra Grande into La Junta, Colonel Chivara's men peppered the Terrazas military escort with rifle fire. Once safely into Ojinaga, Terrazas crossed the border to Presidio and motored to Marfa, where he boarded a train for El Paso. He had already reserved all of the available rooms in the Paso del Norte Hotel, where he resided until he could move into more appropriate surroundings at the El Paso mansion of United States Senator Albert B. Fall.[12]

Because Orozco's movement was an unholy alliance of oligarchs and anarchists, the ruling-class refugees that entered Ojinaga were escorted by none other than Pascual Orozco and his ragtag Colorados. Orozco's condition confirms that the desert crossing was difficult even for experienced soldiers accompanying an elite convoy:

A lean, gaunt figure half fell from his horse at 9 o'clock tonight and collapsed on the ground beside the general headquarters of the Federals in Ojinaga. It was Gen. Pascual Orozco, who had been riding night and day since Sunday in an effort to keep his irregular forces from bolting for the border and leaving the Chihuahua refugees to the mercy of the rebels who were pressing the rear guard of the Federals, their Mausers barking like coyotes from the hills overlooking La Mula Pass trail.

Orozco had to be assisted to the quarters assigned to him in the little town of sun-dried brick which has suddenly risen from a cow camp settlement to be the provisional Federal State capital of Chihuahua and the one remaining fortress of the Huerta forces in northern Mexico.[13]

Federal general Mercado brought up the rear of the refugee column. He arrived several days after the main body of fleeing soldiers and civilians; runners reported that he was under attack by rebel forces, increasing tensions in Ojinaga.

Stories circulated that federal soldiers and Colorados were threatening to desert unless they were paid. There were constant rumors of schisms between Orozco and Mercado, usually involving a plan by

Orozco to leave Ojinaga and revive his personal revolution. Pascual Orozco vehemently denied any intent to betray: "I am for the Huerta government, first, last and for all the time and will die fighting for it," Orozco proclaimed. "While the government I now serve exists I will never participate in any of the monstrous plans which seemingly, every day, are promulgated by the enemies of my country."[14]

Pascual Orozco and the remainder of the Mexican officer corps in Ojinaga—including eleven generals, twenty-one colonels and forty-five majors—recognized their personal obligation to stay on the Mexican side of the border for appearances' sake, but had no compunction about getting their families into the safety of Texas. General Orozco's wife chose San Antonio. General Mercado sent his wife to El Paso, as did Colorado general Salazar. Ojinaga bulged with 3,500 soldiers, 1,200 soldaderas and as many as a thousand assorted refugees, far beyond its carrying capacity.[15]

American journalist John Reed, on assignment to cover the Mexican revolutions for the muckraking magazine *Metropolitan,* arrived at the border and took stock of the situation:

> At Presidio, on the American side of the river, one could climb to the flat mud roof of the Post Office and look across the mile or so of low scrub growing in the sand to the shallow, yellow stream; and beyond to the low mesa, where the town was, sticking sharply up out of a scorched desert, ringed round with bare, savage mountains.
>
> One could see the square, gray adobe houses of Ojinaga, with here and there the Oriental cupola of an old Spanish church. It was a desolate land, without trees. You expected minarets. By day, Federal soldiers in shabby white uniforms swarmed about the place desultorily digging trenches, for Villa and his victorious Constitutionalists were rumored to be on the way. You got sudden glints, where the sun flashed on field guns; strange, thick clouds of smoke rose straight in the still air.
>
> Toward evening, when the sun went down with the flare of a blast furnace, patrols of cavalry rode sharply across the skyline to the night outposts. And after dark, mysterious fires burned in the town.[16]

Reed was not complimentary about Presidio ("a straggling and indescribably desolate village of about fifteen adobe houses, scattered without much plan in the deep sand and cotton-wood scrub along the river bottom"), but it was in fact a new and improved town: the original settlement had been wiped out in a 1904 flood. Its citizens had moved to higher ground farther down the river.[17]

The next day, ignoring the law and the risk, Reed waded the Rio Grande to Ojinaga and assessed the scene:

The white, dusty streets of the town, piled high with filth and fodder, the ancient windowless church with its three enormous Spanish bells hanging on a rack outside and a cloud of blue incense crawling out of the black doorway, where the women camp followers of the army prayed for victory day and night, lay in hot, breathless sun. Five times had Ojinaga been lost and taken. Hardly a house that had a roof, and all the walls gaped with cannon shot. In these bare, gutted rooms lived the soldiers, their women, their horses, their chickens, and pigs, raided from the surrounding country. Guns were stacked in the corners, saddles piled in the dust. The soldiers were in rags; scarcely one possessed a complete uniform. They squatted around little fires in their doorways, boiling cornhusks and dried meat. They were almost starving.

Along the main street passed an unbroken procession of sick, exhausted, starving people, driven from the interior by fear of the approaching rebels, a journey of eight days over the most terrible desert in the world. They were stopped by a hundred soldiers along the street, and robbed of every possession that took the Federals' fancy.[18]

While the Huertistas were making the best of difficult circumstances in Ojinaga, Villa's Constitutionalists were settling into more comfortable accommodations in Ciudad Chihuahua. Over Villa's protests, the Constitutionalist generals—including Manuel Chao— elected him provisional governor of Chihuahua. He served only four weeks, devoting his brief administration to dramatic acts that implemented his core political principles. He confiscated all the property of the oligarchy and made clear that their lives were at risk. He proclaimed land reform, promising to return land to the military colonies. He began constructing schools, declaring education to be second only to land reform in importance.[19]

Villa carefully protected most foreign investments, pragmatically reducing the risk of foreign intervention, but not all of his directives sat well with the international community. When Villa abruptly ejected all Spaniards from Chihuahua and confiscated their property, the consular community protested strongly. Facing Marion Letcher, the U.S. consul in Chihuahua, Villa exposed the deep roots of his revolution: "Señor Consul, we Mexicans have had three hundred years of the Spaniards. They have not changed in character since the conquistadores. They disrupted the Indian empire and enslaved the people. We did not ask them to mingle their blood with ours. Twice we drove them out of Mexico and allowed them to return with the same rights as Mexicans, and they used these rights to steal away our land, to make the people slaves, and to take up arms against the cause of liberty. They supported Porfirio Díaz. They were perniciously active in politics. It was the Spaniards who framed the plot that put Huerta in the palace. When Madero was murdered the Spaniards in every State in the Republic held banquets of rejoicing. They thrust on us the greatest superstition the world has ever known—the Catholic Church. They ought to be killed for that alone. I consider we are being very generous with them."[20]

Preoccupied with setting the course of the new government, Governor Villa ordered Toribio Ortega to capture Ojinaga. Supported by General Pánfilo Natera, who had commanded Constitutionalists in the state of Zacatecas, Ortega applied five thousand fighters to the task. "Sweep the border clear of Federals, and do not take any prisoners," ordered Villa. "There must not be a Federal left alive on this side of the border." Villa followed up that decree with a written order directing that all federal soldiers and officers—most especially Generals Orozco and Mercado—were to be brought before firing squads immediately after capture.[21]

Ortega was now a Villista general, and Villa trusted him as much as any of his leaders, perhaps because they shared a poor man's view of the revolution. "I am not an educated man," Ortega told journalist John Reed, "but I know that to fight is the last thing for any people. Only when things get too bad to stand, eh? And, if we are going to kill our brothers, something fine must come out of it, eh? You in the United States do not know what we have seen, we Mexicans. We have looked on at the robbing of our people, the simple, poor people, for thirty-five years, eh? We have seen the rurales and the soldiers of Porfirio Díaz shoot down our brothers and our fathers, and justice denied to them. We have seen our little fields taken away from us, and all of us sold into slavery, eh? We have longed for our homes and for schools to teach us, and they have laughed at us. All we have ever wanted was to be let alone to live and to work and make our country great, and we are tired—tired and sick of being cheated."[22]

As Ortega approached, the Mexican Army spread throughout La Junta, moving to secure the entire valley, not just the town of Ojinaga. A federal detachment of about one thousand soldiers was in the vicinity of San Antonio del Bravo on December 28 when Ortega's Constitutionalist advance guard swept down and dealt a surprisingly swift blow. The federales panicked and retreated to Ojinaga, where word of the clash prompted hundreds of faint-hearted soldiers to throw down their arms and cross the Rio Grande into the United States, families in tow. Generals Salazar and Orozco proclaimed that their troops would fight to the death, but observers on the other side of the river had their doubts.[23]

On December 29 Ortega attacked El Mulato, which was defended by four hundred federales. His reason for choosing El Mulato as his first target is obvious: he knew how to use the village as an effective staging ground for a siege of Ojinaga. It took less than two hours for three thousand of Ortega's soldiers to rout the federal troops, many of whom waded the river to El Polvo, where a cavalry sergeant took them into custody, collecting forty-three rifles, fifteen sabers and several thousand rounds of ammunition. A few hours later a U.S. cavalry lieutenant came upon eighty-four more Huertista soldiers who were trying to locate a safe crossing back into Mexico. They were rounded up, taken back to Presidio, disarmed and sent back across the river to Ojinaga. The next day another band of federales was sighted on the Texas side of the river, but they scattered into the hills, leaving fifty-nine rifles and eighteen sabers behind.[24]

Toribio Ortega was not the only person who relied on past experience in preparing for the upcoming battle. Having seen rebels seize Ojinaga before, the United States government expected Mercado's defense to collapse. According to one Border Patrol agent, the Mexican command had already asked to make arrangements for an orderly retreat across the border. The word was that if Constitutionalists launched a major attack, the federal army planned to defend Ojinaga for a respectable length of time, but wanted permission to cross the Rio Grande at an appropriate moment of their choosing.[25]

The United States could foresee the potential cross-border impacts if Mercado's troops did take flight. Serious practical and legal considerations attended the prospect of thousands of refugees—many of them armed soldiers, many of them wounded—swarming into Texas. Foreshadowing future strict immigration policies, on the simplest and most base level the United States did not want five thousand illiterate, impoverished Mexicans streaming into the country. As a matter of security, the idea of a few thousand armed foreign soldiers rushing over the border did not seem like a good idea, and the task of disarming and controlling such a horde was daunting. Legally, there were questions about the Neutrality Act—a foreign army couldn't use United States soil to regroup and return to the fight—but U.S. officials knew that refusing entry to combatants, or forcing them back across the border after a Constitutionalist victory, would lead to hundreds of executions by firing squad, not to mention more crude forms of retribution. It also knew that even under the best of circumstances admitting the refugees would be a humanitarian disaster; any attempt to confine them in groups would require food, shelter, sanitation and health care, and a failure to confine them could lead to mayhem.

Because the great bulk of refugees would be soldiers and their families, international law was a consideration: since 1900, Hague conventions signed by the United States and Mexico required a neutral state receiving belligerent troops to "intern them, as far as possible, at a distance from the theatre of war," and provided that the neutral country could "keep them in camps, and even confine them in fortresses or places set aside for this purpose." Interned soldiers were entitled to "the food, clothing, and relief required by humanity," and "at the conclusion of peace the expenses caused by the internment shall be made good." If the belligerents were wounded or sick, the neutral state could permit the infirm to pass through without internment, but the soldiers "must be guarded by the neutral State, so as to insure their not taking part again in the military operations."[26]

The United States was inclined to apply the Hague conventions, but there was a flaw in its logic: the governing convention applied to conflicts between two "Contracting Powers," meaning two nations that had signed the conventions. It did "not apply except between Contracting Powers, and then only if all the belligerents are parties to the Convention." The Mexican Revolution was a conflict within a Contracting Power, not between two of them, and the rebel forces were not Contracting Powers. There was a sound argument that the Hague conventions had nothing to do with the situation on the border.[27]

Not waiting to sort out the legalisms, the United States Army dispatched Major Michael M. McNamee to Presidio from El Paso with a squadron of the Fifteenth Cavalry. After they arrived, they were reinforced by three more cavalry troops. The American Red Cross sent Special Representative Charles J. O'Connor to Presidio. O'Connor found two thousand to three thousand noncombatant Mexicans encamped on the Texas riverbanks, many of them spouses and children of soldiers and soldaderas that manned stations in Ojinaga. He saw the results of the skirmish at El Mulato and recognized that medical needs would only increase. After taking stock of the situation, he summoned three doctors and five male nurses from El Paso, who set up operations in a wooden school building.[28]

South of Ojinaga, Toribio Ortega prepared his artillery emplacements. This would make the fourth time that Ortega had attacked Ojinaga, but this battle would be on a far larger scale than any before it. Federal forces abandoned their positions in the field and concentrated at Ojinaga. The Constitutionalists commenced rifle and machine-gun attacks on the afternoon of December 30. On the night of December 31 their cannons began lobbing shells into the battered pueblo. The next day ground troops stormed the town, but were repulsed. "Warfare in Mexico has been stripped of its glamour and glory and its bare bones have been shown to the world at the battle of Ojinaga," deplored the front page of the *New York Times*. "Brother has fought brother until the desert of Camargo is strewn with bodies; the buzzards are wheeling overhead lazy with their feasts of human flesh, desperate men are crawling to the American side with stumps of arms appealing for aid and peace from the roar of the cannon and the rattle of Mauser musketry, knit together with metallic whirr of the machine guns."[29]

Ortega and Natera attacked again on January 2, but were hurled back. They shifted their assault to the north on the next day, again battering the town without capturing it. Mexicans continued to flee across the Rio Grande, but army desertions were dwindling; most refugees were camp followers and families. When uninjured combatants reached American soil, Colonel McNamee's men disarmed them, then forced them back across the border to Mexico, where their choice was to be shot as a deserter or shot as an unarmed enemy. Soon, after some debate in Washington and San Antonio, McNamee began providing asylum to uniformed deserters who asked for it, jailing or returning armed soldiers who were fleeing a battle (but not deserting and seeking asylum) and jailing those who adopted civilian dress in an attempt to move back and forth across the border as the situation dictated.

Pancho Villa subordinated Toribio Ortega to Pánfilo Natera, hoping that a change of leadership would improve the rebels' effectiveness. Villa was uncharacteristically diplomatic about the shift, informing reporters that Natera was general of a brigade, superior to Brigadier Ortega, "and that ever since the movement from Chihuahua began, Natera had been chief in command and had planned the investment and assault upon Ojinaga. He had kept in the background, however, but possibly now that the supreme moment had arrived he was taking more active part in the direction of the general movement and that this had created the impression that he had superseded General Ortega." Villa's statement may have been entirely true — Ortega remained a prominent battlefield leader — but by the next day there were already rumors that Villa himself was coming to La Junta to direct the fight.[30]

On the fourth a mass of six hundred cavalry rode out of Ojinaga into the field. Commanded by Colorado general Salazar, their plan was to flank the rebels and dislodge them from their positions. They struck just as confounded Generals Natera and Ortega were withdrawing their troops to regroup. A United States customs inspector watched from across the river:

> *A battle was in progress and apparently at its height. Hundreds of people could be seen along both banks of the Rio Grande, afoot and mounted, rushing hither and thither, although clouds of dust in the river bottoms obscured our vision to such an extent as to render it difficult to determine just what was actually happening. The lines of Federal cavalry which had gone out from Ojinaga to meet and engage the advancing Rebel forces were plainly visible on a rolling plateau several miles outside of Ojinaga. Here occurred one of the most, if not the most, gallant and spectacular engagements of the revolution. Three times the Federal cavalry charged a ridge without success. It looked like annihilation to persist; but, rallying their forces, the Federals made another dash up the long incline and this time victory crowned their gallantry. The Rebels were swept from their position, and both pursued and pursuers were soon lost to view.*
>
> *The day was perfect, clear and sunny, and from our position it was at times difficult to realize that the scenes being enacted were those of actual warfare. Through it all ran the rattle of rifle fire, at times almost a roar, punctuated every moment or two by the report of a big gun —first a puff of white smoke marking the spot where the shell exploded, then the initial report.*

Though the federal cavalry suffered a "considerable lack of mobility and cohesion" in Major McNamee's opinion, they bested the disorganized Constitutionalists, then fell back to Ojinaga under the cover of darkness, taking more than two hundred prisoners with them. Salazar ordered the Constitutionalist captives executed.[31]

Unlike the first siege of Ojinaga when Ortega quickly shut down the river crossings, the government troops maintained control of the border even though Constitutionalists launched attacks upon the customhouse. Wives and disguised soldaderas crossed back and forth, bringing supplies from Presidio. When the fighting became intense, noncombatants would seek refuge in the United States; when the gunfire diminished, they would return to Mexico. Mexican federal forces managed to cache great quantities of ammunition in the hills on the Texas side of the border. Soldaderas would travel to the cache and return to Ojinaga with ammunition concealed beneath their skirts. Not taking sides, the United States opened a border crossing two miles below Presidio so that the Constitutionalist forces could obtain food—but not arms or ammunition, at least in theory.[32]

J. L. Kleinman was still selling ammunition in bulk. Perhaps because of the kind of traffic done in his store, government officials used competitor Spencer's store as their informal headquarters. To that point the Constitutionalist attacks had failed, but observers still considered the collapse of the federales and Colorados inevitable. On January 5 Major McNamee, Presidio County Sheriff Chastain, a county health officer, an immigration inspector, Red Cross Special Representative O'Connor and Mexican Consul Maillefert gathered to coordinate. A case of smallpox had broken out among the Mexicans; the officials decided to separate the refugees with a "broad, unoccupied strip of land between them and the town." Travel between Presidio and the refugee camp was restricted. In a few days it became necessary to quarantine a handful of smallpox victims, and the medical authorities began inoculations of Presidio citizens and refugees. The situation was brought under control: only seven cases arose, resulting in just two deaths.[33]

On January 6, after the Constitutionalists had spent two days licking their wounds and waiting for the arrival of ammunition and reinforcements, Pancho Villa rode an old pinto pony over La Mula pass into La Junta. Everything changed: Tired soldiers were energized; reluctant fighters became indomitable. Word of Villa's arrival permeated the rebel ranks, spread across the valley, penetrated federal lines at Ojinaga and reached beyond the river to Presidio. A sense of foreboding spread through the crumbled adobe remnants of the Huertista fortifications.[34]

Villa had said that he had no aspirations to govern, and he was true to his word. Upon assuming command at Ojinaga he resigned his governorship, turning over the office to Manuel Chao. Villa's resignation was spurred by three factors in addition to the need to energize the rebels in La Junta. First, Venustiano Carranza continued to pressure Villa to let Chao govern. Second, Villa was unsuited to his administrative role and disliked the job. Third, once Ojinaga was secure Villa needed to direct an attack on the federal stronghold at Torreón.[35]

Villa paused before assaulting Ojinaga. There were good reasons for the delay—ammunition was being carted from Chihuahua, battle plans had to be made, the wounded needed to be tended to, his troops needed to be redeployed around Ojinaga—but there may have been a less becoming reason as well. Villa had just signed a contract with the Mutual Film Corporation of New York under which he would receive 50 percent of the profits from films of his battles. Rumor had it that Villa was stalling until the cameramen could reach Ojinaga. Whether the rumor was true or not, the cameramen did manage to reach La Junta in time to film parts of the final fight.[36]

There was no shortage of rumors in the valley. One had three automobiles full of Constitutionalist ammunition seized by federales at La Mula pass. Another had Pancho Villa captured in the same event. A third had federal general Argumendo fighting his way across La Mula pass with four thousand reinforcements. None were true.[37]

Villa, Ortega and Natera attacked Ojinaga in the afternoon of January 10, heading a swarm of Constitutionalist fighters that some reporters estimated to number ten thousand, but military men on the scene appraised as about 1,500. Among them was the armed and dangerous María Gómez Gutierrez, who had become "one of General Ortega's most trusted lieutenants," dubbed "the Joan of Arc of Mexico" by the newspapers. Villa's assault was backed by twenty-four heavy cannon; the four thousand federales holding Ojinaga had only eight cannon, but held defensible high ground.[38]

The ensuing firefight was intense and frightening; the Huertistas knew full well who they were up against. Around eight o'clock in the evening, the front lines of the federal defense fell back to replenish their ammunition. The nervous soldiers behind them panicked, mistaking the movement for a retreat. Mercado assessed the chaotic situation; he knew that ammunition was low, and he knew the penalty for being taken prisoner by Pancho Villa. Never one to make a futile stand, Mercado ordered an orderly abandonment of Ojinaga. By nine o'clock a weary federal army lined up to cross the river. Major McNamee's cavalry rounded up the soldiers and disarmed them as they slogged up the riverbanks.[39]

One observer described the nighttime evacuation: "Here before us where the moon lighted up the white desert sand was an Oriental scene. There passed a slow procession, now singly, now in groups, horsemen in mantles, a train of pack mules, women on foot carrying babes on their backs in the fold of a shawl, men on foot close wrapped in blankets, patient burros loaded with family goods or bearing children. The occasional commands of troopers or the jingling of spurs and bridles were lost in the silence that seemed to subdue all sounds."[40]

A tally taken a few days later in Presidio showed 3,700 officers and soldiers, 1,100 women and more than five hundred children. Confiscations included 1,200 rifles and carbines, 156 sabers, nine pistols and a plethora of other equipment. Crude corrals held 1,800 animals in various stages of distress.[41]

Only about four hundred refugees escaped. Among the escapees was Pascual Orozco, who made himself scarce until he and a small contingent of Colorados arrived at Torreón on January 25, just in time for the Mexican government to announce that they had created a new military decoration to bestow upon him.[42]

Mexican general Mercado was taken into custody in Presidio. The Huertista government asked for his return, but not so they could give him a medal: they wanted to try him for dereliction of duty in the abandonment of Ciudad Chihuahua and Ojinaga. Mercado explained his decision to a reporter: "It was hopeless. Our men had left only seventy-eight rounds of ammunition each and we could not have resisted a charge by the rebels; it would have been a massacre. . . . When I saw there was no hope, I had to command the soldiers to leave. I chose to place the lives of my men in the care of the United States rather than to risk them to the rebels. We are grateful for our hospitable asylum here." [43]

In his first interview after the battle, Pancho Villa confirmed the importance of ammunition supplies in the battle, but attributed the federal shortage to clever Constitutionalist leadership, graciously emphasizing the role of the local boy made good:

The credit for this victory is due to Gen. Toribio Ortega. He led the original attack a week ago. We knew the Federals had only a limited supply of ammunition. Our tactics were to exhaust that supply. Gen. Ortega started an attack to draw the Federal fire. He succeeded well.

For a whole week the Federal garrison kept firing back at us with little effect. We did not go near enough to endanger our men. Then we withdrew for six days to obtain more ammunition. Our renewed attack settled the conflict. The Federals were exhausted and the flight to the United States began just as we had planned it would. [44]

Presidio was chaos on January 11. Thousands of refugees camped in the scrub. Despite advance preparations, facilities for food, sanitation and medical care were woefully inadequate. Noncombatants were given the option of returning to Mexico, but few did. Surveying the circumstance, the U.S. authorities decided that managing the situation required relocating the refugees to Marfa, where food and supplies could be brought by rail, or to El Paso, where Fort Bliss could provide comprehensive infrastructure. In the meantime, the defeated soldiers were gathered into a corral, guarded by United States cavalry. "These men have no more fight left in them," one observer related. "They obey the commands of the Americans like children. Their suits are the Summer slate-colored fatigue uniform of the Federal Army, and few have underwear or shoes, sandals covering their feet. They squat around the big fires or sleep on beds made of poles and brush." [45]

Noncombatants were not formally confined, but they gathered into camps provided by the military. "All the sorrows of Mexico seem centered around the great fire of mesquite logs and cottonwood to-night," said the *New York Times*. "Here the women who must wait are trying to keep their little ones warm by holding them up to the blaze. These women do not weep, for their sorrow is too deep for outward evidence. Many have lost their husbands and others their sons. Many more do not know the fate of their menfolk, for families have been separated. Food has been doled out to these women and children meagrely today by a generous Government, for the pack trains have been unable to bring enough supplies from the railroad."[46]

On January 12 the War Department ordered the soldiers interned at Fort Bliss. It takes only a moment's thought to realize what was about to happen: five thousand people were going to walk seventy miles to the railroad station at Marfa. The sick and wounded were left in Presidio field hospitals until they were well enough to make the trip. Those who had horses or wagons could ride, and a limited number of wagons were available for those who were too old, weak or footsore to travel on foot, but most—men, women and children of all ages—walked.[47]

There is an opportunity here for a bold accusation: Imprisoned Mexican soldiers and the women and children who accompanied them were forced to march scores of miles across a wintry desert to a concentration camp. The accusation is only part of the story, but the rest of the story provides little amelioration. On the one hand, virtually all of the refugees traveled from Ciudad Chihuahua—or at least Falomir—in exactly the same way that they made the journey to Marfa; on the other hand, that only means that their misery was being compounded. It was winter. Days could be warm, but nights were always cold, and the cold intensified as they moved toward Marfa, three thousand feet higher than Presidio. Photographs of the scene show people in long-sleeved shirts, some with sweaters or jackets, but heavy coats and blankets were in short supply during frigid nights. The United States Army made an effort to stock three overnight campsites with food and firewood, but rations and supplies were limited by the capacity of pack trains organized on short notice. The four-day march was broken into segments of twenty-four, nineteen, fourteen and thirteen miles, but even those are brutal distances for people of the sort that made the march. Major McNamee tells the story of the first day's march:[48]

It was noon before the rear guard had reached the top of the first hill out of Presidio, a distance of about two miles.

The day was one of the hottest days of the season; a great many men and women were heavily loaded with personal belongings, pots and pans and worthless articles; some were carrying thirty to forty pounds of food stuffs which they had in some unknown manner accumulated; there was no water along the road for the first fifteen miles and at this point an unhealthy water hole was found.

When about twelve miles from Presidio one woman gave birth to a child. The child was dead born and had to be buried near the road side.

These conditions caused great hardships and suffering and resulted in a lengthening of the column for many miles. Practically without exception, both men and women made every effort to complete the march. Wagons loaded with water were sent out from Shafter shortly after the Army wagons reached camp.

All but about 200 reached Shafter by 10:00 P.M. Those unable to continue the march were permitted to camp along the roadside a mile or two outside of town.

About sixty animals either died or had to be abandoned along the road.

There is seldom a satisfactory humanitarian resolution to an influx of refugees; the situation inevitably worsens when the refugees are being moved. Major McNamee and a contingent of cavalry led the way to Marfa. Behind him rode a phalanx of Mexican officers—General Mercado was ensconced in an automobile—followed by soldiers and their families. At the rear were two troops of United States cavalry. When they reached Marfa, the refugees watched helplessly as their horses, saddles and wagons—including those that were privately owned—were confiscated and sold at auction by the United States government to offset the cost of internment. The people were loaded onto passenger cars and mail cars—one step above freight cars—and shipped to Fort Bliss.[49]

Their destination was a camp measuring 1,880 feet by 720 feet—about thirty acres. It was surrounded by a ten-foot-high barbed wire fence, capped with eighty floodlights. Sentry boxes rose at each corner and in the middle of each side. Smaller fences were erected to create an unoccupied zone flanking the ten-foot barrier. Federales were on one side of the camp, Colorados on the other, with a wide road running between them. General Mercado named the road "Avenida General Huerta." In accordance with Mexican custom, the prisoners cooked their own meals using the food provided them each day: 1,800 pounds of beans and chilis, 2,400 pounds of meat, 5,000 pounds of flour and proportionate quantities of canned milk, sugar, salt, onions, potatoes, prunes and vinegar. The cost was about thirty-three cents per person per day.[50]

The prisoners may have been remote from Ojinaga, but they were still close to Mexico. As the United States grew less cordial to the Huertista cause, concerns arose about having that many potential combatants so close to the border. The internment camp was relocated to abandoned Fort Wingate, fifteen miles outside Gallup, New Mexico. When the Constitutionalists drove Huerta from power in August 1914, the United States transported all the interned enlisted men and civilians east to Piedras Negras for repatriation. The members of the officer corps, who would have been executed if they had returned to Mexico, were given asylum. General Mercado retired to a ranch he owned near Las Cruces, New Mexico.[51]

Still on the loose, Pascual Orozco declared revolt against the interim government that replaced Huerta and against the Constitutionalist regime to come. His support dwindled quickly, and he went into hiding in the United States, scheming to reinvigorate his movement.[52]

Toribio Ortega took ill during the last stages of the Constitutionalist campaign. He was transported to Ciudad Chihuahua for medical care, but died on July 16. His remains were interred in a Mexican pantheon of heroes.[53]

Carranza, Villa and Zapata jointly drove Huerta from power. In October 1914 their representatives held a convention at Aguascalientes to formulate a unified plan for governing the nation. The outcome, as an experienced observer might expect, was internecine warfare among the three. On paper, Villa and Zapata were united as "Conventionists" against the less radical Carrancistas, but the two Conventionists fought their wars independently—Villa in the north, Zapata in the south.

Financing revolutions became difficult in Mexico. In 1910, businesses, banks and wealthy landowners had supported a variety of movements, but after years of revolutions and counterrevolutions many financial interests sidelined themselves. Pancho Villa obtained some indirect support from the United States government, which loosened import and export restrictions for his benefit, but his core constituency was the impoverished and dispossessed, thus he had few sources of direct cash infusions. Because he was trying to respect the central authority of the convention, he was unable unilaterally to enact laws confiscating property of the wealthy, but he showed little hesitation about shaking down Mexico City's businesses for money. Flush with victory over the Huertistas, Villa became a bully, resorting to kidnapping and extortion to fund his campaigns.

Villa came under a great deal of criticism and pressure on account of his uncouth behavior in Mexico City. Cracks began to appear in the Conventionist alliance. Villa, still possessed of a vision that was more regional than national, moved his operations to Chihuahua and northern Mexico, where he chased down Carrancistas. He declared himself the head of a "northern administration" that he claimed was still loyal to the Conventionist cause.

Carranza was not without resources, and he received an immense boost when President Woodrow Wilson delivered the port of Veracruz—which the U.S. Marines occupied—into his hands. Carranza was as intent on sweeping Villistas from northern Mexico as Villa was on doing the reverse; Carranza dispatched distinguished general Alvaro Obregón to manage the task. Obregón trounced Villa at Ceyala, León and Aguascalientes in the spring of 1915, eviscerating Villa's army.

Punitive

Expeditions

Wilson's policy was to maintain some sort of balance among the various political elements in Mexico, hoping to force a reconciliation and emergence of a coalition government. The United States called for a meeting of all revolutionary leaders to select a provisional president, but the conclave never happened. Exasperated, Wilson swung his backing to Carranza, who seemed to have the upper hand, and declared an arms embargo against Villa.

Villa's battered troops moved to attack Agua Prieta, on the Arizona border. There were only 1,200 Carrancista troops there, and Villa felt confident. Unknown to him, Wilson permitted five thousand Carrancista reinforcements to enter the United States in Coahuila, travel to Arizona and recross the border to defend Agua Prieta. Villa was hammered in the battle; accounts portray him as dazed and baffled afterward.

When he recovered his wits, Villa took an unexpected tack. In Santa Isabel, Chihuahua, his men pulled fifteen U.S. mining engineers from a Kansas City, Mexico & Orient passenger car and executed them. Two months later, in March 1916, his troops crossed the international border into the pitiful town of Columbus, New Mexico, terrorized the residents, burned the village and murdered eighteen people. His actions seem to have been in part revenge for what he saw as betrayal by Wilson and in part an effort to force the United States to invade Mexico, which he felt would ultimately work to his advantage. The two incidents confirmed people's worst impressions of Villa and severely damaged his credibility as a national leader.

Wilson sent General John "Blackjack" Pershing into Mexico with six thousand troops to capture Villa. Known as Pershing's Punitive Expedition, the invasion had no chance of catching the wily Mexican general-rebel-bandido, who still enjoyed wide support among northern campesinos. Pershing spent nine months and US$130 million traipsing around the Sonoran and Chihuahuan Deserts without success.

This is the point in the Mexican revolutions when supporters of Pancho Villa let out a collective sigh. Other than successfully eluding Pershing and hanging on to control of parts of the northern frontier for a few more years, Villa never recovered his revolutionary footing. His political motives became overshadowed by the banditry that he used to fund his movement. Bit by bit, Carranza, actively aided by the United States, chipped away at Pancho Villa's control of the north. Villa was — and is — a folk hero, but his national political and military clout were gone.

Carranza's troops took control of Chihuahua's population centers; Villistas dominated the countryside. Carranza's army garrisoned Ojinaga while Villistas and apolitical outlaws roamed La Junta and the Big Bend. It was a difficult time on Chihuahua's northern frontier. Poverty and conflict were rampant, leading to violence and banditry that spilled over the border into Texas.

Local sheriffs lacked the resources to stem the raids. Sometimes a posse would assemble and pursue bandits, but more often the robbers escaped unscathed. In 1913 Texas governor Oscar Colquitt asked President Taft to send troops to the border, but the army reassured the President that West Texas was not in enough of an uproar to merit military intervention. Two years later new governor James Ferguson asked new president Woodrow Wilson to station cavalry along the Rio Grande. Wilson's secretary of war admitted that the situation was "very near to justifying martial law," but he saw the matter as one for the civil authorities to handle, and recommended no action. As a palliative, the army sent a few patrols into the region. Behind the army's reluctance lay a realization that even they could not control the lengthy and rugged border; the secretary of war admitted as much, saying that the land from El Paso to Brownsville "is about as inaccessible and difficult a country as can be imagined, so that it will not in any circumstances be possible to station troops throughout that entire stretch."[1]

Pancho Villa's rampages at Santa Isabel and Columbus changed the army's mind about militarization of the border, and incidents near La Junta exacerbated the alarm that was growing in the United States. In May 1916, eighty bandits crossed the Rio Grande downstream of La Junta near the old Presidio de San Vicente and raided ranches and stores at Glenn Springs and Boquillas. There were a handful of U.S. soldiers in Glenn Springs, but they were completely overwhelmed by the Mexicans. Three soldiers and a child were killed. Two men were kidnapped at Boquillas, and another six captives were taken at a nearby silver mine. Fortunately, the hostages from the silver mine not only escaped but also disarmed their captors and delivered them to the Brewster County sheriff. The other two captives—Boquillas store owner Jesse Deemer and his clerk, Monroe Payne—remained in the hands of the bandits.[2]

While the Mexicans were pillaging Glenn Springs and Boquillas, representatives of the United States and Mexico were meeting in El Paso to discuss Pershing's ongoing Punitive Expedition, which had soured relations between the two nations. The raids in the Big Bend hardened the United States viewpoint. Two troops of cavalry—about two hundred men—under Major George Langhorne went to punish the Big Bend raiders. They arrived in Boquillas accompanied by journalists, photographers and a film crew. Langhorne was a cavalry major and a fine horseman, but he rode in a Cadillac touring car. The media team took two Ford sedans. The odd caravan crossed into Mexico on what has become known as the Little Punitive Expedition. Trying to catch Mexican bandidos on their home turf—in clumsy automobiles, no less—was impossible. The closest that Langhorne came was when his men surrounded the pueblo of El Pino, only to find out that their prey had vacated the town hours earlier. Fortuitously, however, the bandits left Deemer and Payne behind in El Pino to be "rescued" by the army. After sixteen days of chasing around in the desert, Langhorne could claim two captives returned, three bandidos killed and most of the stolen plunder recovered. There had been no casualties among the cavalry, reporters, photographers or film crew. Compared to Pershing's Punitive Expedition, Langhorne's Little Punitive Expedition was a success.[3]

Two days before Langhorne invaded Mexico, President Wilson called up the Texas, New Mexico and Arizona National Guards and assigned them to border duty. Soldiers deployed through La Junta and the Big Bend, and cross-border raids gradually diminished. In the natural cycle of things, the military relaxed, the intensity of their patrols waned and depredations soon resumed.[4]

On November 30, 1917, a band of raiders struck a ranch near Ruidosa owned by a man named Tigner, stealing cattle and killing a ranch foreman. Langhorne sent Captain Leonard Matlack to pursue with twenty-one men. Matlack's patrol ran into more than two hundred bandidos, who were planning an ambush. Not faint of heart, Matlack charged into their midst, killing dozens and losing one man and five horses in the process. The next day the bandidos fired across the river at another cavalry patrol, which gave chase into Mexico and killed about a dozen of them. For good measure, the cavalry burned the Mexican villages of Los Mimbres and Buena Vista, which they considered bandit hideouts.[5]

Two weeks later a group of Carrancista soldiers under the command of General José Murguía crossed to the Texas side of La Junta to steal two horses and a mule from Francisco Estricero. When the general denied taking the animals, cavalry major Langhorne denied Mexican access to Presidio until compensatory payment was forthcoming. Langhorne lacked the authority to close the port of entry, but as he put it, "We had to regulate traffic."[6]

On Christmas day about forty-five bandidos crossed the Rio Grande and raided the Brite Ranch between Marfa and Candelaria. The postman had the bad luck to drive his mail stage through the ranch with two passengers during the raid; all three were killed. The bandits, led by a man named Jesus Rentería, looted the Brite ranch store and lugged their gains back toward the Rio Grande. A neighboring rancher alerted the Presidio County sheriff, who raised a posse that took chase in automobiles. The posse was only a few miles behind the bandidos, but the roads became impassable near the Candelaria rim (the rocky ledge that divides Candelaria and La Junta from the ranch country near Marfa), and Rentería's horseback thieves escaped easily.[7]

The next day an augmented posse rode horseback to Pilares, Mexico, where they suspected the gang was hiding out. The vigilantes attacked the pueblo, killing a number of people, burning a few houses and recovering some of the booty taken at the Brite Ranch. There was a mild brouhaha over the border transgression, and some Texas Rangers that participated in the raid were discharged from service, but West Texans understandably approved of the expedition.[8]

The Presidio County retribution didn't halt incursions. Three months later Mexican bandidos launched another raid, this time upon the Nevill Ranch, which ran for eighteen miles along the river across from Pilares. The bandits killed the son of rancher Ed Nevill, murdered a ranch hand's wife, then gathered up all the livestock, supplies and goods they could carry and headed back to Mexico.[9]

George Langhorne, now a colonel in command of the district, dispatched two troops of cavalry to the Rio Grande. They crossed the river and headed for Pilares, but were ambushed by the bandidos en route. The soldiers trounced their ambushers—killing more than thirty by one estimate—then carried the battle into Pilares, where they found some of the property taken from Ed Nevill's ranch.[10]

Spurred by continuing border conflicts—and two Villa attacks on Ciudad Juárez—the United States Army became more serious about protecting the Rio Grande. In late 1917 Langhorne dispatched troops of cavalry for long-term assignments at the river; in La Junta they erected tent camps at Candelaria, Ruidosa, Indio, Presidio and Redford, establishing a cordon through the valley.

On November 14, 1917, Pancho Villa himself led an attack on Ojinaga. A morning assault failed, but a nightfall charge drove the Carrancistas across the Rio Grande into the waiting arms of the U.S. Army. The refugee count was much smaller than the thousands of Huertistas that fled to Presidio in 1914, and the army dealt with the new arrivals differently. Langhorne disarmed the Mexican troops and moved them to Marfa by truck, where they were confined. Before transporting them further, he contacted the Mexican consul and required payment of all anticipated expenses in advance. Once the funds were on deposit, Langhorne put the Carrancistas and their confiscated weapons on a train and shipped them under guard to El Paso, where they were returned across the river to Juárez.[11]

Villa placed Ojinaga under the command of General Alfonso Sánchez, who set about clearing out pockets of Carrancistas. A squad led by Carrancista lieutenant colonel Jorge Meranga was stationed at San Antonio del Bravo. Sánchez attacked, driving Meranga's men across the Rio Grande to Candelaria, where a cavalry troop intercepted them. The cavalry fed and quartered the Mexican soldiers until it appeared safe for them to go back across the river. The United States was taking a more pragmatic approach after the 1914 concentration camp spectacle.[12]

Major Langhorne refused to open the Presidio port of entry to the Villistas, practically eliminating the strategic value of Ojinaga. After about a month of ruling the valley, the Villistas departed, leaving it to Carranza's troops.

Even with the presence of the United States cavalry, it was chaotic and dangerous in La Junta from 1917 to 1920 — as wild as the Apache days. Raids on ranches and stores were frequent, and lives were lost. The folk-hero status of Pancho Villa led newspapers and the citizenry to equate most of the depredations with Villistas, but the soldiers on the ground reported that Carrancistas were the biggest problem, followed by unaffiliated bandidos. During the time that Villistas held Ojinaga, the cavalry reported no incidents.[13]

The Carranza government was bankrupt and disorganized, as was most of the country it governed. Carrancista soldiers were persistent raiders because they were untrained, undisciplined, hungry and maltreated. Their morale was miserable. In March 1917 fifty-seven soldiers from the Ojinaga garrison defected across the river and refused to return. They insisted on staying in captivity at the Presidio cavalry base, where they were decently fed and housed. They preferred forced labor making adobe bricks to serving in the Mexican Army.[14]

Carrancista Colonel Ruiz visited Colonel Langhorne in Marfa, and Langhorne related how he returned the favor: "And then I had to — at Candelaria — to go over and return the visit of Colonel Ruiz and his officers, and a very pathetic thing happened; he sent over to see if he could not borrow some sugar and coffee in order to extend hospitality to our officers, who were visiting him. They were actually down; they ate their burros; they had nothing to eat at all."[15]

Over time, the situation in La Junta degenerated to the point that attaching labels to the various bandits made little practical difference.

U.S. cavalry officers reported incidents in which garden-variety bandidos were reinforced by Carrancista soldiers. Chico Cano's name surfaces repeatedly in the annals of the Big Bend as a notorious bandido, sometimes a Villista bandido. In fact, Cano was a Carrancista captain and the men he led were loyal to Carranza, though in Mexico's fluid political situation it is more than possible that at various times he held other loyalties or none at all.[16]

The cavalry adopted a practice of chasing bandidos across the river when it seemed appropriate, requiring only authorization from Marfa to proceed. The presence of an official Carrancista garrison in Ojinaga prevented the United States from making incursions in the central part of La Junta, but hot pursuit was the rule in Redford, Indio, Ruidosa and Candelaria. San Antonio del Bravo and Pilares became known bandido strongholds, the scenes of repeated skirmishes.[17]

Jesus Rentería, who led the Brite Ranch raid, was generally considered a Carrancista, sometimes linked with Chico Cano. He had a wooden leg, and a steel hook replaced his right hand. The injuries were due to a railroad accident in Kansas, not battle wounds in the revolution. Because of his prosthetics, locals called him *El Mocho* (the maimed one) or *Gacho* (hook). Rentería was terrible; legend holds that he once sat on a victim's chest and cut his throat with a pocket knife.[18]

Bandidos of Rentería's type committed depredations on both sides of the Rio Grande, but they gained greatest notoriety for organizing in Mexico, dashing across the Rio Grande, raiding ranches and stores in the United States, then returning to their Mexican sanctuaries. Although bandidos roamed far into West Texas, most at risk were towns and ranches near the Rio Grande.[19]

Candelaria, across the river from San Antonio del Bravo, was run by the Kilpatrick family. Mary Kilpatrick was the first of her clan to move there. She purchased a small store in 1903 and taught in the local schoolhouse. Soon her brothers Dawkins ("D. D.") and James ("J. J.") took up cotton farming nearby. They built a cotton gin in 1910, a larger one in 1914 and another in 1917. From an initial crop of seven bales raised on twelve acres, by 1919 the Kilpatricks expanded to producing three hundred bales plus a bountiful supply of corn from their eight hundred cultivated acres. The Kilpatrick brothers opened a store in Candelaria. J. J. became justice of the peace, and his son Jim served as the town constable.[20]

Mary Kilpatrick wed Jack Howard, a well-known and respected customs agent. Howard's job was dangerous; he rode horseback throughout the border region, covering an immense stretch of territory. Risks were omnipresent in La Junta then; J. J. Kilpatrick mounted a .30-caliber Colt machine gun on the roof of the Candelaria store to keep things under control.[21]

In 1913 Jack Howard was patrolling with fellow customs agent Joe Sitters and local cattle association inspector J. W. Harwick. They came upon Chico Cano and arrested him for suspected theft and horse rustling; on their way toward jail, they were ambushed by a band of Cano's men. Howard was mortally wounded and Sitters was shot. Sitters recovered, but two years later was killed in a mountain shootout with Cano's bandidos between Candelaria and Pilares.[22]

Captain Leonard Matlack, a hard-bitten veteran of the Spanish-American War, commanded the cavalry troop stationed in Candelaria. Despite the Kilpatricks' roles as constable and justice of the peace, Matlack was the only effective law there. Locals from both sides of the border brought their disputes to him for resolution. On occasion he even granted divorces. Matlack's assumption of local authority grated upon the demoted Kilpatricks.[23]

Small-time smuggling, which was not Matlack's primary concern, was done mostly by women and children. Men were afraid to smuggle, because if caught the punishment would likely be summary execution. Matlack had a creative solution for handling women who smuggled: "they would be arrested and placed in the small jail in the town of Candelaria, which was not connected with the army camp. I would put a thirty-five-cent lock on the door and place no guard over the jail. The next morning I would find that the friends of the women had broken the jail and sent them into Mexico, but, of course, they never came back because they thought we had a good case for jailbreaking."[24]

The Kilpatricks—particularly J. J. Kilpatrick—became increasingly offended by Matlack's presence. Candelaria was Kilpatrick turf, and the Kilpatricks—aided by their Colt machine gun—were keeping a lid on things, even with a nest of bandidos living right across the river in San Antonio del Bravo. The Kilpatrick clan didn't need the military stirring up trouble. They probably didn't mind the cavalrymen's contributions to liquor sales in their pool hall, but drunken soldiers and their firearms were a problem, and the problem became acute when Constable Jim Kilpatrick shot and killed a cavalryman in circumstances outside his official duties. Kilpatrick was indicted for murder. Though he was never convicted, the incident inflamed relations between civilians and military in the tiny community.[25]

The Kilpatricks' greatest objection to the army's presence remained unstated. Anyone familiar with the history of Ben Leaton understands the Kilpatricks' store. Carrancistas, Villistas and bandidos were the

Kilpatricks' customers. The store would never trade for cattle or horses stolen from American ranches (for doing so would be suicide) but there was certainly less compunction about trading ammunition, food and supplies for livestock rustled from Chihuahuan hacendados. Before Matlack's arrival, Candelaria was as much a bandido haven as San Antonio del Bravo—bandits raided and traded on both sides of the river, trading on one side what they raided on the other. The Kilpatricks' store was Leaton's fortín, right down to the heavy weaponry mounted on the roof. J. J. Kilpatrick wanted the cavalry out of town because the cavalry were upsetting a delicate and dangerous equilibrium.

Most ranchers and farmers in Presidio County welcomed the military presence. They were particularly grateful in 1919, when the Army Air Service began flying the border in DeHavilland DH-4s—flimsy biplanes locally known as "Big Chickens." The pilots routinely crossed the Rio Grande to look for roving bands of predators, continuing the United States' aggressive policies.[26]

The air patrols seemed to do a remarkably good job of suppressing banditry. Based out of El Paso, the aircraft would take off, follow the Rio Grande to Presidio then turn north to a crude landing strip at Marfa. After refueling in Marfa, they would fly back to the river and either turn toward El Paso or jog downriver and cut across the rough inland of the Big Bend to Sanderson, where another dirt airstrip had been leveled for refueling.[27]

A DeHavilland DH-4 had a spruce wood frame joined with glue, bolts and guy wires. Its skin was linen cloth. The inherent unreliability of its 450–horsepower water-cooled Liberty engine was worsened by the poor grades of fuel and lubricating oil available in West Texas. The ninety gallons of fuel stored between the pilot's and observer's two cockpits would keep the plane airborne about four hours, if the engine didn't burn out first. The craft's two nonretractable wheels hung below the plane, joined by an axle called a "spreader bar," which had a notable tendency to get hung up on trees, brush, cactus or rocks as the plane approached the earth. When that happened, the spreader bar would fracture and the aircraft would often flip over on its back.[28]

For communication, the DH-4s were equipped with one-way air-to-ground radios that had a fifty-mile range—useless anywhere near La Junta. Most air-to-ground communication was done by flying over cavalry detachments and dropping messages in canvas bags that had long red streamers attached. Ground-to-air communication was done by waving arms and cursing.[29]

When on patrol, the DeHavillands were outfitted with two Marlin machine guns, mounted forward of the pilot's cockpit and synchronized to fire between the spinning propeller blades. The pilot aimed the guns by going into a dive and pointing the nose of the aircraft at the target, using the radiator cap as a gunsight. The Marlins would typically function well through two or three dives, then jam. There was no safe way to clear the jams while in flight. In addition to the Marlins on the nose of the plane, a twin Lewis machine gun was swivel-mounted on the rear cockpit. The Lewis was more reliable than the Marlins, and could be aimed more flexibly. When the Lewis gun jammed, the observer could usually remedy the malfunction.[30]

Lieutenants Harold Peterson and Paul Davis clambered into their DH-4 on August 10, 1919, and flew southward from Marfa to pick up the Rio Grande at Lajitas. When the river was beneath them, they turned northwest, following it upstream toward El Paso. Like most patrol fliers, they swung toward the Mexican side of the river, then back to the United States bank, looking for bands of riders in the desert. Patrols over the Rio Grande developed a creative way of distinguishing bandidos from ordinary rancheros: the plane would fire a burst from its machine guns at horsemen. If they fired back, they were fair game.[31]

Except for the river, there aren't many distinctive landmarks in the Chihuahuan Desert, and the airmen's maps of the Mexican side of the border were virtually useless. Whether for that reason or some other, Peterson and Davis made a critical error as they flew over La Junta: they mistook the Rio Conchos for the smaller Rio Grande and began following the Conchos into Mexico. Intruding upon Mexican airspace was not a problem (air patrols did it regularly), but following the Conchos was an unlikely way for the fuel-limited plane to reach El Paso.[32]

Somewhere between Coyame and Falomir the airplane exhausted its engine oil. Four connecting-rod bearings burned out, and the rods rammed through the engine's crankcase, ruining the motor. The DH-4 went into a glide. Peterson and Davis looked for a safe landing spot, and picked the best available. When the plane descended into a thicket of mesquite and greasewood, its spreader bar caught and snapped; the stress on the landing gear fractured the fuselage. Fortunately, the two fliers were uninjured. They climbed out of the plane and took stock of their situation, believing themselves to be somewhere in Texas. Before setting out for help, they buried the plane's machine guns and ammunition to prevent their falling into the hands of bandits.[33]

The plane had landed in some hills. Davis and Peterson began walking downhill toward the Rio Conchos, which they thought was the Rio Grande. The distance to the river was greater than they estimated, and traveling overland was difficult; leaving the wrecked plane in the early afternoon, they still had not made it to the Conchos by 3:00 A.M., when they came upon a small ranch house. They roused the ranchero, purchased some food and water and asked for directions to the river. When they reached the Conchos they turned downstream, toward Coyame, thinking they were heading down the Rio Grande to Candelaria.[34]

An alarm went out when Davis and Peterson didn't return from their patrol. The Army Air Service launched an intensive search along their intended route: from Marfa to Lajitas, then upstream to El Paso. The downed fliers were almost one hundred miles distant from the primary search area, but the army recognized that they might have gone astray and included the Rio Conchos drainage in their search pattern, disregarding the niceties of international jurisdiction. The downed airmen saw one of the search craft and waved, but they were in a brush thicket and couldn't be spotted by the fliers. The two men moved out of the brush onto the open riverbank, hoping to be noticed on the airplane's return flight, but the searchers took a different route home.[35]

The lost airmen came upon a small village, where they hired Alfonso Quintana, who had three burros, to take them to Candelaria. The three mounted up and rode toward the Rio Grande. They came across an armed man, who greeted Quintana. A discussion ensued, but the fliers couldn't understand the Spanish. The armed man rode off. Soon more armed men appeared. The gun-toting men directed the flyboys to pay ten dollars to Quintana and give him his burros back. The bandidos would be handling matters from here on.[36]

On Sunday August 17—a week after the fliers disappeared— Tomás Sánchez appeared in the Kilpatricks' Candelaria store. He gave Dawkins Kilpatrick a note. It was from Jesus Rentería and it demanded US$15,000 for the return of the fliers. The ransom was to be paid by midnight on the eighteenth or the two captives would die. Adding credibility to the demand, Sánchez handed Kilpatrick several messages written by Davis and Peterson that Kilpatrick was to telegraph to military officials and the fliers' family members.[37]

Dawkins Kilpatrick contacted the authorities, who authorized payment of the ransom. The military didn't have enough funds locally available, but local ranchers directed the Marfa National Bank to disburse the money on their credit. A bank vice president, accompanied by an army major, drove from Marfa to Candelaria with the cash and a letter from Colonel George Langhorne to Captain Leonard Matlack explaining the source and purpose of the money. Langhorne put his cavalry troops in Presidio, Indio, Ruidosa and Candelaria on alert.[38]

Using Tomás Sánchez as a go-between, Matlack and Rentería negotiated about how and where the ransom would be exchanged for the hostages. As the midnight deadline approached on the eighteenth, no agreement had been reached. Matlack warned Rentería that if the aviators were harmed the U.S. cavalry would come to San Antonio del Bravo to make things right. Rentería's next communication directed Matlack to wait for a signal light after dark on the nineteenth; when he saw it, he should proceed to an old cottonwood tree by a cornfield on the trail to San Antonio del Bravo. There, one prisoner would be exchanged for half the money, followed by the second flier for the remainder. Matlack agreed.[39]

But the signal light never appeared. Concerned, after midnight Matlack took half the ransom money, stuffed it in his shirt and rode to the rendezvous point. About a mile into Mexico he encountered a mounted bandido accompanied by a man on foot—Peterson. Matlack made the exchange. Peterson got on Matlack's horse behind him, and they returned safely to Candelaria. "Here's one of them, thank God," the officer reported.[40]

Matlack went back across the river with the remaining US$7,500. The design of the exchange made this the high-risk moment—a solitary cavalry officer, a mile into hostile territory with ransom money on his person. He returned to the place where he had rescued Peterson and waited in the dark. According to the account that Matlack gave later, he saw two riders cut through a cornfield on the edge of the trail. He overheard the instruction "*Mata los dos gringos*" (Kill the two gringos), the reply "*Seguro*" (Sure) and something about *bosque* and *rio* (underbrush and river). According to Matlack, that's when he decided that he was facing an ambush.[41]

In a few minutes a horse and rider approached, then another, followed by a man on foot. It was Lieutenant Davis. Matlack told Davis to mount up behind him. Handing the flier one of his pistols, he whispered that they might have to fight their way out. Matlack extracted the ransom money from inside his shirt, flashed it, then pulled his pistol. "Tell Gacho to go to hell," Matlack said, "He's had his last dollar." The bandits backed off at gunpoint; Matlack and Davis galloped for the river.[42]

When he reached safety in Candelaria, Matlack held up the money for all to see. "Look at that," he said. "I'm going back tomorrow and get the rest of that money." As the bank vice president made ready to return to Marfa, he counted up the currency that Captain Matlack had brought back. It was only US$6,500, a thousand dollars short. Matlack said he had given the missing thousand to Tomás Sánchez for his dangerous and diligent work as a go-between. Given how things turned out, Matlack explained, Sánchez was going to have to relocate from Mexico to the United States and start his life over. The thousand dollars was well deserved. There is no record of anyone confirming with Sánchez that he received the money.[43]

General Joseph Dickman, commanding officer of the army's Southern Department, criticized Matlack for not paying the full ransom, fearing that a reputation for breaking promises would endanger the lives of future captives. But at the time of his criticism neither he nor anyone else had heard Captain Matlack's version of events on the trail to San Antonio del Bravo. Those facts only came out when Dickman and Langhorne summoned Matlack to Marfa for an explanation. Once he heard Matlack's story, General Dickman withdrew all criticism of the officer, but continued to assert that full payment was in order, saying "Nothing will be done about the matter until later, but when the right time comes the government will undertake to carry out its agreement for the ransom of the aviators."[44]

At daybreak on the nineteenth, just hours after Matlack's return, three columns of cavalry under the command of Major James P. Yancey crossed the Rio Grande at Candelaria, Ruidosa and Indio. They were accompanied by just-released Lieutenants Peterson and Davis, plus Dawkins Kilpatrick, two customs inspectors, Marfa town marshal A. G. Beard, Presidio County deputy sheriff Mark Langford and a number of civilian scouts, including former Texas Ranger John Kerr. Captain Matlack led the Candelaria detail.[45]

Like the earlier punitive expeditions, La Junta's mostly involved chasing around in the desert without any tangible results. Unlike the other two, the expedition was conducted among frequent downpours and hailstorms. And there were some remarkable moments. The first came just after the Ruidosa column crossed the river. In a tiny hamlet on the Mexican side the cavalry found five draft evaders—La Juntans who were U.S. citizens living in Mexico. It is hard to imagine the cavalry pausing to check identification, ask for draft cards, and then escort suspected draft violators back across the river—instead of chasing after Rentería—but that is what they did.[46]

On the morning of the second day of the incursion, scouts for Matlack's Candelaria column came upon three armed Mexicans and took them captive. Another patrol found a solitary armed man, making the total four. Matlack knew them. They weren't part of Rentería's band, but they *were* wanted men: Jesus Janír and his son Francisco, who had escaped from jail after stealing cattle and horses from the Brite Ranch; Bernardino Salgado, a bandit and horse thief; and Juan José Fuentes, who had killed civilian scout Pablo Chaves's brother. The prisoners were passed along a chain of command, then, following what he said was local custom, Major Yancey turned them over to civilians—including Marshal Beard and Deputy Langford—to be taken back to the United States and handled under criminal law.[47]

Yancey knew full well that one of the civilian scouts was Pablo Chaves, whose brother had been killed by Juan José Fuentes. He admonished the civilians to keep an eye on Chaves lest he try to exact revenge. As soon as Yancey was out of sight, John Kerr suggested, "Just take them off down there and we'll shoot them." Kilpatrick and the customs agents wanted no part of it, but frontier justice was quickly done. A cavalryman later said that he "saw the scouts shooting at the prisoners. I was about five hundred yards distant and the Mexicans were running about twenty-five yards away from the scouts. Two of them I saw fall."[48]

The search for Jesus Rentería continued on the ground and in the air. Lieutenants F. S. Estill and R. H. Cooper, flying one of the Air Service's DeHavillands, spotted three riders on a mountain trail. After making a few passes to check out the riders, and perhaps after loosing a few rounds to see how they reacted, the fliers realized that the horsemen were firing back. The aviators circled, then dove, aiming the twin Marlin machine guns at their quarry. Estill pushed the trigger button on his stick and ripped off a string of bullets; Cooper aimed the swivel-mounted Lewis machine guns and fired. One of the presumed bandits fell from his white horse, apparently dead. The other two riders fled into the canyons, out of sight.[49]

It can be difficult to pin down the truth when it comes to bandidos in northern Mexico. Everyone agrees that the man on the white horse was Rentería. Some say he was killed. Others say that he survived. A veteran of the Army Air Service who flew searches for Peterson and Davis conducted intensive research and agrees with the official army position that Estill and Cooper had by sheer dumb luck killed Rentería, making the La Junta punitive expedition the only one that meted out its intended punishment. Another army veteran who served in the pack trains on the La Junta punitive expedition, and who later became a respected authority on the Big Bend, cites "one of the most trusted and efficient informers in the Big Bend, above suspicion," as having tossed back shots of tequila with Rentería a month after his supposed death.[50]

Whether or not the cavalry successfully exterminated Rentería, the punitive expedition in La Junta enjoyed another important distinction from the previous two. It was the only one undertaken with Mexican consent, albeit late and disputed Mexican consent. Shortly after his troops crossed the border, Colonel Langhorne contacted the Carrancista commanding officer at Ojinaga, General Antonio Pruneda, and informed him of the movement. Surprisingly, Pruneda — supported by his commanding officer in Ciudad Chihuahua — agreed that Rentería needed to be chased down. He sent a column of his own cavalry toward Cuchillo Parado to backstop the U.S. push. At Fort Bliss, General Robert Howze notified his Mexican counterpart General Francisco González, commander of northern Chihuahua, and González agreed to cooperate. The rationale for the U.S. adventure, and the foundation for Mexican cooperation, was the compact signed by both nations in the 1880's that allowed border crossings in hot pursuit of Apache raiders. Mexico had angrily contested that same justification when it had been posited during Pershing's 1916 Punitive Expedition; the difference in 1919 was that Mexico and the United States had been discussing bandido border incursions for three years, and a consensus was emerging that cooperation was the best course. The issue was not settled, however; Mexico City's newspapers waxed indignant over the La Junta punitive expedition; *El Universal* discontinued its English-language section in angry protest. President Carranza formally objected to the United States State Department, even though the military commander of the state of Chihuahua had granted Langhorne formal permission to enter Mexico (albeit two days after Langhorne did so).[51]

The cavalry withdrew from Mexico on August 24, the sixth day of their expedition and three days after President Carranza's diplomatic protest.[52]

A few words need to be said about the unquestionably brave and hardy Captain Leonard Matlack. It is a shame to smudge the reputation of such a man, and we would not do so over the foggy questions of whether he really heard Mexican death threats while waiting to rescue Lieutenant Davis or whether Tomás Sánchez really received the missing thousand dollars. But the record is clear on one point: when he reported the deaths of the four murdered Mexican prisoners to Colonel Langhorne, he stated that they died during a wild gunfight at a fortified adobe hideout. That was the version adopted by Major Yancey in his official report. We cannot tell whether one officer was covering for the other, or whether they had mutually agreed on a modified set of facts. Antagonist J. J. Kilpatrick disputed the veracity of the Matlack-Yancey version, leading to a court-martial of Major Yancey in which the truth came out. Matlack's known prevarication about the Mexicans' deaths casts some doubt on the matter of the missing money and the attempted ambush.[53]

In 1919 life in La Junta hadn't changed all that much over the previous seventy years. The Mexican central government still held the fort at Ojinaga, surrounded by hostile warriors, regularly emerging from the fortress to apply violence to their own ends. Nomadic looters still used the border's political boundary to their advantage, raiding on one side and trading on the other. A few isolated towns became outlaw havens where stores did business with all comers and bandits could live in peace. The only difference was that the United States added a cordon of cavalry and air surveillance to the mix, with limited success.

The bandidos finally died out under pressure from troops of both governments, but it took much longer than necessary because nationalism and borderism prevented an integrated, cooperative approach to the problem.

Borders have consequences. Among the consequences are increased incentives to commit cross-border crime and an impaired ability of law enforcement to do anything about it. Borders create havens from which the guilty can taunt the injured. As a result, niceties are sometimes set aside and offended parties sometimes feel compelled to make illegal incursions into places like Chihuahua, Cambodia, Lebanon and Afghanistan. But it is painfully difficult—and not infrequently counterproductive—to pursue folk heroes on their home turf.

The feuds and shootings among Ben Leaton, John Burgess, Edward Hall and their progeny steal the spotlight from other early settlers who did as much—perhaps more—to shape the Texas side of La Junta. Candelaria's J. J. Kilpatrick receives some notice, but mostly because he got in a feud of his own with the United States Army. William Russell was almost invisible, spending his life working hard on his farm.

Only John W. Spencer seems to have left a mark on the community without attracting notoriety. His past was somewhat shady—he was said to have joined James Kirker's scalp-hunting squadron, and he would never be specific about how he spent his first year in La Junta—but his life after reaching Presidio was generally peaceful. He lent five hundred dollars to Ben Leaton for land acquisition. He supplied horses and cattle to Fort Davis. Henry Skillman used Spencer's farm as an informal headquarters during the Civil War. Perhaps most notably, John Spencer located what became the Presidio Mine at Shafter, but he sold his interest to San Francisco mining speculators for US$1,600 and five thousand shares of stock in the Presidio Mining Company; Spencer never became wealthy from silver.

There are historical references to "Spencer's Farm," which can mean either of two places. John Spencer's first homestead was directly across from the river junction, extending downstream to the original town of Presidio. As his holdings expanded, Spencer moved his base of operations up the Rio Grande about thirteen miles. A little settlement called Indio sprouted there to house people working on his farm and others. It was Indio, not Presidio, that became Spencer's home. He ran a trading post there—the first Spencer's store. When he died in 1898, his widow buried him in a small cemetery on a mesilla overlooking his Indio ranch. His is the only marked grave in the plot—the others are simple mounds of stones.[1]

At his death John Spencer owned six tracts of land totaling 1,650 acres—a goodly amount of irrigable farmland, but less significant to the extent that it included dry grazing acreage. Reflecting the changes brought to Texas by the railroad rush, four of Spencer's six tracts were within railroad surveys. The surveys had been performed by four different railroads, none of which ever laid tracks in La Junta.[2]

John Spencer was eighty years old when he died. Either

The Spencers

he had ceased active ranching and farming or his family disposed of most of his livestock between his death and the filing of his will for probate; other than land, his estate inventory lists only seven horses, two cattle, a carriage and 4,263 shares in the Presidio Mining Company. The company was behind in paying its dividends, owing Spencer US$3,730. Spencer's land, livestock and personal property were valued at US$3,272. His mining company stock was worth US$8,600.[3]

John Spencer was survived by his widow, Felicitas Molina de Spencer, and seven surviving adult children ranging in age from twenty-seven to forty-three. Arcadio, Carlos, Guillermo and Salome lived in Ojinaga. Ricardo lived in Ciudad Chihuahua, Presilliano lived in Presidio and Carolina lived in Shafter. The seven children produced a gaggle of grandchildren who produced a flurry of great-grandchildren, scattering the Spencer name and genes across West Texas.[4]

Operating a store in La Junta is a Spencer family tradition. John W. Spencer had his trading post at Indio. His son Carlos ran an Ojinaga store in partnership with Moses Kelly (the customs inspector shot by Juan Faver). Carlos's son Francisco moved the store to Presidio, then moved it again to higher ground after the 1904 flood. It was Francisco's general store that became the informal United States military headquarters during the 1913–1914 battle of Ojinaga. Francisco lost his supply of kerosene when stray bullets from the fray punctured a storage tank.[5]

Francisco was still operating his store in Presidio when Arthur Stilwell's Kansas City, Mexico & Orient Railway completed its Mexican line to Ojinaga in 1927. The town scheduled a great celebration. Governor Marcelo Caravel boarded the KCM&O in Ciudad Chihuahua for a ceremonial trip to the border, but a railroad bridge collapsed, killing three people. The governor survived, but the fete was canceled.[6]

That turned out to be the last gasp of the troubled KCM&O; the Atchison, Topeka & Santa Fe Railroad Company bought up its disjointed trackage in 1928 and completed the Texas side of the link to La Junta in 1930, running track down the Alamito Creek valley to Presidio.[7]

Presidio and Ojinaga expected a boom from the new railroad. In large part, their hopes were pinned on developing deposits of gold, silver, copper and zinc in the surrounding mountains. There was talk that the recently abandoned Shafter silver mine might reopen now that it could economically ship ore to El Paso for smelting. Agriculture was the valley's second hope; one study indicated that La Junta held more than 325,000 irrigable acres of farmland. Anticipation was high; some

Kansas City investors showed up in Presidio one day, talking about building a three-story office building. Newspapers looked into Presidio's future and predicted that the railroad's arrival would "make its 2000 inhabitants into a second El Paso."[8]

Weary of instability in Mexico, the Santa Fe no sooner completed the link across the Rio Grande than it announced that its 311 miles of Mexico trackage were for sale. Purchaser Benjamin F. Johnston, a United States citizen whose United Sugar Company had prospered in Mexican farming, bought the asset for US$1.55 million.[9]

Because its tracks were too flimsy to permit high-speed transport, the KCM&O was a leisurely line. One of its conductors was said to teach school in the small Texas town of Hovey. When the train came through, he would dismount, walk over to the schoolhouse, review the students' work, assign new lessons and take a batch of their papers back to the train for grading during the long, slow journey. Another story has a cowpoke making a suggestion to the conductor: "Those shop boys in San Angelo ought to unhitch the cowcatcher from the front end and wire it onto the rear end. We ain't liable to catch up with no cows, but what's to stop them from walkin' in the back door?"[10]

The Big Bend's hard-rock mineral boom never happened. Presidians watched a wildcat oil well being drilled by the Linderman Oil Corporation four miles from Presidio, but that turned out to be a dry hole. By 1936 the outlook for agriculture was dimming too. Upstream water diversion—especially the Elephant Butte Dam that controlled the Rio Grande's flow—diminished water quantity and quality. J. J. Kilpatrick's farm, which once produced 600 bales of cotton annually, yielded about half that much. The normal valleywide annual production of 6,000 bales dropped to 2,500.[11]

In 1939, following the rise of the Mexican unionist movement, a sugar price drop, Benjamin Johnston's death and the disastrous depression, United Sugar sold its railroad to the Mexican government for a pittance. The Santa Fe held on to its line to Presidio, but business was poor.[12]

In retrospect, the railroad came too late in the game—routes had already been established to the east and west—and it was hampered by several steep grades that escalated fuel costs and freight rates on the line. The first refrigerated load of produce didn't cross the river in La Junta until 1967. Rail cars of Mexican zinc concentrate occasionally moved through La Junta on their way to smelters in El Paso, but the Santa Fe line and the Mexican National line that met in La Junta carried primarily local traffic—including goods for Spencer's store—

and a few passengers who embarked in Presidio or Ojinaga for the trip south. Traffic dwindled, then surged briefly in the 1980's, but finally ceased.[13]

As Francisco Spencer grew older, he began to rely on his son — another Carlos Spencer — to run the store. According to ads in local newspapers, F. Spencer & Bros. would deliver purchases from its general merchandise store in Presidio: groceries, dry goods, hardware, Stetson hats, shoes and novelties. You could even pay your telephone bill at the store.[14]

Though the valley was beyond the reach of television or radio, and though there was only one paved road into town (from Marfa), bilingual local newspapers brought global issues into the valley's consciousness. For the most part, however, front-page stories stayed close to two concerns: agriculture and transportation.

Cantaloupes, cotton and lettuce were always topics of conversation and concern. Would a hailstorm ruin the crop? Would blowing sand damage fragile melons? Ten carloads of lettuce, forty rail cars of cantaloupes, five thousand bales of cotton — that was news. Presidio noted the promised construction of a dam on the Rio Conchos near Peguis Canyon — the beginning of a Mexican irrigation project that would water the farms along the Conchos. There is no indication that La Juntans on the Texas side of the valley realized the problems that could come if Mexico captured the waters of the Rio Conchos before they reached the Rio Grande.[15]

Far downriver, Big Bend became a Texas state park in 1933 — created primarily to tap funds and jobs available through FDR's Civilian Conservation Corps — and gained the status of a national park in 1944. By the 1950's tens of thousands of people were coming to see the natural wonders of the park, and Presidio eyed the revenue-generating traffic jealously. Even though virtually no cars jounced down the dirt road from the park to La Junta by way of Terlingua, Lajitas and Redford, La Juntans hoped that improvements to the road would someday bring visitors. As it was, driving forty miles on the "steep and rocky road" could take five hours, and was considered a "breath-taking adventure."[16]

Equally important was the matter of a paved road from Ojinaga to Ciudad Chihuahua. The existing rutted trail was suited only for jeeps. There were hopes that the road would be graded by the summer of 1956, though paving the route would take longer — until the 1970's as it turned out. Presidians laid plans to snag tourists from the American side of the Rio Grande before they crossed over to Ojinaga; some thought that old Fort Leaton, which sat in decay, would make a good night club, or maybe a tourist headquarters. It ended up becoming a state park.[17]

The Rio Grande was the biggest obstacle to vehicle traffic between the two banks of La Junta. In 1928 H. E. Dupuy built a bridge across the river and began charging tolls to cross it. The bridge was rickety and inadequate, but Presidio County lacked the financial means to erect a substitute. Dupuy had found a bird's nest on the ground; he could charge whatever tolls the traffic would bear, reportedly sometimes as high as US$100 for a commercial truck. In 1958 Dupuy got in an argument with a Presidio County commissioner over proposed construction of a county bridge. Standing on Dupuy's private span, the commissioner concluded the argument by shooting and killing Dupuy. The shooting was ruled self-defense, and no charges were ever brought.[18]

The occasional local scandal diverted people's thoughts from international conflicts and the daily difficulty of life in the valley. Francisco Garza Solis, "el brujo de Ojinaga" (the sorcerer of Ojinaga), hit his twenty-year-old son René four times in the head—with an axe—then buried the body under the floor of the house they shared, where it lay for nine months. When the police discovered the crime, they took Solis not to jail, but to the local clinic for a psychiatric examination. Perhaps that decision was prompted by the accused's remark to the police at his arrest: "Let me go to Ojinaga to get an herb; when it's on fire, you will see the whole picture. It's a modern television." Solis, who was seventy-seven years old, was painted as an "ancient bartender and imaginary monster"; even his own children wrote a letter to the judge saying that their father was "a man with an evil heart, without scruples, very clever and bright, with a wicked mind, but we wouldn't say that he was crazy." By the time Solis was convicted and sentenced to a Mexican penitentiary, he was being called "the Ogre of Ojinaga," which has a certain alliterative ring.[19]

Sometimes there was organized entertainment. The Ojinaga Lions Club sponsored a bullfight, requiring the construction of a bull ring to hold five thousand people. It was all for a good cause—purchasing Salk polio vaccine, which was a major concern after the terrible polio epidemics only a few years earlier. The opening day at the bullring featured Carmelita Hernandez, "a beautiful brunette who fights on foot and on a horse the most wild bulls," as well as a more conventional male toreador. The Lions Club in Presidio took a tamer route, hosting a Memorial Day Carnival featuring a Turtle Derby, a dunking pond and a friendly game of roulette. The valley's founding family was well represented: Oscar Spencer worked the dunking pond, Ismael Spencer kept an eye on the kiddy car ride and Frank and Carlos Spencer handled the hamburgers and soft drinks.[20]

Joe (José) Spencer, brother of Frank and Carlos, wasn't at the Lions Club event because he had moved his family to El Paso after World War II. The brothers were close, though. Frank was shot down over Germany in the war and spent time in a POW camp. When Joe learned that his big brother was being held prisoner, he quit his job working for Carlos in the store, lied to the Marines about his age and signed up for duty. Joe was going to save Frank. He had completed training at Paris Island and was awaiting orders when the crew of the *Enola Gay* dropped Little Boy on Hiroshima.[21]

After the war, Joe went to work at the Falstaff brewery in El Paso. When the brewery closed, he took a job at a building materials company. Meanwhile, Carlos had changed Spencer's store from a grocery into a clothing store. The peso was strong, business was good, and in the 1970's Carlos asked Joe if he would consider returning to Presidio and helping out. For several years Joe commuted two hundred miles from El Paso weekly rather than uproot his wife and four children. By 1979 only his youngest, Gilbert, was still in school and the store was doing well, so the El Paso Spencers moved back home to La Junta, just in time for the next cycle of cross-border conflict.[22]

Smuggling is the epitome of border problems. La Juntans have smuggled things since the moment the border was drawn. They smuggled cattle in both directions. They smuggled ammunition, usually southward. Before, during and after Prohibition they smuggled sotol liquor, pulque and tequila northward. When Mexico kept prices for candelilla wax artificially low, they smuggled the stuff into Texas. But there's something special about drug smuggling.

Maybe it's because marijuana, cocaine and heroin are illegal on both sides of the border—double contraband. Maybe it's because smuggling drugs, unlike smuggling candelilla wax or Swiss watches or Japanese boom boxes, requires an extended network of criminals and corrupt public officials from one end of the chain to the other. Or maybe it's the "Smuggler's Blues":

Pablo Acosta

The sailors and pilots, the soldiers and the law,
The pay-offs and the rip-offs, and the things nobody saw.
No matter if it's heroin, cocaine, or hash,
You've got to carry weapons 'cause you always carry cash.
There's lots of shady characters, lots of dirty deals;
Every name's an alias in case somebody squeals.
It's the lure of easy money, it's got a very strong appeal.[1]

Ojinagan Domingo Aranda began his smuggling career during World War II, portaging tires, sugar, coffee and other hard-to-come-by commodities across the Rio Grande. After the war he moved to Portales, New Mexico, where he learned to smuggle heroin and assembled a modest distribution network. One night in 1969 he was playing cards with a business partner of his named Pancho Carreón. Liquor was involved, and Carreón said something impolite about Aranda's sister. Aranda jumped to his feet, angry. Carreón lunged with a knife. Aranda pulled a small-caliber pistol and shot Carreón in the mouth. Carreón drowned in his own blood. It seemed like a good time for Aranda to return to Ojinaga, and he did.[2]

The heroin-smuggling business in Ojinaga was profitable. Aranda operated out of the telephone exchange. As his enterprise grew, he brought nephew Manuel Carrasco into the fold. Carrasco was ambitious. Soon he had his own operation, with a reach larger than Aranda's. When Uncle

Domingo's business suffered several setbacks, Manuel took him into his employ, reversing roles.[3]

Smugglers weave tangled webs. Manuel Carrasco became convinced that his uncle was stealing from him. It's not clear whether Carrasco's suspicions were justified, but they were enough to prompt him to cooperate with a couple of gentlemen who had come to town — Pancho Carreón's sons, looking for revenge.

The police found Domingo Aranda's remains near the Polvo crossing. He had been shot, garroted, doused with gasoline and set aflame. The killers lingered to consume a six-pack of beer in the firelight, then went on their way.[4]

Manuel Carrasco is notable as Ojinaga's first violent, unpredictable borderlands drug lord. He is also notable because he advanced the drug-smuggling business model; he was the first Ojinaga operator to have the *plaza*. The critical question in a Mexican drug-dealing town is "*¿Quién está manejando la plaza?*" — literally, "Who is managing the town square?" but figuratively, "Who's in charge here?"

The plaza is a drug-dealing franchise granted by powerful government officials. There might be more than one plaza in a busy area — for example, one overseen by the military and the judicial police and another under the jurisdiction of the governor and the state police. That arrangement can create healthy — or deadly — competition.

On the local level, it sometimes appears that the dealer controls the police or the local military. He becomes a drug lord, openly ruling the town. But even the most powerful drug lords have controllers, people who provide money or protection — bigger drug lords, oligarchs, generals, governors, attorneys general, presidents. At this higher level, the police and the military control the drug lord. Controllers want to remain in the background, and they prefer to give the plaza to someone who understands the importance of circumspection. It is acceptable for the drug lord to become known, for that draws attention away from the controllers, but it is a bad idea for the drug lord's profile to become too high, lest someone wonder who his controllers might be. If the plaza holder steps out of line, the controllers will arrange for his replacement. Preferring to avoid direct involvement, they might create a powerful competitor, or they might signal law enforcement that the dealer's immunity has been stripped. Then they let nature take its course.[5]

Manuel Carrasco was the first person to hold the Ojinaga plaza. He owned the mayor and he bribed the local military commander, but he did not control the municipal police — who were headed by a reformer—and he was dependent on a Parral operator for product and financing. The mix worked, but even the best drug dealers sometimes experience cash flow problems. In March 1976 Carrasco met with Heraclio Avilez to discuss just that. Heraclio represented Carrasco's Parral connection, who had sold a lot of product to Carrasco on credit. Unfortunately, thirty pounds of Carrasco's heroin and a ton of his marijuana had been nabbed in United States drug busts. Avilez was paying a polite visit to make sure prompt payment would be forthcoming nonetheless.[6]

Apparently Carrasco soothed Avilez's concerns, for evening found them in an Ojinaga cantina, drunk and rowdy. Enjoying the company of several bar girls, the pair amused themselves by firing their pistols into the air. One of the bullets ricocheted, hitting a hooker in the foot. Being responsible citizens, Carrasco and Avilez took her to the offices of Dr. Artemio Gallegos for medical care. Someone must have sounded an alarm of some sort, because the doctor had barely begun bandaging the woman up when the police chief came through the door, backed by a squad of patrolmen. Since the chief was not on Carrasco's payroll, this was trouble. Avilez, still intoxicated, started shooting. The cops shot back. The doctor, the nurse and the whore dived behind the counter. Machine guns sprayed the room. A policeman took a bullet in the arm, and Carrasco was wounded in the lower back. Someone shot Heraclio Avilez through the heart. The fight spilled into the street. A voice shouted that soldiers were coming from the comandancia. The drug runners ran.[7]

The next morning Carrasco was lying in a hospital in Ciudad Chihuahua. He knew his main problems were not going to be with the police or the military. It was his Parral connection that was going to be a problem. Manuel Carrasco thought things over. Was it possible to turn this disaster into a windfall? The connection called and asked what had happened to Heraclio. Carrasco told him, and offered his condolences. "And what about the money?" the connection asked. Manuel Carrasco lied, reassuring his controller that he had paid Heraclio in full, but he didn't know where Heraclio had put the cash.[8]

Not a bad story, dead men being somewhat difficult to interrogate. But when Heraclio Avilez's bodyguards got back to Parral, they said that they had never seen any money change hands. Worse—much worse— one of the bodyguards said he saw Carrasco put an opportune bullet in Heraclio Avilez during the shootout. And so the word went out that Carrasco was a dead man. To drive the point home, the entire Ojinaga police force was marked for death too. Carrasco skipped town, as did the frightened reformer police chief and all his men. Carrasco laid low somewhere in Mexico. The United States Immigration and Naturalization Service smoothed the way for the police officers and their families to take refuge across the border.[9]

Carrasco had relied heavily on Martín "Shorty" Lopez to run his plaza, which extended from Pilares on the north all the way to Boquillas on the south—all of La Junta and more. Shorty handled the mechanics of the operation, managing an airstrip-equipped ranch for Carrasco and hauling loads of marijuana up Highway 67 to Fort Stockton. When Carrasco vanished, Shorty Lopez stepped in to fill the gap. At first he assumed that he was running Carrasco's plaza during his absence, but as the months went by and Shorty forged his own relationships with suppliers, controllers and protectors, everyone began looking at the plaza as Shorty's.[10]

Shorty Lopez's income soared. He bought himself a ranch—a piece of the old Hacienda de Orientales near San Carlos that had once belonged to Enrique Creel. As 1976 turned to 1977, Lopez became more comfortable in his new role as drug lord. But there were persistent rumors that Carrasco saw Lopez as a usurper, and planned revenge. A chance encounter between the two men on the streets of Ciudad Chihuahua turned ugly, but not violent.[11]

Many people along the border believe that there are good drug dealers and bad drug dealers. Local citizens like Shorty Lopez, who rise from poverty and contribute part of their drug proceeds to the church and the schools, are good drug lords. They are heirs to the legacy of Pancho Villa: dangerous men who fight the system but have hearts of gold. The bad drug lords are "*la mafia*": rich gangsters, corrupt politicians, outsiders who do not respect the local community. Somewhere along the line Manuel Carrasco became identified with the Mafia— a tool of the powerful, not a champion of the poor. After his embarrassment in the doctor's office shootout, he worked his way back into the good graces of the underworld powers. When he regained enough clout to deal with Martín "Shorty" Lopez, he sent his gunmen to avenge the loss of his plaza. A translation of a Mexican *corrido*, the folk song of the campesino, tells the story:

*They passed through Providencia
And now came from Santa Elena,
Where they had been paid.
Thirty kilos of the good stuff.
Manuel Valdez and Martín
Suffered a terrible punishment.*

They were traveling on the road.
The men were waiting for them.
An innocent person warned them,
And so they separated.
Martín got back in the bed of the truck
While Manuel continued driving.

The awaited moment arrived
As had the enemies.
There was a hail of bullets
And three fell sprawling.
Afterward Martín also
Took a bullet through the brain.

They grabbed Martín
And searched his clothes.
They didn't find anything.
They split open his head,
Because they had to follow
The Mafia's orders.

He was named Martín Lopez
But they called him "Shorty."
He was a well known man
At the Hacienda de Orientales,
And he was also respected
By the judicial police.

From the Mafia nor from fate,
Has anyone ever escaped.
He who walks the path of evil
Ought to go well armed.
But as for Manuel and Martín,
The Mafia has killed them.[12]

When Lopez turned up dead, the second tier of the Ojinaga plaza—men like Pablo Acosta, Rogelio Gonzalez and Victor Sierra—met to decide how to go forward. They chose Sierra, another local boy, to apply for the franchise. Sierra had been raised by his mother, a pious woman who put him in the seminary, but at some point he fell under the spell of his deceased father's brothers. Victor's principal source of income came from serving as emcee at his uncles' Ojinaga strip clubs. On occasion he moved some marijuana for Shorty Lopez.[13]

Following his nomination, Sierra went to Ciudad Chihuahua to present his application to the comandante of the federal judicial police. After several days of waiting to see the comandante, an intensive interview process commenced with some oblique conversations in which the most important issues were never mentioned, followed by three days of beatings and torture. It must have been a confusing time for Victor Sierra, but when the interview was finished—when the comandante was convinced that Sierra could keep a secret under pressure—he was granted the plaza.[14]

Sierra held the plaza for about four years before being arrested in late 1980. The United States Drug Enforcement Agency nabbed him on his way to Las Vegas to deliver a half-ton of marijuana. Sierra wanted to check out how Vegas ran the bigtime strip clubs.[15]

During Sierra's tenure, Pablo Acosta worked to build his own drug organization in Ojinaga. The effort was undertaken openly, with Sierra's consent. So long as Pablo paid Sierra and Sierra paid his controllers, there was no problem.

Pablo Acosta was a native of Santa Elena, on the river below La Junta. His grandfather and father were farmers and migrant workers who occasionally smuggled candelilla wax or sotol liquor across the border. Pablo's father was killed outside a Fort Stockton bar, the result of a long-standing feud with the Baiza family. Pablo was twenty-one at the time. Shortly after his father's murderer received probation instead of a prison sentence, a member of the Baiza family was shot dead in another Fort Stockton watering hole.[16]

Pablo got arrested for a bar fight in 1963 and for a shooting outside a bar in 1964. In 1968 he took his first stab at drug running, leaving Ojinaga with an ounce of black-tar heroin in a balloon tied under his arm. An informant turned him in just after he crossed the river. Acosta was stopped at a Border Patrol roadblock near Marfa. At age thirty-one he began serving eight years in the federal penitentiary.[17]

Acosta left the penitentiary after five years, freed early for good behavior, and looked up a friend he had met in prison: Shorty Lopez. Shorty offered to help Pablo. Pablo took up residence in Odessa, Texas, and went into the roofing business, but he made regular trips to Ojinaga and back. When a former county commissioner failed to pay Pablo for a roofing job, Pablo used a piece of rubber hose to explain his position; he was arrested for assault. Acosta moved to Eunice, New Mexico, where he continued roofing and kept his channels to Shorty Lopez open.

While in Eunice, Acosta did well in shingles and opiates. In November 1976 he attempted to close the sale of a pound of heroin that he had placed in a mayonnaise jar for safekeeping. Pablo, the buyers, a couple of go-betweens and some hangers-on met in the cold desert—pickup trucks and cowboy hats and automatic pistols and a mayonnaise jar of black-tar heroin. Something went wrong. Pablo smelled a trap. One of the buyers pulled a badge and a gun. Pablo took off running. A federal grand jury indicted Acosta, but by then he was safely in Ojinaga, working with Shorty.[18]

During the reigns of Manuel Carrasco, Shorty Lopez and Victor Sierra, Ojinaga had been a two-plaza town. A drug organization under the protection of the state judicial police, thus reporting to powerful figures in Ciudad Chihuahua, existed independent of the plaza licensed by the army and the federal judicial police. This independent plaza, which obtained most of its product from Sinaloa, was run by Fermín Arevalo. For a few years Arevalo had to supervise his organization from the federal penitentiary in Ciudad Chihuahua—he robbed an Ojinaga bank, and protection by state officials only goes so far. Arevalo was out of prison by the time Victor Sierra was busted in the United States, and he had his eye on Ojinaga's federal plaza. But the federal plaza went to Pablo Acosta, who had established the necessary credibility and relationships during his work with Lopez and Sierra.[19]

A drug plaza is not unlike a multilevel marketing organization. As glorious as being a "drug lord" may sound, Pablo Acosta was on one of the lower rungs of the MLM structure. He was the person who keeps ten cases of water filters in his basement, distributing them case-by-case to his affiliates, who break them out piecemeal among front-line marketers, who sell the water filters to users. Upstream of Pablo were some people who stocked water filters by the thousands, but most upper levels of the organization never touched a water filter and never wanted to; they merely sold territories and collected royalties. Pablo paid commissions to Ojinaga's federal police commander, who passed the payments up the chain of authority, and to an honorary army comandante who fed the money into the army pipeline.[20]

Because Ojinaga was on the ragged edge of the Mexican frontier, Acosta enjoyed latitude that might not have been allowed closer to civilization. The military and the federal police both gave him badges to carry. His men were commissioned as federal police officers. Acosta and his entourage openly toted automatic pistols and assault rifles on Ojinaga's streets. If Pablo needed to hold a meeting, he might well sit down with his visitor in the military garrison offices, or in the federal police station. In the early 1980's, Pablo Acosta had the run of Ojinaga.[21]

Fermín Arevalo was frustrated at his inability to secure the federal plaza. A feud developed between Arevalo and Acosta, and it was exacerbated when Acosta decided that Arevalo's son Lilí had informed

DEA agents of an Acosta-owned planeload of marijuana flown into the United States. The snitch cost Acosta a plane, a pilot and a lot of marijuana. Then Lilí and Pablo got into an argument about payment for another load of drugs. On a hot August afternoon in 1982 two of Acosta's enforcers, Marco DeHaro and Damaso Martínez Prieto, went looking for Lilí Arevalo. They found him in downtown Ojinaga, coming out of an ice-cream parlor called Nevería Alegría. DeHaro pointed his AR-15 out the driver's window of his vehicle and opened fire. Martínez hopped out the passenger side, laid an old M-1 across the hood and contributed to the thicket of bullets. Lilí died at the scene; his brother Lupe was taken to the hospital. The Chihuahua state police made noises about the incident, but no one was charged with the shootings.[22]

Two months later a carload of Arevalo's men ambushed Pablo Acosta and Marco DeHaro in front of Samborn's Restaurant in Ojinaga. Pablo was wounded and passed out. DeHaro carried on a gun battle with the three attackers. At one point a school bus drove into the firefight. When the driver realized what he had done, he hit the brakes and, instead of speeding out of danger, told the kids to duck for cover. The battle continued. DeHaro killed one attacker and wounded another. The remaining assailant used the shelter of the school bus to drag his wounded compadre into their car and dash for safety. DeHaro, hiding behind one of the bus's wheels, stepped into the street and loosed a fusillade at the fleeing vehicle. The car swerved, then crashed. When the commotion was over, DeHaro flagged down a passing pickup and persuaded the driver to help him take Pablo to safety.[23]

Fearing that more of Arevalo's men might be lurking in Ojinaga, DeHaro drove Acosta to a private clinic in San Carlos. After Pablo had been stitched up, DeHaro and Acosta went to Pablo's nearby ranch to recover, but by three o'clock in the morning the injured leader was back on his feet, ready for action. He knew that one of his attackers was lying wounded in the Ojinaga hospital; Pablo meant to kidnap the villain and make him confirm who was behind the attack. Back to Ojinaga, where Acosta rounded up several of his enforcers, armed with assault rifles. Over to the hospital. The gunman's room was guarded by two municipal policemen. When Pablo's men approached, the cops carefully extracted their revolvers and placed them on the floor. In the truck on the way back to Pablo's ranch the kidnapped gunman admitted that the Arevalos were behind the attack. He was dead by the next morning.[24]

A month later two Arevalos were sitting in a car on Ojinaga's main drag with the state police comandante. A pickup screeched to a halt. There were three men in the cab, four in the truck bed, and all seven opened fire with automatic weapons. A nearby Arevalo relation saw the gunfight erupt and returned fire from behind with a 9 mm semi-automatic pistol. Four of the seven attackers fell; the remaining three threw the dead and wounded in the back of the truck and raced off. The two Arevalos were shot up pretty bad, but they recovered. The comandante was miraculously unscathed. Witnesses said the attackers included Marco DeHaro and Pablo Acosta's brother Juan. No arrests resulted. Five months later Juan Acosta and his bodyguard were killed at a dance hall in San Carlos.[25]

In the three years after Lilí Arevalo's murder more than twenty-five people associated with Acosta or Arevalo were assassinated. Things were getting out of hand. Pablo Acosta always maintained that he had nothing to do with Lilí's shooting, that it was a rogue act by DeHaro. He claimed the same about the seven men in the pickup-truck attack. The explanation didn't wash with Arevalo. Acosta made peace overtures to Arevalo, who rejected them.[26]

Pablo decided to drive out to Fermín Arevalo's ranch to try to settle matters peaceably. To demonstrate his good faith, Acosta took only four armed men with him in his Ford Bronco. The peace emissaries paused for some target practice before donning bulletproof vests and heading to Arevalo's. It is easy to detect approaching vehicles on desert dirt roads; they leave a plume of dust that is visible for miles. When Acosta and his four goodwill ambassadors reached Arevalo's ranch house, his wife said he had gone to Ojinaga. Pablo said he would wait, suspecting that Arevalo was hiding inside. After an hour of tense discussions with Señora Arevalo, Acosta decided that Fermín had already ducked out the back door and that there was no point in waiting further.[27]

There were two roads out of the ranch: one smooth, one rough. Acosta decided to take the rugged, less-traveled route, figuring that if there were an ambush waiting it would be on the graded road. As the Bronco slowed to cross a cattle guard, a white pickup approached from the other direction. Acosta's men were focusing on the approaching vehicle when Fermín Arevalo and a ranch hand popped up out of an arroyo, assault rifles firing on full automatic. Acosta and his men dived for the floor. Tires blew out, the windshield shattered, the radiator gushed coolant and bullets zinged and clanged into the Bronco. One occupant of the bullet-riddled vehicle lifted his assault rifle over the back of the front seat, returning fire. The driver of the white pickup stepped out behind his door, taking careful shots at the Bronco with a hunting rifle. Fermín Arevalo expended his clip of ammunition and paused to reload; one of Acosta's men nailed him with a burst of bullets, then another took out the pickup driver. The ranch hand fled into the chaparral. Neither Pablo nor any of his men were seriously injured, though they were going to have some new battle scars. They inspected Fermín Arevalo's body, laced it with a few more bullets, drove over it a few times with the white pickup, then slit his belly open, spilling his innards into the sand.[28]

Fermín Arevalo's widow filed a criminal complaint against Pablo and his four henchmen. Her defiance was astounding, but not as astounding as when a judge issued arrest warrants for Pablo and the others. Pablo later claimed that it cost him MEX$2 million to get the warrants quashed, but he was the undisputed and exclusive owner of the Ojinaga plaza.[29]

Pablo Acosta had weaknesses. He had always been attracted to alcohol, judging by the number of scrapes he got into in and around bars. And he was known to light up a joint now and then. But he developed two other habits that proved more dangerous and ultimately more deadly. The first was his addiction to crack cocaine. He smoked it in the Mexican way, rolling part of the tobacco out of a cigarette and stuffing rocks of crack inside. Crack made the already mercurial and violent man bleary-eyed and unpredictable. Mood swings, feelings of invincibility, loss of perspective, fear of conspiracies — his already imperfect personality took a turn for the worse.

His second deadly attraction was to Mimi Webb Miller. Mimi was not your typical borderlands resident. With a degree in art history from Southern Methodist University, the petite blonde had lectured at Rice University and organized exhibits in Houston galleries. In 1977 the developer of the regrettable resort at Lajitas asked her to come down and oversee a showing. Then he invited her to stay and establish an artists-in-residence program, and she accepted. It was love at first sight — with the Big Bend, not the developer. Mimi had a romantic streak, and it was fed by the rugged landscapes and lifestyles of West Texas. She bought a ranch on the Mexican side of the river. It was a remote spread — no electricity, no running water, just a big spring-fed cistern. Mimi's Rancho Milagro was seventeen miles — two hours — from the nearest telephone.

Mimi took a Mexican lover, and they lived together at Rancho Milagro. Her *novio* had occasional business dealings with Pablo Acosta, who became a regular visitor to the ranch. It turned out that Mimi's lover was a heroin addict. He said that it had started when heroin slipped under his fingernails while he broke down blocks of dope for shipment. That might have been true, but the addiction intensified into a needle-fed nightmare. She rid herself of her drug mule boyfriend, but retained her friendship with Pablo.[30]

Mimi developed a fascination with the border drug trade. It was dangerous and exciting. There is no evidence that she ever dealt in contraband herself, but the illicit business was part of what made the borderlands such a heady place to live. It fit perfectly into romantic notions of bandidos and federales, good drug dealers and bad drug dealers, murderers with hearts of gold. Webb Miller exhibited a rosy naïveté about Pablo Acosta and his enterprise, seeming to believe the heart-of-gold stuff, seeming to believe that everyone would love — or at least accept — Pablo if they just got to know him.

And so Mimi Webb Miller introduced her new boyfriend David Regela to Pablo. Regela was a U.S. customs agent assigned to penetrate the Acosta organization. Everyone knew that Regela was a narcotics officer. Pablo recognized him as the one who had sent a couple of his relatives to the penitentiary. Mimi seemed to think that the two could work things out if only they would spend some time together. Somehow the uneasy relationship between Acosta and Regela continued without either of them killing the other.

In 1985 writer Alan Weisman and photographer Jay Dusard came through Lajitas. They were working on a book about the borderlands. Mimi helpfully offered to introduce them to Pablo Acosta, border legend. They went to Ojinaga together, where they waited in the honorary military comandante's office for Pablo to appear. The comandante contacted Pablo over the police radio, then reminisced about the good old days: "Everything was under control then. Now there are so many different police. Every little while another special force shows up, all wanting money and cars and television sets. Each one says it's here to enforce some new law. You'd think the authorities would tell us. You don't know whether to pay attention or not. In the U.S. you can ask. Here, you just don't know." After badmouthing the supposed innocence and integrity of law enforcement in the United States, he penetrated to the heart of the matter: "You know, the system is so rotten that it's what lets us live in peace. It's so bad, it's good. The law doesn't let you do anything. It encourages you to be crooked. You are guaranteed much more that way."[31]

Acosta arrived, dressed in western fashion, begrimed with dust and sweat, a cocked and locked .45-caliber automatic pistol clipped to his belt. It was ten in the morning. He poured himself a glass of scotch and began rolling some tobacco out of a cigarette. He left the room to stuff in a few rocks of crack cocaine, then returned with the bulging mega-reefer, which he consumed in three enormous tokes. "The law has no charge against me," said Acosta, adopting the posture of the misunderstood. "I've never fought with the law or with honest people. What I do is wrong, but I do it to remedy many things, like education for young people who lack resources. I put on benefit horse races and cockfights. It's for them. The government never gives them anything. I buy them sports equipment.[32]

"The same governors and mayors in the U.S. are in the Mafia. If they wanted to stop drugs, they could do it in a day," asserted the increasingly stoned Acosta. "Look at me. You don't think the United States could control me if they wanted to? How can that rich country say that I am smarter than they are?"[33]

When the interview was over, Pablo and Mimi took Weisman and Dusard to see the Bronco that Pablo had been riding in when Fermín Arevalo ambushed him. The gunfire-ventilated automobile sat on concrete blocks, rusting. Pablo had preserved it, testimony to his invincibility. He enjoyed showing it to visitors.

A few months later a reporter for the *Washington Post Magazine* appeared in Presidio County. He was trying to chase down a story about vigilantes who had broken into the Ojinaga jail and abducted a prisoner accused of a vicious rape on the Texas side of the river. They handcuffed the scoundrel to a tree, naked, in a park outside Alpine, where the county sheriff picked him up. Inevitably, the reporter ran into Mimi Webb Miller, who drove him to Rancho Milagro. He was entranced with the ranch's rustic beauty, and with hers. Noting that she had been a debutante in Wichita Falls, Texas, he said, "The Mexicans call the beautiful woman who lives alone in the Chihuahuan Desert 'La Gringa Guera'—the blond American." In Mimi he saw an artistic soul drawn to the borderlands by "the undertow of human and natural danger, the exotic mingling of cultures, the meaninglessness of class and status, the appeal of strong, lawless men. But this intrigued her most: If there was a place where right and wrong weren't self-evident, it was the border." The reporter had caught a dose of Mimi's romance.[34]

Webb Miller didn't take the reporter directly to Pablo, even though he seemed well primed for the encounter. Instead, she introduced him to someone who introduced him to someone who took him to the radio dispatcher at the Ojinaga military comandancia, who radioed Pablo in his truck. In Ojinaga, which is quite different from Washington, D.C., the reporter surveyed the scene: "The dust envelops Ojinaga like a choking fog. As night falls, the refracting sunlight is replaced by the refracting headlights of old cars and trucks, always Fords and Chevys. We park outside the dirty white building and wait in the car. A street lamp on the corner showers the skeleton of a chinaberry tree that will soon be thick as an umbrella with springtime leaves. Three Mexican men, one wearing a cowboy hat, sit talking on the doorstep ten feet away. A dog and two empty Coke bottles are on the ground before them. The crickets are deafening. A Ford truck passes with a burned-out taillight. Across the street a man sits in a beat-up Chevy Impala." [35]

That was quite a buildup for what happened next. Pablo drove up in his pickup truck, rolled down his window, talked to the reporter's contact and refused to give an interview. He was tired and had been drinking tequila, he said. This effort of Mimi's to introduce the world to the fascinating conundrum of Pablo Acosta aborted, perhaps because she had failed to personally escort the reporter and manage the situation. [36]

Five days after the *Washington Post Magazine* article appeared, an El Paso paper did a decidedly unflattering story on Acosta. It quoted a DEA report that said that Acosta was "believed responsible for most of the narcotics flowing into Texas from Chihuahua." A DEA agent characterized Acosta as "a vicious, extremely dangerous person with little regard for human life." It mentioned that following a five-month undercover investigation eight presumed members of Acosta's organization had been indicted in Fort Stockton for heroin and cocaine trafficking. If Mimi Webb Miller was trying to polish Acosta's image, she had some work to do. [37]

Eight months later, Mimi persuaded Pablo to sit down with another reporter from the same El Paso newspaper. The interview took place in an Ojinaga apartment owned by the military comandante. Magically, Mimi somehow convinced the reporter to see things more or less the way she did: the article opened with a big picture of Pablo and Elva Fernandez, a blind woman who had been reduced to begging on Ojinaga's streets. According to the article, Pablo was going to arrange a cornea transplant for Fernandez. "Sure, what I do is wrong," Acosta admitted, "but for every bad thing I do, I do six hundred good things." But there was also a quote from a U.S. narcotics agent who said that "when [Acosta] gets bored, he goes out and shoots someone." And the reporter mentioned that Acosta had a reputation for "shooting down would-be assassins, slicing them open, then dragging their bodies through the desert behind his truck." [38]

The question is, what in the world were Mimi and Pablo thinking? One is drawn to the conclusion that Mimi Webb Miller was astoundingly naïve; she must have thought that people would embrace Pablo as a benign and intriguing contradiction amid the wild and mysterious borderlands. It is equally attractive to conclude that Pablo Acosta was so strung out on tequila, marijuana and crack cocaine that he entirely overlooked the profound stupidity of getting his name in the papers. For Pablo personally, it was a bad idea to taunt the drug-enforcement authorities in both countries. But for Pablo's handlers, the idea of a high-profile press-courting operative was absolutely unacceptable. True, the man who ran the plaza was put out there to take the heat, but he was supposed to be intelligent enough to keep the heat to a minimum. If he drew too much attention, someone was sure to ask about the multilevel marketing tiers above him. Someone would begin chasing down corrupt government officials.

To anyone involved in the illegal distribution chain who was not a complete drug-addled moron, "Yes, I smuggle cocaine and murder people, but I give basketballs to kids" was not an effective public relations message. Pablo did not come across as Robin Hood. He came across as a murderous common thug, and a not especially bright one at that. He had outlived his usefulness.

Killing Pablo quietly was not the answer. The honest drug-law enforcers would know that his organization continued, and they would shift their attention to his successor. Those determined to root out corruption would know that he had been killed to shut him up, and would be more determined than ever to find out who was behind Pablo Acosta. No, it was time to give the good guys a big, splashy victory, one that would let them claim to have cleaned up the border. And, to lessen the likelihood of pursuit beyond Pablo, the Mexican power structure had to take a visible role in making it happen.

Pablo's self-promoting interview appeared in the El Paso newspaper on December 3, 1986. Two days later the Mexican federal judicial police—his protectors—put out orders for his arrest. Mexico's attorney general gave the comandante in Juárez special authority over Ojinaga with a singular order: get Pablo.[39]

The comandante in Juárez was Guillermo Gonzalez Calderoni, an interesting man. Born into the Mexican elite, he served only four years as a federal police officer before being promoted to the Juárez comandancia. To American narcotics agents, he seemed to be a reformer. When he arrived in Juárez, he unceremoniously told his predecessor to clear out of town, then he went after the city's highest-profile drug dealer. The drug dealer had threatened, kidnapped and tortured a couple of El Paso journalists who had taken his picture and written articles about him. Everyone assumed that Calderoni busted the doper for roughing up the journalists. It never occurred to anyone that the dealer's original sin might have been having his name and face appear in the newspapers.[40]

Calderoni sent a squad of men to Ojinaga, but Pablo Acosta had already fled. Reverting to his roots, Pablo took refuge in Santa Elena, the tiny village where he had been born. It was a passable hideout—a small swath of agricultural land in the canyons of the Big Bend—but anyone who knew Pablo's life story would know to look there first. Worse, Pablo didn't exactly keep his presence a secret. Mimi Webb Miller knew. David Regela knew. The trading post across the river had long ago learned that when the Mexicans from Santa Elena bought up all their cigarettes, Pablo was in town. And the Border Patrol had figured out that noisy fiestas across the river in Santa Elena meant that Pablo was buying beer and roasting cabrito. Guillermo Calderoni and his men from Juárez were probably the last people in La Junta to find out where Pablo Acosta was hiding.[41]

When Calderoni finally caught on, he still faced a difficult task. Acosta was surrounded by men, guns and ammunition in Santa Elena. The roads into the town were rough and dusty; Acosta would know of a task force's approach well in advance. Coming in by boat through the rugged Big Bend canyons was impossible. A helicopter attack might work, but bringing helicopters into Ojinaga would set telephone wires buzzing. Flying from Ciudad Chihuahua wasn't an option: Pablo's network would notice a helicopter task force crossing the desert and tip him off before the long flight to Santa Elena was half over.

Acosta had too many friends in too many places, especially in rural pueblos that saw him sympathetically as another peon being chased by the Mafia. The image was ironic. Pablo Acosta existed only because state and national drug organizations and their corrupt police and military had penetrated La Junta. He was a creature of a postrevolutionary narco-oligarchy. He was the Mafia's point man, their fall guy, an expendable asset. But campesinos love their bandidos, and they adopted Pablo as a good drug lord.

Knowing that it would be impossible to approach Acosta from the Mexican side of the border, Calderoni called his new friend Matt Perez, acting agent in charge of the FBI office in Juárez. Perez recognized the opportunity for building a better drug-enforcement mechanism based on cross-border cooperation. He called his superiors in Washington, D.C., who authorized him to help Calderoni, even though the Mexican comandante had attached an unusual condition: only the FBI could be involved; the mission must be kept secret from the DEA, the Customs Service, the Border Patrol, even the State Department. Calderoni did not want to risk a leak.[42]

On April 24, 1987, airport workers in Marfa watched with surprise as an olive drab U.S. Army Huey set down, followed by two blue-and-white Bell 212s bearing the insignia of the Mexican federal police. The two Mexican helicopters held Calderoni and seventeen rough-looking armed men in civilian garb. Matt Perez and fifteen plainclothes FBI agents were in the army chopper. The aircraft refueled, then flew to a remote spot in Big Bend National Park, where they took on guides, four more FBI agents and some equipment that they had brought for the Mexicans. After a quick final briefing, the three copters took off and headed for the Rio Grande. The Huey landed on the United States side of the river; FBI agents spread out along its banks. The two Mexican craft darted for Santa Elena, low and fast.[43]

Santa Elena was taken entirely by surprise. Helicopters swooped and disgorged armed men onto rooftops and plazas. Pablo's men scattered, but were rounded up by machine-gun fire from helicopters that circled the village after unloading. The village was secure and quiet within ten minutes. Calderoni's men stood guard over dozens of men facedown in the dirt. But none of the men was Pablo Acosta. He had barricaded himself inside his fortified adobe house. Two of his men were in there with him, and they had an abundance of arms and ammunition. Calderoni's force surrounded Pablo's citadel. They ordered him to surrender; he did not. The ensuing gun battle lasted more than an hour. The Mexican force fired smoke grenades and tear gas. They rammed the house with a pickup truck. They charged through the door and captured one of Pablo's men, but were driven back by a blistering fusillade. Acosta's second compadre surrendered, but the drug lord would only shout defiant threats at Calderoni.[44]

Out of options, the police poured gasoline on the adobe's brushy roof and set it afire. Still Pablo did not emerge. An agent peered through a window; he thought he saw Pablo lying on a bed, bleeding. As the fire grew more intense, another agent looked. Pablo hadn't moved. He was dead. They pulled him from the fire. He had only one wound. It was to the back of the head.[45]

Pablo Acosta was his name,
He was born a U.S. citizen,
And he started playing with fire,
Knowing that one could get burned
on the banks of the Río Bravo,
in the state of Chihuahua.

There were fifteen federal policemen
That arrived in Santa Elena
On the banks of the Río Grande,

The spot where they landed.
They had come from Ciudad Juárez
To arrest the accused.

The leader of the police,
By the name of Calderoni,
Yelled "Give up Pablo,
This is your last chance!"
"You'll have to kill me
to take me to prison!"

The gun fight started,
According to the newspapers,
It was April 24,
Marked Friday on the calendar,
The day that cost the life
Of the Great Czar of smugglers.

If anyone reveres his memory,
And wants to send flowers
To the man who made legends,
And who helped the poor,
My cross is standing
In Rancho El Tecolote.[46]

Gral. Ortega   Gral. Villa   Gral. Herrera

One cannot always trust the historical record. Toribio Ortega is actually the man on the right, not the left. The man on the left appears to be Rodolfo Fierro, not Maclovo Herrera. Fierro was a notoriously vicious cutthroat. Corbis photograph.

Most leaders of the Mexican revolutions were simple people inspired by a cause. Sitting, second from the left, is Toribio Ortega. To his left, with the abundant beard, is José de la Cruz Sánchez. Photograph courtesy of the Aultman Collection, El Paso Public Library.

They came in wagons, buggies, on the backs of burros and on foot. Marfa Public Library, Marfa, Texas.

When oligarch Luis Terrazas crossed the river from Ojinaga in 1914, his clothes were dusty, but otherwise he looked none the worse for wear. Photograph courtesy of the Aultman Collection, El Paso Public Library.

Conditions for the Ojinaga refugees were better at Fort Bliss, but the accommodations were still spartan. These refugees are lining up to receive clothing.

Soldiers of the United States Eighth Cavalry based in Candelaria in 1918. The civilian who appears so easy in the saddle is scout Jim Watts, made of sterner stuff than the young cavalrymen. Though Watts usually carried a Winchester rifle in a scabbard on the left side of his horse, he is holding an army Springfield in this photo. W. D. Smithers Collection, Harry Ransom Humanities Research Center, the University of Texas at Austin.

Captain Leonard F. Matlack (reclining) and soldiers of the United States Eighth Cavalry at their base in Candelaria. Matlack ransomed two captive U.S. Army Air Service aviators from Jesus Rentería. The photo was taken in 1918, before the La Junta punitive expedition. W. D. Smithers Collection, Harry Ransom Humanities Research Center, the University of Texas at Austin.

Narrow, high-sided commercial prairie schooners still frequented Presidio's streets in 1917. W. D. Smithers Collection, Harry Ransom Humanities Research Center, the University of Texas at Austin.

By 1924 automobiles were replacing wagons on Presidio's streets, but dirt roads were still the rule. W. D. Smithers Collection, Harry Ransom Humanities Research Center, the University of Texas at Austin.

Except for the pavement and recent-vintage pickup trucks, downtown Presidio does not look much different today than it did eighty years ago. Photograph by author.

Ojinaga still had dirt streets in the 1920's and—though automobiles had made their appearance—horses and burros were still the most reliable mode of transportation. Several of the men on the street corner are dressed like merchants or clerks, not campesinos or rancheros. W. D. Smithers Collection, Harry Ransom Humanities Research Center, the University of Texas at Austin.

In 1924 Ojinaga's presidencia (city hall) was among the town's most imposing buildings. The wind continually relocated the loose La Junta soil, eroding streets and undermining sidewalks; maintenance required shoveling dirt back under the slabs. W. D. Smithers Collection, Harry Ransom Humanities Research Center, the University of Texas at Austin.

In 1924 the customhouse in Ojinaga was well built and was adorned with pebble decoration around the windows and doors. Probably constructed after the 1913–1914 battle of Ojinaga, it stood on the edge of the mesilla, offering a view across the valley floor to the Sierra de la Santa Cruz beyond. W. D. Smithers Collection, Harry Ransom Humanities Research Center, the University of Texas at Austin.

These Mexican soldiers are standing in front of Ojinaga's comandancia, or military post. The doorway to the right is labeled jefatura—a name for the offices of the chief of police—but since that doorway opens to the center courtyard, it probably refers to the entire headquarters building. The sign over the third door says detall—the disbursement office. The soldiers (arranged by height) are facing the plaza in front of the Ojinaga church. The year is 1926. W. D. Smithers Collection, Harry Ransom Humanities Research Center, the University of Texas at Austin.

This 1926 view of the jefatura *shows the courtyard inside (which remains today) and the Mexican eagle and serpent over the door. W. D. Smithers Collection, Harry Ransom Humanities Research Center, the University of Texas at Austin.*

This 1926 school photo taken in Ojinaga tells us a lot. Every shoe is covered in dust. Some children are barefoot. Boys and girls seem about equally represented. Every face is serious. Skin tones cover the spectrum. The school walls are crumbling; they bear bullet pockmarks from the revolutions. What is that look in the children's eyes? W. D. Smithers Collection, Harry Ransom Humanities Research Center, the University of Texas at Austin.

John Spencer's white gravestone lies among the modest stone cairns on a mesilla overlooking the former farmlands at Indio. The fields have returned to desert. Photograph by author.

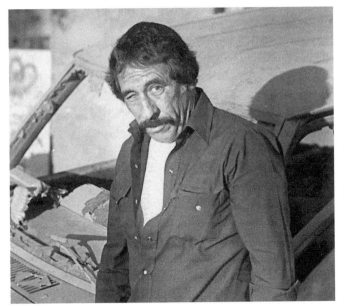

Drug smuggler Pablo Acosta enjoyed showing visitors the shot-up Ford Bronco that he was driving when Fermín Arevalo ambushed him. Photograph by Terrence Poppa.

Enrique Madrid holds forth in the book-cluttered living room of his family's Redford home. Photograph by author.

Using La Junta's version of a dune buggy, local teenagers cross at El Polvo to visit friends in El Mulato. Photograph by author.

The United States Border Patrol erected two flimsy highway barriers at the El Polvo crossing and dumped some boulders on the riverbank. Like most border-control efforts, it was a waste of time and money. Photograph by author.

In the United States we accept the notion of corrupt Mexican government officials who permit drugs to flow through their nation into the United States. How else could Colombian cocaine be transported into Mexico, across hundreds or thousands of miles of highways, reach our borders and penetrate our defenses? The Mexicans have a thousand chances to interdict the illegal drugs, but they seldom do so. When they do run a drug lord to ground, their motives often seem mixed, as with Pablo Acosta.[1]

Yet in the United States, the wealthiest and most powerful nation on earth, the same drugs somehow manage to cross our borders, travel hundreds or thousands of miles, get warehoused, parceled out, distributed and sold even though our law enforcers are the least corrupt in the world. How can that be? Only four possibilities exist: (1) we need more cops, more equipment and more ideas; (2) there's no point in trying to interdict drugs, because it's impossible; (3) our law enforcers are honest but incompetent; or (and) (4) some of our cops and politicians are just as crooked as some of Mexico's.

Take the Texas side of La Junta, for example: Presidio County, the first line of defense against drugs smuggled from Ojinaga. The county is a nest of law enforcers. The Customs Service, the Border Patrol, the FBI, the DEA, the United States Air Force, the County Sheriff, the municipal police and sometimes even the United States Marines. Why can't they stop the drugs?

Rick Thompson spent a lot of time in the drug war trenches. Born and bred in West Texas, the six-foot-six, tobacco-chewing Thompson served eighteen years as Presidio County's sheriff. Thompson was tough, burly and plainspoken and he cut a wide swath through Texas law-enforcement circles. Under his watch Presidio County enjoyed one of the lowest per capita crime rates in the state. An ex-Marine and a graduate of the criminal justice program at nearby Sul Ross State University, Thompson was chairman of the Region Eight Law Enforcement Academy in El Paso and chairman of a multicounty narcotics task force. He was elected president of the Sheriffs' Association of Texas. Senator Phil Gramm of Texas appointed him to a screening committee for United States marshals.[2]

Rick Thompson was the sheriff responsible for the Texas

Rick

Thompson

side of La Junta before, during and after Pablo Acosta's reign. When the drug war between Fermín Arevalo and Acosta was raging, things were tense in Presidio County. One night officers stationed at the Polvo crossing came under machine-gun fire from the Mexican side of the river. Thompson sent word to Pablo to contain the violence. "I asked one thing of Pablo," said Thompson. "I asked him that anything explosive, the killings and things, remain outside of my county. I didn't want any bodies scattered on this side of the river with no explanations."[3]

Towns along the United States side of the river, like Presidio and Redford, experienced a lot of action during the years that Thompson and Acosta overlapped. A customs agent shot a drug smuggler at the Polvo crossing in 1982. Later that year, the Border Patrol seized 1,300 pounds of marijuana being transported in a travel trailer twelve miles from Redford. In the late summer, a man from El Mulato nicknamed *El Gato* wounded a Border Patrol agent in a gunfight eight miles below Redford. Jesus M. Hernandez was found dead in Redford in 1984, shot three times with a .22-caliber gun. A couple of months later two La Juntans were arrested for murdering a Mexican game warden. The Border Patrol busted people with 700 pounds of cocaine in October 1986; another 663 pounds were nabbed in February 1987. Three men were caught with 142 pounds of marijuana at the Presidio airport in March. An Oklahoman was caught with 114 pounds of marijuana at the Presidio port of entry in April. On the Monday after Acosta's death four men were nabbed with 28 pounds of marijuana.[4]

That's a lot of action for someplace as remote and sparsely populated as La Junta, but it must be said that except for a couple of good-sized cocaine busts, most of the incidents were minor, especially considering the reputation developed by Pablo Acosta for smuggling tons of heroin, cocaine and marijuana into the United States. Though Sheriff Thompson's first drug task force claimed to have interdicted US$1.5 million in narcotics (itself not an especially large amount), an audit suggested that the value of drugs seized was less than US$5,000. Of the 147 arrests chalked up by the task force, only 50 could be verified, of which 3 were for illegal beer purchases.[5]

On the evening when Guillermo Calderoni swept into Santa Elena to get Pablo Acosta, Rick Thompson was in Lajitas taking part in a task force drug bust. The sweep netted mostly little fish. Some of them complained that Robert Chambers, reputed to be the biggest drug importer in Presidio County, had once again gone unscathed.[6]

Thompson knew Chambers. They were both ex-marines, and they both lived in the small-town atmosphere of Presidio County. Chambers owned a modest ranch just above Candelaria. In 1988 he was charged with shooting at an acquaintance near there and shouting, "Stay off my river!" In 1989 he was brought up on federal charges of providing false information in a gun purchase. That same year, he was tried for two felony counts of weapons possession. Chambers was given probation, in part because of a letter of recommendation from Sheriff Thompson. It was widely rumored that Robert Chambers was the person who had busted the rapist out of the Ojinaga jail and handcuffed him to a tree for Thompson to find. Chambers was a versatile type; with the consent of his probation officer he would travel to Mazatlán, where he claimed to work as a captain in a fleet of fishing boats.[7]

Robert Chambers's Candelaria ranch was near the historically lawless town of San Antonio del Bravo. It was on the flats below the Candelaria Rim—the lofty escarpment that looms over the Texas side of the Rio Grande. That was important, because the United States maintained an aerostat—a tethered, unmanned blimp with radar equipment—near Valentine, on the other side of the rim. The aerostat was supposed to pick up any drug smugglers' airplanes, but it couldn't detect flights in the rimrock's radar shadow. Chambers's ranch was a perfect location for a plane to fly across the border undetected and unload. The same could be said of the dirt strip maintained by the town of Candelaria, but landing at the Candelaria strip risked an upstanding citizen calling the sheriff to report suspicious activity.

It turned out that Robert Chambers was involved in drug smuggling and that he was not above the law. After he was arrested the DEA estimated that between 1986 and 1991 he had transported ten tons of cocaine and another ten tons of marijuana through Presidio County. That was Chambers's specialty: transporting through Presidio County. Sometimes he bought and sold, but his greatest value was in moving drugs from the Rio Grande to someplace less carefully watched, such as a back road near an interstate highway.[8]

The DEA used an informant to catch Robert Chambers. In December 1991 the informant helped Chambers move 2,400 pounds—more than a ton—of cocaine across the river from San Antonio del Bravo to Candelaria. Chambers told the informant to truck the cocaine to his ranch and gave him a telephone number to call when he was done. Whoever answered, he was to say that "the deal was down." The informant did as he was told, but kept his DEA handlers informed.[9]

The DEA wanted more than just Robert Chambers. They wanted to know where the cocaine was going. In a day or so, someone called and told them that they ought to go have a look at a red horse trailer out at the County Fairgrounds. When they checked out the tip, they found the cocaine stacked in the trailer—a billion dollars' worth using the DEA's inflated street-value calculations. The cocaine was packaged in wrappers bearing a polo pony logo, the signature of the Medellín cartel.[10]

Someone said the horse trailer looked familiar. Wasn't it the custom job that was seized from a drug dealer in Redford a while back? Didn't the sheriff take custody of the trailer? The DEA probably didn't need that bit of sleuthing to know who they were dealing with: the telephone number given to the informant was Rick Thompson's home phone.[11]

At first Sheriff Thompson insisted that the drugs were part of a secret, one-man reverse sting operation that he was engineering. He said that at a press conference, and some of the reporters present started snickering. Then Robert Chambers cut a plea bargain that called for him to testify against Thompson; the sheriff's defense collapsed. Thompson and Chambers were both sentenced to life in the federal penitentiary, but Chambers's sentence was reduced to twenty-two years due to his cooperative attitude.[12]

At sentencing, Thompson admitted that he had been working with Chambers since 1986, taking payments of US$15,000 to US$18,000 at a time. He was an active participant; the 2,400 pounds of cocaine had gotten from Chambers's ranch to the fairgrounds in Thompson's Sheriff's Department Chevy Suburban. It took three trips, one involving a chat at a Border Patrol checkpoint. According to the DEA, Thompson's drug running began long before 1986. They said he had helped Chambers move 297 pounds of marijuana from the border to Louisiana in 1981 and had assisted in delivering 561 pounds of marijuana near Presidio in that same year.[13]

It doesn't require much imagination to see the similarities between the drug-running operations on the two sides of La Junta, or to speculate that there may have been a business relationship that transcended the border. We can conclude that the drug war does involve cross-border cooperation between governments and private enterprise.

A few pages ago we said that "there's something special about drug smuggling." That something special hampers our understanding of borders. Drug smuggling carries so much emotional, political and international baggage that we lose sight of the fundamentals. The same can be said about international terrorism—smuggling nuclear, chemical and biological weapons. We find ourselves groping for a solution to that problem now, and our task is made more difficult by the baggage that the issue carries.

In the seventeenth century two influential Spanish commanders—the Marqués de Rubí and Teodoro de Croix— disagreed about where to site Nueva España's presidios. The former wanted to establish a defensive line far from Spanish settlements, out along the northern frontier, where migratory nomads could be intercepted and excluded. The latter favored bringing the presidios close, where they could defend the citizenry, and sending out soldiers to chase hostile natives in their homelands. Both approaches had their weaknesses.

Rubí won the debate posthumously in 1848. Since then, two nations have understood that a point of division exists at the Rio Grande. Whether dealing with Apaches, Villistas, bandidos or drug smugglers, we have used the river as a critical point of defense. It is where we put presidios, cavalry, border posts, military colonies, customhouses and United States Marine Corps surveillance teams.

Our thesis is this: as a barrier, the border is much more a problem than a solution. It seduces us into establishing our own Maginot Line. It lures us into attempting the impossible. It renders us perturbed when the impossible proves beyond our reach. It distracts us from more promising solutions.

Our ability to interdict Apaches, cattle, Mausers, bandidos, candelilla wax, bootleg liquor, marijuana, illegal immigrants and nuclear weapons at the border has never been great. Changes in the way things are transported make interdiction increasingly less likely. What would come of a proposal to draw a line across the United States, say along the thirty-eighth parallel of latitude, and fortify the line as a way of catching smugglers, illegal immigrants and terrorists? Why does the proposal make any more sense when the

River and Border

line is moved a few hundred miles south? It will be porous in any location.

This is not to say that there are obvious and overlooked alternative solutions. These are difficult problems. But it may be time to consider whether to entirely abandon the notion of hermetically sealed borders. It may be time to accept that the bad guys are going to get through or around the airport screening points whether we have an international identity database or not. Looking at the small slice of history and humanity that is La Junta, we may be tempted to conclude that Teodoro de Croix was right, and that problems need to be dealt with at their origin and their destination, not somewhere in between.

Lucía Madrid has the traditional view of the Rio Grande: it "has never, never divided the people." Her poetic daughter Denise Chávez says, "The river is a unifier to me in my heart and in my spirit." Romantic Mimi Webb Miller, who commuted across the Rio Grande by pickup truck and rowboat, could wax on—as we have—about the seamless community that gathers along the river's banks.

Touchy-feely as these viewpoints may be, they are entirely true. The river does not divide La Junta. It never has. Neither does the border divide La Junta. It creates a minor administrative delay at the Presidio-Ojinaga international bridge, and has little practical effect on the other half-dozen traditional crossings in the valley.

Borderlands experts whom we respect say things like "The border represents the juncture of two sharply disparate societies." That's not the case in La Junta, though. Socially, the dividing line is somewhere north, near the railroad. People are more or less the same throughout La Junta.

The border hasn't created a material economic division in La Junta. The Mexican La Juntans do not envy the affluence of the Texan La Juntans. Presidio County is one of the poorest in the state of Texas, one of the poorest in the nation, and "south county" is the poorest part of that poor county. Unlike the situation in El Paso or Brownsville, La Juntans don't swarm across the international bridge to day jobs in Presidio, because there are very few jobs in Presidio. Wages are higher on the United States side, but wage structures are abstract when there are no jobs.

Most people still prefer to live on the Mexican side because La Juntans—traditional, long-term inhabitants of La Junta—are agriculturalists. The Mexican side has the Rio Conchos, it has more tillable land and (despite the hideous failings of the Mexican revolutions) it is easier for a peon to get a patch of land in Mexico.

What the border creates is a political division. That is of moderate interest to traditional La Juntans, but it is of immense interest to others. Repeatedly we have seen how political divisions create opportunities to profit, especially opportunities to profit illegally. Pablo Acosta—on the run from a United States drug indictment—was only the latest in a long string of people showing us how political divisions create sanctuaries. Abraham González demonstrated how a political division creates a back door for supply and communication. General Salvador Mercado used the back door to escape. Ben Leaton and Carrancista bandidos showed us how to play one side of a political division against the other.

Inevitably a political division changes a community by bringing with it the government infrastructure used to perpetuate the division. But the greatest community change comes from the other outsiders drawn to the advantages of political divisions: armies, smugglers, refugees, rebels, fugitives and all manner of opportunists. Most of these people accomplish their goals and depart, often leaving a scar behind. Others linger.

The outsiders attracted by the political division have brewed an astounding amount of conflict in the tiny, remote community of La Junta. True, the impacts of arbitrary political division have been felt in other places along the Rio Grande—virtually the same historical events and effects have been felt in Juárez–El Paso, for example—but most places on the border have received milder doses, or at least doses proportionate to their size. This is the case at the smaller agricultural valleys at Pilares and Santa Elena and at the larger paired border towns of Del Rio–Ciudad Acuña and Piedras Negras–Eagle Pass. What is the unique element that has drawn so much turmoil to otherwise insignificant La Junta?

The answer is the Rio Conchos. Explorers and priests wore a path along its banks, following the water into the desert. The trail became a way into the frontier. People considered the geography and the economics and opened the Chihuahua Trail, which led to the ill-fated KCM&O, which led to highways 67 and 16. It is not the ability to grow crops in La Junta that causes problems; it is the ability to go through the place.

Which means, when you think about it, that there are two communities in La Junta. There is the traditional agricultural community that has existed for thousands of years. Its demographics have changed—the original native population was almost exterminated at one point—but it remains as we described it at the outset. It is a riverine agricultural community centered around the junction of the Rio Grande and the Rio Conchos. It has a rich heritage of nominally peaceful, largely sedentary, native settlements dating back more than a thousand years. It has a complex history of Spanish exploration and occupation. When Anglo pioneers first reached the community, they assimilated into the native and mestizo population.

Then there is the community spawned by travelers and transportation across a political division. Its most visible elements are governmental, police and military units. There are less visible legitimate elements: bonded warehouses and customs brokers, for example. There are sometimes-visible illegitimate elements: Pablo Acosta and Robert Chambers come to mind. The bandidos, the U.S. cavalry, the Mexican federal judicial police, the Mexican Army, the U.S. Customs Service, the INS, the Border Patrol, the FBI, the DEA, the U.S. Marines, the drug lords, the corrupt sheriffs and police officers and comandantes — these are creatures of the political division and the road along the Conchos.

The La Junta agricultural community is a remote, impoverished place that is not worth fighting over. The last time people defended the valley for itself was in 1759, when a band of Cholomes tried to thwart construction of the Presidio del Norte. Unlike the traditional agriculturalists, the community spawned by political division and the road along the Conchos is contentious and is not inherently tied to the valley. Most of the revolutionary battles came to La Junta because of the political border and the road; absent that, they would have occurred somewhere else.

At most, agricultural La Junta symbolizes some things that have been repeatedly fought over: local autonomy and fair distribution of land. But the revolutionary battles in La Junta were over those political principles more than they were over the valley. More than once the victorious army, having vanquished its foe, packed up and went home.

Sometimes the two communities get in each other's way. Sometimes one is confused for the other. Sometimes people worry about one extinguishing the other. But that doesn't seem to be a risk. La Junta — the tranquil, agricultural La Junta — has endured for something like five thousand years, and it's not going anywhere. Doubtless it has some hard times ahead — cultivated land will shrink, incomes will dwindle, population will decline — but people will still be out there tending beans, corn and squash, herding a few cattle, raising a few goats, living off the land.

If, as we have suggested, the border is a poor point of control for drugs, weapons, undocumented workers and other contraband, if its physical defense is a poor mechanism for managing political and social problems, then perhaps our nation's viewpoint will shift toward

Teodoro de Croix's. Perhaps we will attack problems at their source and their destination, rather than trying to dam them up somewhere in the middle. If that happens, then the border will soften, become even more porous and thus be less valuable to smugglers, refugees, rebels, fugitives, terrorists and opportunists.

Thirteen-year-old Gilbert Spencer wasn't too happy about leaving his friends in El Paso, but he had always enjoyed visiting his family in the valley. He quickly settled into La Junta. After graduating from high school, he decided to enroll in a summer session at the University of Arizona, where siblings Deena and John were taking courses. It was a shock: the university was more than ten times the size of the entire town of Presidio. At the end of the summer Gilbert transferred to the University of Texas at El Paso, then moved closer to home, enrolling in Sul Ross State University, where he received a degree in wildlife biology with a minor in wildlife management.

Gilbert

Spencer

Gilbert wanted to return to Presidio, but the family store didn't need help and the job market in La Junta was—and is—tough. The once-healthy business of growing melons, onions and cotton has withered. Upstream irrigation projects on both rivers slashed peak flows and increased the water's salinity, making it unsuitable for some crops. United States labor and immigration laws made inexpensive Mexican labor much less available. The North American Free Trade Agreement made growers in Mexico's interior more competitive. The demise of the railroad increased transportation costs. Fields where straight, green rows of crops once grew now lie fallow, their topsoil swirling in the desert wind. Some farmers grow alfalfa for hay because it requires little labor. Just south of Presidio, one landowner took a flat, square onion patch, planted grass and a smattering of trees and called it a golf course. Few people come to play golf.

Despite the lack of economic opportunity, longtime La Juntans cling to the valley. Gilbert Spencer's father and uncle still tend store. Another uncle and aunt operate the original Spencer farm opposite the river junction. The land used to grow melons; now Gilbert's uncle brings in cattle from his ranch in Mexico, fattens them on alfalfa hay and sends them to market in Texas. John Spencer's first farm is a small-time feedlot.

Despairing at the chances of employment in his hometown, Gilbert found a position working for the El Paso medical examiner. He helped with autopsies, which is somewhat outside the boundaries of wildlife biology. Then he married his college sweetheart, Yvonne; the ceremony was performed in her hometown of Shafter, where Gilbert's great-grandfather John Spencer had discovered silver. Yvonne's grandfather had spent his life working in Spencer's mine.

The job market in West Texas showed no signs of improvement, but Gilbert managed to land a biology consulting slot with a California company that employed him on a project basis. He would spend a few weeks in California making a salary that was eye-popping by La Junta standards, then return home until the next project came along. Gilbert and Yvonne rented a small house in Alpine, and soon they were blessed with the birth of a son. Yvonne was working and trying to finish up her degree at Sul Ross while making it plain that it was time for Gilbert to find work somewhere closer than California.

Yvonne landed a good job in Presidio, and it provided the impetus for change. The family moved back to La Junta, and Gilbert focused on finding local employment. He had twice applied to the State Game Warden Academy, but hadn't made the cut. It seemed to him that if he could add some law-enforcement training to his résumé it might improve his chances of a job with Texas Parks and Wildlife. He asked the county sheriff to sponsor him for the next training academy at Sul Ross; to his surprise, the sheriff went one better, sending him to the state-run sheriff's training academy in El Paso—where a much more intensive curriculum prevailed—and hiring him as a deputy sheriff when he graduated.

Deputy Sheriff Gilbert Spencer was based in Presidio, and was soon assigned to work as liaison to the federal officials at the port of entry. Narcotics investigations moved to the forefront of his duties. It was the post-Acosta, post-Thompson era, but a lot of marijuana and cocaine was still moving through Presidio County. The Thompson-Chambers arrests demonstrated that the lonely road to Ruidosa and Candelaria facilitated a lot of illicit traffic, but there was still more law-enforcement emphasis on the busier highway from Presidio to Lajitas. We have already mentioned Enrique Madrid's observation that the supposed drug capital of Redford is too small to be the capital of anything, but there is no denying that a lot of drugs came across—and a lot of drug-related shootings transpired—at Redford, Lajitas and Presidio during the 1980's and 1990's.[1]

Gilbert Spencer was drawn to the better pay and more interesting work available with some of the drug task forces working in the area. He first joined a DEA-funded interagency task force under the Texas Narcotics Control Program, then became part of the Permian Basin Drug Task Force formed by a coalition of West Texas county sheriffs. He worked the highways near Presidio, stopping motorists for any minor infraction in order to assess them and their vehicles. The task is known as interdiction, and it tends to annoy the populace when it is done aggressively.

After working two drug task forces and another stint with the sheriff's department, still trying to make use of his education in wildlife biology and management, Spencer applied yet again to the Texas Parks and Wildlife Department. Fortunately, there were a handful of openings available—none lofty, but openings that might allow a hard worker to advance in the ranks. Ironically, the job he landed was as a ranger manning the visitor center at Fort Leaton Historical State Park. Beginning in October 2001, the great-grandson of John W. Spencer took custody of the fortín fraudulently grabbed by Ben Leaton, usurped by Edward Hall, foreclosed upon by John Burgess, and taken from Burgess by his creditors. It is impossible to know who was turning most rapidly in their grave.

Gilbert Spencer is intelligent and capable; he has advanced in his job, winning a promotion to manager of newly formed Chinati Mountains State Natural Area. The natural area isn't open to the public yet. Gilbert is working on the master plan, occasionally still filling in at Fort Leaton.

Sitting with Spencer in the tiny office at Fort Leaton, you sense relief that his law-enforcement days are behind him. He is pleased to be moving toward a career in wildlife management. He is alert and cheerful in jeans, boots and a crisp uniform shirt, not losing his good humor even as he recounts the difficult days in drug interdiction.

He has had harrowing moments. One afternoon five years earlier, while still part of the Permian Basin Drug Task Force, he was patrolling the highways near Presidio with his radio set on scan, allowing him to listen in on other agencies' radio traffic. Often the transmissions were scrambled, leaving only static, but sometimes they were in the clear. A little after six o'clock in the evening he caught a Border Patrol message about shots fired near Redford. Picking up his microphone, he asked the Border Patrol dispatcher for more information, but there was no response. He heard bursts of static as border patrolmen communicated on scrambled frequencies.[2]

Spencer turned his vehicle around and headed for Redford with lights and siren running. On the way, Deputy Sheriff Oscar Gallegos radioed to let him know that he was about five minutes behind him. At first, the task force dispatcher in Marfa couldn't provide Spencer any additional information, but in a few minutes the dispatcher advised that "the exact location, according to 513 would be at Polvo Crossing, one thousand meters southeast. It's where 513 is located. The man with the rifle is at the abandoned church two hundred meters from the team."[3]

Gilbert Spencer knew what 513 was. He had been briefed a day or two earlier; 513 was Team 7 of Joint Task Force 6. It was four United States Marines under the command of Corporal Clemente Bañuelos.

Hidden in the brush near El Polvo, Marine Corporal Roy Torrez Jr. was watching Bañuelos, who was kneeling in the desert scrub and directing the deployment of Team 7. Torrez heard the Marfa dispatcher's message on Team 7's radio. He knew that both locations were wrong: the man with the rifle was near the old border post on the mesilla, not the church downhill, and Team 7 was spread across an arroyo to the south of the border post, far from the river crossing.[4]

Torrez took his eyes off Bañuelos so he could reply to the dispatcher and correct the erroneous information being given Gilbert Spencer. As he glanced down at the radio, a single shot rang out.[5]

Passing through Redford, Spencer turned off his siren and lights. Pulling off the highway onto the dirt road to the crossing, he stopped his vehicle and lowered his window, listening. The Polvo crossing is low, downhill from the pavement. Surrounding mesillas and scrub make it a perfect site for an ambush. Spencer wasn't about to go farther down the hill until he knew more about the situation. He waited. It was quiet except for the static of scrambled radio transmissions.

In a few minutes Deputy Gallegos pulled up behind Spencer's cruiser. Spencer got out to talk things over with Gallegos. It was a Border Patrol incident, and the situation was unsettled. Only one thing was certain: there were four nervous armed Marines out there somewhere in the silent gathering darkness. Spencer and Gallegos decided to stay put until the Border Patrol arrived.

Ten minutes later two Border Patrol vehicles turned off the highway, carrying four agents. Two of the agents were James DeMatteo and Johnny Urias, who had once warned Junie Hernandez to be more careful with his .22 rifle. After conferring, the six law-enforcement officers got back in their vehicles and drove slowly down toward the Polvo crossing, onto the ancón where the ancient native village of Tapacolmes once stood. They parked near the abandoned church at the bottom of the hill.[6]

Gilbert Spencer grabbed his AR-15 rifle from his cruiser. The Border Patrol agents were carrying M-16s. Together, they began moving cautiously up the nearby mesilla toward the border post while Deputy Gallegos shepherded some curious residents out of the area. Spencer and the agents proceeded in a leapfrog pattern so long as they had adequate cover, but the hill became naked gravel toward the crest.[7]

Spencer had the lead as the officers moved toward the old border post. He describes the moment exactly the same way every time you ask him: "Pffft, this bush stands up out of nowhere, and it's holding an M-16. Then pffft, another bush stands up, and another." The Marines were so perfectly concealed in their guille suits that the officers were almost upon them without noticing. "U.S. Marines!" shouted Corporal Torrez. His rifle was half-raised in a ready position at his waist. Someone shouted back, "U.S. Border Patrol!" The Marines did not relax; their weapons remained at the ready. Spencer and the four Border Patrol agents, all in full uniform, were stunned at the Marines' brazen display of force. The situation was confrontational and tense.[8]

Spencer went around the back of the border post. Corporal Clemente Bañuelos was standing near the old stone trough, his rifle in a ready position. Spencer could just see the legs and feet of Junie Hernandez sticking out of the trough. Spencer checked the boy for vital signs, but there were none.[9]

If the history of La Junta de los Rios is one of a gentle, isolated agricultural people intruded upon by outside forces with independent agendas, if the story is one of borders drawn badly and the jangle of dissonant cultures, if it is about a trilogy of conflict, change and assimilation and about resistance to all three, if it is about the pernicious futility and lamentable consequences of attempting to enforce borders of all kinds, then what moment could be more exquisitely emblematic of La Junta than the tragic conjunction of Gilbert Spencer, Clemente Bañuelos and Junie Hernandez?

The pieces can be taken apart and reassembled into a myriad of symbolisms and ironies. A marine and a goatherd and a reluctant peace officer. A purebred La Juntan, a transplant into his family's heritage and an outsider. Three Hispanics, one with an Anglo surname. A marine and son of a marine and a kid who wanted to be a marine. A cog in the federal machine, a cog in the county machine, and a cog in nobody's machine. A meeting of the agricultural community, the political community and a man with one foot in each. The abandoned border post, the abandoned church, the abandoned native village. Ways of life and rules of engagement. Borders and crossings and enforcement of invisible lines. Three people with so much and so little in common, drawn into a pointless and deadly confrontation on a deserted mound of gravel, dust, ocotillo and cactus. At their backs, the river that delivers flood and drought, life and death, division and unity, past and future.

Presidio, Texas, on a recent day in May. They're filling the swimming pool at the Three Palms Inn. Two men in dirty jeans and faded western shirts lean on a wrought-iron fence, supervising the water.

It's going to be a hot one today. As you back out of your parking space, you see a mega–dust devil sweeping through town. It's coming your way, a hundred feet high, swirling and churning. At a loss for alternatives, you drive on through, worrying about your car's finish. The wind buffets your vehicle and for a moment the town disappears into the brown whirlwind. Then you are through it, on your way to Redford.

When you called Enrique's house this morning Ruby said that he was already at the post office, sorting the mail. She sounded half-awake on the phone, but you listened carefully to her voice. Since you've never met either of the Madrids, you're carefully collecting every available piece of information.

Where is the Redford post office, anyway? When you drove through yesterday, you noticed that both stores in town were shuttered. Twenty minutes of winding road puts you back in Redford. There's the bigger store, the one that was open last fall. A sign in the window says it's closed, and a sign on the side repeats the message. Wait, there's a side door, between the two signs. There's familiar lettering over the door. That's the post office?

Enrique is behind the tiny counter. You recognize him from the photographs and videotapes. In his late fifties, perhaps, beginning to put on weight. Gray streaks dart through his slick black hair. A plastic Postal Service basket of mail is in front of him, a simple set of sorting cubbyholes at his back. He's wearing an old red shirt with a button missing. You introduce yourself, and he responds politely. While you're making small talk, a lean, dusty vaquero walks in and asks for his mail. Switching to perfect English, the vaquero turns to you and excuses himself for interrupting, but he's been gone for seven months and is eager to see what letters and packages have accumulated in his absence. Enrique hands him two envelopes, wrapped with a rubber band. The vaquero seems pleased and makes his exit.

You have your own apologies to make. You want to talk with Enrique, but you can see that he's busy sorting the bas-

An Afternoon with Enrique

ket of mail. "Why don't you come by my house in about an hour," he asks. "Would that be too long to wait?" Of course not. You've already waited more than a year for the right moment. You've read everything he's written about archaeology and native foodways and Spanish explorers and early irrigation devices and social outrages. You've watched him on videotape, and you've listened to him on old Pacifica Network radio interviews. You've read about him in newspaper articles and congressional transcripts. You've learned most of his family tree, marveled at his mother's achievements and heard the story about how his great-grandfather got a land patent from Governor Coke. You've driven seven hundred miles to see him and he's wondering whether you would mind waiting another hour. Not a problem. More a privilege than anything else. You get to talk to Enrique Madrid.

To kill time, you drive downstream along the Rio Grande. A Border Patrol vehicle is parked on a hill overlooking the Redford Bolson. It might make a good photograph. You stop, talk to the patrolman and take the picture, even though there's a big yellow highway sign between the patrolman's car and the valley. The sign is diamond-shaped and has a picture of a bicycle on it, so it's a warning: beware of bicycle. Peculiar at best. Your chances of running into a bicycle on this stretch of road seem about as likely as a bicycle falling out of a cloud onto your car. You waste thirty minutes talking to the border cop. He doesn't know much. Only had the job for a couple of years. Says there's a new breed of snake showing up in the desert that's a combination of a Western Diamondback and something else, with venom that's both a neurotoxin and a hemotoxin, whatever that is. One bite, then five minutes, tops. You thank the officer for sharing that with you, then head back toward Redford.

Enrique's car isn't at his house, so you wait. You park in front of the Redford elementary school, where Lucía Rede Madrid worked her miracles. The Madrid residence is across the road, attached to the dilapidated store where Mrs. Madrid's library was. Mrs. Madrid is in a nursing home now, the store is closed and the library has been broken up. The low, white store has blue window frames and blue security bars on the windows. It's dark inside. Ruby's beater-mobile is parked in the shade of the front awning.

Enrique pulls up and parks his dust-covered dark blue van behind Ruby's car. You cross the road and greet him. "Watch out for the dogs," he says, "they'll bite when you turn your back." Inside the gate are two half-breed Aussie herding dogs. They seem gentle enough, but you've heard stories about this kind of cur before. You briefly consider backing into the house, but throw caution to the wind and follow Enrique past the battered screen door.

It's fly season, and the dogs have punched gaping holes in the screen. Enrique closes the inner door. It's cool inside the cement-block structure, and a window fan on the floor provides a steady breeze. A cat leaps from a windowsill, followed by another. "The cat door," Enrique says. You realize that there's a pane missing in the window, covered by a strip of cloth that the cats can push aside.

You look around while Enrique unfolds Mexican throws — fringed shawls or little blankets — and carefully covers the couch with them. You don't need the ceremony — your own couch looks about as bad, and your dog doesn't smell any better than Enrique's — but given your violent allergies to cats, you decide that the throws might be a good idea. When he's finished, you sit, expectantly.

Ruby appears with a wet rag mop. It's Saturday, and Saturday is house-cleaning day. Wearing shorts and a sleeveless top, she gives the green linoleum floor a once-over. You're embarrassed that she's working while you're sitting, and you try to make yourself small. Enrique seems less concerned and sits down to begin the conversation.

You made a few notes in advance so you won't forget to ask anything important. And you prepared a few icebreakers to get things rolling. The icebreakers prove unnecessary. Enrique has already started. He has a funny way of talking; you noticed it on the videotapes. He talks through his lower teeth, like Marlon Brando doing the Godfather but without any sinister overtones. His dark brown eyes tend to be downcast or averted, but it's quickly apparent that it would be a mistake to read too much into the body language. He's just shy in a loquacious sort of way. Eye contact becomes more frequent as he gets to know you.

Enrique takes you over to a bookcase and shows you photos of his great-grandparents, his grandparents, his parents, his uncle and Chicano activist César Chávez. There's a small painting of Emiliano Zapata and a bronze figure of Pancho Villa. One whole wall is books, and there are smaller bookcases along the other walls. A coffee table is laden with heavy fossils and rocks. There are baskets, pottery and magazines in stacks. Next to the front door hang two Madrid heirlooms: Enrique's great-grandfather's original land patent, laminated onto a faux walnut plaque, and his mother's framed presidential recognition certificate, draped with her two medals. You examine them closely in the dim light.

Sitting again, Enrique pulls photographs and newspaper articles out of files. He's telling you his family history. You're already familiar with it, but it's still mesmerizing. Hispanic pioneers, brave settlers, hard workers and proud teachers. Polvo, Redford, Marfa, Presidio; the Madrids and Redes helped build this corner of the world.

Then Enrique Madrid starts talking about when the marines shot Junie Hernandez. There is genuine emotion in his voice, genuine outrage. He pulls out articles and transcripts and letters. They're underlined, or highlighted in yellow and pink. Junie's shooting isn't your primary reason for wanting to talk to Enrique, but you listen because you know that the tragedy affected the community deeply. Enrique goes on. He goes on too long. You tire of the story—there is so much more that you want to know about La Junta de los Rios.

You can hear Ruby clanking around in the kitchen. Enrique said something about enchiladas. You smell chili gravy cooking. My God, are you really going to get homemade enchiladas?

Enrique is still going on about Junie and the marines and the United States Government. He's pulling out a copy of *The Third Reich* to show you an underlined passage about military immunity from civil law. There's a mannerism that he has: it's never enough to tell you something; it has to be shown you in a book or an article or a document. You're saying it again: "Wow, that really is interesting, Enrique." He goes in the back room and brings out more files. You're starting to worry about whether Enrique's mind has seized up into a Junie obsession.

After an hour of Junie, you find an opening and change the topic. "Tell me about Ydoiaga's journal, Enrique. He mentioned two Ruidosas and a Pilares upstream of La Junta toward El Cajon; where do you think those sites are?" Enrique's not sure; it's hard to identify those places after all this time, and the river has moved, and before you know it he's talking about the marines shooting Junie Hernandez.

One of the ankle-biting dogs limps toward you. It settles onto the cool linoleum, curls up and puts its muzzle on your foot. You can hear Ruby chopping onions. You peek through the kitchen door and see a big white poster taped to the wall: "Stop Military Terror Against Civilians." Enrique is talking about Colin Powell and the Pentagon.

Finally it dawns on you. Just as Gilbert Spencer, Clemente Bañuelos and Junie Hernandez represent the clash of interests that has shaped La Junta, Enrique Madrid embodies the effects of that centuries-long clash. You are sitting in the presence of a metaphor for all you have been studying: a gentle, rural, native-blooded, sensitive person instilled with great dignity and social conscience, traumatized by a violent, senseless, border-spawned intrusion of outside forces beyond anyone's comprehension. A teenage boy was senselessly shot to death by United States Marines in this tiny, ancient, close-knit village. It changed Enrique's world.

Enrique Madrid was a conscientious objector as a teen, perhaps the only Texas conscientious objector west of the Pecos River. He had principles early, and he stood up for them. He learned the ways of the people of La Junta because he loves his heritage. He reveres his people as he reveres his proud and accomplished family. His politics have always been those of the oppressed: the politics of Emiliano Zapata and Pancho Villa and César Chávez. But for most of his life Enrique's populist moral certainty was blessedly theoretical. Then, when Clemente Bañuelos shot Junie Hernandez through the chest, Enrique Madrid's conscience was bludgeoned in real time. His once-academic notions of intrusion, oppression and institutional stupidity became real in a most personal, painful way.

You listen more closely. You watch Enrique. You watch his eyes. You sidetrack him to another subject, and he responds, and you get a pithy quote or a helpful insight, but then it's back to borders and the military and the powerful.

Enrique pulls out more books, more photos, more magazines. He reads more highlighted passages, explains to you how everything ties together. Gradually you realize that his mind is far from locked up; it is churning along a high and abstract plane. Enrique's monologue is evolving. His thoughts are advancing. Now he is talking of borders and of the European Union and of Hispanic demographics. He shows you that the Mega Chihuahuan Desert extends from Alberta to mid-Mexico, and you realize that he is talking about linkages that are cultural and social and economic, not climatic. He shows you a map of the Entrada al Pacifico—a project to create a superhighway from mid-Texas through Chihuahua to the Pacific Coast. You recognize the route with shock—it is the same as Arthur Stilwell's never-realized Kansas City, Mexico & Orient Railway. The Entrada al Pacifico is the road to Topolobampo. The Japanese are building a superport in Topolobampo, Enrique says. He's not making a point about transportation; he's trying to get you to understand the powerful forces that are going to dissolve North American political borders.

It starts getting weird. Your fault, not his. You can almost watch Enrique's intellect work. You're seeing a collision of ideas and mores and images unlike anything you have witnessed before. Enrique is explaining native hallucinogenic traditions and the racist implications of a universal anti-drug stance, then he's showing you sophisticated genetic research that concludes that more than 90 percent of the DNA in Ojinaga's people is native, not Hispanic, then he's explaining the medicinal uses of sotol, then he's pulling out a drawing of a crude native figure found in a cave above La Junta and comparing it to African fetishes and pictures of fish, explaining that the Kiowa-Tanoan root for fish — "pa" — is likely tangled in the word Tapacolmes, the name of people that the Spanish called the *Pescados,* which means the Fish, then he's cursing three hundred years of Spanish occupation, then he's showing you how the spines of the lechuguilla are filled with long, stiff fibers that make rope and sandals and brushes, then he's railing about the marines and the Nazis and the Congress and the Border Patrol and damn, you're beginning to understand how all this fits, and you feel how the death of Junie Hernandez shook this brilliant, gentle man to his core, radicalized his thinking and put him on a journey toward a unified theory of the cosmos. Far from being mired in La Junta's past, Enrique Madrid is divining its future and the future of the border that divides it. The inputs that he is using and the logic that he is employ- ing are complex, sophisticated and entirely alien to your world. You are listening to Stephen Jay Gould muse about evolution or Niels Bohr mull over quantum mechanics, but the intellect before you is applying traditions, mores and principles incomprehensible to Gould, Bohr and most of all you.

And then Ruby says that the enchiladas are ready. Your head is muddled, but the food is wonderful. The enchiladas are old-fashioned — stacked, not rolled — and are accompanied by refritos and sopa de arroz. The conversation takes a more pedestrian turn, partly because it's your turn to talk and you are nowhere near Enrique's league. You go over your La Junta research and explain some of the themes that you see emerging. Enrique purses his lips and eyes his enchiladas. You surmise that some of your ideas don't meet with his approval, and you make a mental note to go back and rethink the entire subject with an infusion of Enrique's unified cosmos theory.

You engage Ruby in conversation. She's bright, informed, articulate and opinionated and probably spends more time debating Enrique than she does cooking or keeping house. Following Rede and Madrid tradi- tion, she has accepted a position teaching the twenty-five students that attend Redford elementary school. Ruby is an Anglo from outside La Junta, but she seems to fit the family mold just fine.

Then Enrique starts talking about the perfectly round tortilla. He did a study with dozens of Hispanic senior women — *abuelas* — and found that every one of them made perfectly round tortillas, but none of them made them in the same way. Whether rolled with a roller or a wine bottle or a beer can, whether patted out or slapped on a table, they all were perfectly round. "I realized," he says, "that there was a scientific principle at work. It wasn't a matter of technique, it was a matter of principle." Before you know it, Enrique has grabbed another magazine article. This one has to do with the astrophysics of wormholes, something about how the collapse of a hollow spherical galaxy into a black hole creates a cross section of something and then some other things happen, and Enrique shows you a mathematical curve that looks like an ostrich's neck, and he produces an equation that explains it all, loaded with deltas and mus and sigmas, and he tells you with a straight face that the equation explains how to make a perfectly round tortilla. He sticks a big copy of the equation on the refrigerator with a magnet.

You look at Enrique. You look at the equation. You look at your enchiladas. Ruby's tortillas are perfectly round. You wonder: is there a punch line coming? Is this a dose of Redford humor? You let it go, let the Zen of Enrique wash over you. Understanding the equation couldn't possibly improve on the moment. You return your attention to the sopa de arroz. It is exquisite.

After lunch you go for a drive with Enrique and Ruby. Of course, you get a tour of where Junie was shot, and Enrique shows you where the marines said they were hiding, and explains how they had to have been lying. He speculates about connections between Oliver North and Rick Thompson, former Presidio County sheriff turned convicted drug smuggler, and you notice that his conspiro-radicalism is starting to make sense, meaning that it's time to take your leave. It's almost four in the afternoon, and you've been basking in Enrique's aura for five hours.

Enrique insists on one more stop before you go. He takes you down to the Polvo crossing. The Border Patrol has dumped a bunch of boulders on the riverbank and has put up a couple of orange-and-white reflective highway barricades. It's a joke of an obstruction, just something for a patrolman to puff about in a report to his commanding officer. Then Enrique and Ruby take you a few dozen yards upstream. There is another crossing and it is unobstructed. If anything, it's shallower and narrower than the old crossing.

The desert sun is bearing down. The temperature has risen to more than one hundred degrees. Ruby is wearing a floppy straw hat. You take her picture with Enrique. Four whooping teenagers zip across the Rio Grande in a homemade dune buggy, headed for good times in El Mulato. You marvel at all the time, money and energy that umpteen government agencies are pouring into a patently futile and arguably pointless exercise.

As you walk back up the road, the perpetual Polvo dust coats your shoes and pantlegs. Enrique sighs. "We're going to have to close this crossing." It startles you. Close the crossing? That doesn't sound like Enrique Madrid talking.

"Why close the crossing?"

"Look around you. Look at this." He picks up a rock. It isn't a rock. It's a potsherd. Eighteenth-century, Enrique says. He picks up another. "A chipped flint," he explains. You stoop and eye the banks of the rutted roadcut. There are broken artifacts everywhere, scattered among the mesquite and acacia that flourish on the riverbank. Enrique gestures. "We're standing in the old Tapacolmes village." It is the law of unintended consequences: when the Border Patrol closed the traditional Polvo crossing, the traffic shunted into a precious and fragile archaeological site.

Enrique is a steward of the Texas Historical Commission, charged with protecting places like this, but he feels this particular sacrilege in his soul. You look at his features and his frustration and you realize that you could take a Pescado, a Chiso, a Cibolo or any of the other inhabitants of Tapacolmes from five hundred or a thousand years ago and draw a line directly through history to Enrique Madrid. In his heart are the lives, loves, rebellions, famines, injustices, celebrations and intrusions that have marked La Junta de los Rios through the centuries. And in his head, in that astounding mind of Enrique Madrid, is a vision of its future.

THREE SPANISH BELLS

A bronze bell was the most important asset of a Franciscan mission. The effort required to haul a heavy bell hundreds of miles into the wilderness symbolized a commitment, permanence and importance that people longed for. There were once as many as six missions in La Junta; the bells from three of them survived and were moved to the church at the Presidio del Norte, predecessor to today's Ojinaga church. The bells bear the dates of their casting and have each been given names.

The Ojinaga church and its three Spanish mission bells around 1914. The man is local insurrecto Toribio Ortega. The town has been devastated by the Mexican revolutions. Marfa Public Library, Marfa, Texas.

By 1918 the wall in front of the Ojinaga church was crumbling and the three Spanish bells had been moved to the side. In the background, left, is the jefatura *and* comandancia. *Note the ornament that caps the column on the right; the columns remain today, but the ornament disappeared within a few years. W. D. Smithers Collection, Harry Ransom Humanities Research Center, the University of Texas at Austin.*

By 1924 Ojinaga had put a new façade on the church and constructed stone pillars to hold the three Spanish bells. The jefatura *and* comandancia *remain in the background. W. D. Smithers Collection, Harry Ransom Humanities Research Center, the University of Texas at Austin.*

A 1957 political campaign photo shows the new tower on the Ojinaga church. The three Spanish bells have been hung in the belfry. W. D. Smithers Collection, Harry Ransom Humanities Research Center, the University of Texas at Austin.

Today's Ojinaga church faces the town's plaza, dominated by a life-size statue of Benito Juárez. One of the three Spanish bells in the church tower has been moved to the right side of the belfry and is not visible. Photograph by author.

1. Bush, George H. W., "Remarks at the Presentation Ceremony," *Public Papers of the Presidents* 16, Weekly Comp. Pres. Doc. 665, Apr. 27, 1990.

2. "Remarks," *Papers of the President.*

3. Barbara Karkabi, "Library of Dreams," *Texas: Houston Chronicle Magazine,* Jan. 27, 1991; Shirley Tipton, "All in the Family," *Texas Historian,* 16–22; Chappell, "El Polvo," 9–10, 13–16.

4. A mesilla, or mesita, is a small, flat-topped mesa that juts out over the river valley. It is an extension of the desert floor above the river valley. It is often what is left between two eroded arroyos that drain toward the river. A true mesa is larger, typically rises out of a plain and is usually, though not always, an independent, insular feature. Mesillas are good places to build villages because they are flat, defensible and above high water. People can leave their villages on the mesilla during the day to tend their fields along the river, to gather water and food and to wash themselves and their clothes.

5. Karkabi, "Library of Dreams"; Monte Paulsen, "Drug War Masquerade," *San Antonio Current,* Sept. 9, 1998.

6. Texas Historical Commission, "Guardians of the Past," *Medallion,* Sept./Oct. 1998.

7. Lucía Madrid, interview, *The Devil's Swing,* videocassette, directed by Alan Govenar (Documentary Arts, 1999).

8. Chávez, interview, *Devil's Swing.*

9. Enrique Madrid, interview, *Devil's Swing.*

10. Denise Chávez, interview, *Devil's Swing.*

11. Melissa Sattley, "Community Pushes for Military Pullout along Border, Remembers Teen's Death," *Odessa American,* Aug. 1, 1999.

12. Paulsen, "Drug War Masquerade"; Andreas, *Border Games,* 74–77. The closest official port of entry to Redford and El Polvo is just twenty miles away, at the Presidio-Ojinaga international bridge. The Presidio port of entry is a bad place to attempt drug smuggling, because it is a low-volume route, permitting the Border Patrol to take its time searching vehicles.

13. Paulsen, "Drug War Masquerade."

14. Sattley, "Community Pushes for Military Pullout"; Julia Prodis, "Fatal Shooting of Goat Herder by Marines Enrages Border Town," *Associated Press,* June 28, 1997.

15. Paulsen, "Drug War Masquerade"; Coyne, *Investigation,* pars. 104–110.

16. Paulsen, "Drug War Masquerade."

17. Coyne, *Investigation,* pars. 435–450. A guille suit (or ghilli suit) covers the wearer from head to toe in long, camouflage-

Notes

colored rags. The suits worn by Bañuelos and his men (JTF-6 Team 7) were made by the marines themselves by sewing strips of burlap to their camouflage uniforms. Coyne, *Investigation,* par. 330.

18. Sam Howe Verhovek, "After Marine on Patrol Kills a Teen-ager, a Texas Border Village Wonders Why," *New York Times,* June 29, 1997.

19. Verhovek, "Texas Border Village Wonders Why"; Paulsen, "Drug War Masquerade."

20. Sattley, "Community Pushes for Military Pullout."

21. *United States of America: Human Rights Concerns in the Border Region with Mexico,* Amnesty International Report AMR 51/03/98 (May 1998); Brendan M. Case, "Amnesty Report Accuses Border Patrol of Abuses," *Dallas Morning News,* May 20, 1998.

22. Sattley, "Community Pushes for Military Pullout"; "Family to Receive US$1.9 Million in Border Shooting; Grand Jury Again Refuses to Indict Marine," *Houston Chronicle,* Aug. 12, 1998.

THE LAND

1. Regarding the Chihuahuan Desert generally, see Mallouf, "Cielo Complex," 49–51; "Chihuahuan Desert," http://nasa.utep.edu/chih/chihdes.htm (accessed Nov. 21, 2001); and "Chihuahuan Desert Research Institute," http://www.cdri.org (accessed Nov. 21, 2001).

2. The Rio Grande does not run the length of the border between Mexico and the United States. West of El Paso, beyond Texas, the border is marked by surveyors' straight lines (and fences), except for a short stretch that follows the Colorado River between the southeast corner of California and the southwest corner of Arizona.

3. Groat, "Presidio Bolson," 5; generally, see Spearing, *Roadside Geology,* 254–321.

4. See map in Groat, "Presidio Bolson," 2, fig. 1.

5. See William S. Strain, "Late Cenozoic Bolson Integration in the Chihuahua Tectonic Belt," in Seewald and Sundeen, *Geologic Framework,* 167–174.

LA JUNTA

1. Kelley, "Historic Indian Pueblos," 21–22. Mesquite is the English spelling for a bush or small tree known in Spanish as mezquite. Mezquital is a clump of mezquite/mesquite bushes. There is a village in La Junta called El Mezquite, and we follow that Spanish spelling for the village. We use the term "Anglo" in its common meaning: people of generally British or Northern European heritage. Thus, someone named Schmidt, DuBois or Stenholm may be an Anglo.

2. Colomo, *Diario,* reports Candelaria Rodriguez getting married in La Junta on Sept. 12, 1853. Madison and Stillwell, *How Come It's Called That?* 104–105, reports a legend that the pueblo "was named for a woman who had

unusual powers," and also mentions that there are tall sandstone pinnacles nearby that could be taken for a *candelaria,* or candelabrum.

BEFORE 1830

1. There has been enormous confusion about the natives who lived in and around La Junta, and not all of the confusion has been dispelled. After lengthy consideration, we have adopted a position that harks back to the classics in the field (Kelley, *Jumano and Patarabueye,* 130–133, 143–144; Hammond and Rey, *Rediscovery of New Mexico,* 11, 19–20, 73–74; and Forbes, *Apache, Navaho and Spaniard,* 56), but we have sorted natives into three groups to enhance comprehension. We diverge from reports about the Espejo entrada stating that the Patarabueyes (Patazagueyes) and Jumanos (Jumanas) were the same people (see Hammond and Rey, *Rediscovery of New Mexico,* 159, n. 2, citing their earlier work, Baltasar Obregon, *Obregon's History of 16th-Century Explorations in Western America,* trans. and ed. Hammond and Rey, 317; and see Espejo, "Report of Antonio de Espejo," in Hammond and Rey, *Rediscovery of New Mexico,* 216). We endorse the participation of La Junta in the Casas Grandes interaction sphere (see Schaafsma and Riley, *Casas Grandes World*), though we have taken liberties with the ideas of the interaction sphere's proponents, as noted elsewhere. We accept the people of the Cielo Complex examined by Mallouf, "Cielo Complex," and wonder whether these might be the Chisos or the otherwise-unassigned Passaguates mentioned by Luxán and Espejo. We agree with Kenmotsu's "Jumano Adaptation," which supports our sense that the Jumanos lived primarily where Kelley put them (on the Edwards Plateau and in the Trans-Pecos) and visited La Junta in much the same fashion that they visited Nuevo Mexico and the Tejas. We doubt that anyone is ever going to resolve the relationship between the Jumanos of Nuevo Mexico (which Forbes, *Apache, Navaho and Spaniard,* calls the Jumano Tompiros, Hickerson, *Jumanos,* calls the Pueblo Jumanos and the Spanish called Humanas) and the Jumanos of Texas (which Forbes calls the Jumano Apaches, Hickerson calls the Plains Jumanos and others, including us, consider distinct, non-Apache Jumanos until they assimilate into the Apaches in the mid-1700s).

2. One early and authoritative interpreter concluded that this village was at El Paso, but that version of the journey leaves an immense narrative gap between crossing the Pecos River and arriving at El Paso. See Hallenbeck, *Cabeza de Vaca,* 214. Others place the pueblo at or near La Junta: Chipman, "Cabeza de Vaca's Route"; Krieger, "Nuevo Estúdio"; Hill, Davenport and Wells cited and mapped in Chipman and reproduced in Cabeza de Vaca, *Relación.* One scholar leans toward La Junta, but diplomatically splits the difference with El Paso (Hickerson, *Jumanos,* 16). A noted archaeologist feels that Cabeza de Vaca passed through La Junta, because the Spaniard's passage was confirmed to the Chamuscado and Espejo entradas by the natives there, but he puzzles over why settled La Juntans, who had trade pottery, would have cooked food by dropping hot rocks in pumpkins as reported by Cabeza de Vaca (see Kelley, *Jumano and Patarabueye,* 16). He speculates that Cabeza de Vaca may have en-

countered Jumanos, not settled La Juntans (whom he calls Patarabueyes), at La Junta, but this raises other questions—Jumanos didn't live in substantial houses of the kind reported by Cabeza de Vaca. If the hot-rocks-in-pumpkins issue rules out settled La Juntans, then it also rules out the people at El Paso (residual Jornada Mogollon), who also had pottery. Kenmotsu, "Helping Each Other Out" (190), speculates that there may be an issue of translation: Cabeza de Vaca may have been saying that the natives did not have large stewpots, but did have shallow bowls. We have difficulty making sense of Cabeza de Vaca's account when that translation is applied, however. Pots, bowls or pumpkins, in our opinion, La Junta's oral history of Cabeza de Vaca's passage through the valley cinches it; we believe that Cabeza de Vaca paused in or near the village that became known as San Bernardino.

3. Cabeza de Vaca, *Relación*, 101.

1. For a period of time under the Mexican constitution of 1836, the Mexican states were governed as "departments" that, with some exceptions, were coterminous with the states. Chihuahua was placed in a department that included New Mexico. We disregard the distinction between departments and states in our discussion.

2. Colonization law of the Free State of Chihuahua, Decree 45, as quoted in "Brief and Argument for the Defendants," U.S. Fifth Circuit, *Owen v. Presidio Mining Co.*, 14–20.

3. "Se permite la introduccion de ciertos géneros de algodon; destinos de los derechos que produzcan y providencias relativa á la colonización y comercío," Apr. 6, 1830, Dublan and Lozano, *Legislacion Mexicana*, No. 809, 2:238; Moquin and Van Doren, *Documentary History*, 144–146.

4. Almada, *Diccionario*, 467–468; Alonso, *Thread of Blood*, 40.

5. Williams, *Pecos County*, uses 1824 as the date that the colony was built, but his stories are openly folklore. It is more likely that the prison colony was established about the time of the 1830 prison colony law, which puts it within Ronquillo's tenure. Thompson, *Marfa and Presidio County*, says the colony was populated in 1824; Tyler et al., *Handbook of Texas*, adopts 1824 as the construction date; and Horgan, *Great River*, loosely links the colony to about 1823. These three accounts appear to be derivative of Williams, and not based on any additional information.

6. Williams, *Pecos County*, 13; Raht, *Romance*, 120–121; Henry T. Fletcher, quoted in "Texas Collection," *Southwestern Historical Quarterly*, 48:295, 296 (Oct. 1944).

7. Williams, *Pecos County*, 13, which appears to be the source for the enhanced versions in Horgan, *Great River*, 471, and Thompson, *Marfa and Presidio County*, 37–38.

8. Depositions of Trinidad Sanchez (13), Mariano Acosta (171) and Francisco Vanagas (201), "Abstract of Record and Evidence," U.S. Fifth Circuit, *Owen v. Presidio Mining Co.* We know that Antonia Oros and her daughter Trini-

dad were in La Junta at the same time as Ronquillo's legitimate family because Trinidad said that she was born in Mexico City in 1826 but had lived in Presidio since the age of six months. This raises the possibility that Captain Ronquillo, who roamed the frontier long before he took command of the Presidio del Norte, met Antonia Oros at Presidio del Norte and that she was already residing there with Trinidad when Captain Ronquillo and his legitimate family took up residence. Local sentiment may have held Rafaela, not Trinidad, to be the trespasser.

9. Depositions of Candido Salgado (9), Vicente Molinar (154) and Juan de Dios Vasquez (184), "Abstract," *Owen.*

10. Depositions of Francisco Vanagas (201–202) and Francisco Arsate (230–231), "Abstract," *Owen.*

11. Depositions of Candido Salgado (6–7), Felix Lerma (10) and C. H. Cratsenberg (79–81), "Abstract," *Owen.* The evidence that the "survey" trip actually occurred is scant but plausible. It seems clear, however, that no one on the trip was a qualified surveyor.

12. Survey by Richard A. Howard, Deputy District Surveyor for the District of Bexar, filed Feb. 27, 1851; "Brief," *Owen,* 2; Bowden, *Spanish and Mexican Land Grants,* 196 and map, 198.

13. Depositions of Candido Salgado (7), Felix Lerma (10), Trinidad Sanchez (13) and Francisca Leaton (18), "Abstract," *Owen.* Contra, see depositions of Mariano Acosta and Querino Sosa, ibid.

14. Deposition of Felix Lerma, "Abstract," *Owen,* 10–12. Lerma was detailed and emphatic in his testimony, insisting that the Ronquillo family lived at Cibolo at least from Jan. 15, 1832 to Nov. 27, 1832, but other witnesses say that Ronquillo never lived east of the Rio Grande, or that he sometimes lived at the fortín but never at Cibolo. Lerma's testimony is generally the most supportive of Owen's position in the litigation and has a certain air of exaggeration. We conclude that Ronquillo tried to set up a ranch house to advance his claim for the land, but we also conclude that the ranchstead was short-lived.

15. Depositions of Vicente Molinar (154) and Trinidad Sanchez (14–15), "Abstract," *Owen.* The name "Fortín de San Jose" doesn't appear to have been widely used; we find it only in the supposed transfer from Juan Bustillos to Ben Leaton dated Feb. 4, 1848 and recorded El Paso County Clerk, Deed Records A:433.

16. "Disposiciones para ayudar a los vecinos que participan en acciones de guerra," Oct. 14, 1830, Orozco, *Las Guerras Indias,* 203.

17. Deposition of Trinidad Sanchez, "Abstract," *Owen,* 14. Some say that Rafaela moved to San Jeronimo, to the east in Coahuila (see deposition of Vicente Molinar, ibid., 154).

18. Almada, *Diccionario,* 468; Smith, "Indians in American-Mexican Relations," 43.

19. José Joaquín Calvo, "Declaración de guerra a los bárbaros," Oct. 16, 1831, in Orozco, *Las Guerras Indias,* 205; "Assignación obligatoria de ciertas zonas a los apaches de paz. Orden para armar a los vecinos," Mar. 1, 1832, ibid., 211.

20. Calvo, "Declaración de guerra," 205; Almada, "Los Apaches," 9; Almada, *Diccionario,* 468; depositions of Candido Salgado (8) and Felix Lerma (11, 12), "Abstract," *Owen.* The location of Ojo Caliente is shown on Capt. W. R. Livermore and Topographical Assistant F. E. Butterfield's "Military Map of the Rio Grande Frontier" (1881), Crimmins Map Collection, Austin: Center for American History, University of Texas. A smaller and less detailed version of the Livermore map (traced by O. L. Wylie in 1883) is part of Shipman, *Taming,* but does not show the location of Ojo Caliente; the traced map also appears as No. 1591 in the collection of the Texas State Archives and Library Commission, Austin, copied from "White God," *Voice of the Mexican Border,* vol. 1, no. 1 (which probably copied the map from Shipman). We have not located the map's original source. Ojo Caliente is shown on U.S. Geological Survey, *Indian Hot Springs, Texas-Chihuahua,* Color Image Map 30105–G3–PI-025 (1982) at approximately 30°49' N, 105°19' W. Ronquillo's grave cannot be found inside the Ojinaga church, which was refloored sometime in the twentieth century.

21. Smith, "Indians in American-Mexican Relations," 43–44.

22. Smith, "Indians in American-Mexican Relations," 35–36.

23. Horgan, *Great River,* 849–852.

24. Smith, "Mexican and Anglo-Saxon Traffic," 99; Smith, "Indians in American-Mexican Relations," 40–42; note David Torrey's proposal to ransom captives held by Comanches: Bolton, *Guide to the History of the United States,* 459, re Archivo de la Secretaría de Gobierno de Chihuahua, Legajo 175, No. 22.

ANGLOS ARRIVE

1. Smith, "Mexican and Anglo-Saxon Traffic," 101.

2. Smith, "Indians in American-Mexican Relations," 51, 57.

3. The original Easterly daguerreotype is in the collection of the Missouri Historical Society. A copy hangs in Fort Leaton, near Presidio. The original Curry mural is painted on the wall of the Kansas State Capitol. A reproduction is in Harpers Ferry, Virginia, and commercial copies have circulated.

4. Smith, "Poor Mexico," 99, regarding contracts executed at the presidio; see discussion inf. regarding scalp hunting by Glanton and Chevallié in La Junta.

5. On use of the term "Anglo," see Chap. 4, n. 1.

6. Palace of the Governors, Museum of New Mexico, "Henry Connelly," http://www.nmcn.org/features/civilwar/sketches/connelly.htm (accessed Jan. 26, 2002); "Connelly, Henry C." in Tyler et al., *Handbook of Texas,* 2:272–273.

7. "Chihuahua Expedition," in Tyler et al., *Handbook of Texas,* 2:76–77; Lister and Lister, *Chihuahua,* 108; Palace of the Governors, "Henry Connelly."

8. Gregg, *Commerce of the Prairies,* 163; *Austin City Gazette,* Apr. 28, 1841.

9. One 1966 book stated that the Presidio del Norte had been approved as

an official port of entry in 1830. This statement has been repeated in other subsequent works. We have not found substantiation for the assertion, and query
whether a port of entry would exist at a place that had only one established
road in or out, that had never once had anyone ask for entrance and that was
several hundred miles from the nearest state or national border. Even El Paso
did not have a customhouse until 1835 (Moorhead, *New Mexico's Royal Road*,
113). We think it is much more likely that Connelly's transit through the presidio was a onetime prearranged affair and that no customs house existed in La
Junta until after the Treaty of Guadalupe Hidalgo. Leaton, Burgess, Spencer,
Hays, Highsmith and Whiting all appeared in La Junta within a year of the
treaty, and those arrivals likely spurred the adoption of border formalities.
See Moorhead, *New Mexico's Royal Road*, 125, re arreglos.

10. Moorhead, *New Mexico's Royal Road*, 125; Gregg, *Commerce of the Prairies*,
165; Santleben, *Texas Pioneer*, 60.

11. *Austin City Gazette*, Apr. 28, 1841; Moorhead, *New Mexico's Royal Road*,
72–75.

12. Colomo, *Diario*, 20 April 1839. The diary (as translated) also has a cryp-
tic entry three days earlier: "The 17th day of April 1839, the General refused
the salute to the Norte de Chihuahua." This may be a mistranslation; the
search for the original diary continues.

13. Gregg, *Commerce of the Prairies*, 163, n.; *Austin City Gazette*, Apr. 28, 1841.

14. Gregg, *Commerce of the Prairies*, 163, n.; *Austin City Gazette*, Apr. 28, 1841;
"Chihuahua Expedition," 2:76–77.

15. Kendall, *Santa Fé Expedition*, 121.

16. Almada, *Gobernadores*, 83–86, 90–97; Smith, "Mexican and Anglo-
Saxon Traffic," 107.

17. Moorhead, *New Mexico's Royal Road*, 126.

IN DONIPHAN'S WAKE

1. For use of the term "Anglo," see Chap. 4, n. 1.

2. Moorhead, *New Mexico's Royal Road*, 152–153.

3. Moorhead, *New Mexico's Royal Road*, 156.

4. Moorhead, *New Mexico's Royal Road*, 163–164; William E. Connelley,
A Standard History of Kansas and Kansans (Chicago, Lewis, 1918), 1:132–134.

5. Moorhead, *New Mexico's Royal Road*, 168–170.

6. Hughes, *Doniphan's Expedition*, 334–335.

7. Doniphan to Wool, Mar. 20, 1847, in Hughes, *Doniphan's Expedition*,
338.

8. Deposition of John W. Spencer, "Abstract," *Owen*, 196. Spencer does
not specifically mention Doniphan, but he says that he knew Leaton's lover,
Pedraza, in Chihuahua, Cerro Gordo and Monterrey—the path taken by
Doniphan. This confirms the existing oral history to the effect that Leaton,
Spencer and Burgess were traders who traveled with Doniphan. See Corning,
Baronial Forts, 20–21. There is a mistake in the dates contained in Spencer's

deposition; the mistake was probably made in transcription. Leaton's surname was pronounced "Lay-ton," though today it is generally pronounced "Lee-ton." See Brown, *Indian Wars and Pioneers*, 105.

9. The Americans reoccupied Chihuahua anyway, driving Governor Trías again from the city and forcing his surrender at Rosales. Moorhead, *New Mexico's Royal Road*, 183.

10. Deposition of John W. Spencer, "Abstract," *Owen*, 195, 198. The statement at 195 that Spencer knew Leaton until 1840 is an obvious mistake, probably a transcriber's error; Spencer says he traveled to La Junta with Leaton in 1848. A soldier based at Fort Davis circa 1855 reported in his later memoirs that there were two ranches on the Texas side of the river, one owned by John Spencer and the other owned by Edward Hall, who "was a discharged soldier who went to Mexico and married the widow of old Ben Leaton, who had a very valuable property. . . . Along the river there were good farming lands, and she was rich, but Hall soon gambled it all away. . . . Spencer had been living there since the Mexican War, and had a good ranch and a train of eight or ten mule wagons, but he spent everything he had in the vain endeavor to open a mine he had discovered, and at last was very poor, but after thirty years the mine has been developed and Spencer holds $500,000.00 worth of stock and may yet die rich." In the town at Presidio del Norte, Mexico, "there were several Americans. John Burgess was at the time the richest of them, and had the finest train on the road. Milton Faver, a Virginian had a little store where he would sell a cents worth of anything but he was laying the foundation of a large fortune, that he now enjoys. A Georgian who went to Mexico with the Army lived on this [the Texas] side in a little jacal, and had quite a pretty Mexican for his wife. . . . There was also a man named Crabbe, and a German named King, who had but one leg, and was known as Peg Leg King." Bliss, *Reminiscences*, 1:260–261.

11. The Texas viewpoint is reflected in "Torrey, David Kilburn," in Tyler et al., *Handbook of Texas*, 6:532. The Mexican view is presented in Smith, "Mexican and Anglo-Saxon Traffic," 102–103; also see the view of Mexican officials about the similar activities of Ben Leaton, discussed inf.

12. Armbruster, *Torreys of Texas*, 27; "Torrey, David Kilburn," in Tyler et al., *Handbook of Texas*, 6:532.

13. Armbruster, *Torreys of Texas*, 27–28; Smith, "Mexican and Anglo-Saxon Traffic," 103; Evans, *Mexican Gold Trail*, 84.

14. *Houston Telegraph*, Mar. 17, 1850; also see Brown, *Henry Smith*, 378–379, which says, "A party of Mescalero Indians, while trading with him in the most friendly manner, learned from a party of their people just arrived, that some of their tribe had been killed a few days before, on the Mexican side, by a party of Americans en route to California. Without a moment's notice they cleft Torrey's head in twain and instantly killed his companions, Strickland and two others. This tragic event occurred on Christmas day, 1849."

15. "Treaty of Guadalupe Hidalgo," Feb. 2, 1848, articles as cited, in Bevans, *Treaties*, 9:791 et seq.; also, Griswold del Castillo, *Treaty*, 183 et seq.

16. "Treaty of Guadalupe Hidalgo," in Bevans, *Treaties*; also, Griswold del Castillo, *Treaty*.

17. Polk, Annual Message of the President to Congress, Dec. 7, 1847: "The terms of a treaty proposed by the Mexican commissioners were wholly inadmissible. . . . It demanded the right for Mexico to levy and collect the Mexican tariff of duties on goods imported into her ports while in our military occupation during the war, and the owners of which had paid to officers of the United States the military contributions which had been levied upon them."

18. Republic of Texas Constitution (1836), Schedule, sec. 1; ibid., General Provisions, sec. 10; Texas Constitution (1845), Art. 13, sec. 3; "An Act to Adopt the Common Law of England, to Repeal Certain Mexican Laws, and to Regulate the Marrital Rights of Parties," Jan. 20, 1840, Gammel, *Laws of Texas*, 2:178; Griswold del Castillo, *Treaty*, 53–55; McKitrick, "Public Land System," 49; "Land Grants," in Tyler et al., *Handbook of Texas*, 4:56–58.

19. Griswold del Castillo, *Treaty*, 53–55.

20. Re formation of Presidio County, see "An Act Creating the Counties of Presidio, El Paso and Worth," Jan. 3, 1850, Gammel, *Laws of Texas*, 3:462, and "An Act to Provide for the Civil Organization of the Counties of Presidio, El Paso, Worth and Santa Fe," Jan. 4, 1850, ibid., 464; re the commission, see "An act to Provide for the Investigation of Land Titles in Certain Counties Therein Mentioned," Feb. 8, 1850, ibid., 582; regarding the low priority of Presidio County, note that the act for investigation of land titles specified dates for hearings in Kinney, Webb, Starr, Cameron and Nueces Counties (at times through 1851), but left the question of timing open in the Trans-Pecos realm of Presidio, El Paso, Worth and Santa Fe Counties (sec. 3, 583). See more detailed discussion of county formation and organization, inf.

21. Re scrip, see, for example, "Joint Resolutions Authorizing the President to Negotiate a Loan for Twenty Thousand Dollars," Dec. 10, 1836, and "Joint Resolutions Authorizing the President to Issue Scrip to the Amount of Five Hundred Thousand Acres of Land," Dec. 10, 1836, Gammel, *Laws of Texas*, 1:1136–1137; re surveying, see, for example, "An Act Providing for the Location of Land Scrip Issued by an Act of Congress, Dated the 6th Day of December, 1836, and for Redeeming the Same," May 18, 1838, ibid., 1488; McKitrick, "Public Land System," 79–83.

22. "An Act Granting to Settlers on Vacant Public Domain Pre-emption Privileges," Jan. 22, 1845, Gammel, *Laws of Texas*, 2:1073; "Land Grants," in Tyler et al., *Handbook of Texas*, 4:56–58.

23. Deposition of Leno Baisa, "Abstract," *Owen*, 169. The deposition of Elanerio Baiza spells the family name with a "z"; the deposition of Leno Baisa spells the family name with an "s." The spellings, which are phonetically identical, were probably selected by the court reporter, not the deponents.

24. Deposition of Elanerio Baiza, "Abstract," *Owen*, 168.

25. "Presidio County Letter" in the trial record of U.S. Fifth Circuit, *Owen v. Presidio Mining Co.*, 1276; El Paso County, Texas, Deed Records, document 370, A:405, 407, 411, 414, 415.

26. El Paso County, Texas, Deed Records, documents 372, 373 and 374, A:430, 433, 434, 439, 442, 444, 447, 449, 452. A transcription of the fortín grant is recorded in Presidio County, Texas, Deed Records 11:29.

27. Deposition of John W. Spencer, "Abstract," *Owen*, 195.

28. El Paso County, Texas, Deed Records, document 371, A:421, 425, 426, 427, 428. Also filed in Bexar County, Texas, Deed Records, J-1: 48–52. An English translation appears in "Brief," *Owen,* Exhibit A, 159.

29. "Presidio County Letter," 1276.

30. "Presidio County Letter," 1277. The six brave rancheros deserve to be identified. They were Dionisio Evano, Sabino Quintela, Querino Sosa, Juan Baesa, Dario Rodriguez and Telesforo Lujan.

31. Depositions of Mariano Acosta (172), Francisco Vanagas (202) and Francisco Arsate (231), "Abstract," *Owen.* Herrera reappeared in La Junta within a year, apparently having avoided incarceration. It is possible that he dodged conviction by pointing out that the titles he fraudulently created were to land in the United States, not Mexico, and thus were not crimes under Mexican law.

JACK HAYS GETS LOST

1. "Reglamento de la direccion de colonizacion," Dec. 4, 1846, Dublan and Lozano, *Legislacion Mexicana,* 6:229, 233.

2. Bolton, *Guide,* 458; Colomo, *Diario,* Sept. 21, 1851, reports a request for a "force to fight the Indians" that resulted in an additional 57 men being sent.

3. "Sobre establecimiento de colonias militares, y su reglamento," July 19, 1848, Dublan and Lozano, *Legislacion Mexicana,* 6:422; Mexico, *Colonias militares,* map and table; trans. as Faulk, "Projected Mexican Military Colonies for the Borderlands, 1848," 39–45, map and table.

4. Faulk, "Projected Mexican Colonies in the Borderlands, 1852," 115–128.

5. Gregg, *Presidio County,* 47; Livermore, "Military Map of the Rio Grande Frontier," in Shipman, *Taming.*

6. Gregg, *Presidio County,* 49.

7. Corning, *Baronial Forts,* 23.

8. Depositions of Francisca Leaton (18), Francisco Vanagas (201), Francisco Arsate (230), Querino Urivas (233), Miguel Montes (236) and John Spencer (195), "Abstract," *Owen;* Swift and Corning, *Three Roads to Chihuahua,* 76; U.S. Bureau of the Census, *Eighth Census.*

9. Depositions of Francisca Leaton (18), Francisco Vanagas (201), Francisco Arsate (230), Querino Urivas (233) and Miguel Montes (236), "Abstract," *Owen;* Corning, *Baronial Forts,* 41. One account says "Joe Leaton killed several Mexicans and finally died in jail in San Antonio, where he was held for murder, and died of small pox." Bliss, *Reminiscences,* 1:265.

10. See the inventories and sales receipts contained in Bexar County, *Leaton Estate;* these are transcribed in Corning, *Baronial Forts,* 77–105.

11. Hays report to Bell, *Houston Democratic Telegraph and Texas Register,* Dec. 28, 1848, and *Clarksville Northern Standard,* Feb. 10, 1849; Maverick, "Journal, Chihuahua Expedition," 338; Greer, *Colonel Jack Hays,* 222.

12. Austin to Williams in Barker, *Austin Papers*, 3:43; Greer, *Colonel Jack Hays*, 215–216.

13. Brown, *Indian Wars*, 104; Hays report to Bell; Maverick, "Journal, Chihuahua Expedition," 338; Maverick, *Memoirs*, 102; Hays and Caperton, *Life and Adventures*, 61–64.

14. Maverick, "Journal, Chihuahua Expedition," 336–338; Maverick, *Memoirs*, 102; Hays and Caperton, *Life and Adventures*, 64.

15. Hays report to Bell, *Houston Democratic Telegraph and Texas Register*, Dec. 28, 1848, and *Clarksville Northern Standard*, Feb. 10, 1849; Highsmith report to Bell, *San Antonio Western Texian*, Jan. 12, 1849; Greer, *Colonel Jack Hays*, 217–218; Hays and Caperton, *Life and Adventures*, 64. The 1879 memoirs of Hays and Caperton report that they received "beef, corn, and many things of which they were in need" at San Carlos. This may overstate the situation somewhat. Samuel Maverick reported himself "recruiting on bread and milk" at San Carlos, but did not say that his sustenance was limited to those items. Whiting (see inf.) found only dried beef, cornmeal and pinole at Fort Leaton. At about the same time, when Evans reached San Carlos (see inf.) he reported, "With the exception of [green] wheat and a very few beans just ripening, there is nothing to supply our wants, and eighty-four men must live five days longer without bread."

16. By 1879, when Hays was collecting his memoirs, he and Caperton asserted that the Presidio del Norte had been their destination all along, but Hays's own statements in 1849 contradict that assertion. Hays and Caperton, *Life and Adventures*, 63; "Col. Hays' Report," *Clarksville Northern Standard*, Feb. 10, 1849.

17. Hays and Caperton, *Life and Adventures*, 65.

18. Hays report to Bell; Maverick, "Journal, Chihuahua Expedition," 338; *Corpus Christi Star*, Dec. 23, 1848. Hays and Caperton, *Life and Adventures*, 65, says, "They had a Quarter Master with them named Ralston, who made purchases, through Leaton, for the party, from the Bishop of Chihuahua who came down to that place, and furnished them with animals and such provisions as the country would afford." The idea of a bishop as provisioner is not impossible, but has a certain unlikely grandeur; thus we choose to understate the occasion.

19. Brown, *Indian Wars*, 104.

20. Hays and Caperton, *Life and Adventures*, 66.

21. Brown, *Indian Wars*, 104, 106; Greer, *Colonel Jack Hays*, 224; Frontier Times, *Jack Hays*, 26; Bexar County, *Leaton Estate*. The co-owned cattle were branded PL, presumably for Peacock-Leaton. Note the probate accounting for the sale of thirty-nine head of cattle to E. Trimble, subject to a deduction for the expense in herding and driving the cattle from Peacock's ranch. It would not make sense for the estate to have driven the co-owned mares, sheep and cattle from La Junta to San Antonio, and the estate papers contain no evidence of that. The co-owned livestock were kept by Peacock.

22. Greer, *Samuel Maverick*, 338; Frontier Times, *Jack Hays*, 26; Brown, *Indian Wars*, 105; Hays and Caperton, *Life and Adventures*, 66–67.

23. Hays report to Bell; Hays to Marcy, in U.S. Senate, *Report of the Secretary of War, Communicating in Compliance with a Resolution . . .* , 64–65.

24. Highsmith report to Bell.

25. Hays report to Bell; Hays to Marcy, 64–65.

WHITING DRAWS THE LINE

1. Whiting, William Henry Chase, "Journal of 1849," in Bieber and Bender, *Exploring Southwestern Trails,* 30–31.

2. Whiting, "Journal of 1849," 34.

3. Whiting, "Journal of 1849," 34. See ibid., 267, where Whiting crosses Connelly's trail, recognizes it and refers to it as "Connelly's wagon trail to Presidio."

4. Lieut. Whiting to Gen. Totten, June 10, 1849, in U.S. House, *Message,* 281–282; see ibid., 285, re fifteen men; Whiting, "Journal of 1849," 243.

5. Whiting, "Journal of 1849," 281–284.

6. Whiting, "Journal of 1849," 284–288.

7. Whiting, "Journal of 1849," 290–291.

8. Whiting, "Journal of 1849," 291, 294; Whiting to Totten, 281–287, 288, 291–292.

9. Whiting to Totten, 290–291.

10. Whiting to Totten, 291.

11. Whiting to Totten, 292.

12. Whiting to Totten, 288; also, see similar remarks in Whiting's subsequent report regarding reconnaissance of the western frontier of Texas: Lieut. Whiting to Maj. Deas, Jan. 21, 1850, in U.S. Senate, *Reports of the Secretary of War . . .* , 237, 249–250.

FORTY-NINERS

1. Deposition of Vicente Molinar, "Abstract," *Owen,* 154; Centers for Disease Control, U.S. Department of Health and Human Services, http://www.cdc.gov/travel/cholera.htm (accessed Jan. 21, 2002).

2. British Broadcasting Corporation, "Medicine through Time; the Industrial Revolution; Public Health; Slum housing and cholera epidemics," http://www.bbc.co.uk/education/medicine/nonint/indust/ph/inphcs1.shtml (accessed Jan. 21, 2002).

3. Note the reference to "1849–1850. Expedientes concerning the epidemic of cholera ('or cholera morbus')" contained in Legajo 174, Regular Files of the Archivo de la Secretaría de Gobierno, in Bolton, *Guide,* 458. The Chihuahua Archives are said to have been lost in a fire in 1941, after Bolton's inventory was taken.

4. Colomo, *Diario.*

5. "Epidemic Diseases," in Tyler et al., *Handbook of Texas,* 2:877–878; Colomo, *Diario.*

6. Maverick, *Memoirs,* 98–99.

7. Maverick, *Memoirs,* 100.

8. Maverick, *Memoirs,* 98, 101–102.

9. Maverick, *Memoirs,* 103–104.

10. Evans, *Mexican Gold Trail,* 14; ibid., preface by Robert Glass Cleland, xiv.

11. Evans, *Mexican Gold Trail,* 18; ibid., preface by Robert Glass Cleland, xv–xvii.

12. Evans, *Mexican Gold Trail,* 75–76.

13. Evans, *Mexican Gold Trail,* 76–77.

14. Evans, *Mexican Gold Trail,* 78–79.

15. Evans, *Mexican Gold Trail,* 79.

16. Evans, *Mexican Gold Trail,* 83–86.

17. Evans, *Mexican Gold Trail,* 81–82.

18. Hunter, *Texan in the Gold Rush,* 13–14, and introduction by Robert W. Stephens, 8–9.

19. Hunter, *Texan in the Gold Rush,* 14–15.

20. We know that Hunter did not follow the Rio Grande to El Paso because he mentions that "we are compelled to cross the river here as there is no route to be found on this side to El Paso del Norte." The usual path along the river (the Whiting Trail) began on the Texas side, not the Mexican bank, and stayed on that side for most of the journey. Hunter, *Texan in the Gold Rush,* 14.

SCALP HUNTING REDUX

1. Almada, *Gobernadores,* 133–134; Almada, "Los Apaches," 12; Smith, "Scalp Hunt," 118.

2. Smith, "Poor Mexico," 82–83; "Glanton, John Joel," in Tyler et al., *Handbook of Texas,* 3:180.

3. Smith, "Poor Mexico," 96. The concealed-cannon story, which is true (or at least ingrained in history), apparently gave rise to a similar story about Leaton killing Apaches at Fort Leaton using the same trick. The latter story has the ring of folklore. It appears to have been concocted by Victor Leaton Ochoa, who was known for his creative storytelling (see Thompson, *Marfa and Presidio County,* 68). We relegate it to the category of apocrypha.

4. Bliss, *Reminiscences,* 1:295–296.

5. Extract of letter from Babbitt, Oct. 15, 1849, in Winfrey and Day, *Indian Papers,* 5:49–50.

6. Jones to Brooke, Aug. 20, 1849, in Winfrey and Day, *Indian Papers,* 5:48–49.

7. Van Horne to Deas, Nov. 8, 1849, in Winfrey and Day, *Indian Papers,* 5:50. Skillman's is not specifically identified as the military expedition that passed through, but there is no record of a military visit to La Junta during 1849 other than Whiting/Skillman, and Whiting's 1849 report mentions that Apache Chief Gomez, "fearing lest we might come back with a stronger

party, had made a treaty with Mr. Leaton, and permitted Skillman to pass unmolested through his whole tribe." Whiting to Totten, 291.

8. Van Horne to Deas, 5:51.

9. Langberg to Van Horne, Oct. 23, 1849, in Winfrey and Day, *Indian Papers,* 5:52.

10. Trías to Langberg, Oct. 10, 1849, in Winfrey and Day, *Indian Papers,* 5:53.

11. "Demanda de la Diputación Permanente del Congreso in relación al tratado de paz con Estados Unidos y los indios 'bárbaros,'" Orozco, *Las Guerras Indias,* 256.

12. Van Horne to Deas, 5:51.

13. Treaty of Guadalupe Hidalgo, Feb. 2, 1848, Art. 11, in Bevans, *Treaties,* 9:791 et seq.; also, Griswold del Castillo, *Treaty,* 190; Crawford to Clayton, Nov. 8, 1849, in U.S. Department of State, *Diplomatic Correspondence,* 43–44, n. 4.

14. The correspondence from Crawford in Washington bore the same date as the letter from Van Horne in El Paso; Crawford was reacting to the Babbitt letter, not the Van Horne letter. Crawford to Clayton, 51; Clayton to Letcher, Nov. 10, 1849, in U.S. Department of State, *Diplomatic Correspondence,* 43–44, and footnoted letter Crawford to Clayton, with extract from Babbitt letter, Oct. 15, 1849.

15. Smith, "Poor Mexico," 99, reports that John Allen Veatch (a noted Texas frontiersman who founded Eagle Pass, Texas) and some other Americans entered into a scalp-hunting contract at Presidio del Norte in July 1849.

16. Colomo, *Diario,* Apr. 18, 1850, May 15, 1850, May 17, 1850, June 17, 1850, July 4, 1850.

A SUDDEN DEATH

1. "An Act to Create and Organize the County of Santa Fe," Mar. 15, 1848, Gammel, *Laws of Texas,* 3:95; "Preamble and Joint Resolutions," Mar. 20, 1848, ibid., 3:218; "Joint Resolution," Feb. 11, 1850, ibid., 3:645. Despite the designation of Santa Fe as the county seat, San Antonio was effectively the county seat until actual organization of El Paso County. Deeds, court files and other documents for La Junta are in San Antonio (Bexar County), El Paso (El Paso County) and Marfa (Presidio County).

2. "Compromise of 1850," in Tyler et al., *Handbook of Texas,* 2:253; "Ford and Neighbors Trail," ibid., 2:1076; "An Act Making an Appropriation for the Payment of Outstanding Liabilities of the Mission of Maj. R. S. Neighbors . . . ," Aug. 28, 1850, Gammel, *Laws of Texas,* 3:786; "An Act Accepting the Propositions Made by the United States to the State of Texas . . . ," ibid., 3:832.

3. "An Act Creating the Counties of Presidio, El Paso and Worth," Jan. 3, 1850, Gammel, *Laws of Texas,* 3:462.

4. "Compromise of 1850," 2:253; "Joint Resolutions," Nov. 20, 1855, Gammel, *Laws of Texas,* 4:263.

5. "An Act to Organize the County of Presidio," Jan. 2, 1858, Gammel, *Laws of Texas,* 4:906; "An Act to Organize the County of Presidio," July 19, 1870, ibid., 6:206; "An Act to Organize the County of Presidio," May 12, 1871, ibid., 6:988; "An Act to Perfect the Organization of the County of Presidio," Mar. 13, 1875, ibid., 8:481. The first (1871) statutory county commissioners were Patrick Murphy, Moses E. Kelley and Daniel Murphy. The second (1875) statutory county commissioners were Daniel Murphy, O. M. Keesey, H. W. Tinkson, T. A. Wilson and W. M. Ford.

6. "Brewster County—Creation and Organization," Feb. 2, 1887, Gammel, *Laws of Texas,* 9:802; "New Counties Created out of Presidio County," Mar. 15, 1887, ibid., 9:824; Shipman, *Taming,* 56–57; Gregg, *Presidio County,* 209–211. The five counties were Presidio, Brewster, Jeff Davis, Buchel and Foley. Buchel and Foley Counties were never organized and were merged into Brewster County.

7. Bexar County, *Leaton Estate,* evidences Leaton's travels and Peacock's advances of money to Leaton for those trips. Cesario Ureta averred to the validity of signatures on Leaton's fraudulent grants in San Antonio during 1849.

8. Peacock's involvement in the process of attempting to prove up Leaton's title is evidenced in Bexar County, *Estate of Ben Leaton,* which reflects expenses for hiring assistants to travel to El Paso (for recording), and "expenses Mexican witnesses proving up land claims." A May 31, 1852 accounting of expenses incurred by Peacock for Leaton's account during 1850 expressly includes the cost of land claim witnesses and expressly relates to amounts already due Peacock at the time of Leaton's death. "Recorders," Dec. 20, 1836, Gammel, *Laws of Texas,* 1:1215. Re color of title, see *Lambert v. Weir,* 27 Tex. 359 (1864).

9. "An Act to Provide for the Registry of Deeds, and Other Instruments of Writing," May 12, 1846, Gammel, *Laws of Texas,* 2:1542.

10. Depositions of Juan de Dios Vasques (185), Francisco Arsate (233) and Miguel Montes (239), "Abstract," *Owen.*

11. Deposition of Francisca Leaton, "Abstract," *Owen,* 17–19; affidavits of Ureta in Bexar County Clerk, J1:40, 43, 47, 51 and 58 (same instruments also appear in El Paso County and are transcribed in Presidio County).

12. *Holliday v. Cromwell,* 26 Tex. 188 (1862).

13. Depositions of Juan de Dios Vasques (185), Querino Sosa (188), John W. Spencer (198) and Francisco Vanagas (204), "Abstract," *Owen;* Exhibit A, "Brief," ibid.; affidavits of Hall in Bexar County Clerk, J1:40, 44, 47, 51 and 58 (same instruments also appear in El Paso County and are transcribed in Presidio County).

14. Will of Ben Leaton in Bexar County, *Leaton Estate;* Deposition of John W. Spencer, "Abstract," *Owen,* 195.

15. Bexar County, *Leaton Estate.* Francisca Leaton said that her husband Joe Leaton had died in San Antonio (in jail) while on a trip to visit his uncles (deposition in "Abstract," *Owen,* 19). Brown, *Indian Wars,* 105, says Ben Leaton was the senior of two or three brothers.

16. Bexar County, *Leaton Estate;* Hall-Pedraza marriage license, Oct. 15, 1852, office of the Bexar County Clerk, C:13. The probate file is incomplete,

and it is conceivable that Hall was appointed administrator in parallel with Pedraza as administratrix.

17. Texas Constitution (1845), Art. 7, Sec. 22, Gammel, *Laws of Texas,* 2:1294. The deed from Hall, Pedraza et al. to Devine dated Apr. 10, 1853 was recorded Apr. 12, 1853 in Bexar County Clerk, J2:402 and was recorded July 7, 1869 in El Paso County Clerk, D:56. Juana Pedraza confirmed the deed as executrix of Ben Leaton's estate with a quitclaim dated Apr. 4, 1854, recorded Apr. 8, 1854, in Bexar County Clerk, J2:403 and recorded July 7, 1869, in El Paso County Clerk, D:59. Daniel Devine (not Joseph H. Devine) conveyed the land to Robert H. Neilson by deed dated June 4, 1869 and recorded in El Paso County Clerk, D:61. Because the Leaton probate file is incomplete, and because land records were chaotic at the time, the exact lands sold are difficult to determine. It is clear, however, that Pedraza first elected to retain the fort and a surrounding two hundred acres, then sold all but the fort and a surrounding five acres to Devine.

THE END OF ISOLATION

1. Rebert, *Gran Línea,* 139.

2. Treaty of Guadalupe Hidalgo, Art. 5, in Bevans, *Treaties,* 9:791 et seq.; also, Griswold del Castillo, *Treaty,* 187; Rebert, *Gran Línea,* 2–7.

3. Rebert, *Gran Línea,* 139–140.

4. Rebert, *Gran Línea,* 139.

5. Rebert, *Gran Línea,* 141.

6. Rebert, *Gran Línea,* 142.

7. Emory, *Report,* 85; Rebert, *Gran Línea,* 143.

8. Emory, *Report,* 85–86.

9. Emory, *Report,* 89; Colomo, *Diario,* Aug. 17 and 26, 1852. We conclude that the raiders were Apaches because of their location, well above Comanche raiding routes.

10. Emory, *Report,* 86.

11. Rebert, *Gran Línea,* 145–147.

12. Rebert, *Gran Línea,* 147.

13. Rebert, *Gran Línea,* 145, 153–154.

14. Emory, *Report,* 89.

15. Swift and Corning, *Three Roads to Chihuahua,* 109–110.

16. Evans, *Mexican Gold Trail,* 89.

17. Fröbel, *Seven Years' Travel,* 406. Fröbel also reported that at Fort Clark (on the "lower" military road from San Antonio to El Paso, being the outbound route of Whiting) "preserved fruits, anchovies, pickled oysters, and champagne, were to be had at a store adjoining the fort." Ibid., 428–429.

18. Fröbel, *Seven Years' Travel,* 408.

19. Fröbel, *Seven Years' Travel,* 408. Another legitimate question is whether Fröbel could tell the difference between an Apache and a Comanche.

20. Fröbel, *Seven Years' Travel,* 409–410.

21. Fröbel, *Seven Years' Travel,* 410.

22. Fröbel, *Seven Years' Travel,* 410–411.

23. Santleben, *Texas Pioneer,* 100–101.

24. Santleben, *Texas Pioneer,* 101–102.

25. Santleben, *Texas Pioneer,* 102.

26. Santleben, *Texas Pioneer.*

27. Santleben, *Texas Pioneer,* 99.

28. Santleben, *Texas Pioneer,* 103–104.

29. Santleben, *Texas Pioneer,* 167.

30. Santleben, *Texas Pioneer,* 161–162, 180–183.

31. Santleben, *Texas Pioneer,* 168–169.

32. Santleben, *Texas Pioneer,* 169–170. Santleben also mentions the presence of "Hugh Kelly" that night. This was probably Hiram Kelly, brother of Moses Kelly, the first representative of the United States Customs Service in Presidio. The Kellys arrived around 1867, seven years before the beans-and-coins incident, and opened stores on both sides of the Rio Grande. Gregg, *Presidio County,* 59.

RAILROADS AND RANCHES

1. Depositions of Joseph Magoffin (261) and John W. Spencer (199), "Abstract," *Owen;* Almada, "Los Apaches," 11.

2. Paul W. Gates, *History of Public Land Law Development* (Washington, D.C.: Public Land Law Review Commission, 1968), 345, 350, 360.

3. McKitrick, "Public Land System," 57–59.

4. McKitrick, "Public Land System," 59–60.

5. McKitrick, "Public Land System," 68–71.

6. Deed dated Jan. 29, 1858, from Edward Hall and Juana P. Hall to Milton Favors [*sic*] in records of El Paso County Clerk, B:111, and transcribed into records of Presidio County Clerk, 11:41; deed dated Aug. 9, 1858, from A. C. Hyde to Milton Favor [*sic*] in records of El Paso County Clerk, B:110, and transcribed into records of Presidio County Clerk, 11:40.

7. Gregg, *Presidio County,* 51–52; Corning, *Baronial Forts,* 44–45; Poindexter, *Cibolo Creek Ranch,* 15–17.

8. Poindexter, *Cibolo Creek Ranch,* 19; Madrid, "Expedition of Captain Ydoiaga," 63–64.

9. Corning, *Baronial Forts,* 47–48; Faver did not acquire legal title to La Cienaga and La Morita until 1882, according to Poindexter, *Cibolo Creek Ranch,* 18.

10. Corning, *Baronial Forts,* 46, 55, concludes that there was no fort at La Morita. Poindexter, whose corporation purchased the ranches between 1990 and 1992, conducted archaeological work disclosing the existence of a fortín at La Morita. Poindexter, *Cibolo Creek Ranch,* 24–26. In his 1967 book, Corning observed that Cienaga was "worthy of becoming the site of a modern resort area" (46). Today Poindexter operates a breathtakingly restored retreat on

the three ranches and opens them to the public for between US$300 and $600 per night. La Morita is one of the more expensive lodgings; it is remote and lacks electricity.

11. Poindexter, *Cibolo Creek Ranch*, 21–23.

12. Corning, *Baronial Forts*, 55–64; Gregg, *Presidio County*, 62.

13. Gregg, *Presidio County*, 69; Corning, *Baronial Forts*, 59–60; Texas, *Condensed Reports*, 10–14.

14. Corning, *Baronial Forts*, 63–64; Poindexter, *Cibolo Creek Ranch*, 41–43.

15. We use the term "Hispanic" in its imprecise colloquial way, just as we do "Anglo." A Hispanic may be a pure-blooded Tecolote who speaks Spanish and lives in La Junta, a thoroughly cross-bred mestizo who speaks fluent English and broken Spanish, or a perfectly bilingual La Juntan with an Anglo surname, brown skin, brown eyes and straight, black hair. Robert Benchley once said that the world is divided into two kinds of people: those who believe there are two kinds of people, and those who don't.

16. The spouses' names are taken from deeds of record and from Colomo, *Diario*, Feb. 10, 1851.

17. Gregg, *Presidio County*, 59–60; Shipman, *Taming*, 41; Corning, *Baronial Forts*, 58–59.

18. Gregg, *Presidio County*, 63–64.

THE ARMIES

1. It is difficult to keep track of what was where near El Paso. In addition to the confusing switch of names between El Paso del Norte (Juárez), Mexico, and El Paso, Texas, there are periods of time when one must deal with as many as five different settlements clustered together on the Texas side of the river. Fort Bliss stood (stands) at today's El Paso. At the time of the fort's construction, the adjacent town was called Magoffinsville, but correspondence and documents to and from the fort often refer to its location as Franklin, which was earlier known as Coons' Ranch. There was a related garrison a few miles downriver at San Elizario. Fort Quitman was farther down, where the Ford-Neighbors Trail left the river.

2. Raht, *Romance*, 127; Bliss, *Reminiscences*, 1:242.

3. Bliss, *Reminiscences*, 1:170, 260.

4. Bliss, *Reminiscences*, 1:170, 175, 260; Tyler, *Big Bend*, 103–104.

5. For example, see Echols, Report, Oct. 10, 1860, U.S. Senate, *Message*, 44, re Colonel Bomford, who may have been traveling through La Junta to Fort Quitman, though that would be a difficult route. Colonel Bomford also shows up in Fort Leaton on the day that the 1860 census enumeration was taken, along with an army medical team. U.S. Bureau of the Census, *Eighth Census*.

6. Raht, *Romance*, 144; Gregg, *Presidio County*, 52–53; Echols, Report, Oct. 10, 1860, 44–45, re produce supplied to Fort Davis. The 1860 census does not show a miller living in Presidio or at Fort Leaton, but Daniel Geddis

claimed that occupation in the 1870 Census. U.S. Bureau of the Census, *Ninth Census.*

7. Echols, Report, Oct. 10, 1860, 44–45.

8. Echols, Report, Oct. 10, 1860, 45.

9. Lee to Cooper, Oct. 18, 1860, U.S. Senate, *Message,* 3; see Boyd, *Noble Brutes;* Faulk, *U.S. Camel Corps.*

10. Echols, Report, Oct. 10, 1860, 45.

11. Echols, Report, Oct. 10, 1860.

12. Echols, Report, Oct. 10, 1860.

13. Echols, Report, Oct. 10, 1860, 46, 49.

14. Twiggs to Scott, Dec. 13, 1860, U.S. War Dept., *War of the Rebellion,* ser. 1, 1:579; Letter Twiggs to Thomas, Dec. 27, 1860, ibid.

15. Circular, Feb. 18, 1861, U.S. War Dept., *War of the Rebellion,* ser. 1, 1:516.

16. Twiggs report, Feb. 19, 1861, U.S. War Dept., *War of the Rebellion,* ser. 1, 1:503; Whiteley report, Feb. 16, 1861, ibid., 516; Abadie report, Feb. 17, 1861, ibid., 517; Waite report, Feb. 26, 1861, ibid., 521; Waite report, Feb. 12, 1861, ibid., 522; Burleson to Johnson, Feb. 24, 1861, ibid., 595; General Orders, No. 5, Mar. 1, 1861, ibid., 597; "Twiggs, David Emanuel," in Tyler et al., *Handbook of Texas,* 6:602–603; Bliss, *Reminiscences,* 2:233–234.

17. "Summary of the Principal Events," U.S. War Dept., *War of the Rebellion,* ser. 1, 1:502; Special Orders, No. 32, ibid., 594; Special Orders, No. 36, ibid., 596; Special Orders, No. 44, ibid., 597; Scott to Waite, Mar. 19, 1861, ibid., 598; Bliss, *Reminiscences,* 3:3A; Shipman, *Taming,* 34.

18. Clark to Davis, Apr. 4, 1861, U.S. War Dept., *War of the Rebellion,* ser. 1, 1:621.

19. Hemphill and Oldham to Walker, Mar. 30, 1861, U.S. War Dept., *War of the Rebellion,* ser. 1, 1:618–620; Walker to Hemphill and Oldham, Apr. 1, 1861, ibid., 620.

20. General Orders, No. 8, May 24, 1861, U.S. War Dept., *War of the Rebellion,* ser. 1, 1:574–575; Van Dorn to Ford, May 27, 1861, ibid., 577–578.

21. Sibley to Loring, June 12, 1861, U.S. War Dept., *War of the Rebellion,* ser. 1, 4:55–56; Canby to Lynde, June 24, 1861, ibid., 56–57; Canby to Lynde, June 30, 1861, ibid., 57; "Baylor, John Robert," in Tyler et al., *Handbook of Texas,* 1:423–424.

22. Order Baylor to Adams, Oct. 3, 1861, U.S. War Dept., *War of the Rebellion,* ser. 2, 2:1527.

23. Adams to McCulloch, Oct. 21, 1861, U.S. War Dept., *War of the Rebellion,* ser. 2, 2:1526–1527.

24. Wulff to Adams, Oct. 16, 1861, U.S. War Dept., *War of the Rebellion,* ser. 2, 2:1528–1530; Adams to McCulloch, 2:1526–1527.

25. Wulff to Adams, 2:1528–1530; Adams to McCulloch, 2:1526–1527.

26. In addition to knowing that Ben Leaton sent his young son Joe to school in 1849, we know that in 1870 Joe's oldest daughter, Ohamita, was thirteen and his wife Francisca was thirty, and we know that his younger sister Isabella was twenty-one in 1860. If Joe were two years older than Isabella

(uncertain), he would have been born in 1837, would have gone to school at age twelve in 1849, would have been twenty-four in 1861, and would have fathered Ohamita at age twenty. These numbers seem plausible. U.S. Bureau of the Census, *Ninth Census* and *Eighth Census*.

27. Wulff to Adams, 2:1528–1530; Adams to McCulloch, 2:1526–1527.

28. Wulff to Adams, 2:1528–1530; Adams to McCulloch, 2:1526–1527.

29. Gibbons to Contreras, Oct. 16, 1861, U.S. War Dept., *War of the Rebellion,* ser. 2, 2:1527. Elected municipal chief executive officers in Mexico were *presidentes,* as opposed to appointed alcaldes, and their headquarters were *presidencias.*

30. Contreras to Gibbons, Oct. 16, 1861, U.S. War Dept., *War of the Rebellion,* ser. 2, 2:1527–1528.

1. "Sibley Campaign," in Tyler et al., *Handbook of Texas,* 5:1040–1041; Steele to Cooper, July 12, 1862, U.S. War Dept., *War of the Rebellion,* ser. 1, 9:721.

2. Carleton to Canby, Sept. 9, 1862, U.S. War Dept., *War of the Rebellion,* ser. 1, 9:695–696.

3. Carleton to Thomas, Oct. 10, 1862, U.S. War Dept., *War of the Rebellion,* ser. 1, 15:578.

4. West to Cutler, Nov. 13, 1862, U.S. War Dept., *War of the Rebellion,* ser. 1, 15:598; Rigg to West, Nov. 11, 1862, ibid., 598; Carleton to West, Nov. 18, 1862, ibid., 599–601; Carleton to Bowie, Nov. 18, 1862, ibid., 605.

5. Caniffe to Tully, Nov. 26, 1862, U.S. War Dept., *War of the Rebellion,* ser. 1, 15:606.

6. Willis to Rynerson, Nov. 26, 1862, U.S. War Dept., *War of the Rebellion,* ser. 1, 15:606–607.

7. Willis to Rynerson.

8. West to Fergusson, Jan. 3, 1863, U.S. War Dept., *War of the Rebellion,* ser. 1, 15:635–636.

9. Fergusson to West, Feb. 13, 1863, U.S. War Dept., *War of the Rebellion,* ser. 1, 15:674–675.

10. Report, French to Smith, *Santa Fe New Mexican* (weekly), May 7, 1864; Terrazas to Carleton, Apr. 11, 1863, U.S. War Dept., *War of the Rebellion,* ser. 1, 15:701.

11. Re the artillery, see Fergusson to West, Feb. 13, 1863, U.S. War Dept., *War of the Rebellion,* ser. 1, 15:687; Carleton to Thomas, Feb. 23, 1863, ibid., 681.

12. Carleton to Terrazas, Feb. 20, 1863, U.S. War Dept., *War of the Rebellion,* ser. 1, 15:687.

13. Burgess to Scurry, Mar. 17, 1863, U.S. War Dept., *War of the Rebellion,* ser. 1, 15:1065. Burgess sent the letter to San Antonio in the custody of his business partner, J. Hubbell. Upon arriving, Hubbell learned that General

Scurry had left town, so he delivered the letter to Colonel S. M. Baird of the Arizona Brigade in San Antonio, with an explanatory cover letter. Baird then forwarded the letters to Captain Edmund Turner, assistant adjutant general in Brownsville. Hubbell to Baird, Apr. 28, 1863, ibid., 1065; Baird to Turner, Apr. 30, 1863, ibid., 1064.

14. Baird to Turner, May 5, 1863, U.S. War Dept., *War of the Rebellion*, ser. 1, 15:1075–1076.

15. Carleton to Creel, Apr. 23, 1864, U.S. War Dept., *War of the Rebellion*, ser. 1, 15:708–709.

16. Two letters West to McFerran, May 8, 1863, U.S. War Dept., *War of the Rebellion*, ser. 1, 15:720–722.

17. Report, French to Smith, *Santa Fe New Mexican* (weekly), May 7, 1864; Swift and Corning, *Three Roads to Chihuahua*, 200. French refers to Cottonwood Spring as "Alamo Spring." *Alamo* is the Spanish word for "cottonwood." The spring in question is at the corner of Ronquillo's land grant, fifty-plus miles from Presidio, and is also known as Ojo de Alamo.

18. Report, French to Smith; Swift and Corning, *Three Roads to Chihuahua*, 200.

19. Report, French to Smith.

20. Report, French to Smith.

THE RISE AND FALL OF JOHN BURGESS

1. Fergusson to West, 15:684–687.

2. Shipman, *Taming*, 40–41; deposition of Joseph Magoffin, "Abstract," Owen, 261, 263 (misnumbered 163).

3. Mortgage (conveyance subject to condition subsequent), El Paso County Clerk, A:745 and B:195, and transcribed in Presidio County Clerk, 11:46. The grantors were actually Edward Hall as administrator of the estate of Benjamin Leaton, deceased, and for the minor William Leaton, Juana P. Hall, wife of Edward Hall, Isabella Leaton and Joseph Leaton. The odd amount of the loan was probably because interest was computed in advance.

4. Patents dated Oct. 21, 1862, Oct. 22, 1862 and Nov. 13, 1862, Bexar County Clerk, S2:445–451, and El Paso County Clerk, C:421. Regarding the exact location of the patented lands, see the map records of the Texas General Land Office regarding Lots 190–201, Section 2 (later surveyed as Survey No. 1, T.C. Ry. Co. Block JB), Presidio County, Texas. Regarding the exact location of Fort Leaton on the lands (it is within Lot 200), see Warranty Deed dated Dec. 8, 1967 from Frank O. Skidmore and Tottie L. Skidmore to the Parks and Wildlife Department of the State of Texas, Presidio County Clerk, reception no. 0910042. It is revealing that Burgess was recording mortgages in San Antonio and obtaining patents in Austin during 1862 despite the turmoil of the Civil War.

5. Shipman, *Taming*, 39, 157–158; Swift and Corning, *Three Roads to Chihuahua*, 218–219; Raht, *Romance*, 157–158.

6. Shipman, *Taming,* 39, 157–158; Swift and Corning, *Three Roads to Chihuahua,* 218–219; Raht, *Romance,* 157–158; Travers, "Great Chihuahua Cattle Drive," 85, 87, 89, 96–103.

7. Deed of trust dated July 30, 1868 from John D. Burgess to Robert Burns for the benefit of Halff & Levy ($8,038.90) and Norton & Deutz ($2,425.60), El Paso County Clerk, C:479; deed from Daniel Devine to Robert H. Neilson dated June 4, 1869, El Paso County Clerk, D:61.

8. Bliss, *Reminiscences,* 201. The Halff & Levy note was declared in default by declaration dated Dec. 19, 1873, El Paso County Clerk, E:231; a public trustee's deed of that same date issued to Halff & Brother, El Paso County Clerk, E:232. Koenigham's judgment dated Feb. 24, 1874 appears in El Paso County Clerk, E:637. A writ of execution for a judgment rendered against Burgess in *Buchoz v. Burgess,* foreclosing on 160 acres upstream of the Leaton farm, is dated Apr. 6, 1875, El Paso County Clerk, F:233.

9. *Pedis possessio* — right by possession — is a recognized principle in U.S. mining law, where a shotgun is the best evidence of title to an unpatented claim.

10. Others put Pedraza in Ojinaga after Hall's murder, but the report of her relocation to Fort Davis is reliable. Bliss, *Reminiscences,* 5:201–202. The murder of Hall at the behest of Burgess is entrenched La Junta lore, but the names of the accused, the fact that they were tried and the outcomes of the trials have not previously been published. See James Leaverton and Kathleen Houston, "Presidio County's Oldest Building, Fort Leaton," *Voice of the Mexican Border* (Marfa, 1936), 86; Corning, *Baronial Forts,* 38.

11. A second son of John Burgess (Vidal) and Pablo Baisa were also indicted, but the district attorney declined to prosecute those two. Appearance bonds reciting indictment, El Paso County Clerk, E:305, 307. The El Paso County Criminal Docket for the Jan. 1874 term, 86, reflects indictment no. 254, applicable to John Burgess, Tomás Burgess, Vidal Burgess, Santiago Ruiso (Baisa?), Pablo Ruiso (Baisa?) and W. H. Tinkham. The records reflect that the charges against Vidal Burgess were dropped, and that was apparently the case with Pablo Baisa too. Judge Mies was indicted on Nov. 5, 1874 (indictment no. 53 in Menard County Criminal Docket 1:88); that indictment was quashed. He was indicted again on Mar. 3, 1875 (indictment no. 56 in Menard County Criminal Docket 1:107) but was found not guilty. The Mies-Halff debt is evidenced in case no. 38, default judgment against Mies entered Mar. 3, 1875 in the amount of $325.90.

12. The best spellings of the witnesses' names must be picked carefully from the record, which presents many variations. Case nos. 31, 32 and 33, Menard County Criminal Docket 1:79, 80, 86, and 89.

13. Case nos. 31, 32 and 33, Menard County Criminal Docket 1:98, 104–108, 120, 121, 124.

14. Leaverton and Houston, "Presidio County's Oldest Building," 86.

15. One account says that "Burgess had plenty of money when the war broke out but lost everything in the rebellion, and was finally shot and killed at Fort Davis in 1875, I think, by Bill Leaton, the stepson of Hall." Bliss, *Reminiscences,* 1:264–265. The theft filigree comes from Gregg, *Presidio County,*

124, citing a 1927 interview with J. H. Fortner of Marfa. That account puts Burgess's death in 1870, which is wrong, so maybe the rest of that version is flawed as well.

16. Bliss, *Reminiscences,* 5:201–202.

17. Presidio County Clerk, Docket 1:5, Apr. term 1877; Presidio County Clerk, Criminal Minutes 1:37, 39, 40, 42–51, 62, 63, 70–75, 78–81, 92, 93, 120, 121.

18. State of Texas pardon no. 2835, Oct. 30, 1879 (Austin: Texas State Library and Archives); Swift, *Baronial Forts,* 41; Leaverton and Houston, "Presidio County's Oldest Building," 86; Bliss, *Reminiscences,* 1:265. Swift and Corning, *Three Roads to Chihuahua* (citing an interview of J. A. Nieto), says Bill Leaton was shot in the late 1870's, which would mean he died very shortly after being released.

19. Warranty Deed John B. Burgess to Nestor Mendoza, dated Apr. 23, 1884, Presidio County Clerk, Sept. 30, 1889.

THE END OF THE MESCALEROS

1. Machado, *Barbarians of the North,* 15–22; Almada, *Gobernadores,* 219–271; Wasserman, *Capitalists, Caciques and Revolution,* 15–31.

2. Almada, *Gobernadores,* 268; Machado, *Barbarians of the North,* 19–20; Wasserman, *Capitalists, Caciques and Revolution,* 5, 27, 44–45.

3. Almada, *Gobernadores,* 230–231; Wasserman, *Capitalists, Caciques and Revolution,* 44, 50, 48 text and n. 24; Elam, "Madero Revolution," 176.

4. Almada, *Gobernadores,* 231; Wasserman, *Everyday Life and Politics,* 108.

5. Machado, *Barbarians of the North,* 17; Almada, *Gobernadores,* 235.

6. Almada, *Gobernadores,* 301–306.

7. Almada, *Gobernadores,* 310.

8. "Todo se ha perdido; con mi muerte la causa nacional va a sufrir bastante." Almada, *Gobernadores,* 310.

9. Almada, *Gobernadores,* 241–242, 245.

10. Wasserman, *Capitalists, Caciques and Revolution,* 35.

11. U.S. Bureau of the Census, *Ninth Census.*

12. Russell to *Daily Herald,* May 25, 1874, in *Voice of the Mexican Border,* 187.

13. Daly to *Daily Herald,* July 12, 1874, in *Voice of the Mexican Border,* 188.

14. Letter to *Daily Herald,* Jan. 11, 1878, in *Voice of the Mexican Border,* 188.

15. Grierson to *Daily Herald,* June 29, 1878, in *Voice of the Mexican Border,* 188.

16. Koch, "Federal Indian Policy," 109–110; Newcomb, *Indians of Texas,* 354; Marcy and Neighbors to Bell, Sept. 30, 1854, in Winfrey and Day, *Indian Papers,* 3:190; Tyler, *Big Bend,* 115; Machado, *Barbarians of the North,* 21.

17. Machado, *Barbarians of the North,* 21; Almada, "Los Apaches," 14; Tyler, *Big Bend,* 115, 118.

18. "Translation of a Note from the Charge d'Affairs in Mexico Reporting the Defeat of Chief Victorio's Band of Mescalero Apache and the Death of Victorio in Chihuahua by Mexican Forces," Oct. 30, 1880, NWCTB-393-

DMOPI172E2547–8493DMO1880, National Archives, Washington, D.C.; Almada, "Los Apaches," 14; Tyler, *Big Bend,* 118–119.

19. Almada, "Los Apaches," 14.

20. Williams, *Stories from the Big Bend,* 15–21; Daugherty and Elizondo, "New Light." The original source for the story of Arzate, called Alsate in the Big Bend, was the various pamphlets published by O. W. Williams, some of which have been compiled in Williams, *Stories from the Big Bend.* The compiler's footnotes make it clear that there are some factual discrepancies in Williams's story. (Williams himself published more than one version of Arzate's demise.) Williams's version has been followed by other local writers. See, for example, Raht, *Romance,* 273 et seq., Madison and Stillwell, *How Come It's Called That?* 26–27. Williams, *Stories from the Big Bend,* n. 31, observes that the traditional Big Bend name Alsate is probably a corruption of Arzate. That is confirmed by Almada, "Los Apaches," 13, which relates an 1874 encounter in Santa Rosa (probably the same incident described by Williams, *Stories from the Big Bend,* 13–15), but does not mention the San Carlos ambush and march to Presidio del Norte.

21. Almada, "Los Apaches," 15; Tyler, *Big Bend,* 133.

22. Swift and Corning, *Three Roads to Chihuahua,* 276, 282, 287.

23. Swift and Corning, *Three Roads to Chihuahua,* 301–307.

VICTOR OCHOA

1. U.S. Bureau of the Census, *Eighth Census;* http://educate.si.edu/scitech/impacto/Text2/victor (accessed Apr. 2, 2002; hereafter cited as "educate.si.edu"). The cited Internet page, created by the Smithsonian Institution, is based on materials in *Victor L. Ochoa Papers, ca. 1894–1945,* Washington, D.C.: Archives Center, National Museum of American History, Smithsonian Institution, 0590.

2. Deposition of C. H. Cratsenberg, "Abstract," *Owen,* 94; educate.si.edu.

3. Wasserman, *Capitalists, Caciques and Revolution,* 36–42.

4. Chavez, *Diccionario,* 153; educate.si.edu.

5. educate.si.edu.

6. United States Patents nos. 1,417,196, 1,454,333, 873,587, 718,508 and 1,319,174; educate.si.edu.

7. educate.si.edu.

8. educate.si.edu.

9. Gregg, *Presidio County,* 143–149.

10. Bowden, *Spanish and Mexican Land Grants,* 199.

11. Bowden, *Spanish and Mexican Land Grants,* 199–200.

12. See transcription of the forged decree, Presidio County Clerk, 13, on July 3, 1889; Bowden, *Spanish and Mexican Land Grants,* 199; *Owen v. Presidio Mining Co.,* 61 F. 6 (5th Cir. 1893), 14–15, 23–24.

13. Bowden, *Spanish and Mexican Land Grants,* 200.

14. See various deeds to Estanislas N. Ronquillo, from Ronquillo to

James J. Fitzgerrell and from Fitzgerrell and Seth F. Crews to Earnest Dale Owen, Trustee, recorded in Presidio County Clerk, bk. 13, during July and Aug. 1889; Bowden, *Spanish and Mexican Land Grants,* 201.

15. *Owen v. Presidio Mining Co.,* 16; "Appellee's Brief," U.S. Fifth Circuit, *Owen v. Presidio Mining Co.,* 53; Bowden, *Spanish and Mexican Land Grants,* 201.

16. See various revocations of power of attorney recorded in Presidio County Clerk, bk. 13, during June 1899; Bowden, *Spanish and Mexican Land Grants,* 201–202.

17. *Owen v. Presidio Mining Co.,* 14–16; Bowden, *Spanish and Mexican Land Grants,* 199, 202.

18. *Owen v. Presidio Mining Co.,* 14–17; Bowden, *Spanish and Mexican Land Grants,* 202–203.

19. See various deeds to Ernest Dale Owen, Trustee, recorded in the Presidio County Clerk, bk. 13, in May, July and Oct. 1890 and Jan. 1891; Bowden, *Spanish and Mexican Land Grants,* 203.

20. *Owen v. Presidio Mining Co.,* 20–22.

21. "Abstract," *Owen; Owen v. Presidio Mining Co.,* 23.

22. A *criollo* is a Mexican born in Mexico of pure Spanish blood. An *Indio* is a Mexican of pure native blood. A *gauchupín* is a Mexican born in Spain of pure Spanish blood. A *mestizo* is a mix of Spanish and native blood, one of far too many "castas" that the Spaniards carefully tracked.

TORIBIO ORTEGA'S REBELLION

1. Wasserman, *Capitalists, Caciques and Revolution,* 20, 41, 148–149.

2. Wasserman, *Capitalists, Caciques and Revolution,* 20, 41.

3. Kerr, *Destination Topolobampo,* 39–48, 97–99, 123, 127. The epitome of this principle was Grenville Dodge's Union Pacific Railroad.

4. Kerr, *Destination Topolobampo,* 45–48.

5. Kerr, *Destination Topolobampo,* 48–55.

6. Kerr, *Destination Topolobampo,* 33–35, 48–55.

7. Kerr, *Destination Topolobampo,* 54.

8. See Mar. 7, 1912 capitalization table in Kerr, *Destination Topolobampo,* 235, and discussion of finances at 125–129. We do not share Kerr's forgiving view of Stilwell's time at the trough. We cannot reconcile all of the financial numbers provided by Kerr and are uncertain why he refers to Stilwell's claim of US$28 million raised as an obvious exaggeration. The US$25 million equity capitalization of the company is at par value; the stock could have been sold for more, but not less, although stock could have been issued to Stilwell and others for services.

9. "Marfa to the Front," *Marfa New Era,* Aug. 6, 1910; "Orient News," ibid., May 20, 1911.

10. The Terrazas front man for the spa was Santos Terrazas, who was also involved in the Shafter silver mine. "Candelaria Items," *Marfa New Era,* May 1, 1909; "Marfa to the Front"; "Mexico Mineral Hot Springs," ibid., Aug. 13, 1910.

11. Wasserman, *Capitalists, Caciques and Revolution,* 88, 112; http://ojinaga .com/morehistory/nine/nine.html (accessed Apr. 8, 2001; hereafter cited as "ojinaga.com").

12. Wasserman, *Capitalists, Caciques and Revolution,* 136.

13. Wasserman, *Capitalists, Caciques and Revolution,* 95–97; Meyer, Sherman and Deeds, *Mexican History,* 445–446.

14. Wasserman, *Capitalists, Caciques and Revolution,* 100–101; Meyer, *Museo Historico,* 32.

15. Meyer, Sherman and Deeds, *Mexican History,* 475, attributing the quote to Frederick Starr, *Mexico and the United States* (Chicago, 1914).

16. Johnson, *Madero in Texas,* 19–21; Fehrenbach, *Fire and Blood,* 491.

17. "Plan de San Luis," in Fabela, *Documentos Históricos,* 69, 72; "Says Madero Made Plans," *El Paso Morning Times,* Nov. 19, 1910.

18. "Marathon Citizens Alarmed over Report," *El Paso Morning Times,* Nov. 18, 1910; Ellsworth to Secretary of State, Nov. 5, 1910, in Hanrahan, *Documents,* 1 (1): 51, 52; Memorandum, Embassy of Mexico, Nov. 19, 1910, ibid., 66.

19. ojinaga.com.

20. Meyer, *Museo Historico,* 46; Altamirano and Villa, *Chihuahua,* 187–188; Ontiveros, *Toribio Ortega,* 12–15; Almada, *Diccionario,* 383; http://www.cnca .gob.mx/cnca/nuevo/reporta/reporta99/chih002.html (accessed Apr. 3, 2002); ojinaga.com.

21. Ontiveros, *Toribio Ortega,* 15; Chavez, *Diccionario,* 151; http://www .cnca.gob.mx/cnca/nuevo/reporta/reporta99/chih002.html.

22. Altamirano and Villa, *Chihuahua,* 188–189.

23. Ellsworth to State Department, Nov. 20, 1910, in Hanrahan, *Documents,* 1 (1): 69; "Madero Flies From Texas," *El Paso Morning Times,* Nov. 20, 1910; "Mexico Has No Uprising," ibid., Nov. 21, 1910.

24. Altamirano and Villa, *Chihuahua,* 185–187; Johnson, *Madero in Texas,* 79.

25. Ontiveros, *Toribio Ortega,* 16; Altamirano and Villa, *Chihuahua,* 188; "Ellsworth in the City," *El Paso Morning Times,* Dec. 16, 1910; "Red Revolution," *Marfa New Era,* Dec. 10, 1910. We believe that Gonzalez and Perfecto are the "two of the most prominent of the revolution leaders" mentioned in the *Marfa New Era* as having "left Marfa for the river" on Dec 8. They would have come by train from El Paso or San Antonio.

26. "Taking Town of Ojinaga," *El Paso Morning Times,* Dec. 19, 1910; Elam, "Madero Revolution," 177.

27. "Red Revolution"; "Severe Loss," *El Paso Morning Times,* Dec. 5, 1910; "Ellsworth in the City."

28. Carman, *Customs and the Madero Revolution,* 24–25; Elam, "Madero Revolution," 176.

29. Ontiveros, *Toribio Ortega,* 16–17; "From Presidio," *Marfa New Era,* Dec. 24, 1910.

30. Ellsworth quoting an article in an El Paso newspaper, "Letter from an Insurgent," Dec. 22, 1910, in Hanrahan, *Documents,* 1 (1): 107; "From Presidio,"

Marfa New Era, Dec. 24, 1910; "Battle Occurred Near Presidio Yesterday," *El Paso Morning Times,* Dec. 17, 1910; "Ojinaga Battle Is Reported a Draw," "Insurrectos Say They Don't Want Ojinaga," and "Colonel Dorantes Killed One Young Man," ibid., Dec. 18, 1910.

31. "Taking Town of Ojinaga"; "No Reports from Field," *El Paso Morning Times,* Dec. 20, 1910; Elam, "Madero Revolution," 177.

32. Johnson, *Madero in Texas,* 78–79.

33. "Extra from Presidio," *Marfa New Era,* Dec. 24, 1910; Elam, "Madero Revolution," 177.

34. Johnson, *Madero in Texas,* 81–82.

35. Ontiveros, *Toribio Ortega,* 18; Cole to Chief, Bureau of Investigation, Jan. 5, 1911, in Hanrahan, *Documents,* 1 (1): 120–123; Ellsworth to Secretary of State, Dec. 28, 1910, ibid., 1 (1): 105–106. Cole misstates Perfecto Lomelín's last name as Lomelí, perhaps confusing him with El Paso's Mexican consul Antonio Lomelí, who was a Maderista secret agent. Johnson, *Madero in Texas,* 111–112.

36. "Federal Officers Arrive in Town of Ojinaga," *El Paso Morning Times,* Jan. 5, 1911; Elam, "Madero Revolution," 180.

37. Carman, *Customs,* 24, 27; Edwards to Secretary of State, Nov. 20, 1912, in Hanrahan, *Documents,* 6:171; Edwards to Secretary of State, Dec. 21, 1912, ibid., 6:173.

38. Ellsworth to Secretary of State, Feb. 10, 1911, in Hanrahan, *Documents,* 1 (1): 148, 149; Johnson, *Madero in Texas,* 108–111, 119.

39. "Trouble on the Rio Grande," *Marfa New Era,* Feb. 11, 1911; Carman, *Customs,* 23, 33; Elam, "Madero Revolution," 173–174.

40. "Letter from Abram Gonzales, Near Ojinaga," *El Paso Morning Times,* Jan. 9, 1911; "Governor Gonzales Off for Ojinaga," ibid., Jan. 12, 1911.

41. "Part of Luque's Forces Reported Bottled Up," *El Paso Morning Times,* Jan. 21, 1911; "Severe Engagement Tuesday Near La Aldea," ibid., Jan. 22, 1911; "Majority of Troops Killed or Wounded" and "Nearly Annihilated the Entire Force," ibid., Jan. 23, 1911; "Insurrectos Win Another Victory," ibid., Feb. 3, 1911; "Challenged Gen. Luque to Come into Open," ibid., Jan. 23, 1911; "Federals Refuse an Open Fight," ibid., Mar. 3, 1911.

42. Johnson, *Madero in Texas,* 116–117.

43. Secretary of War to Secretary of State, Feb. 6, 1911, in Hanrahan, Documents 1 (1): 142–143; Elam, "Madero Revolution," 181.

44. "Second Battle of Mulato," *Marfa New Era,* Feb. 11, 1911; "Notes from the Border," ibid., Feb. 18, 1911; Elam, "Madero Revolution," 179. Emilio Salgado was Ortega's co-commander in this battle.

45. "Second Battle of Mulato"; "Notes from the Border"; Ellsworth to Secretary of State, Feb. 10, 1911, *Documents,* 1 (1): 148, 151. Colonel Dorantes was also reported to have been involved in the battle, but we think it is more likely that he remained in command at Coyame; local papers tended to allocate command to the officers known to be in the region.

46. Telegram, Terrazas to Creel, Jan. 19, 1911, in Fabela, *Documentos Históricos,* 1:173–174; "The Battle of Cuesta del Peguis," *Marfa New Era,* Jan. 28,

1911; Ontiveros, *Toribio Ortega,* 20–21. The *Marfa New Era* identifies the Cuesta de Peguis as a canyon, but we believe that the newspaper confused it with the Cañón de Peguis. We identify the Cuesta (slope) de Peguis with the conical hill mentioned by Ontiveros, who says that the federales approached Cuchillo Parado by way of the Cañón del Gato. We believe that Dorantes's relief column probably came from Coyame, not Ojinaga, having gone there earlier in response to harassment of Coyame by rebels as reflected in the Terrazas telegram to Creel.

47. Ontiveros, *Toribio Ortega,* 5.

48. Elam, "Madero Revolution," 180; *San Antonio Light and Gazette* article quoted in Ellsworth to Secretary of State, Jan. 31, 1911, in Hanrahan, *Documents,* 1 (1): 139. The AP reporter was probably E. S. O'Riley, who covered the battles in and near La Junta.

49. Ellsworth to Secretary of State, Feb. 27, 1911, in Hanrahan, *Documents,* 1 (1): 193, 196; "From Presidio," *Marfa New Era,* Mar. 4, 1911; "Candelaria Scared," ibid., Feb. 25, 1911.

50. Ellsworth to Secretary of State, Feb. 10, 1911, *Documents,* 1 (1): 148, 151.

51. Elam, "Madero Revolution," 182; "The Mexican Revolution," *Marfa New Era,* Jan. 28, 1910.

52. "Siege of Ojinaga by Insurrectos," *El Paso Morning Times,* Mar. 16, 1911; "Spectacular Trick Worked on Federals," ibid., Mar. 17, 1911.

53. Carman, *Customs,* 60–61; Elam, "Madero Revolution," 182; Aydelotte to Adjutant General, Department of Texas, Apr. 24, 1911, in Hanrahan, *Documents,* 1 (2): 333–335; "Fierce Battle Raging at Ojinaga Yesterday," *El Paso Morning Times,* Mar. 13, 1911; "Sanchez Hemmed Luque at Ojinaga," ibid., Mar. 15, 1911; "Siege of Ojinaga by Insurrectos"; "Spectacular Trick Worked On Federals"; "Eleven Federals Killed," *El Paso Morning Times,* Mar. 19, 1911; "Moonlight Battle Enlivened Ojinaga," ibid., Mar. 21, 1911; "Bullets Fell among Troops," ibid., Mar. 23, 1911. The *El Paso Morning Times* reported in March that the rebels controlled the Ojinaga-Presidio crossing and that U.S. customs officials refused to permit another crossing to be opened; later, in April, the second crossing was opened as reflected in the report relayed by military source Aydelotte.

54. "Siege of Ojinaga," *Marfa New Era,* Apr. 8, 1911; Elam, "Madero Revolution," 178.

55. "Antonio Carrasco Insurgent and Bandit," *El Paso Morning Times,* Apr. 6, 1911; "Siege of Ojinaga"; Elam, "Madero Revolution," 179.

56. Elam, "Madero Revolution," 182–183; Aydelotte to Adjutant General, *Documents,* 1 (2): 333–335; "Five Federals Were Killed," *El Paso Morning Times,* Mar. 28, 1911.

57. "The Siege of Ojinaga," *Marfa New Era,* Mar. 25, 1911; Elam, "Madero Revolution," 183; "Bullets Fell among Troops"; "Moonlight Battle Enlivened Ojinaga."

58. "The Siege of Ojinaga," *Marfa New Era,* Apr. 22, 1911; ibid., Apr. 29, 1911; Ontiveros, *Toribio Ortega,* 23; Elam, "Madero Revolution," 184; Carman, *Customs,* 56–57; "Blue Whistler Cannon Story," *El Paso Morning Times,* Apr. 13, 1911; "Rebels Will Rush Federals at Ojinaga," ibid., Apr. 20, 1911; "Sanchez

Advised to Attack Ojinaga," ibid., Apr. 23, 1911; "Ojinaga Assaulted Saturday Morning," ibid., Apr. 30, 1911.

59. Meyer, Sherman and Deeds, *Mexican History,* 485–486.

60. "Federals Have Report of Rebel Defeat," *El Paso Morning Times,* Apr. 30, 1911; "Siege of Ojinaga Failure," ibid., May 2, 1911.

61. "Ojinaga Reinforced by 600 Federals," *Marfa New Era,* May 6, 1911; Elam, "Madero Revolution," 185.

62. "Ojinaga Reinforced by 600 Federals"; "Sanchez Has Lost in Ojinaga Siege," *El Paso Morning Times,* May 3, 1911; Elam, "Madero Revolution," 185.

63. "Federal Forces Occupy the Town of Mulato," *El Paso Morning Times,* May 7, 1911.

64. "Federals Abandon Town of Ojinaga," *El Paso Morning Times,* May 20, 1911; "Peace Prevails in Mexico Today as Result of Signing Agreement," ibid., May 22, 1911; "Ojinaga Abandoned," *Marfa New Era,* May 13, 1911.

65. "Ojinaga Abandoned"; Ellsworth to Secretary of State, May 11, 1911, in Hanrahan, *Documents,* 1 (2): 365; Elam, "Madero Revolution," 186.

OROZCO AND HUERTA

1. Meyer, *Mexican Rebel,* 15–17.

2. Fehrenbach, *Fire and Blood,* 498–499.

3. Meyer, *Mexican Rebel,* 38–52; Osorio, "Death of a President," 105–107.

4. Osorio, "Death of a President," 105–112; Meyer, *Mexican Rebel,* 67–87.

5. Del Toro to Secretary of Exterior Relations, Aug. 27, 1912, in Fabela, *Documentos Históricos,* 14, doc. no. 249, p. 53.

6. Del Toro to Secretary of Exterior Relations, Aug. 27, 1912, 53.

7. Del Toro to Secretary of Exterior Relations, Aug. 29, 1912, in Fabela, *Documentos Históricos,* 14, doc. no. 250, p. 54.

8. Del Toro to Secretary of Exterior Relations, Sept. 2, 1912, in Fabela, *Documentos Históricos,* 14, doc. no. 251, p. 55. Although our normal style would be to refer to Salvador Martinez del Toro as Consul Martinez, we defer to the manner in which he signed his communications: S. M. del Toro.

9. Fehrenbach, *Fire and Blood,* 502; Osorio, "Death of a President," 112– 113.

10. Del Toro to Secretary of Exterior Relations, Sept. 5, 1912, in Fabela, *Documentos Históricos,* 8, doc. no. 887, p. 114. Thirty-eight police (*gendarmes*) is far more than the town of Ojinaga required; the police were likely responsible for the *municipio* of Ojinaga, which is akin to a county, not a city, making the police more like sheriff's deputies.

11. Del Toro to Secretary of Exterior Relations, Sept. 5, 1912, 114; "Ojinaga Taken by Orozco Sr.," *El Paso Morning Times,* Sept. 4, 1912.

12. Del Toro to Secretary of Exterior Relations, Sept. 5, 1912, 114.

13. Del Toro to Secretary of Exterior Relations, Sept. 19, 1912, in Fabela, *Documentos Históricos,* 14, doc. no. 259, p. 68; "Ojinaga Falls One More Time," *El Paso Morning Times,* Sept. 13, 1912.

14. Del Toro to Secretary of Exterior Relations, Sept. 19, 1912, 68, 69.

15. Del Toro to Secretary of Exterior Relations, Sept. 5, 1912, Sept. 19, 1912, 68, 70; "Trucy Aubert Near Ojinaga," *El Paso Morning Times,* Sept. 10, 1912; "Ojinaga Falls One More Time."

16. Del Toro to Secretary of Exterior Relations, Sept. 19, 1912, 68, 71; Nolto to Attorney General, Sept. 17, 1912, in Hanrahan, *Documents,* 7:141; Beezley, *Insurgent Governor,* 147; "Red Flaggers Are Driven from Ojinaga," *El Paso Morning Times,* Sept. 16, 1912. In the United States, Colorados were often called "Red Flaggers."

17. Meyer, *Mexican Rebel,* 87.

18. "Red Flaggers"; "General Trucy Aubert Occupies Ojinaga," *El Paso Morning Times,* Sept. 17, 1912; Del Toro to Secretary of Exterior Relations, Sept. 19, 1912, 68, 72. Some respected historians have reported that the Orozquistas made Ojinaga their headquarters through the early months of 1913; based on del Toro's detailed account and contemporary news reports, we conclude otherwise.

19. Del Toro to Secretary of Exterior Relations, Sept. 19, 1912, 68, 72–73.

20. Del Toro to Mexican Consul in El Paso, Dec. 9, 1912, in Fabela, *Documentos Históricos,* 8, doc. no. 962, pp. 238, 239.

21. Del Toro to Mexican Consul in El Paso, Dec. 9, 1912, 239.

22. Meyer, *Mexican Rebel,* 88–89.

23. Meyer, *Mexican Rebel,* 94–95; Meyer, Sherman and Deeds, *Mexican History,* 499–502.

24. Meyer, *Mexican Rebel,* 96–97; Osorio, "Death of a President," 116–117. The first Huertista military governor of Chihuahua was General Antonio Rábago, who had been the commander of the Second Military Zone, but he was soon replaced by Mercado.

25. Licéaga to Secretary of Exterior Relations, Mar. 26, 1913, in Fabela, *Documentos Históricos,* 14, doc. no. 298, pp. 136, 137.

26. Licéaga to Secretary of Exterior Relations, Mar. 26, 1913, 137.

27. Licéaga to Secretary of Exterior Relations, Mar. 26, 1913, 137.

28. Licéaga to Secretary of Exterior Relations, Mar. 26, 1913, 136, 138.

29. Licéaga to Secretary of Exterior Relations, Mar. 26, 1913, 136, 138. Licéaga communicated with Antonio Rábago, who had been commander of the Second Military Zone following Huerta's removal from the Division of the North. On Mar. 26, 1913, when Licéaga communicated with Rábago, Rábago was both commander of the Second Military Zone and military governor of Chihuahua; he was soon replaced by Salvador R. Mercado. Osorio, "Death of a President," 117; Meyer, *Mexican Rebel,* 96; "Ojinaga Falls to Loyal Band," *El Paso Morning Times,* Mar. 26, 1913; "Ojinaga Was Captured," ibid., Mar. 30, 1913.

30. Katz, *Pancho Villa,* 208–209, 212–215.

PANCHO VILLA

1. Katz, *Pancho Villa,* 210–215, 229–236, 332–333; Reed, *Insurgent Mexico,* 138–139.

2. Osorio, "Death of a President," 120–124; Meyer, *Mexican Rebel,* 103–108; Reed, *Insurgent Mexico,* 30; "Federals Desert Chihuahua City," *New York Times,* Dec. 2, 1913; "Flees with $2,500,000," ibid., Dec. 3, 1913; "Seven Generals Desert Huerta; Ready to Surrender to the Rebels; Envoys in Juárez to Meet Gen. Villa," ibid.; "Plan Advance on Mexico City," ibid., Dec. 4, 1913; "Villa Hears that Chihuahua City Has Been Evacuated," *El Paso Morning Times,* Dec. 1, 1913; "Federals Fly," ibid., Dec. 2, 1913.

3. Katz, *Pancho Villa,* 228, 230; Osorio, "Death of a President," 125.

4. Diebold to Secretary of War and Navies and Secretary of Exterior Relations, Dec. 22, 1913, in Fabela, *Documentos Históricos,* doc. no. 478, pp. 418–420; Altamirano and Villa, *Chihuahua,* 238; "Villa near Chihuahua," *New York Times,* Dec. 5, 1913; "Villa Seized $5,000,000," ibid., Dec. 15, 1913; "Refugees from Chihuahua Perish of Hunger and Cold," *El Paso Morning Times,* Dec. 4, 1913.

5. Reed, *Insurgent Mexico,* 143; Katz, *Pancho Villa,* 218–221, 241–242, 295–296; Osorio, "Death of a President," 124; Altamirano and Villa, *Chihuahua,* 238; Meyer, *Mexican Rebel,* 107; "Seven Generals Desert Huerta; Ready to Surrender to the Rebels; Envoys in Juárez to Meet Gen. Villa." *New York Times,* Dec. 3, 1913.

6. "Fugitives Are Nearing the Border," *New York Times,* Dec. 4, 1913; "Bullion Train Reaches Border with Million Ounces Silver," *El Paso Morning Times,* Dec. 7, 1913.

7. Diebold to Secretary of War and Navies and Secretary of Exterior Relations, 418–420; "Money Train near Border," *New York Times,* Dec. 7, 1913; "In Hostage," *El Paso Morning Times,* Dec. 5, 1913; "2,000 Refugees Are Still Wandering on Mexican Desert," ibid., Dec. 6, 1910.

8. "In Hostage."

9. "Rebels Approach; Federals in Fear," *El Paso Morning Times,* Dec. 10, 1913. The newspaper reported her name as "Mariana Gutierrez."

10. "Money Train near Border"; "Bullion Train Is Safe," *New York Times,* Dec. 8, 1913; "Refugees Wandering on Mexican Desert."

11. "Starving Refugees Reach Ojinaga; Women and Children Die on the Trip," *El Paso Morning Times,* Dec. 8, 1913; "Federals Set Up Provisional Government in Ojinaga," ibid., Dec. 9, 1913; "Rebels Approach; Federals In Fear."

12. Katz, *Pancho Villa,* 228, 230; Osorio, "Death of a President," 125; Raun, "Refugees or Prisoners of War," 136–137; "Flees with $2,500,000"; "Money Train near Border"; "Bullion Train Is Safe"; "Rebels Harried Refugees," *New York Times,* Dec. 9, 1913; "Refugees Wandering On Mexican Desert"; "Bullion Train Reaches Border with Million Ounces Silver," ibid., Dec. 7, 1913; "Rebels Approach; Federals In Fear." Terrazas is variously said to have traveled by automobile, stagecoach, foot, horse and "scavenger cart." It is sometimes said that he gave up his auto (or his stagecoach) to old women who needed it more. The *New York Times* and the *El Paso Morning Times* both reported his arrival by automobile; the latter also said that he rode horseback the entire distance while his sons, grandsons and nephews rode in automobiles ("Have Cannon," *El Paso Morning Times,* Dec. 11, 1913). Photos of Terrazas arriving in

Presidio show him fit and well-kempt in a three-piece business suit (though a bit dusty), uncharacteristic of an octogenarian who had done much walking or horseback riding.

13. "100 Dead in Desert March," *New York Times,* Dec. 10, 1913.

14. "Closing In on Ojinaga," *New York Times,* Dec. 13, 1913; "Orozco May Leave Huerta," ibid., Dec. 14, 1913; "Have Cannon"; "Federals Whipped at La Mula Pass," *El Paso Morning Times,* Dec. 12, 1913; "Mercado's Forces Are in Flight," ibid., extra edition, Dec. 12, 1913; "2,500 Men Leave Ojinaga," ibid., Dec. 17, 1913; "Federal Troops Are Not Yet Paid and May Make Trouble," ibid., Dec. 18, 1913; "Soldiers at Ojinaga Are Given Their Back Pay," ibid., Dec. 21, 1913.

15. Reed, *Insurgent Mexico,* 29; Osorio, "Death of a President," 125; Raun, "Refugees or Prisoners of War," 135–137; untitled article under headline "Villa Impounds Vast Estates," *New York Times,* Dec. 17, 1913; "Have Cannon"; "More Troops," *El Paso Morning Times,* Dec. 17, 1913; "Soldiers Given Their Back Pay."

16. Reed, *Insurgent Mexico,* 29.

17. Reed, *Insurgent Mexico,* 32; Willeford, "American Red Cross," 169; *Alpine Avalanche,* Sept. 16, 1904.

18. Reed, *Insurgent Mexico,* 32–33.

19. Katz, *Pancho Villa,* 229–252, 417–419; "Villa Impounds Vast Estates."

20. Reed, *Insurgent Mexico,* 131–132; "Villa Begins His Advance," *New York Times,* Dec. 18, 1913; "Aliens Safe, Says Villa," ibid., Dec. 18, 1913.

21. " 'Move on Ojinaga; Give No Quarter,' " *New York Times,* Dec. 25, 1913; "Fierce Fight at Ojinaga," ibid., Dec. 31, 1913; "Decrees Orozco's Death," ibid., Dec. 27, 1913; "5,000 Rebels Rushed to Ojinaga," *El Paso Morning Times,* Dec. 25, 1913; "On to Ojinaga," ibid., Dec. 26, 1913; "Looks like Defeat for Federals," ibid., Dec. 30, 1913.

22. Reed, *Insurgent Mexico,* 135.

23. "Federals Driven Back to Ojinaga," *El Paso Morning Times,* Dec. 29, 1913.

24. "Looks Like Defeat For Federals"; "Ojinaga Federals Desert," *New York Times,* Dec. 30, 1913; Raun, "Refugees or Prisoners of War," 139–140; Willeford, "American Red Cross," 169–170, relies on accounts by American Red Cross Special Representative O'Connor and Enrique Madrid (the father of Enrique Rede Madrid mentioned in Chapter 2) in describing the event as *la batalla del rebote* (the battle of the backstop) and locating it at El Salitre, downstream from El Mulato. Willeford says that the federal troops were driven into an upstream phalanx of heavy machine guns manned by Constitutionalists, and he identifies the Constitutionalist forces as local bands perhaps led by Colonel José de la Cruz Sánchez.

25. Reed, *Insurgent Mexico,* 34–35.

26. "Convention with Respect to the Laws and Customs of War on Land" (Hague 2), July 29, 1899, Arts. 57–59, in Bevans, *Treaties,* 1:261–262; "Convention Respecting the Rights and Duties of Neutral Powers and Persons in Case of War on Land" (Hague 5), Oct. 18, 1907, Arts. 11, 12, 14, ibid. 1:663–664.

27. "Convention Respecting the Rights and Duties of Neutral Powers and Persons in Case of War on Land" (Hague 4), Oct. 18, 1907, Art. 2, in Bevans, *Treaties,* 1:640.

28. O'Connor, "Capture of Ojinaga," 85–86, 91; Willeford, "American Red Cross," 167–169; "Great Alarm in Ojinaga," *El Paso Morning Times,* Dec. 15, 1913.

29. "Fierce Fight at Ojinaga," *New York Times,* Dec. 31, 1913; "Rebels Shell Ojinaga," ibid., Jan. 1, 1914; "1,000 Men Slain in Ojinaga Fight," ibid., Jan. 2, 1914; "Ortega Orders Battle Renewed," *El Paso Morning Times,* Dec. 31, 1913; "Rebels Open Attack on Ojinaga," ibid., extra edition; Willeford, "American Red Cross," 171–172; Osorio, "Death of a President," 127; Raun, "Refugees or Prisoners of War," 140–142.

30. "2,000 in Flight under Rebel Fire," *New York Times,* Jan. 4, 1914; "Villa Will Lead Ojinaga Attack," ibid., Jan. 5, 1914; "Assault upon Ojinaga Has Begun," *El Paso Morning Times,* Jan. 3, 1914.

31. "Villa Will Lead Ojinaga Attack"; "Rebels Fall Back from Ojinaga," *New York Times,* Jan. 6, 1914; "Federals Are Driving Rebels Back," *El Paso Morning Times,* Jan. 5, 1914; "Rebels Now 12 Miles From Ojinaga," ibid., Jan. 6, 1914; McNamee to Commanding General, Southern Department, Jan. 10, 1914, RG393, pt. 1, ent. 4440, Box 1, National Archives, Washington, D.C.

32. "Fierce Fight at Ojinaga"; "Villa Is Taking His Time at Ojinaga," *El Paso Morning Times,* Jan. 10, 1914; McNamee to Commanding General, Southern Department, Jan. 10, 1914; Willeford, "American Red Cross," 171; Raun, "Refugees or Prisoners of War," 141.

33. O'Connor, "Capture of Ojinaga," 88–89; Braden, "Work of the Surgeons," 96; Willeford, "American Red Cross," 173; Raun, "Refugees or Prisoners of War," 142. O'Connor identified Sr. Maillefert as consul, but no more information about him is available. The Jan. 3, 1914 *El Paso Morning Times* mentioned that Pedro C. Garma, the Mexican consul at Marfa, was killed in a Dec. 31, 1913, automobile accident. That same newspaper mentioned the presence of Inspector of Mexican Consulates Miguel E. Diebold in Ojinaga and Presidio on Dec. 12, but according to a Dec. 18 article he soon left.

34. The El Paso newspapers reported Villa's arrival as happening on the eighth, not the sixth, but suggested that he might have arrived earlier. The earlier date fits better with events as reported, thus is more likely. Admittedly, though, the *New York Times,* which had Villa arriving on the sixth, reported that he "disappeared" on the eighth, and on the ninth said that Villa was "reported to be approaching through the south end of La Mula Pass." The New York newspaper may have been amending an erroneous earlier report. "Villa at the Front; 'Movies' Sign Him Up," *New York Times,* Jan. 7, 1914; "Villa Has Disappeared," ibid., Jan. 9, 1914; "Villa Rushing Up Troops," ibid., Jan. 10, 1914; "Gen. Francisco Villa," *El Paso Morning Times,* Jan. 6, 1914; "Rebel Battle Front Ten Miles Long," ibid., Jan. 7, 1914; "Villa Directs His Army at Ojinaga," ibid., Jan. 9, 1914.

35. Katz, *Pancho Villa,* 249; Raun, "Refugees or Prisoners of War," 143; Altamirano and Villa, *Chihuahua,* 243. The Villa resignation was on Jan. 7. If Villa had arrived in La Junta on the sixth, the resignation would have been written and transmitted from there. The *New York Times* reported Villa in Juárez just days before reporting his arrival in La Junta, thus he seemed to be operating as a traveling governor. Given the confusion (mentioned in the

previous note) about the exact date of Villa's arrival in La Junta, he could have left Juárez by train, paused briefly in Ciudad Chihuahua to tender his resignation on the seventh, then taken the train to Falomir en route to La Junta, arriving on the eighth.

36. "Villa at the Front"; "Admits He's a 'Movie' Star," *New York Times,* Jan. 8, 1914; "Villa Is Taking His Time."

37. "Rebel Battle Front"; "Quiet Reigns at Ojinaga," ibid., Jan. 8, 1914.

38. "Ojinaga Falls under Attack Led by Villa," *New York Times,* Jan. 11, 1914; "Assault upon Ojinaga Has Begun"; "Villa Drives In Federal Outposts," *El Paso Morning Times,* 2:40 P.M. extra edition, Jan. 10, 1914; McNamee to Commanding General, Southern Department, Jan. 17, 1914, RG393, pt. 1, ent. 4440, Box 1, National Archives, Washington, D.C.

39. "Ojinaga Falls under Attack"; "Villa Starts Army Southward," *New York Times,* Jan. 12, 1914; "Villa Captures the City of Ojinaga," *El Paso Morning Times,* 9:30 P.M. extra edition, Jan. 10, 1914; "Villa Wins; His Victory Complete," ibid., Jan. 11, 1914; McNamee to Commanding General, Southern Department, Jan. 17, 1914; O'Connor, "Capture of Ojinaga," 92–93; Raun, "Refugees or Prisoners of War," 143; Willeford, "American Red Cross," 174; Osorio, "Death of a President," 127; Altamirano and Villa, *Chihuahua,* 243.

40. O'Connor, "Capture of Ojinaga," 93.

41. Raun, "Refugees or Prisoners of War," 143.

42. Meyer, *Mexican Rebel,* 109–110.

43. "Villa Starts Army Southward"; Meyer, *Mexican Rebel,* 109–110.

44. "Villa Starts Army Southward."

45. "Villa Starts Army Southward"; "Mexican Refugees Won't Be Sent Back," *New York Times,* Jan. 13, 1914; "Villa Begins March to Torreon," *El Paso Morning Times,* Jan. 12, 1914.

46. "Suffering in Refugee Camp," *New York Times,* Jan. 13, 1914; "Civilian Refugees Not Prisoners," *El Paso Morning Times,* Jan. 13, 1914.

47. "Refugees Start for Marfa," *New York Times,* Jan. 14, 1914; "Federals to Be Brought to Ft. Bliss," *El Paso Morning Times,* Jan. 13, 1914; Bicknell, "Red Cross Work," 83; Raun, "Refugees or Prisoners of War," 149.

48. "Everything Ready for the Prisoners," *El Paso Morning Times,* Jan. 15, 1914; "Prisoners Are Coming," ibid., Jan. 17, 1914; McNamee to Commanding General, Southern Department, Jan. 17, 1914; Raun, "Refugees or Prisoners of War," 149.

49. "Singing Caravan to Marfa," *New York Times,* Jan. 17, 1914; "4,000 Come in Rags to Be Our Wards," ibid., Jan. 19, 1914; "Mexico Must Pay," ibid., Jan. 20, 1914; "Prisoners in Ft. Bliss Camp," *El Paso Morning Times,* Jan. 21, 1914; Whittington, *Road of Sorrow,* 48; O'Connor, "Capture of Ojinaga," 93; Raun, "Refugees or Prisoners of War," 149–150.

50. "Mercado Camp Commander," *New York Times,* Jan. 23, 1914; "Gen. Scott Reassures the City Fathers," *El Paso Morning Times,* Jan. 16, 1914; "Prisoners in Ft. Bliss Camp"; Raun, "Refugees or Prisoners of War," 150–151; O'Connor, "Capture of Ojinaga," 86.

51. Raun, "Refugees or Prisoners of War," 153–158; "Salazar's Sons Here," *El Paso Morning Times,* Dec. 13, 1913.

52. Meyer, *Mexican Rebel,* 115–120.

53. "Ortega, Toribio," in Almada, *Diccionario,* 383.

PUNITIVE EXPEDITIONS

1. Tyler, *Big Bend,* 163–164. Substantially the same information about the Little Punitive Expedition contained in that book appears in Tyler's "Little Punitive Expedition in the Big Bend."

2. There are several versions of the Glenn Springs and Boquillas incidents. Miles, *Stray Tales,* 86–108; Madison and Stillwell, *How Come It's Called That?* 39–41; Tyler, *Big Bend,* 165–169.

3. Miles, *Stray Tales,* 109–118; Madison and Stillwell, *How Come It's Called That?* 41–42; Tyler, *Big Bend,* 169–174.

4. Tyler, *Big Bend,* 177.

5. "Testimony of Col. Geo. T. Langhorne," U.S. Senate, *Investigation,* 1632; "Testimony of Capt. Leonard L. Matlack," ibid., 1649.

6. "Testimony of Col. Langhorne," 1633–1634; "Testimony of Capt. Matlack," 1649–1650.

7. Tyler, *Big Bend,* 177–179.

8. Tyler, *Big Bend,* 180.

9. Tyler, *Big Bend,* 180–181.

10. Tyler, *Big Bend,* 181.

11. "Testimony of Col. Langhorne," 1631.

12. "Testimony of Capt. Matlack," 1648; "Testimony of Col. Langhorne," 1642.

13. "Testimony of Col. Langhorne," 1630–1643; "Testimony of Capt. William V. Ochs," U.S. Senate, *Investigation,* 1643–1647; "Testimony of Capt. Matlack," 1649–1655.

14. "Testimony of Col. Langhorne," 1641–1642; "Testimony of Capt. Ochs," 1645.

15. "Testimony of Col. Langhorne," 1636.

16. "Testimony of Col. Langhorne," 1635, 1638; "Testimony of Capt. Matlack," 1651, 1655.

17. "Testimony of Col. Langhorne," 1634–1635, 1638; "Testimony of Capt. Ochs," 1644; Smithers, *Chronicles,* 35; Madison and Stillwell, *How Come It's Called That?* 102; Justice, "Candelaria," 10, 12.

18. "Testimony of Capt. Matlack," 1656; Smithers, *Chronicles,* 36; Tyler, *Big Bend,* 163; "Troopers Wipe Out Nest of Bandits," *El Paso Morning Times,* Aug. 22, 1919.

19. Justice, "Candelaria," 12; Tyler, *Big Bend,* 163; Smithers, *Chronicles,* 36.

20. Justice, "Candelaria," 8–12.

21. Justice, "Candelaria," 9, 11.

22. Tyler, "Little Punitive Expedition," 275; Smithers, *Chronicles,* 36; Madison and Stillwell, *How Come It's Called That?* 102–104; Tyler, *Big Bend,* 162; Justice, "Candelaria," 11.

23. "Testimony of Capt. Matlack," 1659–1660.

24. "Testimony of Capt. Matlack," 1659–1660. We have edited the punctuation and style of the Matlack quote as it appears in the hearing transcript.

25. Justice, "Candelaria," 9–10.

26. Hinkle, *Wings and Saddles,* 3–5; Tyler, *Big Bend,* 182–183; Justice, "Candelaria," 11–12.

27. Hinkle, *Wings and Saddles,* 5.

28. Hinkle, *Wings and Saddles,* 7, 10.

29. Hinkle, *Wings and Saddles,* 21.

30. Hinkle, *Wings and Saddles,* 6.

31. "Mexicans Hold Flyers for Ransom," *El Paso Morning Times,* Aug. 18, 1919; Gómez, *Most Singular,* 132; Hinkle, *Wings and Saddles,* 8, 32–33; "Ransom Paid and Americans Freed," *Alpine Avalanche,* Aug. 28, 1919.

32. Smithers, *Chronicles,* 36; Hinkle, *Wings and Saddles,* 19–22.

33. Hinkle, *Wings and Saddles,* 21–22; Smithers, *Chronicles,* 36.

34. Hinkle, *Wings and Saddles,* 22.

35. Hinkle, *Wings and Saddles,* 9–11, 23.

36. Hinkle, *Wings and Saddles,* 23–24.

37. "Mexicans Hold Flyers for Ransom," *El Paso Morning Times,* Aug. 18, 1919; Smithers, *Chronicles,* 36, 38; Hinkle, *Wings and Saddles,* 11–12; "Testimony of Col. Langhorne," 1638–1639; "Testimony of Capt. Matlack," 1655. Matlack said that he intercepted the note on its way to Kilpatrick.

38. "Mexicans Hold Flyers for Ransom"; Hinkle, *Wings and Saddles,* 13–14; Smithers, *Chronicles,* 41; "Testimony of Col. Langhorne," 1638–1639; "Testimony of Capt. Matlack, 1656.

39. "Testimony of Capt. Matlack," 1656; Hinkle, *Wings and Saddles,* 15–16; Smithers, *Chronicles,* 41.

40. "Testimony of Capt. Matlack," 1656–1657; Hinkle, *Wings and Saddles,* 16–17.

41. "Testimony of Capt. Matlack," 1656–1657; Smithers, *Chronicles,* 42; Hinkle, *Wings and Saddles,* 17.

42. Smithers, *Chronicles,* 44; Hinkle, *Wings and Saddles,* 18.

43. "Testimony of Capt. Matlack," 1657; "Ransom Paid and Americans Freed"; "Cavalry Pursues Bandits in Storm," *El Paso Morning Times,* Aug. 20, 1919; Hinkle, *Wings and Saddles,* 18–19.

44. "Bandits Elude Pursuing Troops," *El Paso Morning Times,* Aug. 23, 1919; "Captain Matlack Saves Own Life in Saving Ransom," ibid., Aug. 22, 1919.

45. Hinkle, *Wings and Saddles,* 26–27; Smithers, *Chronicles,* 44.

46. Hinkle, *Wings and Saddles,* 28.

47. "Troopers Wipe Out Bandits"; Hinkle, *Wings and Saddles,* 39–40.

48. Smithers, *Chronicles,* 44–45, 55; Hinkle, *Wings and Saddles,* 40.

49. "Cavalry Pursues Bandits In Storm," *El Paso Morning Times,* Aug. 20, 1919; Hinkle, *Wings and Saddles,* 31–32; Smithers, *Chronicles,* 47.

50. "Renteria, Bandit Leader, Is Reported Killed by Aviator," *El Paso Morning Times,* Aug. 25, 1919; "Americans Turn Back to Avoid Clash with Federals at Coyame," ibid., Aug. 26, 1919; "Newspaper Gets Alleged Letter from Renteria," ibid., Aug. 30, 1919; Hinkle, *Wings and Saddles,* 32 and epilogue; Smithers, *Chronicles,* 51–53; "Testimony of Col. Langhorne," 1639.

51. "Mexicans Praise Action of American Troops," and "Mexico City Papers Tell about Withdrawal in Large Headlines," *El Paso Morning Times,* Aug. 26, 1919; "American Troops Return to Border," and "Papers Say Dieguez Denied Permission for U.S. Troops to Cross," ibid., Aug. 25, 1919; "Americans to Leave Mexico in 24 Hours," ibid., Aug. 24, 1919; "Gen. Dieguez Says U.S. Is within Rights," ibid., Aug. 22, 1919; "Captured in Texas, Says Aviator; Aviators to Reach Border Today," ibid., Aug. 19, 1919; Hinkle, *Wings and Saddles,* 36 and 37; "Testimony of Col. Langhorne," 1639.

52. "Mexico City Papers Tell about Withdrawal"; "American Troops Return to Border."

53. "Troopers Wipe Out Bandits."

THE SPENCERS

1. Davenport, "Spencer," 2–3. Spencer's grave is not in the Indio Ranch cemetery, but in a smaller nearby cemetery with only a few graves.

2. "Appraisers Report," Presidio County, *Estate of John W. Spencer.*

3. "Appraisers Report" and "Application for Community Administration," Presidio County, *Estate of John W. Spencer.* The application for community administration states that Spencer died on September 17; his headstone bears the date September 18.

4. "Application for Community Administration"; Ross McSwain, "John Blazed Trail, Many Followed," *San Angelo Standard-Times,* Aug. 29, 1965.

5. Davenport, "Spencer," 6; McSwain, "John Blazed Trail."

6. Miles, *Stray Tales,* 62.

7. Kerr, *Destination Topolobampo,* 155–169.

8. "Presidio Is Looking Forward to Becoming Second El Paso," *El Paso Herald,* Oct. 9, 1930; "Presidio Expects New Development to Follow Completion of Orient Project," *El Paso Times,* Oct. 24, 1929; "Railroad Comes to Border Town of Cattle Fame," *Christian Science Monitor,* Oct. 10, 1930.

9. Kerr, *Destination Topolobampo,* 165.

10. Miles, *Stray Tales,* 74.

11. Untitled article datelined Presidio, Texas, *El Paso Times,* Oct. 21, 1936.

12. Kerr, *Destination Topolobampo,* 168–169.

13. "Kansas City, Mexico & Orient Railroad Company of Texas and Its Predecessors," *Southwestern Historical Quarterly* 54 (Apr. 1951): 490; "The Orient," ibid. 53 (Apr. 1950): 480; Miles, *Stray Tales,* 67. The Santa Fe sold the line to the short line South Orient Railroad Company in 1992, which ended up terminating service and selling its assets to the Texas Department of Transportation in 2001. The Texas Department of Transportation (TxDOT) leases the line to Texas Pacifico Transportation Ltd, a subsidiary of Nuevo Grupo Mexico, S.A. de C.V., which plans to restore service. "Kansas City, Mexico and Orient Railway," in Tyler et al., *Handbook of Texas,* 3 : 1029–1030; "Purchase agreement for South Orient Railroad Completed," press release, TxDOT, Feb. 2, 2001.

14. Among many other advertisements for the establishment, see *Presidio*

International, July 30, 1955; "Carlos Spencer New Agent for Telephone Co. in Presidio," ibid., 30 April 1956.

15. "10 Carloads of Lettuce Shipped Out to Market," *Presidio International,* May 31, 1955; "40 Rail Cars of Cantaloupes Shipped Out by June 29," ibid., June 30, 1955; "The Rio Conchos Peguis Dam to Be Constructed," ibid., Aug. 27, 1955; "5,025 Bales of Cotton Been Ginned up to Dec. 30," ibid. Dec. 31, 1955; "La irrigacion debe ser oportuna en todo caso," ibid., Mar. 31, 1956; "Wind and Sand Damage Presidio Valley Lettuce Crop," ibid., Apr. 30, 1956.

16. Jameson, *Big Bend National Park,* 23–24, 49–50; "$6000 Allotted for New Campground at Boquillas," *Presidio International,* May 31, 1955; "Build the River Road," ibid.; "Marfa Delegates Made a Trip of True Inspection," ibid.; *Alpine Avalanche,* May 13, 1955; "Big Bend National Park Activities," *Presidio International,* June 30, 1955, sec. A; "5.10 Miles to Be Paved from Redford," ibid., Aug. 27, 1955; "Visitors to Big Bend Park Increases [*sic*] in August," ibid., Sept. 24, 1955.

17. "Presidio-Chihuahua Hi-way," *Presidio International,* Sept. 24, 1955; "Mexican Officials Support Proposed Highway Extension," ibid.; "Ojinaga-Chihuahua Travel Seem [*sic*] by August 1956," ibid., Mar. 31, 1956; "La Propuesta Carretera Ojinaga-Chihuahua," ibid., May 31, 1956, sec. B; "Hopes for Ojinaga-Chih. Highway Prevail after Meeting with Borunda," ibid., June 30, 1956; "Ojinaga-Chihuahua Roadbed to Be Finished Sept. 30," ibid., Aug. 25, 1956.

18. David Hancock, "New Bridge Brings New Hope to Presidio," *El Paso Times,* Apr. 16, 1986.

19. "El brujo de Ojinaga fue puesto en las casa salud," *Presidio International,* July 30, 1955, sec. D; "¡El brujo Pancho Garza de Ojinaga no esta loco!" ibid., Sept. 24, 1955, sec. B; "De 14 a 20 anos de prision piden para el ogro de Ojinaga," ibid., Mar. 31, 1956.

20. "Bull Fights to Be Held in Ojinaga Late in February," *Presidio International,* Jan. 31, 1956; "Lions Carnival to Be Held in Presidio Thursday, May 30th," ibid., Feb. 28, 1957.

21. McSwain, "John Blazed Trail"; Gilbert Spencer, interview by author, tape recording, Fort Leaton, Tex., May 13, 2002.

22. Unless otherwise noted, all information about Gilbert Spencer and his family is from the author's interview (see previous note).

PABLO ACOSTA

1. Glenn Frey and Jack Tempchin, "Smuggler's Blues," from *The All-nighter,* MCA LP 5501, MCA CD 31158 (1984).

2. Poppa, *Drug Lord,* 6–7.

3. Poppa, *Drug Lord,* 8–9.

4. Poppa, *Drug Lord,* 9–11.

5. Poppa, *Drug Lord,* 44–45.

6. Poppa, *Drug Lord,* 45–46.

7. Poppa, *Drug Lord,* 45–46; Weisman and Dusard, *La Frontera,* 76.

8. Poppa, *Drug Lord,* 47–48.

9. Poppa, *Drug Lord,* 48.

10. Poppa, *Drug Lord,* 49–52.

11. Poppa, *Drug Lord,* 52–56.

12. Translation by author of arrangement by Santiago Tercero, Los Jilgueros del Arroyo, "Corrido de Martín 'El Shorty' López," Los Tres Amigos de Isidro Ruiz, *The Devil's Swing,* Arhoolie LP 480.

13. Poppa, *Drug Lord,* 61–65.

14. Poppa, *Drug Lord,* 65–67.

15. Poppa, *Drug Lord,* 70–71.

16. Poppa, *Drug Lord,* 19–26.

17. Poppa, *Drug Lord,* 26–33; Weisman and Dusard, *La Frontera,* 80.

18. Poppa, *Drug Lord,* 37–43; Weisman and Dusard, *La Frontera,* 80; "Mexican Godfather," *El Paso Herald-Post,* Dec. 3, 1986.

19. Poppa, *Drug Lord,* 78–83; Weisman and Dusard, *La Frontera,* 77; "Leadership of Border Gangs Rarely Able to Just Retire," *El Paso Herald-Post,* Dec. 5, 1986.

20. Poppa, *Drug Lord,* 75–76; "A No-Holds-Barred Interview with Acosta," *El Paso Herald-Post,* Dec. 3, 1986.

21. Poppa, *Drug Lord,* 72–77.

22. Poppa, *Drug Lord,* 85–90; Weisman and Dusard, *La Frontera,* 77; "Suspected Drug 'Enforcer' Faces New Set of Charges," *El Paso Herald-Post,* Apr. 11, 1986; "Mexican Godfather"; "Duel in the Desert," *El Paso Herald-Post,* Dec. 4, 1986.

23. Poppa, *Drug Lord,* 90–94.

24. Poppa, *Drug Lord,* 94–98.

25. Poppa, *Drug Lord,* 98–99.

26. Poppa, *Drug Lord,* 100–101.

27. Poppa, *Drug Lord,* 101–107; Weisman and Dusard, *La Frontera,* 77; "Duel in the Desert."

28. Poppa, *Drug Lord,* 107–110; Weisman and Dusard, *La Frontera,* 77, 80; "Duel in the Desert."

29. Poppa, *Drug Lord,* 111.

30. Poppa, *Drug Lord,* 227–229; Weisman and Dusard, *La Frontera,* 78.

31. Weisman and Dusard, *La Frontera,* 78, 79.

32. Weisman and Dusard, *La Frontera,* 80.

33. Weisman and Dusard, *La Frontera,* 81.

34. Walt Harrington, "The Last Days of the Lawless West; What the Guerilla Kidnapping of Refugio Gonzalez Really Means," *Washington Post Magazine,* Apr. 6, 1986.

35. Harrington, "Last Days of the Lawless West."

36. Harrington, "Last Days of the Lawless West." Terrence Poppa, author of *Drug Lord,* says that Mimi Webb Miller escorted the reporter, Walt Harrington. We present Harrington's version.

37. "Area Cocaine Bust Tied to Chihuahua Organized Crime," *El Paso Herald-Post,* Apr. 11, 1986.

38. Terrence Poppa, "Mexican Godfather" and " 'For Every Bad Thing I Do, I Do 600 Good Things'," *El Paso Herald-Post,* Dec. 3, 1986; "Area Cocaine Bust."

39. Poppa, *Drug Lord,* 279–280.

40. Poppa, *Drug Lord,* 281–282. Calderoni is customarily called by his maternal surname.

41. Poppa, *Drug Lord,* 287–291.

42. Poppa, *Drug Lord,* 294.

43. Poppa, *Drug Lord,* 294–298; "Acosta Killed in Ambush," *El Paso Herald-Post,* Apr. 27, 1987; "Dead Drug Lord's Empire Goes On," *El Paso Times,* Apr. 28, 1987. The Mexican helicopters were from La Procuraduría General de la República, in charge of investigation and enforcement of Mexican federal law.

44. "Acosta Killed in Ambush"; "Paper: Mexican Drug Kingpin Slain," *El Paso Times,* Apr. 26, 1987.

45. "Acosta Killed in Ambush."

46. Translation by author of arrangement of "El Corrido de Pablo Acosta," by Los Palomares del Bravo, *The Devil's Swing,* Arhoolie LP 480.

RICK THOMPSON

1. We do not mean to suggest that the Mexican system is not corrupt. See Luís Astorga, "Drug Trafficking in Mexico: A First General Assessment," UNESCO Discussion Paper No. 36, www.unesco.org/most/astorga.htm (accessed May 1, 2002); Peter Lupsha, "Transnational Narco-Corruption and Narco-Investment: A Focus on Mexico," *Transnational Crime,* spring 1995 (see pbs.org/wgbh/pages/frontline/shows/mexico/readings/lupsha.html); Andrew A. Reding, "Political Corruption and Drug Trafficking in Mexico: Impunity for High-Level Officials Spurs Lawlessness and Growth of Drug Cartels," Senate Committee on Foreign Relations, Aug. 8, 1995; Silvana Paternostro, "Mexico as a Narco-Democracy," *World Policy Journal,* spring 1995 (see worldpolicy.org/journal).

2. Terrence E. Poppa, "Sheriff in Swirl of Drug Allegations," *El Paso Herald-Post,* Dec. 28, 1991; "Thompson Takes Reins as State President," *Marfa Big Bend Sentinel,* Aug. 2, 1984; "Lies, Cocaine and Dirty Money," *Marfa NIMBY News,* Dec. 1992.

3. Poppa, *Drug Lord,* 119.

4. "Man Injured in Polvo Shooting," *Marfa Big Bend Sentinel,* Feb. 9, 1982; "Marijuana Found in Travel Trailer," ibid., June 17, 1982; "Drug Investigation Continuing," ibid., Aug. 19, 1982; "Bond $1 Million for Shooting Suspect; Reward Offered," ibid., Aug. 26, 1982; " 'El Gato' Convicted in Border Patrol Shooting," ibid., Dec. 2, 1982; "Man Fatally Shot," ibid., Apr. 12, 1984; "Two Held in Murder Case," ibid., June 14, 1984; "Three Found Guilty," ibid., Mar. 12, 1987; "Marijuana Found in False Fuel Tank," ibid., Apr. 9, 1987.

5. "BUSTED!" *Marfa NIMBY News,* winter 1991.

6. "We're Back," *Marfa NIMBY News,* Oct. 21, 1997.

7. "Lies, Cocaine and Dirty Money"; "Chambers Denied Bail," *Marfa NIMBY News,* winter 1991.

8. "Thompson and Chambers Get Life," *Alpine Avalanche,* May 14, 1992.

9. "Whose Coke Bust? DEA Informant Implicates Sheriff," *Marfa Big Bend Sentinel,* Dec. 12, 1991.

10. DEA officials don't tell everything they know. There is a certain amount of conjecture involved in figuring out how they found the cocaine in the trailer and how they linked the trailer to Thompson. It is entirely possible that they watched Thompson the entire time, waiting to make a move, but at the time of Chambers's arrest the U.S. attorney handling the case said that he did not know how the cocaine got from the ranch to the fairgrounds. "Whose Coke Bust?"

11. "Whose Coke Bust?"

12. "Presidio Sheriff under Drug Scrutiny," *Dallas Morning News,* Jan. 5, 1992; "Drugs Seized in County Probe, Thompson says," *Marfa Big Bend Sentinel,* Dec. 12, 1991; "Chambers Plea Includes Agreement to Testify against Thompson," ibid., Jan. 30, 1992; "Thompson Pleads Guilty," ibid., Feb. 13, 1992; "Thompson and Chambers Get Life."

13. "Thompson Corruption Began in 1986–1987," *Marfa Big Bend Sentinel,* May 14, 1992; "Thompson and Chambers Get Life."

GILBERT SPENCER

1. "Man Injured in Polvo Shooting"; "Marijuana Found in Travel Trailer"; "Bond $1 million for shooting suspect"; "'El Gato' Convicted in Shooting"; "Man Fatally Shot"; "Two Held in Murder Case."

2. Coyne, *Investigation,* par. 391.

3. Coyne, *Investigation,* par. 448.

4. Coyne, *Investigation,* pars. 449–451.

5. Coyne, *Investigation,* par. 451.

6. Coyne, *Investigation,* pars. 480–485.

7. Coyne, *Investigation,* pars. 490, 498; Gilbert Spencer, interview.

8. Coyne, *Investigation,* pars. 499, 501; Gilbert Spencer, interview.

9. Gilbert Spencer, interview by author, tape recording, Fort Leaton, Tex., May 13, 2002.

Almada, Francisco R. "Los Apaches," *Boletín de la sociedad chihua-huaense de estudios históricos* 2 (1): 5–15 (1939).

———. *Diccionario de Historia, Geografía y Biografía Chihua-huenses.* 2nd ed. Ciudad Juárez: Impresora de Juárez, S.A., 1968.

———. *Gobernadores del Estado de Chihuahua.* 3rd ed. Ciudad Chihuahua: Centro Librero La Prensa, 1981.

Almonte, Juan Nepomuceno. "Proyectos de Leyes sobre Coloniza-ción," within "Projected Mexican Colonies in the Border-lands." Translated and edited by Odie B. Faulk. *The Journal of Arizona History* 10:115 (1969).

Alonso, Ana María. *Thread of Blood: Colonialism, Revolution, and Gender on Mexico's Northern Frontier.* Tucson: The University of Arizona Press, 1995.

Altamirano, Graziella, and Villa, Guadalupe. *Chihuahua: Una his-toria compartida, 1824–1921.* Mexico City: Gobierno del Es-tado de Chihuahua, Instituto de Investigaciones, Universidad Autónoma de Ciudad Juárez, 1988.

Andreas, Peter. *Border Games: Policing the U.S.-Mexico Divide.* Ith-aca: Cornell University Press, 2000.

Armbruster, Henry C. *The Torreys of Texas: A Biographical Sketch.* Buda, Tex.: The Citizen Press, 1968.

Barker, Eugene C., ed. *The Austin Papers, October, 1834–January, 1837.* Vol. 3. Austin: University of Texas, 1927.

Batalla, Guillermo Bonfil. *Mexico Profundo: Reclaiming a Civiliza-tion.* Translated by Philip A. Dennis. Austin: University of Texas Press, 1996.

Beezley, William H. *Insurgent Governor: Abraham González and the Mexican Revolution in Chihuahua.* Lincoln: University of Ne-braska Press, 1973.

Bevans, Charles I., ed. *Treaties and Other International Agreements of the United States of America, 1776–1949,* vols. 1 and 9. Wash-ington, D.C.: Department of State, 1937.

Bexar County, Texas. *Estate of Ben Leaton, Deceased.* Case No. 309, Clerk of the Probate Court.

Bicknell, Ernest P. "Red Cross Work on the Mexican Border." *The American Red Cross Magazine* 9:78–83 (1914).

Bliss, Zenas R. *Reminiscences of Zenas R. Bliss, Major General United States Army,* vols. 1–3 and 5. Austin: Center for American His-tory, University of Texas at Austin, Box 2Q441, n.d.

Bolton, Herbert E. *Guide to the Materials for the History of the United States in the Principal Archives of Mexico.* Washington, D.C.: 1913.

Bowden, J. J. *Spanish and Mexican Land Grants in the Chihuahuan Acquisition.* El Paso: Texas Western Press, 1971.

Boyd, Eva Jolene. *Noble Brutes: Camels on the American Frontier.* Plano: Republic of Texas Press, 1995.

Bibliography

Braden, C. F. "Work of the Surgeons and Nurses in the Red Cross Hospital at Presidio." *The American Red Cross Magazine* 9:93–97 (1914).

Brown, John Henry. *Indian Wars and Pioneers of Texas*. Austin: L. E. Daniel, 1895.

———. *Life and Times of Henry Smith, the First American Governor of Texas*. Dallas: A. D. Aldredge & Co., 1887.

Carman, Michael Dennis. *United States Customs and the Madero Revolution*. Monograph No. 48. El Paso: Texas Western Press, 1976.

Chappell, Jack Richard. "El Polvo." Research paper, Sul Ross University, 1964.

Chavez, Armando B. *Diccionario de Hombres de la Revolucion en Chihuahua*. Ciudad Juárez: Universidad Autonoma de Ciudad Juárez, 1990.

Chipman, Donald E. "In Search of Cabeza de Vaca's Route Across Texas: An Historiographical Survey." *Southwestern Historical Quarterly* 91:127–148 (1987).

———. *Spanish Texas, 1519–1821*. Austin: University of Texas Press, 1992.

Clayton, Lawrence, Jim Hoy and Jerald Underwood. *Vaqueros, Cowboys and Buckaroos*. Austin: University of Texas Press, 2001.

Colomo, Francisco. *Diario de Don Francisco Colomo, 1821–1859*. Translated by Lupe Carrasco Hernandez. Marfa: Marfa Public Library, [1937?].

Corning, Leavitt, Jr. *Baronial Forts of the Big Bend*. San Antonio: Trinity University Press, 1967.

Coyne, Major General John T., United States Marine Corps. *Investigation to Inquire into the Circumstances Surrounding the Joint Task Force-6 (JTF-6) Shooting Incident that Occurred on 20 May 1997 Near the Border Between the United States and Mexico,* 5800 JAGT/jtc, Camp Pendleton, Ca., 1998.

Daugherty, Franklin W., and Luis López Elizondo. "New Light on Chisos Apache Indian Chief Alsate." *Journal of Big Bend Studies* 8:33–49, 1996.

Davenport, Dorothy. "John W. Spencer." Unpublished account of interview with Ricardo Spencer, son of John W. Spencer. Archives of the Big Bend, Sul Ross University, 1931.

Dublan, Manuel, and Jose Maria Lozano, comp. *Legislacion Mexicana, o collección completea de las disposiciones legislativas expedidas desde la independencia de las Republica,* vol. 1–6. Mexico City: Imprenta del Comercio, 1876–1904.

Elam, Earl H. "The Madero Revolution and the Bloody Bend." *Journal of Big Bend Studies* 13:167–194 (2001).

Emory, William H. *Report on the United States and Mexican Boundary Survey,* vol. 1. Washington, D.C.: A. O. P. Nicholson, 1857.

Evans, George W. B. *Mexican Gold Trail, the Journal of a Forty-Niner*. Edited by Glenn S. Dumke. San Marino: The Huntington Library, 1945.

Fabela, Isidro, ed. *Documentos Históricos de la Revolución Mexicana,* vols. 1, 5, 8, 14 and 20. Mexico City: Fondo de Cultura Económica and Editorial Jus, S. A., 1965, 1968, 1970.

Faulk, Odie B. *The U.S. Camel Corps: An Army Experiment*. New York: Oxford University Press, 1976.

Fehrenbach, T. R. *Fire and Blood: A History of Mexico*. 1973; reprint, New York: Da Capo Press, 1995.

Forbes, Jack D. *Apache, Navaho and Spaniard*. Norman: University of Oklahoma Press, 1994.

Fröbel, Julius. *Seven Years' Travel in Central America, Northern Mexico and the Far West of the United States*. London: R. Bentley, 1859.

Frontier Times. *Jack Hays, the Intrepid Texas Ranger*. Bandera, Tex.: Frontier Times, 1927.

Gammel, Hans Peter Marius, comp. *The Laws of Texas, 1822–1897*. 10 vols. Austin: Gammel Book Co., 1898.

Gerald, Rex E. *Spanish Presidios of the Late Eighteenth Century in Northern New Spain*. Museum of New Mexico Research Records, no. 7. Santa Fe: Museum of New Mexico Press, 1968.

Gomez, Arthur R. *A Most Singular Country: A History of Occupation in the Big Bend*. Salt Lake City: Brigham Young University, 1990.

Greer, James Kimmins. *Colonel Jack Hays, Texas Frontier Leader and California Builder*. 2nd ed. Waco: W. M. Morrison, Pub., 1973.

Gregg, John Ernest. "The History of Presidio County." M.A. thesis, University of Texas at Austin, 1933.

Gregg, Josiah. *Commerce of the Prairies, or the Journal of a Santa Fe Trader*. New York: Henry G. Langley, 1844.

Griffin-Pierce, Trudy. *Native Peoples of the Southwest*. Albuquerque: University of New Mexico Press, 2000.

Griswold del Castillo, Richard. *The Treaty of Guadalupe Hidalgo: A Legacy of Conflict*. Norman: University of Oklahoma Press, 1990.

Groat, Charles G. *Presidio Bolson, Trans-Pecos Texas and Adjacent Mexico: Geology of a Desert Basin Aquifer System*. Report of Investigation No. 76. Austin: Bureau of Economic Geology, University of Texas at Austin, 1972.

Hallenbeck, Cleve. *Alvar Nunez Cabeza de Vaca: The Journey and Route of the First European to Cross the Continent of North America, 1534–1536*. Glendale: Arthur H. Clark Company, 1940.

Hammond, George P., and Agapito Rey. *The Rediscovery of New Mexico, 1580–1594*. Albuquerque: University of New Mexico Press, 1966.

Hanrahan, Gene Z. *Documents on the Mexican Revolution*. Vols. 1 (pts. 1 and 2, "The Origins of the Revolution in Texas, Arizona, New Mexico and California, 1910–1911"), 6 ("Abajo el Gringo!"), 7 ("The Counter-Revolution") and 9 (pts. 1 and 2, "The Bad Yankee, el Peligro Yankee"). Salisbury, N.C.: Documentary Publications, 1976, 1982, 1983, 1985.

Hays, John C., and John Caperton. *Life and Adventures of John C. Hays, the Texas Ranger*. (Alternate title: *Sketch of Colonel John C. Hays, The Texas Ranger: Incidents in Texas and Mexico, from materials furnished by Col. Hays and Major John Caperton*.) Comp. unknown. Berkeley: Bancroft Library, University of California at Berkeley, 1879.

Hickerson, Nancy Parrott. *The Jumanos: Hunters and Traders of the South Plains*. Austin: University of Texas Press, 1994.

Hinkle, Stacy C. *Wings and Saddles: The Air and Cavalry Punitive Expedition of 1919*. University of Texas at El Paso Southwestern Studies Monograph No. 19. El Paso: Texas Western Press, 1967.

Hobby, Edwin. *A Treatise on Texas Land Law.* St. Louis: The Gilbert Book Company, 1883.

Horgan, Paul. *Great River: The Rio Grande in North American History.* 1954; reprint, Austin: Texas Monthly Press, Inc., 1984.

Hughes, John T. *Doniphan's Expedition: Containing an Account of the Conquest of New Mexico.* 1848; reprint, Chicago: The Rio Grande Press, 1962.

Hunter, Robert. *A Texan in the Gold Rush: The Letters of Robert Hunter, 1849–1851.* Bryan, Tex.: Barnum and White Publications, Inc., 1972.

Ing, J. David, and George Kegley. *Archeological Investigations at Fort Leaton Historic Site, Presidio County, Texas.* Austin: Texas Parks and Wildlife Department, 1971.

Jameson, John. *The Story of Big Bend National Park.* Austin: University of Texas Press, 1996.

John, Elizabeth A. H. "Spanish-Indian Relations in the Big Bend Region during the Eighteenth and Early Nineteenth Centuries." *The Journal of Big Bend Studies* 3:71–80 (1991).

Johnson, David Nathan. *Madero in Texas.* San Antonio: Corona Publishing Co., 2001.

Justice, Glenn. "Candelaria, Texas: Life in the Wild, Wild West." *Texas Heritage* 18 (3): 8–12 (2000).

Katz, Friedrich. *The Life and Times of Pancho Villa.* Stanford: Stanford University Press, 1998.

Kelley, J. Charles. "The Historic Indian Pueblos of La Junta de los Rios." *New Mexico Historical Review* 27:257–295 (1952) and 28:21–51 (1953).

———. "Juan Sabeata and Diffusion in Aboriginal Texas." *American Anthropologist* 57:981 (1955).

———. *Jumano and Patarabueye: Relations at La Junta de los Rios.* Anthropological paper No. 77. Ann Arbor: The Museum of Anthropology, University of Michigan, 1986.

Kendall, George Wilkins. *Narrative of the Texan Santa Fé Expedition, Comprising a Description of a Tour through Texas and across the Southwest Prairies . . .* Austin: The Steck Company, 1935.

Kenmotsu, Nancy Adele. "Helping Each Other Out: A Study of the Mutualistic Relations of Small-Scale Foragers and Cultivators in La Junta de los Rios Region, Texas and Mexico." Ph.D. diss., University of Texas at Austin, 1994.

———. "Seeking Friends, Avoiding Enemies: The Jumano Response to Spanish Colonization, A.D. 1580–1750." *Bulletin of the Texas Archeological Society* 72:23–43 (2001).

Kerr, John Leeds, with Frank Donovan. *Destination Topolobampo, The Kansas City, Mexico & Orient Railway.* San Marino, Calif.: Golden West Books, 1968.

Koch, Clara Lena. "The Federal Indian Policy in Texas, 1845–1860." *The Southwestern Historical Quarterly* 29:98ff. (1926).

Krieger, Alex D. "Un Nuevo Estúdio de la Ruta Seguida por Cabeza de Vaca a Través de Norte América." Ph.D. diss., Universidad Nacional Autónoma de México, 1955. English typescript, Southwest Collection, Texas Tech University.

Leaverton, James, and Kathleen Houston. "Presidio County's Oldest Building, Fort Leaton." *Voice of the Mexican Border.* Centennial Edition. Marfa:
n.p., 1936.

Lister, Florence C., and Robert H. Lister. *Chihuahua: Storehouse of Storms.*
Albuquerque: University of New Mexico Press, 1966.

Machado, Manuel A., Jr. *Barbarians of the North: Modern Chihuahua and the
Mexican Political System.* Austin: Eakin Press, 1992.

Madison, Virginia. *The Big Bend Country of Texas.* New York: October House,
Inc., 1968.

Madison, Virginia, and Hallie Stillwell. *How Come It's Called That? Place Names
in the Big Bend Country.* Marathon, Tex.: Iron Mountain Press, 1997.

Madrid, Enrique Rede. "The Expedition of Captain Joseph de Ydoiaga to
La Junta de los Rios." *West Texas Historical Association Year Book* 70:88–
101 (1994).

Mallouf, Robert J. "Archaeology of the Cinega Mountains of Presidio County,
Texas." *Artifact* 31:1–44 (1993).

———. "Arroyo de las Burras: Preliminary Findings from the 1992 SRSU
Archaeological Field School." *Journal of Big Bend Studies* 1:3–38 (1992).

———. "Comments on the Prehistory of Far Northeastern Chihuahua, the
La Junta District, and the Cielo Complex." *Journal of Big Bend Studies* 2:49–
92 (1999).

———. "Prehistoric Cultures of the Northern Chihuahuan Desert." In *Second Symposium on Resources of the Chihuahuan Desert Region.* Alpine, Tex.:
The Chihuahuan Desert Research Institute 69–78, 1983.

Mallouf, Robert J., and Virginia A. Wulfkuhle. "An Archaeological Reconnaissance in the Rosillos Mountains, Brewster County, Texas." *Journal of
Big Bend Studies* 1:1–24 (1992).

Maverick, Mary A. *Memoirs of Mary A. Maverick.* Edited by Rena Maverick
Green. San Antonio: Alamo Printing Co., 1921.

Maverick, Samuel. "Journal, Chihuahua Expedition." In *Samuel Maverick,
Texan: 1803–1870, a Collection of Letters, Journals and Memoirs.* Edited by Rena
Maverick Green. San Antonio: n.p., 1952.

Maxwell, Ross A. *The Big Bend of the Rio Grande: A Guide to the Rocks, Landscape, Geologic History, and Settlers of the Area of Big Bend National Park.* Austin:
Bureau of Economic Geology, University of Texas at Austin, 1968.

McKitrick, Reuben. "The Public Land System of Texas, 1823–1910." *Bulletin of
the University of Wisconsin,* no. 905, Economics and Political Science Series,
9 (1): 1–172 (1918).

Mexico. *Colonias militares: Proyecto para su establecimiento en las fronteras de oriente
y occidente de la republica.* Mexico City: Imprenta de I. Cumplido, 1848.

Meyer, Eugenia, ed. *Museo Historico de la Revolucion en el Estado de Chihuahua.* Mexico City: Secretaría de Gobernación, Secretaría de la Defensa
Nacional, Secretaría de Educación Pública, Instituto Nacional de Antro-
pología e Historia, 1982.

Meyer, Michael C. *Mexican Rebel: Pascual Orozco and the Mexican Revolution,
1910–1915.* Lincoln: University of Nebraska Press, 1967.

Meyer, Michael C., William L. Sherman and Susan M. Deeds. *The Course of Mexican History.* 6th ed. Oxford: Oxford University Press, 1999.

Miles, Elton. *Stray Tales of the Big Bend.* College Station: Texas A&M University Press, 1993.

Moorhead, Max L. *New Mexico's Royal Road: Trade and Travel on the Chihuahua Trail.* Norman: University of Oklahoma Press, 1958.

——. *The Presidio: Bastion of the Spanish Borderlands.* Norman: University of Oklahoma Press, 1975.

Moquin, Wayne, and Charles Van Doren. *A Documentary History of the Mexican Americans.* New York: Praeger Publishers, 1971.

Newcomb, W. W., Jr. *The Indians of Texas.* Austin: University of Texas Press, 1961.

O'Connor, Charles J. "Capture of Ojinaga and Red Cross Care of the Sick and Wounded." *The American Red Cross Magazine* 9:84–92 (1914).

Ontiveros, Francisco de P. *Toribio Ortega y la Brigada Gonzalez Ortega.* Translated by Victor Manuel Martinez Ortega. Austin: Martinez Publishing Company, 1991.

Orozco, Victor Orozco. *Las Guerras Indias en la Historia de Chihuahua.* Ciudad Juárez: Instituto Chihuahuense de la Cultura, Universidad Autónoma de Ciudad Juárez, 1992.

Osorio, Ruben. "The Death of a President and the Destruction of the Mexican Federal Army, 1913–1914." *Journal of Big Bend Studies* 12:105–132 (2000).

Palladini, Eric Louis, Jr. "Making Fortunes on the Frontier of Enemies: The Agrarian Economy of San Felipe el Real de Chihuahua, 1709–1831." Ph. D. diss., Tulane University, 2000.

Poindexter, John B. *The Cibolo Creek Ranch.* Shafter, Tex.: Southwest Holdings, Inc., 2000.

Poppa, Terrence E. *Drug Lord: The Life and Death of a Mexican Kingpin.* Seattle: Demand Publications, 1998.

Pospisil, JoAnne. "Chihuahuan Desert Candelilla: Folk Gathering of a Regional Resource." *Journal of Big Bend Studies* 6:59–74 (1994).

Presidio County, Texas. *Estate of John W. Spencer, Deceased.* Case No. 46, Office of the Presidio County Clerk.

Raht, Carlysle Graham. *The Romance of Davis Mountains and Big Bend Country.* Edition Texana. Odessa: The Rahtbooks Company, 1963.

Raun, Gerald G. "Refugees or Prisoners of War: The Internment of a Mexican Federal Army after the Battle of Ojinaga." *Journal of Big Bend Studies* 12:133–166 (2000).

Rebert, Paula. *La Gran Línea, Mapping the United States-Mexico Boundary, 1849–1857.* Austin, University of Texas Press, 2001.

Reed, John. *Insurgent Mexico.* New York: International Publishers, 1969.

Sandels, Robert Lynn. "Silvestre Terrazas, the Press, and the Origins of the Mexican Revolution in Chihuahua." Ph. D. diss., University of Oregon, 1967.

Santleben, August. *A Texas Pioneer: Early Staging and Overland Freighting Days on the Frontiers of Texas and Mexico.* Edited by I. D. Affleck. New York: Neale Publishing Company, 1910.

Schaafsma, Curtis F., and Carroll L. Riley, eds. *The Casas Grandes World*. Salt Lake City: University of Utah Press, 1999.

Seewald, Ken, and Dan Sundeen, eds. *The Geologic Framework of the Chihuahua Tectonic Belt*. Midland: West Texas Geological Society, 1970.

Shipman, Mrs. O. L. (Alice Jack Dolan Shipman). *Taming the Big Bend: A History of the Extreme Western Portion of Texas from Fort Clark to El Paso*. Austin: Van Boeckmann-Jones Co., [1926?].

Smith, Ralph A. "Indians in American-Mexican Relations before the War of 1846." *Hispanic American Historical Review* 43 (1): 34–64 (1963).

————. "Mexican and Anglo-Saxon Traffic in Scalps, Slaves, and Livestock." *West Texas Historical Association Year Book* 36:98–115 (1960).

————. "Poor Mexico, So Far from God and So Close to the Tejanos." *West Texas Historical Association Year Book* 44:78–105 (1968).

————. "The Scalp Hunt in Chihuahua." *New Mexico Historical Review* 40 (2): 117–140 (1965).

Smithers, Wilfred Dudley. "The Border Trading Posts." *Sul Ross State College Bulletin* 41 (8): 11 (1961).

————. *Chronicles of the Big Bend: A Photographic Memoir of Life on the Border*. Austin: Texas State Historical Association, 1999.

Spearing, Darwin. *Roadside Geology of Texas*. Missoula, Mont.: Mountain Press Publishing Company, 1991.

Swift, Roy L., and Leavitt Corning Jr. *Three Roads to Chihuahua: The Great Wagon Roads That Opened the Southwest, 1823–1883*. Austin: Eakin Press, 1988.

Taylor, Thomas U. *Irrigation Systems in Texas*. U.S. Department of the Interior, U.S. Geological Survey, Washington, D.C., 1902.

Texas. *Condensed Reports of State School Land Agents to School Land Board*. Austin: State Printing Office, 1885.

Thompson, Cecilia. *History of Marfa and Presidio County*. 2 vols. Austin: Nortex Press, 1985.

Travers, Douglas N. "The Great Chihuahua Cattle Drive of 1868." *The Journal of Big Bend Studies* 13:85–105 (2001).

Tunnell, Curtis. *Wax, Men and Money: A Historical and Archaeological Study of Candelilla Wax Camps Along the Rio Grande Border of Texas*. Report 32. Austin: Texas Historical Commission, Office of the State Archeologist, 1981.

Tyler, Ron C. *The Big Bend: A History of the Last Texas Frontier*. College Station: Texas A&M University Press, 1996.

————. "The Little Punitive Expedition in the Big Bend." *Southwestern Historical Quarterly* 78 (3): 271–291 (1975).

Tyler, Ron C., Douglas E. Barnett, Roy R. Barkley, Penelope C. Anderson and Mark F. Odintz, eds. *The New Handbook of Texas*. Austin: Texas State Historical Association, 1996.

U.S. Bureau of the Census. *Eighth Census of the United States, 1860*, Population Schedule, Presidio County, Tex. Washington, D.C.: National Archives and Records Administration, RG029, M653.

————. *Ninth Census of the United States, 1870*, Population Schedule, Presidio

County, Tex. Washington, D.C.: National Archives and Records Administration, RG029, M593.

U.S. Department of State. *Diplomatic Correspondence of the United States, Inter-American Affairs 1831–1860,* vol. 9—Mexico 1848 (Mid-Year)–1860, documents 3772–4476. Washington, D.C.: Carnegie Endowment for International Peace, 1937.

U.S. Fifth Circuit Court of Appeals. *Ernest Dale Owen, Complainant v. The Presidio Mining Company, Defendants.* Case No. 58 in Chancery, appeal from the U.S. Circuit Court for the Western District of Texas. RG 276, National Archives Branch Depository, Fort Worth, Tex.

U.S. House of Representatives. *Message from the President of the United States to the Two Houses of Congress at the Commencement of the First Session of the Thirty-First Congress,* 31st Cong., 1st sess., 24 Dec. 1849, Ex. Doc. 5.

U.S. Senate. *Message from the President of the United States to the Two Houses of Congress at the Commencement of the Second Session of the Thirty-Sixth Congress,* vol. 2, 36th Cong., 2nd sess., 4 Dec. 1860, Ex. Doc. 1.

————. *Report of the Secretary of War, Communicating in Compliance with a Resolution of the Senate, a Map Showing the Operations of the Army of the United States in Texas and the Adjacent Mexican States on the Rio Grande . . . ,* 31st Cong., 1st sess., 18 Feb. 1849, Ex. Doc. 32.

————. *Reports of the Secretary of War with Reconnaissances of Routes from San Antonio to El Paso . . . ,* 31st Cong., 1st sess., ordered to be printed 24 July 1850, Ex. Doc. 64.

U.S. War Department. *The War of the Rebellion: A Compilation of the Official Records of the Union and Confederate Armies.* Ser. 1, vols. 1, 4, 9, 15 and ser. 2., vol. 2. Washington, D.C.: Government Printing Office, 1886.

Wasserman, Mark. *Capitalists, Caciques and Revolution: The Native Elite and Foreign Enterprise in Chihuahua, Mexico, 1854–1911.* Chapel Hill: University of North Carolina Press, 1984.

————. *Everyday Life and Politics in Nineteenth Century Mexico: Men, Women and War.* Albuquerque: University of New Mexico Press, 2000.

————. *Persistent Oligarchs: Elites and Politics in Chihuahua, Mexico, 1910–1940.* Durham: Duke University Press, 1993.

Weisman, Alan. *La Frontera: The United States Border with Mexico.* Photographs by Jay Dusard. New York: Harcourt Brace Jovanovich Publishers, 1986.

West, Elizabeth Howard. "Bonilla's Brief Compendium of the History of Texas." *Quarterly of the Texas State Historical Association* 8:9–78 (1904).

West Texas Geological Society. *Geology of the Big Bend Area, Texas.* Midland: West Texas Geological Society, 1965.

Whiting, William Henry Chase. "Journal of 1849." In Ralph P. Bieber and Averam B. Bender, eds. *Exploring Southwestern Trails, 1846–1854.* Glendale, Calif.: Arthur H. Clark Company, 1938.

Whittington, Lona Teresa O'Neal. "The Road of Sorrow: Mexican Refugees Who Fled Pancho Villa through Presidio, Texas, 1913–1914." M.A. thesis, Sul Ross University, 1976.

Willeford, Glenn P. "American Red Cross Activities at the Battle Of Ojinaga, December 1913–January 1914." *Journal of Big Bend Studies* 12:167–180 (2000).

Williams, Oscar Waldo. *O. W. Williams' Stories from the Big Bend.* Monograph No. 10. El Paso: Texas Western College Press, 1965.

—————. *Pecos County: A History.* N. p., 1918.

Winfrey, Dorman H., and James M. Day, eds. *The Indian Papers of Texas and the Southwest, 1825–1916.* Vol. 3 and 5. Austin: Pemberton Press, 1966.

Abriaches (tribe), 21
Acosta, Hipolito, 47, 134
Acosta, Juan, 215
Acosta, Pablo, 211, 212–223, 225, 226, 231, 232
Acousta, Crisanto, 46
Adams, W. C., 105
Agriculture: and Anglos, 50; and Apaches, 127; and Chihuahua, 25–26, 138, 142–143; and communal and traditional landholding, 121; and Cuchillo Parado, 145; and Fort Davis as market, 100–101; and irrigation, 203, 204; and La Junta de los Rios, 1–2, 5, 14, 15, 19, 21, 22, 41, 42, 230, 231, 232, 234, 237, 238; and Ojinaga, 17; and railroads, 141, 202–203; and Rio Conchos, 67, 127, 230, 231; and Rio Grande, 18–19, 231; and Vado de Piedra, 85
Aguilar, Lucas, 46
Aguirre, Cipriano Márquez, 162
Alamito Creek, 86, 87, 89, 100, 101
Alamo Chapo (ranch), 27
Alamos, Mexico, 140
Almonte, Juan, 49–50
Amarillas, Ciro, 142, 154
American Red Cross, 176, 179
Amnesty International, 9
Anasazi pueblos, 21
Ancón Grande, 26, 28
Anglos and Anglo settlement: and Chihuahua, 25, 39; and Chihuahua Trail, 93, 97; and Civil War, 115; and Comanches, 23; and La Junta de los Rios, 16, 19, 39, 40–41, 50, 232; and Leaton, 74; Mexican Revolution, 150; and rail-

roads, 62; relations with Hispanics, 97, 98, 136; and roads, 56, 60–61; and scalp hunting, 34; and trading, 34, 35, 50
Anti-Reelectionist Party, 143, 144, 145, 147
Apaches: and border, 128, 199; and Chihuahua, 25, 29, 30–32, 33, 49, 115, 121, 128, 146; and Civil War, 103, 104, 115; and Evans, 68; and Faver, 96, 98; and Fröbel, 88, 89; and Hunter, 69; and Leaton, 51, 69, 71–74, 85, 88; as nomadic or seminomadic hunters and gatherers, 21; and Presidio, 58; and Quintanilla, 93; and railroads, 129; and Ramirez, 98; and ranching, 115, 126–127, 129; and reservation life, 42, 70, 127, 128, 129; and route to El Paso, 55; and scalp hunting, 33, 34, 70, 73; and Spaniards, 23; and Spencer, 50; and Terrazas, 123, 128; and trading, 41, 51, 72, 73–74, 85, 127; and Vado de Piedra, 85; and wars of extermination, 128. See also Mescaleros
Aradia, Clato, 125
Aranda, Domingo, 207–208
Arevalo, Fermín, 213–216, 218, 226
Arevalo, Lilí, 213–214, 215
Arevalo, Lupe, 214
Arevalo family, 214–215
Arizona National Guard, 188
Armijo, Governor, 38
Arms traffic, 160–161, 165, 166, 178–179, 207, 232
Army Air Service, 195, 198
Army of the West, 39
Arreglo, 36, 38, 49

Arroyo, Francisco, 145
Arzate (Chisos Apache leader), 128, 146
Atchison, Topeka & Santa Fe Railroad Company, 202–203
Aubert, Trucy, 161, 162
Aubrey, Francis Xavier, 87
Austin, Stephen F., 51
Austin, Texas, 60
Avilez, Heraclio, 209

Babbitt, E. B., 71
Baesa, Eugenio, 46
Baird, Spruce McCoy, 112
Baisa, Santiago, 117–118
Baiza, Esmerijildo, 45, 46
Banditry: and air patrols, 193–198, 200; and border, 187, 191, 199, 200, 231, 232; and Carrancista soldiers, 190, 191; and Kilpatrick family, 191–193; and Mexican Revolution, 153–154; and United States Army, 187–188, 189, 190–193, 199; and Villa, 185, 186, 187, 190, 191
Bañuelos, Clemente Manuel, 2, 4, 8–9, 237, 238, 242, 243
Bartlett, John, 83
Baylor, John R., 103, 104–105, 108–109
Beard, A. G., 197, 198
Belgium, 50
Bell, Peter, 44, 54, 127
Bent's Fort, 41–42
Bexar County, Texas, 78–81
Big Bend, 15, 16, 31, 52, 62, 187, 191
Big Bend National Park, 204, 222
Blake, E. D., 103
Bliss, Zenas, 100
Blood, James M., 8
Bofecillos Mountains, 12, 31
Bohr, Niels, 244
Bolson de Mapimí, 31, 49, 66
Bolsons, 12–13
Bomford, Colonel, 101
Boquillas, 187
Border: advantages of, 41, 48; and

Apaches, 128, 199; and arms traffic, 147, 149, 150, 151, 160–161, 165, 166, 178–179, 207, 232; and banditry, 187, 191, 199, 200, 231, 232; characteristics of, 218, 229; and Civil War, 104, 107, 111; establishment of, 39, 41, 75; and fencing operations, 41–42, 74; and law enforcement, 48; and Madrid, 243; and Mercado, 175, 231; and Mexican Revolution, 146, 150–151, 153–154, 157, 175–178, 186; militarization of, 9, 232; and Orozco, 158; and political divisions, 230–232, 238; porosity of, 6, 230, 233; and Rio Grande, 5, 6, 12, 25, 41, 83–84, 107, 229, 230; and scalp hunting, 73–74; and smuggling, 6, 207, 231, 232, 233; and surveys, 83–84, 86, 107; and Treaty of Guadalupe Hidalgo, 43, 74–75, 83; and United States Army, 18, 187–188, 189. See also United States Border Patrol
Bowie, G. W., 113
Brite Ranch, 188–189
Brooke, George, 71
Brooks, George, 125–126
Brown, John, 33
Brownsville, Texas, 230
Burgess, John D.: and Confederate forces, 111–112; death of, 119–120; and feuds, 201; and Fort Davis, 100, 117, 118–119; and Fort Leaton, 116, 117, 236; and Hall, 68, 115–118, 133; and interethnic marriage, 97; and law enforcement, 48; and Bill Leaton, 118–119; and Torrey, 42; and trading, 40, 50, 116; and Wulff, 106
Burgess, John D. (son), 120
Burgess, Tomás, 117–118, 133
Burgess, Tomasa Baeza, 97
Bush, George Herbert Walker, 3
Bush, George W., 3
Bustillos, Juan, 46

Cabeza de Vaca, Álavar Núñez, 21–22, 23, 26
Cabris (tribe), 21
Calderoni, Guillermo Gonzalez, 220–223, 226
California: and El Paso road, 61, 62; and forty-niners, 66–69, 87; and Hays, 52, 53; and railroads, 129–130
Calvo, José Joaquín, 30–31, 33
Camels, 101, 102
Camino Real, 24, 34, 34, 66, 69, 87, 130
Camp Hudson, 60
Camp San Saba, 99
Candelaria, Texas, 16, 17–18, 153, 189, 191–193, 227, 235
Candelilla wax, 207, 212
Cano, Chico, 191, 192
Caperton, Jack, 53, 54
Caravel, Marcelo, 202
Carleton, James, 108, 109, 111, 112
Carranza, Venustiano: and banditry, 199; and Chihuahua, 168, 186–187; government of, 190; and Huerta, 185; and Villa, 179, 185, 186, 189–190; and Wilson, 185, 186
Carrasco, Antonio, 153–155
Carrasco, Manuel, 207–211, 213
Carreón, Pancho, 207, 208
Catholic Church, 174
Cerro Gordo, Mexico, 40
Chambers, Robert, 226–228, 232, 235
Chao, Manuel, 168, 173, 179
Chastain, Sheriff, 179
Chaves, Pablo, 197, 198
Chávez, César, 241, 243
Chávez, Denise, 5, 6, 230
Chevallié, Michael, 53, 70–71, 74
Chicago & Texas Land & Cattle Company, 134
Chichimecas, 21, 121
Chihuahua, Mexico: and agriculture, 25–26, 138, 142–143; and Apaches and Comanches, 25,
29, 30–32, 33, 49, 115, 121, 128, 146; colonization of, 25–26; and Connelly, 35–38; and Díaz, 131; economy of, 25, 142; Fort Davis as protection for, 116; and González, 146, 153, 163; and Huerta, 163, 165; La Junta de los Rios as part of, 25; and land grants, 44; and land issues, 25, 27–28, 136–137; and Mexican-American War, 39–40; and Mexican Army, 169; mining industry of, 138; and Ojinaga, 124; recession of 1908, 142–143; and regional identity, 121; and roads, 51, 65, 86, 89; and scalp hunting, 70, 71, 72–73; and trading, 58, 66, 90; and Villa, 173, 185; and Whiting, 57
Chihuahuan Desert, 11–12, 11, 15, 21, 96, 116
Chihuahua Trail: and Anglo settlement, 93, 97; and Civil War, 115; and Confederate forces, 112; and economics, 231; and Faver, 95, 96; and Fort Davis, 95, 100; map of, 37; and railroads, 129; and trading, 61–62, 87, 117
Chinati Mountains, 12, 31
Chisos Apaches, 21, 128
Chisos Mountains, 31
Chivara, Emilio, 170, 171
Cholera, 63–64, 65, 66, 68, 79
Cholomes, 232
Cibolo Creek, 28, 53, 56, 96
Cibolo (ranch), 29
Cibolos (tribe), 21
Cielo Complex people, 21
Cisneros (Mescalero leader), 93
Ciudad Acuña, Mexico, 231
Ciudad Chihuahua, Chihuahua: and cholera, 63; and drug smuggling, 210, 213; and evacuation to Ojinaga, 170; and Evans, 67, 68; and Fröbel, 87; and Hunter, 69; and land records, 28; and Leaton, 87; and Madero, 156; and Mercado,

181; and Mexican-American War, 39, 40; Mexican Army, 157; military hospital of, 29; and Orozco, 163, 168; and railroads, 129, 140, 141; and roads, 24, 34–35, 54, 55, 56, 61, 62, 66, 204; and Sánchez, 164; and Santleben, 90; and scalp hunting, 34; and supplies for Ojinaga, 154; and Villa, 169, 173

Ciudad Juárez, Mexico: and border, 231; as center of authority, 142; and drug smuggling, 220; and González, 146–147, 151; and Madero, 156–157; and Ojinaga's evacuation, 160; and Orozco, 156, 158, 159, 163; and Villa, 156, 168, 189

Civilian Conservation Corps, 204

Civil War: effects of, 102, 115; and Mexico, 107, 109–111; and military road forts, 99, 103–105, 115; and Presidio del Norte, 105, 107, 110, 111, 115; and Texas' secession, 102–103; and trading, 87. *See also* Confederate forces; Union forces

Clark, Edward, 103

Clark, James, 92

Clayton, John, 73

Coahuila y Texas, Mexico, 44

Cocaine, 6, 219, 225, 226, 227–228

Coin smuggling, 90–91

Coke, Richard, 240

Colonization laws, 25, 27, 42, 47

Colorado (Chisos Apache leader), 128

Colorado (state), 12, 14

Colorados, 168–169, 171, 179, 180, 183

Colorado Territory, 108

Colquitt, Oscar, 150, 187

Columbus, New Mexico, 186, 187

Comanches: and Chihuahua, 25, 29, 30–32, 33, 49, 115, 121, 128, 146; and Civil War, 103, 104, 115; and Evans, 68; and Faver, 96; and Fröbel, 88; and Hays,

52; and Hunter, 69; and Leaton, 72; and nomadic or seminomadic hunters and gatherers, 21; and Ronquillo, 27; and San Carlos, 86; and scalp hunting, 33, 70, 73; and Spaniards, 23; and trading, 41, 58

Committee of Public Safety, 102–103

Communal and traditional landholding, 121–122, 141, 142

Compromise of 1850, 77

Conchos (tribe), 21

Conde, Francisco García, 38, 49

Confederate forces: and Burgess, 111–112; and military road forts, 104–105; and Skillman, 109, 110, 111–114; and supplies, 112, 113; and sympathizers in Mexico, 107, 108, 110; and Wulff, 105–107

Confederate States, 103–105, 108, 110

Confederate Territory of Arizona, 104

Congress of Chihuahua, 29

Connelly, Henry C., 35–38, 39, 40, 49, 87, 90

Connelly's Trail, 37, 89

Conservatism, in Mexico, 122, 145

Constitutionalist movement: and Chivara, 170; and Ojinaga, 175, 177, 178–179, 180, 181; and Ortega, 163, 164, 165–166, 181; and Villa, 163, 166, 168, 169, 172

Contreras, Benigno, 106–107

Conventionist movement, 185

Cooper, R. H., 198

Coronado, Francisco Vasquez de, 22

Cottonwood Spring, 28, 113

Coyame, Mexico, 19, 150, 152, 153, 159, 164

Crawford, George, 73

Creel, Enrique, 122, 123, 138–140, 150, 210

Creelman, James, 143

Crews, Seth, 134

Croix, Teodoro de, 229, 230, 233

Crosson, George, 116

Cuchillo Parado, Mexico: and Gordillo, 156; and La Junta de los Rios settlement, 19; and liberalism, 153; and Luque, 152; and Ortega, 144, 145, 159, 160, 163, 164; and Sánchez, 150

Curry, John Steuart, 33

Daly, Richard, 126

Davis, Jefferson, 100, 103, 108

Davis, Paul, 194–195, 196, 197, 198, 199

DEA. See United States Drug Enforcement Agency

Deemer, Jesse, 187, 188

DeHaro, Marco, 214, 215

DeHavilland DH-4s, 193–194, 198

Delaware, 20

Delaware Indians, 36

Del Rio, Texas, 231

Del Toro, Salvador Martinez, 159, 160–161, 162, 164

DeMatteo, James, 8, 237

Dengue fever, 63, 64

Derecho de consumo, 38

Derecho de extracción de oro y plata, 38

Derecho de internación, 38

Devine, Daniel, 117

Devine, Joseph H., 81

Dianda, Joseph, 125

Díaz, Domingo, 23, 27, 174

Díaz, Porfirio: and Chihuahua, 131; and Ciudad Juárez, 156; and Juárez, 121, 125; and local oppression, 141–142; and Luque, 149; and Madero, 143–144; as oligarch, 145; and Ortega, 166; power of, 143; resignation of, 157, 158; and Stilwell, 140; and Terrazas, 125, 131, 138; and United States, 150, 163; and Villa, 169, 174

Dickman, Joseph, 197

Diphtheria, 64

Doniphan, Alexander, 39–40

Dorentes, Alberto, 147–148, 152

Dougherty, J. S., 133

Douglas, Stephen A., 93

Drawback Act (1845), 36

Drug lords, 208, 210, 213, 221, 225, 232

Drug smuggling: and Acosta, 211, 212–223, 225, 226; and Aranda, 207–208; and border, 6, 232; and Carrasco, 207–211; and drug lords, 208, 210, 213, 221, 225, 232; and Ojinaga, 17, 207–221; and plaza, 208, 210–211, 212, 213, 216, 220; and police, 208, 209–210, 212, 213, 214, 221; and Presidio County, 225–227, 235; and Thompson, 225–228; and weapons, 7

Dupuy, H. E., 205

Dusard, Jay, 217, 218

Eagle Pass, Texas, 66, 231

Easterly, Thomas, 33

Echols, William H., 100–102

Education, and Villa, 173

Eighth United States Infantry, 100

El Chino (Mescalero leader), 93

Elephant Butte Dam, 203

El Gordo (Mescalero leader), 93

Elguezábal, Juan Bautista, 23, 27

Ellis, W. O., 133

Ellsworth, Luther T., 147, 149, 150–151

El Mezquite, Mexico, 18, 19

El Morrión Pass, 31

El Mulato, Mexico: and Cohuilan rebels, 153; and González, 147, 149, 152; and Gordillo, 156; as La Junta de los Rios settlement, 19; and Ortega, 148, 149, 152, 175; wounded in, 176

El Paso, Texas: and border, 42, 83, 230, 231; and Connelly, 39; and drug smuggling, 220; and Hunter, 69; and Madero, 151, 152; and Ojinaga's refugees, 181, 190; as port of entry, 6; and railroads, 129; and Rio Grande, 12;

and roads, 24, 51, 54–55, 56, 60, 61, 66, 76, 86, 89; and Ronquillo, 30; and Skillman, 109; and Terrazas, 123, 124, 171; and trading, 59, 87; and Union forces, 110; and United States Army, 99
El Paso County, Texas, 78
El Polvo, Texas, 4, 5, 6, 17, 149, 175
El Polvo river crossing, 3–4, 6, 208, 226, 236–237, 245
El Tecolote, Mexico, 19
Emory, William H., 83–86, 87, 88, 107
Entrada al Pacifico, 243
Equestrian entertainers, 38
Espejo, Antonio de, 22, 23
Espejo (Mescalero leader), 93
Espinosa, Andrew, 118
Estill, F. S., 198
Estricero, Francisco, 188
Evans, George, 66–68, 87
Evaro, Rosendo, 7

Fall, Albert B., 171
Falomir, Mexico, 140
Faver, Francísca Ramirez, 95, 96, 97
Faver, Gavina Ramirez, 97–98
Faver, Gumercinda Zubia, 97
Faver, Juan, 96–98
Faver, Milton, 95–96, 97, 98, 126, 133
FBI (Federal Bureau of Investigation), 149, 221–222, 225, 232
Federales: and Colorados, 168–169; and Cuchillo Parado, 152–153; desertions of, 156; and El Mulato, 149, 175; and Fort Bliss internment, 182, 183; and Juárez, 125; and Ojinada, 147, 148, 149, 153, 154, 155, 166, 170, 174, 179, 180; and Orozco, 158; rurales and jefes distinguished from, 141–142; and Villa, 174. See also Mexican Army
Ferguson, James, 187
Fergusson, David, 109–110, 115, 122

Fernandez, Elva, 219
Ferrocaril Chihuahua al Pacifico, 140
Fifth Law, 70, 74
Fitzgerrell, James J., 134
Ford, John "Rip," 76, 104
Ford-Neighbors Trail, 76
Foreign investments: and Terrazas, 123, 138; and Villa, 173
Fort Bliss: and Confederate forces, 104, 108, 109; founding of, 99; and military road, 60; and Ojinaga's refugees, 182, 183; and Union forces, 103, 108, 109, 110, 113
Fort Clark, 60, 89, 104
Fort Davis: and Apaches, 96; and Burgess, 100, 117, 118–119; and Confederate forces, 105, 108; and Faver, 95; founding of, 28, 93, 99, 100; and Hall, 110; and military roads, 60, 77, 99, 100, 129; and Pedraza, 118; as Presidio County seat, 77; and ranching, 50, 100; reopening of, 126; and Spencer, 100, 201; and Union Forces, 103, 108; U.S. reoccupation of, 116
Fort Fillmore, 99, 104
Fort Hancock, 60
Fortín del Cibolo, 96
Fortín de San José, 29, 42, 44–46
Fort Inge, 60, 104
Fort Lancaster, 60, 89, 99
Fort Leaton: and Burgess, 116, 117, 236; and Civil War, 110, 111; construction of, 50; and Gibbons, 105; and Glanton, 72; and Hays, 51, 52–53; and Highsmith, 54; and Maverick, 65; and Pedraza, 81, 93; and Presidio County, 76, 78; as state park, 205, 236; and trading, 58, 74; and Whiting, 57, 58, 59–60
Fort McKavett, 60, 99
Fort Quitman, 60, 76, 99
Fort Sam Houston, 152

Fort Stockton, 60, 77, 89, 99
Fort Towson, 37, 38
Fort Wingate, 183
Forty-niners, 66–69, 87
Foster, Edward, 125
France, 50
Franciscans, 23, 95, 121, 145
French, Albert H., 113–114
French Intervention (1861—1867),
    121, 123–125
Fröbel, Julius, 87–88, 90
Fuentes, Juan José, 197, 198
Fuero, Carlos, 128

Galindo, Januario, 46
Gallegos, Artemio, 209
Gallegos, Oscar, 236, 237
Galveston, Harrisburg and San
    Antonio Railway, 129
Galveston, Texas, 63
Garcia, Thomas, 46
García-Bartlett compromise, 83, 86
García Conde, Pedro, 83, 84
Gasden Purchase, 61
Geddis, David, 125
Germany, 50
Gibbons, Emory, 105–107
Glanton, John, 70–72, 74
Glasgow, Edward, 39
Glenn Springs, Texas, 187
Gomez (Mescalero chief), 56–57,
    59, 60
Gonzales, Esculpio, 118
Gonzales, Refugio, 125
González, Abraham: and Anti-
    Reelection Party, 144; and Ciu-
    dad Juárez, 146–147, 151; and El
    Mulato, 147, 149, 152; as gover-
    nor of Chihuahua, 146, 153, 163;
    and Huerta, 163; and Madero,
    146, 148, 149, 151, 152; and Oji-
    naga, 147, 149, 166; and Ortega,
    147; and political division of
    border, 231; and United States,
    150
González, Celso, 123
González, Francisco, 199

Gonzalez, Juan, 118
Gonzalez, Rogelio, 211
Gordillo y Escudero, Manuel, 156–
    157, 166
Gould, Stephen Jay, 244
Gramm, Phil, 225
Grand Kingdom of Quivira, 22
Grierson, Benjamin, 127, 128
Guadalupe, Mexico, 26, 59
Gutiérrez, María Gómez, 165, 170,
    180

Hacienda de Orientales, 122, 210
Hacienda Los Angeles, 123
Hague conventions, 176
Hall, Edward: and Burgess, 68,
    115–118, 133; and Civil War, 115;
    death of, 118–119; and Doniphan,
    40; and Evans, 68; and feuds,
    201; and Fort Leaton, 93, 236;
    and land claims, 95; and law en-
    forcement, 48; and Leaton, 41,
    79–80, 136; and Pedraza, 80–
    81; and raiding in Mexico, 110,
    111, 115; and trading, 50, 68; and
    Wulff, 106
Harwick, J. W., 192
Hays, John Coffee: and Chevallié,
    70; and cholera, 66; and Fort
    Leaton, 51, 52–53; and Presidio
    del Norte, 52, 54, 68–69; and
    road to Chihuahua via El Paso,
    51–52, 54–55, 56, 57, 59, 65; and
    San Carlos, 52, 66
Hearst, William Randolph, 138
Heredia, Eugenio, 30
Hernandez, Belen, 9
Hernandez, Carmelita, 205
Hernandez, Esequiel, Jr. (Junie):
    Bañuelos' killing of, 2, 4, 8–9,
    237, 238, 242, 243; and El Polvo,
    7; and Madrid, 1, 4, 9, 242–243,
    244, 245; and U.S. Border Patrol
    agents, 7–8
Hernandez, Esequiel, Sr., 9–10
Hernandez, Jesus M., 226
Heroin, 6, 207, 209, 212, 219, 226

Herrera, Cesario, 28, 45–47, 48, 78–79, 133, 136
Herrera family, 16
Highsmith, Samuel, 51–52, 54
Hilderband, H. R., 133
Hippel, Maurice von, 83–84
Hispanics: and Mexican Revolution, 150; relations with Anglos, 97, 98, 136. *See also* Mexicans
Homestead laws, 45
Houston, Sam, 41, 70, 103–104
Howard, George T., 53
Howard, Jack, 191–192
Howard, Richard A., 56, 57
Howze, Robert, 199
Huerta, Victoriano: and Chihuahua, 163, 165; and Constitutionalist movement, 183–184; fall of, 185; and Ojinaga, 173, 180–181; and Orozco, 158, 159–160, 163, 164, 166, 168, 172; schism in Huertistas, 168; and Villa, 174, 185
Hunter, Robert, 68–69
Huntington, Colis, 129
Hyde, Archibald, 95

Indianola, Texas, 78, 79, 90, 103
Indian reservations, 42, 70, 127, 128, 129
Indio (village), 50, 189, 191, 201
Influenza, 64
Interethnic marriage, 97
Irigoyen de la O, José, 36, 38
Italy, 50
Iturbide, Augustin de (emperor), 26

Janír, Francisco, 197
Janír, Jesus, 197
Jefes, 141–142
Jefes muncipales, 142, 145
Jefes politicos, 142, 145
Jeff Davis County, Texas, 77, 100
Jiménez, Viviano, 154
Johnston, Benjamin F., 203
Ju (Mescalero leader), 128
Juárez, Benito, 17, 121, 123–124, 125

Juárez, Pedro, 125
Julimes, Mexico, 19, 87
Julimes (tribe), 21
Jumanos (tribe), 21, 22, 55

Kansas City, Mexico & Orient Railway, 139–140, *139*, 202, 231, 243
Kansas City Southern Railroad, 138, 139
Kearney, Stephen W., 39, 76
Keller, Juan, 125
Kelly, Moses, 97–98, 202
Kerr, John, 197, 198
Kilpatrick, Dawkins (D. D.), 141, 191, 195, 197, 198
Kilpatrick, James (J. J.), 191, 192, 193, 199, 201, 203
Kilpatrick, Jim, 191, 192
Kilpatrick, Mary, 191
Kilpatrick family, 191–193, 195
Kiowas (tribe), 33, 69
Kirker, James (Santiago), 33, 70, 201
Kleinman, J. L., 150, 151, 154, 159, 160–161, 166, 178–179
Krain, Tom, 105, 106

La Ciénega, 95, 96
La Esmeralda, Mexico, 19
La Follette, Mel, 9
Lajitas, Texas, 19, 31, 204, 226
La Junta de los Rios: age of, 21; and agriculture, 1–2, 5, 14, 15, 19, 21, 22, 41, 42, 230, 231, 232, 234, 237, 238; and Anglo settlement, 16, 19, 39, 40–41, 50, 232; and Apaches and Comanches, 29, 31, 32, 49; and bolsons, 13; and border, 39, 230; boundaries of, 14–16, 17; map of, *1;* meaning river junction, 14; mountains and bolsons of, 12–13, *13;* native people of, 21–23; and Rio Conchos, 12, 14, 15, 85, 88, 230, 231; and Rio Grande, 5–6, 12, 14, 15, 18, 85, 88; and roads, 41, 60, 62; settlements near, 17–19, *18;* and

Spaniards, 16, 19, 21–24, 232; and trading, 15, 41, 42, 59, 89

La Morita, 95, 96, 98

La Mula, 91, 156

Landa, Manuel, 162, 166

Land grants: and Leaton, 45–48, 78–80, 106, 116, 136; and military colonists, 49, 146; and official surveys, 42–43, 45, 46, 47; and railroads, 93–94, 116; and Ronquillo, 27–28, 46, 47, 95, 133–136; and Treaty of Guadalupe Hidalgo, 43–44

Land issues: and Chihuahua, 25, 27–28, 136–137; and Ciudad Chihuahua, 28; and communal and traditional landholding, 121–122, 141, 142; and La Junta de los Rios, 41, 232; and Mexican Revolution, 131, 136, 144, 145, 146, 230; and Ortega, 167; and railroads, 93–94, 116; and regional oligarchies, 136–137, 141, 144; and Terrazas, 123, 131, 141, 146; and Texas, 44–45, 93–94, 136–137; and Treaty of Guadalupe Hidalgo, 43–44; and Villa, 173–174

Land scrip, 45, 116

Langberg, Emilio, 72, 74, 85

Langford, Mark, 197, 198

Langhorne, George, 187–190, 195, 197, 198–199

Lao, Francisco de, 115

Leaton, Benjamin: as Anglo settler, 97; and Apaches, 51, 69, 71–74, 85, 88; and Bell's investigation of land claims, 44; death of, 79, 85, 88, 119; estate of, 79–81, 117, 134–135; and Evans, 68; and feuds, 201; and Hays, 52–53, 55; Kilpatricks compared to, 192; and land grants, 45–48, 78–80, 106, 116, 136; and law enforcement, 48; and Ochoa, 131, 132; and Pedraza, 40, 47, 50–51, 80, 97; and political division of bor-

der, 231; and Presidio County, 78; and scalp hunting, 70–71; and Spencer, 41; and trading, 40, 42, 50, 51, 67, 69, 72–73, 74, 78, 86–87, 88; and Whiting, 57, 58, 59, 87

Leaton, Bill, 50, 51, 102, 118–119

Leaton, Bino, 125

Leaton, Elizabeth (Isabella/La Chata), 50–51, 131

Leaton, Francisca Ureta, 51, 79, 97, 125

Leaton, Joe: death of, 51; and Echols, 102; and Hays, 53, 54; and raiding in Mexico, 110, 111; as son of Benjamin Leaton, 50; and Ureta family, 79, 97; and Wulff, 106, 107

Leaton, Joseph (son), 125

Leaton, Manuelita, 125

Leaton, Ohamita, 125

Lee, Robert E., 101

Lerdo de Tejada, Sebastián, 125

Letcher, Marion, 173

Liberalism, in Mexico, 121, 122, 124, 145, 153

Licéaga, Avilés, 164–165

Lincoln, Abraham, 35

Linderman Oil Corporation, 203

Little Punitive Expedition, 188

Local political movements, 122

Lopez (Franciscan Friar), 55

Lopez, Martín "Shorty," 210–211, 212, 213

Lorenzo (guide), 51–52

Los Alamos de San Juan, 28

Luque, Gonzalez, 149–150, 151, 152, 153, 154, 155, 156–157

Madero, Francisco: anti-Madero rebel bands, 162; and Carrasco, 155; and Ciudad Chihuahua, 156; and Ciudad Juárez, 156–157; and Díaz, 143–144; and González, 146, 148, 149, 151, 152; government of, 158, 159, 164; and Huerta, 160, 163, 166;

and New Orleans, 148–149, 151;
and Ojinaga, 148, 149, 151, 153,
166; and Orozco, 158, 159, 163;
and Ortega, 144, 145, 167; and
Plan de San Luis Potosí, 144; and
representative democracy, 145;
and United States, 150, 163; and
Villa, 174
Madrid, Enrique, 3, 4
Madrid, Enrique Rede, 1, 4–6, 9,
239–245
Madrid, Lucía Rede, 3, 4, 5, 230,
240
Madrid, Ruby, 9, 239, 240, 241, 242,
244, 245
Mafia, 210–211, 218, 221
Magoffin, James, 39
Magoffin, Joseph, 115
Maillefert (Mexican Consul), 179
Manso, Manuel, 92
Marcos (Mescalero leader), 93
Marfa, Texas: and Ellsworth, 147,
149; and Ojinaga's refugees,
181, 182, 183, 189; and Presidio
County, 20, 77; and railroads,
129, 141; rumors of Mexicans
marching towards, 144
Marijuana, 6, 207, 209–212, 214,
226, 227, 228
Matlack, Leonard, 188, 192, 193,
195–197, 199
Maverick, Agatha, 64–65
Maverick, Augusta, 65–66
Maverick, Mary, 64–65
Maverick, Samuel, 53, 64–66, 102,
103
Maximilian (emperor), 121, 124, 125
Mazatlán, Mexico, 140
McCombs, S. F., 152
McNamee, Michael M., 176, 177,
178, 179, 180, 182–183
Measles, 64
Medellin cartel, 228
Menard County, Texas, 118
Mendoza, Captain, 55
Mendoza, Carmen, 124
Mendoza, Raphael, 125

Meranga, Jorge, 189
Mercado, Salvador: and border,
175, 231; and Colorados, 168;
as governor of Chihuahua, 163;
and Ojinaga, 169–171, 175, 180–
181; and Orozco, 169, 171–172; as
refugee, 183; retirement of, 184;
and Villa, 174, 180
Mescaleros: and Calvo, 30–31; and
Conde, 49; and Glanton, 71–72;
and Hays, 52; and Neighbors,
127; and Presidio del Norte,
68; and Torrey, 42, 67, 73; and
trading, 73–74. *See also* Apaches
Metal (Mescalero leader), 93
Mexican-American War, 39–40,
43–44, 49, 52, 76
Mexican Army: and Apaches, 127–
128; and Chihuahua, 169; and El
Mulato, 149; and Huerta, 163,
164; and Ochoa, 131; and Ojinaga, 147, 148, 149, 153, 154,
156–157, 170, 172, 174, 177–
178, 181; and political division of
border, 232. *See also* Federales
Mexican Border Commission, 84
Mexican Central Railway, 129–130,
131
Mexican colonization law of 1824,
25
Mexican National Railroad, 203
Mexican Revolution: beginning of,
144–145; and border, 146, 150–
151, 153–154, 157, 175–178, 186;
and land issues, 131, 136, 144,
145, 146, 230; and Texas, 144,
147–148, 149, 150–151, 175; and
United States, 150–152, 155, 175–
176, 177, 178, 186. *See also* Díaz,
Porfirio; Madero, Francisco;
Mercado, Salvador; Orozco,
Pascual; Ortega, Toribio; Villa,
Francisco "Pancho"
Mexicans: and Apaches and Comanches, 31–32, 68, 88, 146; and
Civil War, 103, 104; and Evans,
67, 68; and Hunter, 69; and land

grants, 43–48; and Leaton, 45, 46, 47–48, 73, 74; and scalp hunting, 33, 70; and trading posts, 41; and unionist movement, 203. *See also* Hispanics

Mexico: and American Civil War, 107, 109–111; and Apaches, 127–128; and copper coinage, 90; and drug smuggling, 220, 225; and duties on wagons, 69; and export duties, 43, 90–91; and French Intervention, 121; and frontier colonies, 49–50; and import duties, 36, 38, 39, 40, 43, 89–90, 123, 171; political complexity of, 122; recession of 1908, 142; and roads to El Paso, 60; Santa Fe as port of entry, 34; and scalp hunting, 33, 73–74; and trading, 36, 38, 40, 41–42, 90. *See also* Border; Mexican-American War; Mexican Revolution

Mexico City, Mexico, 25, 34, 124–125

Mexico Moon, 31

Mezquite, Mexico, 144

Mezquites (tribe), 21

Mies, Patrick, 118

Military: and border, 9, 232; and Chihuahua, 25, 49; and drug smuggling, 208, 209, 213, 221; and Spaniards, 23. *See also* Mexican Army; United States Army; United States Marines; *and specific presidios*

Military colonies: and Chihuahua, 26–27, 49, 146; and Civil War, 115; and Vado de Piedra, 26–27, 59, 85, 99; and Villa, 173

Military roads: and Aubrey, 87; and Civil War, 104, 113, 115; and Fort Davis, 60, 77, 99, 100, 129; map of, *61;* and railroads, 129; Santleben, 89; and United States Army, 99–100; and Whiting, 56, 60–61, 62

Mimbreño Apaches, 70

Mining industry: and Camino Real, 34; and land issues, 136, 138; and Ochoa, 132, 133, 136; and Parral, 90; and railroads, 141, 202, 203; and Spaniards, 22, 23; and Spencer, 132–134, 135, 201, 235; and U.S. investors, 138

Mississippi River, 37

Montana, 20

Monterrey, Mexico, 40

Montes, Esequiel, 144

Müller, Henry, 115, 122

Muñoz, Manuel, 23, 27

Murguía, José, 188

Murphy (merchant), 105

Mutual Film Corporation, 179

Natera, Pánfilo, 174, 177–178, 180

National political movements, in Mexico, 122

Native Americans: and reservations, 42, 70, 127, 128, 129. *See also* Apaches; Comanches; Mescaleros; *and other specific tribes*

Navajo (tribe), 33

Neighbors, Robert S., 76, 127

Neutrality Act, 132, 161–162, 164, 175

Nevill, Ed, 189

Nevill Ranch, 189

New Mexico: and Confederate forces, 104, 108, 109; and Doniphan, 40; and Indian reservations, 127, 128; and Presidio del Norte, 24; and Rio Grande, 12, 14; and Sibley, 108, 116; and Spaniards, 22; and Texas, 76; and United States Army, 99

New Mexico National Guard, 188

New Military Road, 129

New Orleans, Louisiana, 58, 66, 129, 148–149, 151

New Spain, 23

Nielson, Robert H., 117

Niza, Marcos de, 22

North American Free Trade Agreement (NAFTA), 234

North Dakota, 20
North, Oliver, 245

Obregón, Alvaro, 185
Ochoa, Juan, 131
Ochoa, Victor, 131–136, 145
OchoaPlane, 132
Ochoa Ranch, 131
O'Connor, Charles J., 176, 179
Ojinaga, Chihuahua: and arms traf-
    fic, 151; and bullfights, 205; and
    Carranza, 186–187; as center of
    authority, 142; and Del Toro,
    162–163; description of, 16, 17;
    and drug smuggling, 17, 207–
    221; evacuation of, 160, 161, 170;
    and González, 147, 149, 166;
    and Landa, 162, 166; and land
    issues, 137; and Luque, 152; and
    Mercado, 169–171, 175, 180–181;
    and Mexican Army, 147, 148,
    149, 153, 154, 156–157, 170, 172,
    174, 177–178, 181; and municipal
    officials fleeing to Presidio, 164–
    165; naming of, 124; and Orozco,
    160, 161, 166, 169–172, 180; and
    Ortega, 144–145, 147–148, 154,
    156, 157, 164, 165, 166, 170, 174,
    176–178, 180; as port of entry,
    62; and Presidio del Norte, 23;
    and railroads, 129, 130, 139, 140,
    141; Reed on, 172, 173; and Rio
    Grande and Rio Conchos, 14;
    and roads, 204; and Sánchez, 153,
    156, 157, 159, 160–161, 162, 163–
    164, 166; and Villa, 179–180, 181,
    189, 190
Ojinaga y Castañeda, José Manuel
    María Dionisio León, 123–124
Ojo Caliente, 30
Ojo de Alamo, 28
Ojo Grande del Cibolo, 95, 96
Oklahoma, 36–37
Open-range adherents, 96
Orneles, Ruperto, 125
Oros, Antonio, 27, 30
Orozco, Pascual: and Ciudad

Juárez, 156, 158, 159, 163; and
    Constitutionalist movement,
    184; and González, 146; and
    Huerta, 158, 159–160, 163, 164,
    166, 168, 172; and Madero, 158,
    159, 163; and Mercado, 169, 171–
    172; and Ojinaga, 160, 161, 166,
    169–172, 180; and United States,
    158, 161–162; and Villa, 158, 174
Orozco, Pascual, Sr., 160, 161–162
Ortega, Toribio: and Constitu-
    tionalist movement, 163, 164,
    165–166, 181; and Coyame, 153;
    and Cuchillo Parado, 144, 145,
    159, 160, 163, 164; death of, 184;
    and El Mulato, 148, 149, 152,
    175; and González, 147; ideals
    of, 166–167; and Madero, 144,
    145, 167; and Ojinaga, 144–145,
    147–148, 154, 156, 157, 164, 165,
    166, 170, 174, 176–178, 180; and
    Orozco, 160, 161; and Villa, 166,
    177, 181
Ortiz, Captain, 164–165
Ortiz, Guillermo, 58, 127
Otomoacos (tribe), 21
Owen, Albert Kimsey, 140
Owen, Ernest Dale, 134–136

Pacific Railroad Act (1862), 93
Pais, Feliciano, 118
Parral, 90, 158, 170, 209
Patarabueyes, 21
Payne, Monroe, 187, 188
Peacock, James T., 53, 54, 78–80,
    86
Pecos River, 59, 76, 93, 129
Pedis possessio principle, 117
Pedraza, Juana: and Burgess, 115–
    116, 117, 118; and Fort Leaton,
    81, 93; and Hall, 80–81; and land
    claims, 95; and law enforcement,
    48; and Leaton, 40, 47, 50–51,
    80, 97; and Spencer, 41; and
    Teel, 133
Peña, Henrico, 91
Perez, Francisco, 154

Perez, Matt, 221–222
Perfecto Lomelín, José, 147, 149, 166
Permian Basin Drug Task Force, 235, 236
Pershing, John "Blackjack," 186, 187, 188, 199
Pershing's Punitive Expedition, 186, 187, 188, 199
Peterson, Harold, 194–195, 197, 198
Piedras Negras, Mexico, 140, 146, 184, 231
Pilares, Mexico, 26, 59, 189, 191, 231
Plan de la Noria, 125
Plan de San Luis Potosí, 144
Plan de Tuxtepec, 125
Platón Sánchez, Rafael, 124
Plaza (drug smuggling), 208, 210–211, 212, 213, 216, 220
Police: and drug smuggling, 208, 209–210, 212, 213, 214, 221; and political division of border, 232
Polio, 205
Polk, James K., 39, 43
Poor, David, 116–117
Preemption Act of 1845, 45
Presidio, Texas: and Anglo settlement, 40, 60, 93; and arms traffic, 151; and Confederate forces, 111; description of, 16; and drug smuggling, 226; economics of, 16, 230; and Ellsworth, 150; and Fort Davis, 100; government of, 137; growth of, 87; and Luque, 154; and Ojinaga's battle, 155; and Ojinaga's evacuation, 160, 161; and Ojinaga's families, 17; Ojinaga's municipal officials fleeing to, 164–165; and Ojinaga's refugees, 176, 179, 180, 181, 182, 189; Porfirista loyalists fleeing to, 157; and Presidio County, 77; and railroads, 129, 130, 139, 140–141, 202–203; Reed on, 172; and roads, 60, 61–62; and Ronquillo, 28; and Spencer's store, 50, 202, 204, 206, 234; and United States

Army, 189; and Whiting, 56, 58, 60, 63
Presidio Bolson, 16
Presidio County, Texas: and banditry, 189; and bridges, 205; and drug smuggling, 225–227, 235; economics of, 230; and Fort Davis, 77, 100; and land claims, 44, 96; organization of, 76, 77–78, 117; towns of, 19–20; and United States Army, 193
Presidio del Norte, Chihuahua: and Anglo settlement, 41, 60; and Apaches and Comanches, 49, 128; and border, 84; and Cholomes, 232; and Civil War, 105, 107, 110, 111, 115; and Connelly, 35–38; and Echols, 101–102; and Emory, 84–85; and Evans, 67–68; and Faver, 95; and Fröbel, 88; and Hays, 52, 54, 68–69; and Hunter, 68–69; and Leaton, 74; and Mescaleros, 68; as military presence, 23, 24, 49, 99, 115, 126, 127; as port of entry, 87, 123; and Ronquillo, 26–30; and Santleben, 89–91; and scalp hunting, 33, 34, 71, 74; and Skillman, 110; and trading, 41, 72, 88; and Union spies, 105; and Union sympathizers, 111; and Whiting, 56, 57–58, 66, 68
Presidio de los Rios del Norte y Conchos, 23
Presidio de San Francisco de Conchos, 26
Presidio Mining Company, 133, 134, 135–136, 201, 202
Presidio Nuestra Señora de Bethlem y Santiago de Amarillas, 23
Presidio-Ojinaga international bridge, 14, 16–17, 230
Prieto, Damaso Martínez, 214
Príncipe, Juan Antonio, 145
Prohibition, 207
Provisional Confederate Congress, 104

Pruneda, Antonio, 198–199
Puebla, Mexico, 145
Púliques (tribe), 21

Quintana, Alfonso, 195
Quintanilla, José, 93

Rábago, Antonio, 156
Railroads: and Anglo settlement, 62; and arms traffic, 149; and economics, 142, 203–204, 234; and land issues, 93–94, 116; and Marfa, 129, 141; and Presidio, 129, 130, 139, 140–141, 202–203; and Stilwell, 138–140; and surveys, 94–95, 96, 201
Ramirez, Carmen, 98
Ramirez, Pancho, 98
Ramirez de Dawson, Juliana, 96
Ranching: and Apaches, 115, 126–127, 129; and Chihuahua, 138, 142, 143; and Civil War, 115; and communal and traditional land holding, 122; and Faver, 95–97, 98, 126; and Fort Davis, 50, 100; and Indian depredations, 126–127; and *latifundistas,* 141; and Leaton, 53; and Ochoa, 131; post-Civil War restocking of, 116; and Presidio County, 19, 20; and railroads, 129, 130, 141; and Ronquillo, 27–29, 30; and Spencer, 50, 100, 113, 202; and Terrazas, 115, 116, 122
Randolph, John R., 133
Rede, Eusebio, 3
Rede, María Antonia Luján, 3
Redford Bolson, 15
Redford, Texas: and banditry, 191; description of, 3–4, 5; and drug smuggling, 6, 226, 235, 236; as La Junta de los Rios settlement, 17; and roads, 204; and United States Army, 189
Reed, John, 172–173, 174
Regela, David, 217, 221
Regionalism: and Chihuahua, 121; and Díaz, 138; and Mexican politics, 122
Regional oligarchies: and banditry, 153–154; and Ciudad Chihuahua, 169; and land issues, 136–137, 141, 144; and Mexican liberalism, 121; and mining industry, 138; and Orozco, 171; and Terrazas, 122; and Villa, 173
Rentería, Jesus, 189, 191, 195–196, 197, 198–199
Republic of Texas, 45, 78
Rhode Island, 20
Rigg, Edwin, 109
Rio Bravo, 14, 85, 127
Rio Conchos: and agriculture, 67, 127, 230, 231; and air patrols, 194–195; and Ciudad Chihuahua, 69; and Comanches, 31; and dam, 204; and Fröbel, 87–88; and La Junta de los Rios, 12, 14, 15, 85, 88, 230, 231; and Ortega, 154; and roads, 231, 232
Rio del Norte, 14
Rio Grande: and banditry, 191; and border, 5, 6, 12, 25, 41, 83–84, 107, 229, 230; and bridges, 205; and colonial Spanish, 23–24; and Confederate forces, 104; and La Junta de los Rios, 5, 12, 14, 15, 18, 85, 88; and New Mexico, 76; and Ojinaga battle, 177, 178; and roads, 60, 61, 62; and Ronquillo's land, 28; topographical maps of, 83; and United States Army, 154, 189
Rivera, Quiterio, 30
Rodríguez, Agustín, 22, 23
Rodríguez, José, 58
Rodriguez, Margarita, 125
Ronquillo, Estanislado N., 134, 135
Ronquillo, José Ignacio, 26–30, 42, 45, 46, 47, 95, 133–136
Ronquillo, Josepha, 27, 30
Ronquillo, María de los Angeles, 27, 30
Ronquillo, Paz, 27, 30

Ronquillo, Rafaela, 27, 29–30
Ronquillo, Trinidad, 27
Roosevelt, Franklin Delano, 204
Rubí, Marqués de, 229
Ruidosa, Texas, 17, 189, 191, 235
Ruiz, Colonel, 190
Rurales, 141
Russell, William, 17, 117, 126, 127, 201

Sabeata, Juan, 167
Salazar, José Ines, 170–171, 172, 175, 177–178
Salazar Ylarregui, José, 84–86, 107
Salgado, Bernardino, 197
Saltillo, Mexico, 40, 66
San Antonio, Texas: and cholera, 63, 66, 68; and coinage, 90; and Confederate forces, 108, 111, 112, 113; and Madero, 148–149, 150, 151; and railroads, 129; and roads, 41, 51, 55, 56, 60, 76, 78, 84, 86–87, 89, 129; and trading, 86–87; and Union forces, 102, 103
San Antonio del Bravo, Mexico, 18, 160, 174, 191, 193, 227
San Bernardino, Mexico, 15, 17, 26
San Carlos, Mexico, 26, 52, 66, 85–86, 88, 128, 149–150, 153
Sánchez, Alfonso, 190
Sánchez, Francisco "Chamuscado," 22, 23
Sánchez, José de la Cruz: and Carrasco, 154–155; and Coyame, 153; and Kleinman, 159; and Luque, 151; and Madero, 152; and Ojinaga, 153, 156, 157, 159, 160–161, 162, 163–164, 166; and Orozco, 160; as outsider, 167; retirement of, 165, 166; and San Carlos, 149–150
Sánchez, Manuel, 154
Sánchez, Tomás, 195–197, 199
San Diego, California, 6
San Elizario, Mexico, 26
San Esteban (town), 27

San Francisco, Mexico, 18, 19, 155
San Ignacio, Mexico, 26, 59
San Juan, Mexico, 18, 19, 144, 148
Santa Anna, Antonio López de, 30–31
Santa Bárbara, Mexico, 22
Santa Elena, Mexico, 221, 222, 231
Santa Fe, New Mexico: and Kearney, 76; and roads, 56, 61; and scalp hunting, 34; and Texas, 76; and trading, 38, 39, 58, 59
Santa Fe County, Texas, 76
Santa Fe Trail, 34, *34,* 39
Santa Isabel, Chihuahua, 186, 187
Santa Rita, Nuevo Mexico, 30
Santa Rosa, Mexico, 66, 67
Santleben, August, 89–92, 117, 122
San Vicente, Mexico, 26
Scalp hunting, 33, 34, 70–74, 201
Schleicher, Gustave, 116
Scurry, William, 111–112
Sealy, Rosina, 133
Seawell, Washington, 100
Second Texas Mounted Rifles, 103
Seven Cities of Cibola, 22
Shafter, Texas, 19, 133, 150, 183, 202
Shreveport, Louisiana, 37
Sibley, Henry, 108, 116
Sierra, Victor, 211, 212, 213
Sierra de la Parra, 12
Sierra de la Santa Cruz, 12
Sierra del Carmen, 31
Sierra de Pilares, 15
Sierra de Ventana, 12, 15
Sierra Grande, 12, 14, 15, 19, 59, 151–153
Sierra Madre Occidental, 140
Sierra Pinosa, 12
Sierra Vieja, 12, 31
Sierrita del Alamo, 28
Silver: and Connelly, 35–38; and Crosson, 116; and Fröbel, 87–88; and Santleben, 90–91; and Spaniards, 22; and Spencer, 132–134, 136, 201
Sinaloa, Mexico, 132
Sitters, Joe, 192

Skillman, Henry: and Civil War, 109–111; and Confederate forces, 109, 110, 111–114; death of, 113, 115; and government mail route, 99–100; and Leaton, 60, 71; and Spencer, 201; and Whiting, 59–60, 100

Slaves and slavery, 51, 76

Smallpox, 64, 179

Smuggling: and Aranda, 207; and arms traffic, 160–161, 165, 166, 178–179, 207, 232; and border, 6, 207, 231, 232, 233; and Candelaria, 192; and candelilla wax, 207, 212; and fencing, 41–42, 74; and Santleben, 91; and sotol liquor, 207, 212. See also Drug smuggling

Soldiers of fortune, 155

Solis, Francisco Garza, 205

Solis, René, 205

Solis & Munis caravan, 112

Southern Pacific Railroad, 62, 77, 87, 129, 141, 149

Spaniards: and La Junta de los Rios, 16, 19, 21–24, 232; and Madrid, 244; and Rio Grande, 23–24; and Villa, 173–174

Spencer, Arcadio, 202

Spencer, Carlos (son of Francisco), 204, 206

Spencer, Carlos (son of John W.), 202

Spencer, Deena, 234

Spencer, Felicitas Molina de, 97, 202

Spencer, Francisco, 202, 204

Spencer, Frank, 206

Spencer, Gilbert, 206, 234–238, 242

Spencer, Guillermo, 202

Spencer, Ismael, 206

Spencer, Jesusita Baeza, 97

Spencer, Joe, 206

Spencer, John, 234

Spencer, John W.: as Anglo settler, 97; and Apaches, 50; and arms traffic, 179; and Confederate forces, 111, 113; death of, 201–

202; and Evans, 68; farms of, 59, 201; and Fort Davis, 100, 201; and law enforcement, 48; and Leaton, 46, 59, 201; and mining industry, 132–134, 135, 201, 235; and Ochoa, 132–134, 135; and scalp hunting, 70, 201; and Teel, 133–134; and Torrey, 42; and trading, 40–41, 201, 202; wife of, 97

Spencer, Oscar, 206

Spencer, Presilliano, 202

Spencer, Ricardo, 202

Spencer, Salome, 202

Spencer, Yvonne, 234–235

Stilwell, Arthur, 138–140, 202, 243

Subia, Jesus, 118

Surveys: and border, 83–84, 86, 107; and communal and traditional landholding, 122; and land grants, 42–43, 45, 46, 47; and railroads, 94–95, 96, 201; and Terrazas, 123, 146

Taagua (native rebel), 145

Taft, William Howard, 187

Tapacolmes (ranch), 27, 29

Tapacolmes (tribe), 21, 244

Tapacolmes (village), 5, 27, 246

Tapado Creek, 15

Tecolotes (tribe), 21, 26

Teel, J. J., 118, 133–135

Terlingua, Texas, 19, 204

Terrazas, Joaquí, 128, 146

Terrazas, Luis: and Apaches, 123, 128; and Carleton, 108, 111; and Díaz, 125, 131, 138; and evacuation of Ciudad Chihuahua, 171; and Fergusson, 109–110; and Juárez, 123, 124–125; and land theft, 123, 131, 141, 146; and local oppression, 141–142; as oligarch, 122–123, 131, 138, 141, 145, 146, 158; and Poor, 116; and railroads, 141; and ranching, 115, 116, 122; and Trías, 131

Terrell, Samuel, 125

Texas: and Anglo settlement, 93;
border of, 76–77; and land
issues, 44–45, 93–94, 136–137;
and Mercado, 175; and Mexican
land grants, 44, 46; and Mexican
Revolution, 144, 147–148, 149,
150–151, 175; and New Mexico,
76; and Ochoa, 131–132; and
Orozco, 172; secession of, 102–
103; statehood of, 41, 45; and
trading, 41. *See also* Civil War
Texas Narcotics Control Program,
235
Texas National Guard, and border,
188
Texas Rangers, 70, 160, 189
Texas, Topolobampo & Pacific Railway & Telegraph Company,
140
Thompson, Rick, 225–228, 235, 245
Tierra Blanca, and Villa, 168
Tierras baldíos, 123, 146
Tinkham, H. W., 117–118
Topolobampo, Mexico, 139, 140,
243
Torreón, 179, 180
Torrey, David, 41, 42, 67, 73–74, 85
Torrey, John, 41, 42
Torrez, Roy, Jr., 237, 238
Trading: and Anglos, 34, 35, 50;
and Apaches, 41, 51, 72, 73–
74, 85, 127; and Burgess, 40,
50, 116; and Chihuahua, 58, 66,
90; and Chihuahua Trail, 61–62,
87, 117; and Confederate forces,
112; and Connelly, 35–38; and
fencing, 41–42, 74; and La Junta
de los Rios, 15, 41, 42, 59, 89;
and Leaton, 40, 42, 50, 51, 67,
69, 72–73, 74, 78, 86–87, 88; and
Mexican-American War, 39–40;
and roads, 86–87; and Santleben,
89–92; and Spencer, 40–41, 201,
202; and Treaty of Guadalupe
Hidalgo, 43; and Wulff, 105
Treaty of Guadalupe Hidalgo, 25,
43–44, 48, 49, 74–75, 83

Trías, Angel, 40, 70, 72, 125, 131
Twiggs, David, 102, 103

Union forces: and Confederate
supply line, 112, 113; evacuation of, 103, 104; and Fort Bliss,
103, 108, 109, 110, 113; and San
Antonio, 102, 103; and Skillman, 109, 110, 112, 113–114; and
spies, 105–107; and sympathizers in Mexico, 107; and Texas'
secession, 102–103
United States: and Chihuahua, 25,
72–73; and drug smuggling, 209,
217, 218, 225, 226, 227; and expansionism, 49; and Huerta, 183;
and import duties, 36, 43, 89–
90, 92; and land issues, 137; and
Madero, 150, 163; and Mexican
land grants, 42–43; and Mexican Revolution, 150–152, 155,
175–176, 177, 178, 186; and Ojinaga, 165, 170, 175–176, 177, 180,
181–182; and Orozco, 158, 161–
162; and railroad right-of-way
grants, 93; recession of 1908,
142; and Texas's border, 76–
77; and trading, 36, 37, 41; and
Treaty of Guadalupe Hidalgo,
43; and Villa, 173, 185, 186. *See
also* Border
United States Air Force, 225
United States Army: and air patrols,
193–196; and Apaches, 127–128;
and border, 18, 187–188, 189; and
Burgess, 117; and camels, 101,
102; and Civil War, 102, 103; and
Leaton, 74; and Mexican Revolution, 151–152, 154, 170, 176;
and military road, 99–100; and
Ojinaga's refugees, 182–183;
and Orozco, 161; and Ortiz, 164;
and Rio Grande, 154, 189; and
scalp hunting, 71, 73; and Villa,
170
United States Border Patrol: and
Amnesty International, 9; and

drug smuggling, 212, 221, 225,
226, 236, 237, 238; and El Polvo
river crossing, 245–246; and
Hernandez, 7–8; and La Junta
de los Rios, 14; and Ojinada,
175; and political division of border, 232; and Presidio, 16; and
Redford, 6; role of, 6–7
United States Boundary Commission, 83–84
United States Congress, 77, 93
United States Customs Service: and
Acosta, 221; and Mexican Revolution, 147, 148, 151, 153, 154,
170; and political division of border, 232; and Presidio County,
225
United States Drug Enforcement
Agency: and Acosta, 214, 219,
221; and Chambers, 227–228; and
political division of border, 232;
and Presidio County, 225; and
Sierra, 212; and Gilbert Spencer,
235
United States Immigration and
Naturalization Service, 210, 232
United States Indian Agent, 71
United States Marine Corps: and
Carranza, 185; and Hernandez,
8, 9–10, 237, 238, 242, 243, 245;
and political division of border,
232; and Presidio County, 225;
and Gilbert Spencer, 237, 238
United States Marshals, 132, 160,
170
United States Senate, 44, 48
United States State Department,
44, 199, 221
Ureta, Cesario, 79, 125
Ureta, Jesusa, 125
Urias, Johnny, 8, 237

Vado de Piedra, Mexico: and
Comanches, 30; and Emory, 85;
as La Junta de los Rios settlement, 19; as military colony, 26–

27, 59, 85, 99; and Ronquillo, 28;
and Skillman, 111; and Whiting,
85
Valenzuela, Diana, 9
Valenzuela, Jesus, 9
Valverde, Mexico, 18
Vanagas family, 147
Van Dorn, Earl, 104
Van Horne, Jefferson, 71–73, 74
Varmint rifles, 7
Victorio (Mescalero leader), 128,
146
Villa, Francisco "Pancho": and
Carranza, 179, 185, 186, 189–
190; and Ciudad Juárez, 156,
168, 189; and Constitutionalist movement, 163, 166, 168,
169, 172; drug lords compared
to, 210; funding of campaigns,
185, 186; and González, 146; and
Huerta, 174, 185; and Madrid,
241, 243; and Ojinaga, 179–180,
181, 189, 190; and Orozco, 158,
174; and Ortega, 166, 177, 181;
and Spaniards, 173–174; and
United States, 173, 185, 186
Volunteerism, 3

Wagon trains, 87
Wahm, Doctor, 52
War of Reform (1858–1860), 121
War societies, 33
Water: and Fort Davis, 100; and
irrigation, 14, 15, 17, 83, 85, 141,
142, 204, 234; and military roads,
129; and oligarchies, 141; and
surveys, 95
Webb Miller, Mimi, 216–221, 230
Weisman, Alan, 217, 218
West, J. R., 109–110
Whiting, William Henry Chase:
and Apaches, 73; and cholera,
66; and Fort Leaton, 57, 58, 59–
60; and Leaton, 57, 58, 59, 87;
and military roads, 56, 60–61,
62; and Presidio, 56, 58, 60, 63;

and Presidio del Norte, 56, 57–58, 66, 68; and road to El Paso, 56, 59; and Skillman, 59–60, 100; and Vado de Piedra, 85

Whooping cough, 64

Williams, Andrew, 152, 153–154, 155

Willis, Edward, 109

Wilson, Henry Lane, 163

Wilson, Woodrow, 185–186, 187, 188

Woll (Mexican general), 53

Women: and Constitutionalist movement, 165, 170, 172, 178, 180; and Mexican Revolution, 155; and small-time smuggling, 192

Worth, William J., 56, 60

Wulff (Union spy), 105–107, 110, 111, 116

Yancey, James P., 197, 198, 199

Yaquis, 154

Ydoiaga, Joseph de, 95, 145, 242

Yellow fever, 63, 64

Young Brothers Hardware Company, 150

Zapata, Emilio, 185, 241, 243

Zapatistas, 158

Zaques, 156

Zorillo (Chisos Apache leader), 128

Zuloaga, Felix, 121

317

Index